Paul Cullen,
John Henry Newman,
and the
Catholic University of Ireland,
1845–1865

T

Paul Cullen,

John Henry Newman,

and the

UNIVERSITY OF NOTRE DAME PRESS

Catholic University

of Ireland,

1845–1865

COLIN BARR

Notre Dame, Indiana

Copyright © 2003 by University of Notre Dame
Notre Dame, Indiana 46556
www.undpress.nd.edu
All Rights Reserved

Manufactured in the United States of America

Title page art: Seal of the Catholic University of Ireland,
from a 1954 commemorative pamphlet of
the University College Dublin.

Library of Congress Cataloging-in-Publication Data
Barr, Colin, 1974–
   Paul Cullen, John Henry Newman, and the Catholic University of
Ireland, 1845–1865 / Colin Barr
      p. cm.
   Includes bibliographical references and index.
   ISBN 0-268-03878-3 (paper : alk. paper)
      1. Cullen, Paul, 1803–1878.   2. Newman, John Henry, 1801–1890.
3. Catholic University of Ireland—History.   1. Title

LF915 .B37   2003
378.418'35—dc21   2002151874

∞ *This book is printed on acid-free paper.*

For my grandparents

Donald and Betty Pope

Jeanne Turcotte

Charles Melville Barr, *in memoriam*

Contents

Acknowledgements

THIS BOOK BEGAN LIFE AS A DOCTORAL THESIS, AND AS SUCH I have incurred even more debts than might be expected in the production of a 'normal' academic book. First and foremost I must record my thanks to Dr Eugenio Biagini of Robinson College Cambridge. As a doctoral supervisor, and friend, he made possible both the thesis and now the book. I owe him a great debt of thanks for his unfailing kindness and understanding.

At NUI Maynooth I have enjoyed the friendship and support of my colleagues in the Department of Modern History. I could not have wished for a more supportive and welcoming place to be a postdoctoral fellow. In particular, I would like to thank Professor Vincent Comerford, without whom I would never have come to Maynooth in the first place. His friendship, help, and critical readings made this a much stronger book than it might otherwise have been.

My research was made much easier by the gracious assistance of Mr David Sheehy of the Dublin diocesan archives; Monsignor John Hanly, archivist of the Irish College at Rome; Mr Gerard Tracey of the Birmingham Oratory; Ms Karen White of the Halifax diocesan archives; and the staffs of the National Library of Ireland, Cambridge University Library, Pembroke College (Oxford) Library, and the archives of University College Dublin and the University of Notre Dame. They were all helpful with and interested in my project to a tremendous extent. I also owe especial thanks to the archbishops of Dublin and Cashel for permission to utilise their archives. Monsignor John Fleming, the former rector of the Irish College, proved a most hospitable and tolerant host during my stay in the Eternal City. Dr Sheridan Gilley of the University of Durham, Professor R. F. Foster at the University of Oxford, and Dr Boyd Hilton and Dr Brendan Bradshaw of the University of Cambridge all generously commented on all or part of this book at one stage or another of its gestation. I hope I have done justice to their suggestions and criticisms.

I have been very fortunate to be the recipient of the generosity of many organisations. Neither the book nor the thesis out of which it grew could have been completed without their financial aid. I would like to record my thanks to the Rotary Foundation; the Lightfoot Fund for Ecclesiastical History at the University of Cambridge; and the Master and Fellows of Gonville and Caius College, Cambridge. Without their help, and the generous support of my family, I would not have been either able to come to Cambridge in the first place or finish the thesis once I had arrived. In addition to the financial support of these bodies, the Erasmus Institute of the University of Notre Dame was kind enough to provide me with a quiet place to write at an important point in the completion of this work. James Turner, Robert Sullivan, and the Fellows of the Institute were hospitable and helpful during my time in Indiana. This book would have been most unlikely to have seen the light of day had I not been awarded a Government of Ireland research fellowship by the Irish Research Council for the Humanities and Social Sciences. This excellent and generous program has done much to make Irish universities a centre of research in the humanities and social sciences. Thanks are also due to the National University of Ireland, Maynooth, for a substantial grant towards the preparation of this book.

I could not possibly have finished this project without the help and support of my friends, both at Cambridge and in Ireland. Katie Dean, Miriam Hickey, Dee McCarthy, Caroline McGregor, Grant Tapsell, Brent Whitefield, and Katherine Wiley all gave up their time to help edit this work at one stage or another. Dr Clodagh Tait and Dr Fearghal McGarry provided companionship and support at Maynooth. All the help I received made this book vastly better than it might have been. However, the usual caveat applies: the errors that remain are entirely my own.

Finally, I must thank Caroline and my family—parents, grandparents, and sister—for their love and support over the years. Without them I could neither have finished this book nor enjoyed working on it.

Note on Sources

THIS BOOK IS BASED ALMOST ENTIRELY ON PRIMARY SOURCE
material held in the Dublin diocesan archives, Cashel diocesan archives,
Birmingham Oratory, National Library of Ireland, British Library, Down
and Connor diocesan archives, the archives of the Irish College Rome, the
archives of Pembroke College, Oxford, and the archives of the University
of Notre Dame and University College Dublin. All letters quoted in the
text have been examined in the original unless explicitly stated otherwise.
With the exception of some letters in the Irish College collection, all the
sources quoted are in English. The only other exception are those letters
of Paul Cullen to the Propaganda that are quoted by J. H. Whyte and
Emmet Larkin. In those cases I have used their translation and have acknowledged so doing in the relevant note. For those documents in Italian
from the Irish College, I have relied on the translations specially made by
Dr. Eugenio Biagini of Robinson College, Cambridge. A document that
was originally in Italian will be identified as such in the notes.

The material held in the Irish College falls into four categories: the
Kirby Papers, the Kirby Papers (New Collection), the Cullen Papers, and
the Cullen Papers (New Collection). The 'New Collection' of both the
Kirby and Cullen papers consists of those letters and notes removed from
the Irish College by Patrick Francis Moran, Cullen's nephew and the first
cardinal archbishop of Sydney. Moran took the papers with him to Australia as part of his then planned biography of Cullen. Such a biography
never materialised, and the papers were only returned to the Irish College
in the mid-1950s. They are catalogued in a different manner from the

regular collections, and it is necessary to cite box and folder number in addition to the number of the document itself. In the 'main' collections only the document number is necessary to locate the item in question.

The Dublin diocesan archives does not as yet have a consistent filing system for the papers in its collection. Some parts of the Cullen Papers will have file and document numbers, and some only file numbers. In all cases, documents drawn from the DDA will be cited as they appear in its own catalogues or in such a way that any researcher should easily be able to trace the reference. The DDA also holds all of Cullen's papers from his period as archbishop of Armagh, as he transferred his archive when he was translated to Dublin. The Armagh diocesan archives do not, as a result, hold any Cullen material. The Slattery and Leahy papers of the Cashel diocesan archives were examined on microfilm at the National Library of Ireland.

Peadar MacSuibhne's five-volume *Paul Cardinal Cullen and His Contemporaries* has been treated with caution. Although the work is invaluable in that it both reproduces otherwise unavailable letters and points the way towards collections that might have otherwise remained unknown, it is nonetheless deeply flawed. It is not always clear when MacSuibhne might be editing his documents, and it is impossible to tell if the reproduction is faithful without examining the original; often it is not. MacSuibhne's primary concern was to paint a glowing portrait of Cullen; he was not a trained historian and was not in any real sense acting as one. I have avoided, wherever possible, quoting directly from documents reproduced in MacSuibhne. Where this has been impossible because I was unable to examine the item in the original, I have used my best judgement and quoted sparingly.

The Letters and Diaries of John Henry Newman are an invaluable source for all aspects of Newman's life. In the notes to this book, letters *from* Newman published in the *Letters and Diaries* are indicated by the names of the correspondents, the date of the letter, and the volume in which the letter appears. As the *Letters and Diaries* are arranged in chronological order, this information is enough to locate the letter quoted. In the case of letters *to* Newman, published in whole or in part in the *Letters and Diaries*, I have included the same information along with the pages on which the letter can be found. The editorial practice of the *Letters and Diaries* is to place letters to Newman based on their explanatory value and not necessarily their chronological order.

Throughout the text I have left intact any irregular spellings that appear in quoted documents. Many of the historical actors quoted used what are today American English spellings; for example, 'favor' or 'honor' for 'favour' and 'honour'. Abbreviations appearing between inverted commas have been left intact if they are both obvious and are a regular feature of that writer's style; for example, Paul Cullen often abbreviated 'should' as 'sd.' Only where an abbreviation appears infrequently or might be confusing has it been expanded. The use of *sic* has been limited to those instances where the writer's mistake or irregularity might otherwise be mistaken for a typographical error. Where an emphasis of any kind appears within a quotation, that same emphasis is in the original unless otherwise noted; if an underlined word or words appears within a quotation, then the underlining is in the original; if a word or phrase is italicised within a quotation, then it appears thus in the original.

Abbreviations

Archives of the Oratory of St Philip Neri, Birmingham	BOA
Armagh Diocesan Archives	ADA
Autobiographical Writings of John Henry Newman	*AW*
British Library	BL
Cashel Diocesan Archives	CDA
Catholic University of Ireland	CUI
Down and Connor Diocesan Archives	D&CDA
Dublin Diocesan Archives	DDA
Irish College Rome Archives	ICRA
The Letters and Diaries of John Henry Newman	*LD*
National Library of Ireland	NLI
Pembroke College, Oxford, Archives	PCA
University College Dublin Archives	UCDA
University of Notre Dame Archives	UNDA

Introduction

A FEW YEARS AGO I GAVE A PAPER ON THE CATHOLIC UNIVERSITY of Ireland to the Erasmus Institute at the University of Notre Dame. The institute is interdisciplinary, and one of the fellows—a philosopher—asked me what was 'at stake' in my paper. Now historians are, probably rightly, nervous of such questions. At the time I mumbled something about the importance of *The Idea of a University* in modern education and the necessity of studying the institution for which it was written. I was grateful when the discussion moved on to more empirical matters. Nevertheless, the question has stuck with me. Is there any contemporary relevance to a study of a small, unsuccessful mid-nineteenth-century Irish university?

Certainly, there seems to be little debate as to the importance of Newman's *Idea*. Owen Chadwick has called that book 'a classic of Victorian literature which every student of the philosophy of university education still cites.'[1] G. M. Young was even more fulsome in his praise, remarking that if only two books on education could be kept, 'the rest might, with no loss to humanity and possibly some advantage, be pulped.' Those two books were Aristotle's *Ethics* and Newman's *Idea of a University*.[2] And the Yale University Press in the last decade has felt the need to reissue *Idea* in a critical edition accompanied by five essays with such titles as 'Newman's University and Ours', 'Theology and the University: Newman's Idea and Current Realities', and even 'Newman and the Idea of an Electronic University'.[3]

Nor is interest in Newman's great work limited to historians and public intellectuals. A recent search for the terms 'Newman+Idea of a

University' on 'Yahoo.com' returned more than twelve thousand hits. Of course, anybody who has used the internet to search for information knows that such results can often have little or nothing to do with the thing actually searched for. In this case, however, quite a few of the 150 or so sites I looked at were relevant. Most of the sites belonged to schools or universities from around the world—usually but not always Catholic— who had chosen to put their catalogues or mission statements on the web. Those institutions had all felt the need to quote or at least refer to Newman and his *Idea of a University* when it came time to define themselves and their purposes. Here, clearly, was contemporary relevance.

This book seeks to provide a history of the Catholic University from its origins in the debate over Irish education in the 1840s up to the realisation by the hierarchy in 1865–66 that the Catholic University could no longer be a university in the sense that its founders had intended. The university's history will be examined by focusing on those figures most closely involved in the project, primarily John Henry Newman and Paul Cullen. These two men dominated the university, either alone or together, throughout the period of its creation and early years.

The figure of Newman has overshadowed most treatments of the university, both in his time and later. It is the central contention of this book that it is impossible to gain a full understanding of the Catholic University of Ireland without placing it within its Irish context. To do so, it is necessary to examine both the period of Newman's own tenure at the university as well as the debates and conflicts within the Irish Catholic Church that led up to the university's establishment, and contributed to its failure. By considering the Catholic University as an essentially Irish institution it is possible to achieve a more balanced picture of the university than has been available in previous works on the subject.

Examining the history of the Catholic University in Ireland in such a fashion requires a close study of the part that Paul Cullen, in his various roles as rector of the Irish College in Rome, archbishop of Armagh, archbishop of Dublin, and apostolic delegate, played in its creation, organisation, and affairs. Cullen remains a contentious figure in Irish history, one that can still raise strong feelings. As the poet P. J. Kavanagh has remarked, even today Cullen 'strikes in Irish hearts an ambiguous awe.'[4] Although this book is not intended to be a biography of Cullen, he nevertheless emerges as the central figure in the Catholic University for the period under consideration. Cullen, from his post in Rome, urged and chivvied the Irish bishops to establish a Catholic university; Cullen, as archbishop of Armagh, finally gained episcopal approval for the university and set about raising funds for it; Cullen chose and then wooed John

Henry Newman in an effort to gain him as the university's first rector; Cullen used his influence at Rome to protect the CUI from the damaging effects of internal Irish ecclesiastical politics and ensured its opening; and finally, Cullen, as Newman's tenure drew to an acrimonious end, was forced to urge him to stay and had to arrange for the university's future when he did not.

Cullen's responsibility for, and interest in, the Catholic University of Ireland extended both before and after Newman's own involvement in that institution. Although it is in no sense my intention to downplay or ignore the importance of Newman in the university project, Cullen and his actions necessarily receive the most attention. In focusing on the dominant nature of Cullen's involvement with all aspects of the Catholic University, it will be necessary to reexamine a number of assumptions about Cullen, his educational ideas, and his relationship with Newman that are prevalent in the historiography of this period. Cullen emerges from this study as a man totally committed to the idea of a Catholic university and single-minded in his efforts to create one. It will be seen that he was by no means a narrow, bigoted obscurantist, but rather shared with Newman a vision for a truly *Catholic* university that would be both intellectually rigorous and doctrinally sound. In conflict with Newman, and suffering himself from a lack of scholarly attention, Cullen has come to be seen as a narrow figure who, if he showed vision in appointing Newman in the first place, nevertheless had little sympathy with a truly liberal university education or with anybody who might advocate it. An important aim of this book will be to reconsider this interpretation of Cullen, and his relationship with Newman, in the light of all the available sources, both Irish and English.

There has been little modern work done on the history of the Catholic University of Ireland as such. For nearly fifty years the standard work has been Fergal McGrath's *Newman's University: Idea and Reality*. McGrath's research was hampered by his inability to consult a number of important archival collections dealing with the Catholic University and its founders. He was able to examine neither Cullen's own papers in the Irish College in Rome nor the numerous and important letters from Cullen to his friend Tobias Kirby that are also held there. Other Roman archives, such as the papers of the Propaganda Fide and the Bernard Smith papers held at St Paul's-Outside-the-Walls, were not utilised by McGrath.

In Ireland, McGrath did not consult the papers of two successive archbishops of Cashel, Michael Slattery and Patrick Leahy, which are held in the Cashel diocesan archives but were not then catalogued. As

Slattery was a critical figure in the fight to establish a Catholic University in Ireland and Leahy the university's first vice-rector, these papers form an important source; both men were in regular contact with Cullen, both in Rome and later. Although McGrath did use the Dublin diocesan archives, he does not seem to have been able to examine the full extent of that repository's holdings on Cullen and the university. Those papers have only been fully catalogued in recent years, and it seems likely that there were many important papers held there of which he was simply unaware. Nor could McGrath consult Peadar MacSuibhne's massive, albeit flawed, *Paul Cardinal Cullen and His Contemporaries,* which draws together a large number of letters both from and to Cullen and which began publication in 1961.[5]

The primary source for McGrath's book was the voluminous Newman papers held in the Birmingham Oratory. Newman's own letters and memoranda on the subject of the university, along with numerous letters to Newman, form the heart of McGrath's work. Unsurprisingly, the limited nature of McGrath's sources provided an unbalanced picture of events. Newman believed himself to be in conflict with Cullen through much of the period, and his papers reflect his own views on that conflict. Without access to Cullen's papers or those of his confidants, McGrath was unable to either understand or convey the other side of the question. McGrath himself was aware of this problem, remarking that from the 'historian's point of view, it is regrettable that the chief sources of information concerning Dr. Cullen's character and policy are the writings of [Gavan] Duffy, [Frederick] Lucas and Newman, all of whom were in sharp conflict with him.' Despite this paucity of information on Cullen, McGrath nevertheless felt capable of asserting that '[i]t can hardly be doubted ... that the picture painted of him [Cullen] by his three contemporaries is, in the main, a faithful one.'[6]

These archival collections, held in Rome, Birmingham, Dublin, and Cashel, form the basis of this book. In all but a few cases (primarily, the Bernard Smith papers and the archives of Propaganda Fide) I have examined all the archives personally and have not relied on any published source. With the exception of J. H. Whyte's translations of various letters held at the Propaganda, those letters originally in Italian have been freshly translated for the present work. Although McGrath closely examined the Birmingham collection, and Emmet Larkin, Donal Kerr, J. H. Whyte, Desmond Bowen, Ciaran O'Carroll, E. D. Steele, and Patrick Corish have studied at least portions of the Rome, Cashel, and Dublin collections, no author has considered all the available sources or has done so with a view specifically to the history of the Catholic University.[7]

Since McGrath published his *Newman's University* in 1951, there has been a great deal of work done on both the Irish Catholic Church in the 1840s, 1850s, and 1860s in general and on Cullen in particular; although there is as yet no 'Life' of Cullen.[8] The works of Larkin and Kerr in particular have provided a much fuller understanding of Cullen and his actions, and those of his contemporaries, than had previously been available. Neither author, however, has focused specifically on the Catholic University, although its history plays a part, and often a large part, in their more wide-ranging studies. Kerr, in his *Peel, Priests and Politics* and *A Nation of Beggars?* closely examined the conflicts endemic to the Irish church between 1844 and 1852. In his treatment of the education question, Kerr has covered much of the same ground covered in the first few chapters of this book. Kerr did not, however, focus on the 'pre-history' of the Catholic University, and his *Nation of Beggars?* concludes in 1852, two years before the university formally opened its doors.

Emmet Larkin has built up the most detailed picture available of the Catholic Church in Ireland in the nineteenth century. His focus is primarily political, and he has done more than anybody else to make Paul Cullen a fully three-dimensional figure. Although his *The Making of the Roman Catholic Church, 1850–1860* and *The Consolidation of the Roman Catholic Church in Ireland, 1860–1870* gives ample space to the Catholic University, he did not design either volume to supplant McGrath; he does not focus on the Catholic University as such, but rather on its place within the wider sphere of Irish ecclesiastical politics in the 1850s and 1860s. By beginning his *The Making of the Roman Catholic Church* in 1850, Larkin is also unable to put Cullen's interest in and behaviour towards the Catholic University fully within the context of the educational debates of the 1840s; the creation of the Catholic University, and Cullen's pivotal role in that creation, cannot be properly understood without reference to that earlier period.

In addition to Kerr and Larkin, works by other authors, particularly O'Carroll, Corish, and Steele, have contributed to our understanding of both Cullen and the Irish church in the period under consideration here. None of these writers, however, has combined a close study of the available Irish sources (including those held in Rome) on the Catholic University with an examination of those that give Newman's 'side' of the story. With the exception of a single work, largely derived from McGrath and journalistic in tone, no study of the creation of the Catholic University has been attempted since *Newman's University* in 1951.[9]

The lack of a work that takes into account those sources that have become available since McGrath does not mean that the Catholic University has been ignored by scholars in the interim. Rather, the field has been left to the numerous studies of John Henry Newman that have touched on his career in Dublin. Various biographies, starting with Wilfrid Ward's 1912 authorised biography[10] and continuing on through to Sheridan Gilley's 1990 *Newman and his Age*, have held to the view of the Newman-Cullen relationship put forward by Newman himself in his contemporary letters and his 1870 'Memorandum about my Connection with the Catholic University'.[11] Newman's view of Cullen was an essentially hostile one. He believed that Cullen treated him poorly throughout his time in Dublin and made an already difficult job nearly impossible. Newman's biographers, who often cite McGrath as their authority, have largely accepted this view of Cullen and the university;[12] it is this hostile portrait of Irish obscurantism that has become the popularly accepted one, assumed by most writers who touch on the subject to be accurate.[13] As John Charles McQuaid, another ultramontane archbishop of Dublin, once remarked: if 'we regard Newman as a martyr, we must seek out those who may be thought to have conferred that distinction on him.'[14]

Although Newman's 'side' of the story has dominated, other views have been published. There is a long tradition in Ireland of taking exactly the opposite approach and blaming Newman for the university's failure. Such a response was thought necessary soon after Cullen's death. His half-nephew, Patrick Francis Moran, was quickly commissioned to write a life of his uncle. A respected historian of the Irish church, Moran had also been vice-rector of the Irish College in Rome, Cullen's secretary in Dublin, coeditor of the *Irish Ecclesiastical Record,* and coadjutor bishop of Ossory from 1871 (he succeeded in 1872). In 1882 he published a three-volume collection of Cullen's pastoral letters and other published writings. He was appointed archbishop of Sydney in 1884 and sought to continue the biography in his new post. For many years it was assumed that publication only awaited Ward's own long-overdue life of Newman so that its anticipated criticisms of Cullen might be properly answered. In the event, Moran died both before Ward's book appeared and before he could complete his own work.

Since Moran, other scholars have at least hinted that there might be more to the story than Cullen's obstructionist obscurantism versus Newman's enlightened liberalism. Peadar MacSuibhne's *Paul Cardinal Cullen and His Contemporaries* sought to acquit both Cullen of rudeness towards Newman and Newman of incompetence. Unfortunately, Mac-Suibhne was far too willing to paper over the very real differences that existed between the two men and chose to ignore their effect on the university. Others, like V. A. McClelland, have not bothered to try to protect Newman while they went about the business of exonerating Cullen. In fact, the section on the Catholic University of Ireland in McClelland's *English Roman Catholics and Higher Education* is a sustained and bitter attack on Newman. One gets the sense on reading the book that McClelland was less interested in redressing the balance in the historical treatment of the Newman-Cullen relationship than he was in attacking Newman. In fact, the only work of which I am aware that has sought to reconsider Cullen's role in the university without gratuitous attacks on Newman is an article written in 1961 by Alfred O'Rahilly. Published in the Jesuit journal *Studies*, O'Rahilly's essay identified a crucial truth missed by most historians: 'Newman's own comments on Cullen (as on Faber and others) must not be taken too literally; allowance must be made for Newman's supersensitive character and Cullen's reticence. When the evidence is examined objectively, there is little or nothing to support the widespread thesis of constant interference and thwarting, especially by Cullen.'[15] Unfortunately, O'Rahilly's conclusions did not spread widely; certainly they were missed by all recent works on Newman.

The purpose of this book is to retell the story of the creation and early days of the Catholic University of Ireland; it is consciously designed to supplant McGrath's *Newman's University*. I have attempted to examine the university, both before and after Newman's involvement with it, in the light of the numerous sources that have come to light since McGrath's day. By placing the university firmly within its Irish context, I believe that it is possible to provide a fuller, more nuanced portrait of both the university itself and the critical Cullen-Newman relationship at its heart. In so doing, I hope that the context in which Newman's *Idea of a University* was written will become clear. Only by understanding the actual, existing institution for which that great book was written can we hope to understand the work itself and properly assess its utility as a model for modern university education.

Most important, however, this book aims to return Paul Cullen to his rightful place as the man who founded, sustained, fought for, and mourned the Catholic University of Ireland.

chapter one

First Conflicts

The National Schools
and Charitable Bequests

THE STORY OF THE CREATION OF THE CATHOLIC UNIVERSITY OF
Ireland is one of personalities. John MacHale, William Crolly, Daniel
Murray, Michael Slattery, Paul Cullen, and only a few others both guided
and influenced events for many, many years. Death stopped Crolly in
1849 and Murray in 1852, but those events themselves played a pivotal role
in the university's creation. MacHale and Cullen, once allies become bitter
enemies, continued to spar over education in general and the university
in particular until Cullen's death in 1878. How the university came
about, and how the various members of the Irish hierarchy reacted to the
idea of it, cannot be understood without an examination of the events
surrounding John MacHale's condemnation of the national schools and
the reactions of various members of the Irish church—and Rome—to
both the national system and MacHale's attacks on it. The controversy
over the national schools reveals important similarities as well as some
differences with the later fights over the Queen's Colleges and the
Catholic University.

The personalities of the Irish bishops and their responses to various
issues in the period to 1844 have been brilliantly treated by Donal Kerr in

his *Peel, Priests and Politics.*[1] Any attempt to add substantially to that account here would be superfluous. Instead, the aim is to focus on the various sides and participants in the national system controversy. The conflict over the schools can tell us about the power, beliefs, and activities of those men who would go on to play important roles in the educational debates of the late 1840s, debates that eventually led to the determination by the hierarchy to erect a Catholic university in Ireland.

THE NATIONAL SCHOOLS

Unlike the other parts of the United Kingdom, there had long been in Ireland a tradition of government involvement in the provision of education. From at least the middle of the eighteenth century it was thought neither safe nor right to allow most of the Irish to go without any education at all, or only with that which could be gained illegally and haphazardly from their priests or itinerant schoolmasters. The central difficulty for British governments lay in how an avowedly anti-Catholic state was to provide for the education of a largely Catholic nation. Political and religious feeling in the rest of the United Kingdom (and Protestant Ireland) would not allow the Catholic Church to provide it; the sheer weight of Catholic numbers made it difficult for anybody else to do so satisfactorily.

Since Tudor times, responsibility for education in Ireland had lain with the bishops of the Anglican Church of Ireland and the incumbent of a given parish. In reality, these obligations were little observed, and the mid-eighteenth century saw an effort to revivify primary education in Ireland. Under the various anti-Catholic penal laws (however poorly enforced those were in practice by the mid-to-late eighteenth century), Irish Catholics were prohibited from establishing their own schools. As a result the Catholic population was often forced to provide for their children's education in 'hedge schools'. (Technically illegal, these schools were conducted wherever a place could be found—sometimes an improvised schoolhouse, often the teacher's room, occasionally out of doors. The quality of the teaching, like the quality of the teachers, ranged from the tolerably good to the abysmally poor.)

Both before and after the Union, the government attempted to educate the bulk of the population by means of such bodies as the Incorporated Society or the Kildare Place Society. Albeit private, these organisations were associated with the established church and received substantial government funding. This support enabled them, particularly in the latter case, to open a large number of schools throughout Ireland.

Begun with high hopes, both societies faltered when Catholics with-drew their support in the face of organised and determined attempts on the part of the school authorities to undermine the faith of their Catholic pupils. The relaxation of the penal laws allowed for the opening of some Catholic schools, such as the Jesuit establishment at Clongowes Wood in 1814, but they were never many in number and were aimed at the sons of the Catholic elite and the growing middle class.

The national schools grew out of the recognised failure of earlier efforts to attract Catholic students. Despite a widespread acceptance of its unsuitability, and the withdrawal of Catholic support in 1820, the Kildare Place Society survived until the advent of the Whig ministry of 1830. The most important figure in the creation of the national system of education in Ireland was an unlikely one: Lord Edward Stanley, later the fourteenth earl of Derby and a three-time Conservative prime minister. Stanley was not known for his sympathy for Ireland or the Irish, but he nevertheless proved to be pragmatic and largely fair-minded on the edu-cation issue, a fact that should be borne in mind when we come to con-sider his government's reaction to the request for a charter for the Catholic University in the 1850s and 1860s. In the early 1830s Stanley was chief secretary for Ireland and held, unlike his nominal superior, the lord lieutenant (Lord Anglesey), a seat in the cabinet. Although temperamen-tally inclined to support the Kildare Place Society, in the face of Catholic protests against it Stanley came to the conclusion that a national system was required and set out to design one. The details of the creation of the national system have been described elsewhere,[2] and need not detain us here. Suffice it to say that Stanley was successful in creating a system that partially satisfied the various Irish denominations. Although not perfect, the Catholic hierarchy and laity largely accepted it as the best that was likely to be made available; certainly it was a vast improvement on the Kildare Place Society. This uneasy consensus remained more or less intact until MacHale's outbursts in 1838.

John MacHale's nineteenth-century hagiographer, Bernard O'Reilly, invited his readers to consider the 'deep prophetic sense of the Arch-bishop of Tuam, who divined from the beginning the designs of the British Government and the dangers to national faith [from the National System and the Queen's Colleges], and the short-sightedness and pusilla-nimity of such members of the Catholic clergy and laity as supported the Government and denounced the Archbishop of Tuam as an agitator and a mischief maker.'[3] This remark captures almost perfectly the differences in the Irish church over education in the 1840s. MacHale saw himself as a prophet, whose mission was to save Catholic youth from a perfidious

Protestant and English government; his opponents—O'Reilly's short-sighted and pusillanimous clerics—were the archbishop of Armagh and primate of All Ireland, William Crolly, and Daniel Murray, the long-serving archbishop of Dublin.

John MacHale would long be the most important episcopal figure (aside from Paul Cullen) in the history of the Catholic University of Ireland. Born in county Mayo in 1791, MacHale was the first Irish bishop since the Reformation to be educated entirely in Ireland. He was something of a scholar, and translated both the *Iliad* and the Pentateuch into Irish. As early as his tenure as professor of dogmatic theology at Maynooth in the 1820s, MacHale was an uncompromising polemicist against both the Church of Ireland and British rule in Ireland.[4] He was appointed bishop of Killala in 1825 and was translated to the archiepiscopal see of Tuam in 1834 over British protests. At Tuam he cemented his reputation as the most fiercely partisan of bishops and made himself into the scourge of all things English in Ireland. Despite the adulation MacHale has received from a certain sort of Irish nationalist as the quintessential patriot bishop and 'Lion of the West',[5] the man himself was a quarrelsome, and in later years querulous, person incapable of compromise. Without question a 'good' nationalist, he was neither the best of bishops nor the most pleasant of men.

Although the national school system was originally established in Ireland in 1831, MacHale waited until 1838 to break ranks and condemn the entire system. In tones which must have become all too familiar to British politicians who had cause to tangle with him, MacHale wrote to Lord John Russell (then home secretary under Lord Melbourne) on 12 February 1838, to inform him that the government's 'impression' that it could 'assume and exercise complete control over the education, even the religious education, of the people' was 'an error which would be as fatal to the interests of the State, as it would be to the purity of the Catholic religion.' MacHale's primary objection—beyond a lively mistrust of Englishmen bearing gifts—was to allowing the government, even through the agency of a board or commission of national education, to prescribe which books the Catholic youth of Tuam should read. 'To no authority on earth, save the Pope, shall I submit the books from which the children of my diocese are to derive their religious instruction.'[6] MacHale's concern to maintain the prerogatives of the several bishops remained a central belief for him throughout his long episcopate.

Murray, Crolly, and their allies took a rather different line than MacHale. Both men were bishops of the old school. Murray was born in 1768 at Sheepwalk near the town of Arklow. Educated at the Irish College in Salamanca, he was ordained in 1790. As a curate in Arklow during the 1798 Rising he saw his parish priest murdered and, according to his hagiographer, faced an English 'cannon deliberately levelled at himself, as he stood upon the altar amid his trembling flock.'[7] He was appointed coadjutor to Archbishop Troy of Dublin in 1809, succeeded to that see in 1823, and, despite his experiences in 1798, settled into a long and close relationship with the government. It was his death, in 1852, that cleared the way for the Catholic University to be established in Dublin.

William Crolly also made his greatest contribution to the Catholic University by dying. The vacancy his passing opened in Armagh was to be filled by Paul Cullen, the university's greatest advocate. Born in 1780 to a Catholic landowner and (almost certainly) a Protestant mother, Crolly was one of the earliest students to attend Maynooth. He went on to become a lecturer at Maynooth in logic, ethics, and metaphysics.[8] He was appointed to the primatial see of Armagh in 1835, having been translated from Down and Connor. As archbishop of Armagh he joined Murray in pursuing an accommodationist line towards the government, becoming the greatest episcopal champion of both the national schools and the Queen's Colleges. Both men believed that things were getting better for Catholics in Ireland, that by and large successive British governments were doing the best they could, and that Catholics had more to gain from cooperation than from confrontation. It was a belief that had much truth to it, but one that was out of step with MacHale as well as the new ultramontanism represented by Paul Cullen.

The two archbishops, supported by Michael Slattery in Cashel, saw the national system as the best that Ireland could hope for and as such a positive boon to the Irish people. To these men MacHale's opposition was unfathomable, given the obvious merits of the system. As Murray explained to Cullen, at that time agent of the Irish bishops in Rome and rector of the Irish College there: 'Doctor McHale, you will have perceived, is making a violent outcry, in opposition to the sentiments of the majority of his Episcop[al] Brethren, against the National System of Education.'[9] This was particularly 'surprising' reported Murray, as 'he bases his principal argument on an evident misstatement; namely that the Bible is under the system made a school book.' Murray's despair was obvious as he reminded Cullen that 'we were long struggling to obtain public aid, which could [be] applied towards the education of our poor'. Now that this aid was obtained, however, MacHale 'seems desirous to wrest it from us, and throw it back into the hands of those who would employ it [as a rejection] against us.' MacHale's alternative—his 'pretended hope' to procure 'a separate grant for the education of the Catholic poor'—was considered 'so utterly visionary that no rational person could entertain it for a moment.'[10]

Once he had the bit between his teeth, though, MacHale had no
intention of letting Murray's cogent criticisms either halt his campaign or
temper his rhetoric. He bombarded the government with polemical
letters (quickly published) and told Daniel O'Connell, 'one thing is certain,
that an anti-Catholic Government is laboring to upset an essential principle, and to usurp the right of inculcating religious doctrine, through
books and masters of their own exclusive selection.' Even allowing for
polemic, the seriousness with which MacHale took the matter is revealed
in the same letter: 'The greater number of the present members of the
Board are rank infidels. The books which they put into the hands of the
children are calculated to unsettle their belief, or at least diminish their
reverence for the faith of their fathers; and by the entire system it is intended . . . to place the religious education of Catholics in the hands of
the Crown'.[11]

The battle lines having been drawn in Ireland, Rome became the
scene of much activity as both sides sought to gain official support. It is
important to bear in mind the power of Rome to settle disagreements
and the speed at which dissenting groups within the hierarchy would
appeal thereto. In fact, the history of the Irish church in the 1840s can
often seem to be one long appeal to Rome. This was hardly surprising,
as Catholic Ireland was at this time, and for many years to come, under
the ecclesiastical authority of the Sacred Congregation for the Propagation of the Faith: known, somewhat ominously to modern ears, as the
Propaganda.

In many ways the advent of Irish ultramontanism, manifested most
clearly in the appointment of Paul Cullen to the see of Armagh in 1850,
can be seen as Rome's unwilling response to a hierarchy perpetually divided by British *concessions* to Catholics. Throughout the 1840s (and to
a certain extent the 1830s), successive British governments offered what
they believed to be concessions to individual Roman Catholics and the
institutional Roman Catholic Church. Whether the issue was national
education, charitable bequests, or university education, these grants inevitably plunged the Irish church into turmoil. In the face of a controversial action, all sides appealed to Rome, and the losing side inevitably
reappealed. Rome—and especially the Propaganda—was drawn ever
more closely into Irish affairs; when things were quiet, little enough attention was paid to Ireland. The assertion of Roman control over the
Irish church, primarily by means of the Cullen appointment, can thus be
seen as more of a defensive measure designed to impose some sort of
peace on a fractious Irish hierarchy that had proved itself incapable of
coping with British concessions.

Unlike England before 1850, the Irish church did possess its own hierarchy. There were four ecclesiastical provinces based roughly, but not exactly, on the traditional four Irish provinces of Leinster, Munster, Connaught, and Ulster. Each province had an archbishop (at Armagh, Dublin, Cashel, and Tuam), and there were twenty-three other diocesan bishops. Each archbishop was first among equals in his own province, chairing and convening provincial meetings and synods and representing his province both nationally and in Rome. Despite this, an archbishop had little real authority over his suffragan bishops; he had none at all over other archbishops or their suffragans. Even the title of primate, attached to the see of Armagh, carried with it no other right than that of chairing the annual meeting of the bishops. Those meetings were not synodical (the Synod of Thurles, in 1850, would be the first Irish national synod since the seventeenth century), and decisions taken at them could only be classed as recommendations as far as a dissenting prelate might be concerned. The real power in the Irish church lay in Rome.[12]

The Propaganda took a close interest in Irish affairs and could issue faculties to allow a bishop or bishops to take some action beyond the scope of his normal diocesan duties. The Congregation was also empowered to promulgate rescripts that bound, at least in theory, bishops to follow a given course of action. In addition to the normal *ad limina* visits to Rome expected of all prelates, a bishop was required to report (in writing or in person) to the Propaganda on matters affecting his diocese. Until a papal nuncio was appointed in 1908, Rome had no independent observer in Ireland. This left the Propaganda dependent on the often conflicting reports of a deeply divided hierarchy. Naturally enough, the Sacred Congregation felt the need to consult with an Irish figure it trusted in an effort to sort through the conflicting and often contentious information coming from Ireland.

The Irish hierarchy, too, needed a representative in Rome to act as a kind of envoy to the Sacred Congregation. Conveniently, but sometimes confusingly, the rector of the Irish College, Paul Cullen, fulfilled both roles: agent of all the bishops and expert on a divided Ireland for the Propaganda. If this role left Cullen open to charges of double-dealing or conflict of interest, it also made him uniquely powerful within the Irish church.

The Irish College in Rome was only one, albeit the most important, of a number of Irish Colleges scattered throughout the continent. Created to train priests, the colleges flourished during the penal period, with most declining only after the establishment of Maynooth in 1795. Into the nineteenth century, colleges remained in Lisbon, Salamanca, Paris, and Rome.[13] Indeed, the college in Paris would prove a major headache for Archbishop Cullen in the late 1850s, and the stop-gap rector of the Catholic University after Newman's departure would be drawn from Salamanca. That being as it may, the Irish College in Rome was necessarily the most important of the colleges. The college served as a base for Irish bishops visiting Rome, as well as the preferred establishment for high-flying seminarians anxious to live and train in the Eternal City. Under the rectorships of Paul Cullen (1832–49) and Tobias Kirby (1850–91) the college and its rectors also served as the point of contact between the Irish hierarchy and the Propaganda. Unless a bishop wished to travel to Rome himself or send an envoy—both matters of great expense—he had to rely on the good offices of Cullen or Kirby. Thus Cullen's power was unofficial but vast. As long as he retained the trust of the Propaganda and the pope—and he always did—he could largely control the policy of the Holy See towards Ireland and Ireland's bishops.

The contending camps moved quickly to gain Cullen's help with the Propaganda and his own personal support for their position. The MacHaleites were off the mark early, with the archbishop of Tuam himself writing a rather formal letter to Cullen in February 1838. That letter was most likely designed to be shown by Cullen in the Propaganda and any other useful places, a normal enough practice.[14] 'You may recollect', wrote MacHale, 'that when I was in Rome the new Education Board was formed . . . and that even in its infancy it met with our disapprobation.' 'It has since', he continued, 'become more obnoxious'. 'Dr. Murray does not I think see the extent of its danger.' MacHale went on to tell Cullen, and whomever else might be reading, that 'I felt it my duty lately to express my opinions on its dangerous tendency', as he feared 'that those who often calumniated my opinions before might misrepresent those letters I thought fit to send them to you as published that they may speak for themselves.'[15] William Higgins (later 'O'Higgins'), the bishop of Ardagh and Clonmacnoise since 1829 (and a noted firebrand and close ally of MacHale), followed on, reporting—somewhat optimistically—to Cullen the results of a bishops' meeting on the education question: 'On the principle and operation of the Education System there was a difference of opinion; but I succeeded in putting the whole of the Bishops on the alert and produced such <u>proofs</u> as convinced all, that unless well watched, the Education as now carried on was likely to undermine the authority of the Catholic Church, and ultimately to introduce either positive errors or "Indifferentism"'.[16]

Throughout the summer and early autumn both sides continued to ask Cullen's advice and seek his help. A letter from Murray dated 13 June

1838 sought Cullen's assistance in making the national system intelligible to the prefect of the Sacred Congregation, Cardinal Giacomo Filippo Fransoni, a request that would hardly have been made were Cullen suspected of double dealing.[17] Cullen's own letter to Archbishop Slattery of Cashel (an ally of Murray and Crolly over this issue) in mid-July could give the system's supporters no cause for worry about his loyalty either. It merely reported Propaganda's developing, sceptical views on the system.[18] MacHale continued to write to Cullen, telling him of his contacts with the cardinal prefect and reporting on troubling events within the school system: 'contrary to the express resolutions of the clergy of this Diocese the Board have sent a Protestant inspector to be a resident and permanent agent to regulate the quality and quantity of religious instruction to be given in the Catholic Schools!!'.[19] Such information could hardly be calculated to make Cullen sanguine about the national system.

Cullen, of course, was agent for all the bishops and was well within his rights to report the trend of things within the Propaganda to an interested prelate on an open question. It is true, however, that if Higgins were not sure of Cullen's support, his tone in writing to Cullen was incautious in the extreme. His comments on the January 1839 bishops' meeting are a case in point: 'I say with much affliction that nothing could surpass the <u>secular views</u> and want of candour on the part of our opponents. Could you ever imagine that an Irish Bishop would stubbornly, and not very respectfully refuse to consult the successor of Peter in his doubt and difficulties'.[20] Higgins, however, was noted for his lack of caution and robust epistolary style. His letter can also be read as another attempt to influence Cullen, especially in the remarks about the pro-national schools bishops' refusal to consult the Holy See. Cullen's own devotion to the pope was well known (he closed almost every letter home with a report on the pontiff's health, whatever it might be), and if Higgins could persuade him that Murray and his allies had Gallican tendencies then Cullen's reaction could be easily predicted.

Throughout early 1839 Murray and Crolly continued to enjoy Cullen's services as bishops' agent and kept him informed of the progress of the controversy. Reporting on the same meeting as Higgins, Murray told Cullen that 'Dr. McHale urged, that the matter [of the national schools] was before the Holy See, and that they [the bishops] were not therefore competent to come to a decision on it.' The sixteen bishops in favour of the system, Murray wrote, 'stood firm in their decided approval of the National System of education, and considered it quite unnecessary to annoy the Holy See on a subject which they found by experience to be not only safe but advantageous to Religion.'[21] Crolly wrote in a similar vein on 4 February, 'for the information of the Holy See'. He added an attack on MacHale for good measure.[22]

By March, Murray was clearly hearing things against Cullen but did not as yet credit them. He went so far as to ask Cullen to review the response made by the pro-schools forces to MacHale's charges: 'I wish you would take the trouble of asking to see them, that you may be able to explain whatever obscurity may be found in them.' Essentially, Murray was asking Cullen to be the official interpreter of his case to the non–English-speaking officials of the Propaganda. And this despite the fact that 'the opponents of the National System do not, as I am informed, scruple to reckon you on their side.' Cullen was safe, Murray felt, as 'your judgement will, I am sure, be an honest one; and that is all I would desire.'[23] For his part, MacHale seemed to be receiving advice from Cullen, and, most uncharacteristically, claimed to be taking it.[24] Unfortunately, Cullen's letters to MacHale do not seem to survive before 1840. What is clear is that by July 1839, Murray was beginning to suspect Cullen as he sensed the trend of the Propaganda's thinking towards the schools. Still, it was in Murray's interest to give Cullen the benefit of the doubt for as long as he could. Murray had no one else to turn to in Rome, and it was vastly better to have Cullen as an ally, or even a neutral, than as an opponent.

Throughout 1838 up to the Propaganda's tentative decision (it had not been confirmed by the pope) to condemn the national system in July 1839, Cullen had not only been in communication with both pro- and anti-schools prelates, he had most likely offered advice to both sides. What, then, were Cullen's own views on the subject at this time? The short answer is that we do not know for sure. It seems likely, given his later distaste for any hint of mixed or Protestant-influenced education, his distance from the Irish scene, and the information he received from Higgins and MacHale, that Cullen would be opposed to the national system. Without the vast bulk of Cullen's letters to MacHale (apparently there were none at all to Higgins or John Cantwell of Meath), we simply do not know to what extent Cullen was in league with the episcopal minority.

It is certain that Cullen was consulted by the Propaganda on the matter, and it is quite likely that he offered at least moderate opposition to the plan. What cannot be said is that he engaged in the kind of conspiracy that Murray and (particularly) Crolly came to suspect and that he certainly did engage in when the matter of the Queen's Colleges came up for consideration some five years later.[25] As Ambrose Macaulay has noted: 'there is no written evidence to prove that Cullen so acted [against the schools] at this stage of the dispute, and, as subsequent controversies showed, when Cullen felt strongly about an ecclesiastical problem, he was far from reluctant to put his thoughts on paper.'[26] Macaulay then notes that in 1838 Cullen sent a memorandum to the Propaganda which, although cautious in tone, seemed to indicate that Murray had successfully defended the national system against most of MacHale's charges.[27]

Whatever the nature of Cullen's involvement, the archbishops of Armagh (emphatically) and Dublin (less clearly) believed their man in Rome had betrayed them. David Richard Pigot, an MP and the solicitor-general for Ireland, and Nicholas Wiseman, at that time rector of the English College in Rome, both reported that Cullen's influence had been critical in securing the Propaganda's condemnation.[28] Crolly even went so far as to suggest to Murray that Cullen be removed from his post as the bishops' agent in Rome, telling him that 'Drs H [presumably Higgins] and C[ullen] may yet be sorry for the very unbecoming part they have played in this business.'[29] In assessing Cullen's actions, it seems impossible to improve on Ambrose Macaulay's verdict that Cullen simply gave the best possible advice as he saw it to both sides—and to the Propaganda—even if his own inclinations would have been against the schools.[30]

Despite Cullen's undoubted usefulness, Murray did not see matters in this light. In a letter of February 1840 he not only warned Cullen that he, Murray, was hearing things about Cullen but also revealed the extraordinarily close links between the archbishop of Dublin and Dublin Castle: 'I lately saw a letter addressed to the Government by one of their Diplomatic Agents in Italy (a Protestant) which stated, that nothing could be decided on the Education question until the arrival of Dr McHale's deputy; but that in reality, he did not want one, for that, all thro', he had a most efficient one in the President of the Irish College.' Murray went on to tell Cullen that 'I need not say how galling this intelligence would be to the great majority of the Irish Prelates'.[31] As warnings from Murray went, this one wore only the slightest of veils.

Led by Murray and Crolly, the majority of the Irish bishops continued their campaign in Rome either to prevent the Propaganda's condemnation being confirmed by the pope or to cause the Sacred Congregation itself to rethink the issue. Their success is indicated in a letter of Cullen's to MacHale in early 1840 (written *before* Murray's 'threat letter'), in which Cullen advised MacHale to seek some sort of compromise—optimistic advice to give someone of MacHale's temperament. The Propaganda, Cullen wrote, 'are desirous that the question should be kept before the public as little as possible' and wished 'that the question should be treated with the greatest calmness possible, and that any little excitement that prevailed should subside, in order that the controversy may be carried on peaceably and without any breach of charity.'[32] Considering the vehemence of the opposition got up by MacHale, Higgins, and their allies, the archbishop, if possessed of even the smallest hint of self-knowledge, could only see such requests as a rebuke to himself and his friends.

Instead of continuing with their agitation, Cullen wrote, it would 'be most desirable that the matter were terminated in some way or other, in order that people's minds should not be kept in suspense any longer.' Such a compromise, perhaps reached at the February bishops' meeting, would be advisable to MacHale, as 'I am now convinced that they [Propaganda] will come to no decision, unless it can be proved evidently that the system will be necessarily productive of evil, and great evil, to religion, even when the prelates and priests do their duty and watch its workings narrowly.' Murray and his supporters would thus, Cullen thought, 'succeed in averting a condemnation'. Compromise, then, was necessary, and would carry with it the 'advantage' that 'peace and unity would be again restored' (assuming MacHale saw this as an advantage) and, besides, 'some more favourable opportunity might occur of examining and discussing the merits of the system.'[33]

Visiting Ireland in the summer of 1840, Cullen inspected some of the national schools. He reported back to Cardinal Fransoni that although the 'complaints made against the nature or the theory of the system are generally well founded', the actual practice in the schools could not be any more Catholic. Cullen followed this remark up with a formal report to the Propaganda urging that the status quo be maintained.[34] The conflict over the national schools, then, was not exactly the forerunner of the later debate over the Queen's Colleges, a debate that led directly to the establishment of the Catholic University. Some important lessons, however, can be drawn.

It is clear that there were at least three separate views within the Irish church on the national system. The first two are quite obvious: Murray, Crolly, and the majority of the bishops supported the schools with enthusiasm as a good deal for Ireland, for which the church should be properly grateful (while of course taking care that faith and morals were not threatened). These men would take a similar line over the Queen's Colleges and a consequently hostile approach to the idea of a Catholic university in their place.

Equally clear was the opposition of MacHale, Higgins, Cantwell, and their substantially fewer supporters. It would be uncharitable to suggest that these men were opposed to the system entirely because it emanated from an English source. Certainly MacHale, and most likely the others, had genuine and not altogether unfounded concerns about the nature of the system and its effect on religion. This was especially true with regard to the selection of texts and the inspection of schools. But the primary source of their opposition was a simple unwillingness to accept anything coming from the government as being good. These men would be all for a Catholic university as long as it was to be used as a weapon against the Queen's Colleges. But, to one degree or another, they became dissatisfied with the institution when it was seen as Cullen's own project and when it took on an English face in John Henry Newman and his professors.

The third group took a rather more subtle line and is the more interesting for it. Members of this grouping supported the national schools for pragmatic reasons, as the best possible deal under the circumstances. They did not, however, view government-sponsored education of the Irish (Catholic) population as a good thing in the way, say, that Murray did. Temperamental distrust of 'mixed' or government-controlled education was qualified by pragmatism. Both Cullen and, more problematically, Michael Slattery belonged to this group, as did William Kinsella in Ossory (Kilkenny).[35] The evidence that Cullen took this line has been discussed in some detail above; despite the paucity of information on Cullen in this period, it seems clear that he was cautiously in favour of the national system if temperamentally suspicious of it. Slattery can be placed with Cullen in this grouping only more tentatively; there simply isn't enough information to do otherwise. He certainly supported the national schools, but, like Cullen, he quickly opposed the Queen's Colleges, and on similar grounds. He also, like Cullen, became disillusioned with aspects of the national system in the late 1840s. Slattery too seems to have fallen between the 'Castle' and the 'Patriot' bishops on educational matters.

Michael Slattery had been heavily involved in clerical education before being elevated to archiepiscopal dignity. He was educated at Trinity College and, after identifying his vocation, at Carlow College. Slattery's Trinity education is important in that it demonstrates both the possibility that devout Catholics might attend there and also the reaction that at least one very devout Catholic had to the nature of his education in Ireland's only university. After ordination Slattery was appointed a professor at Carlow (where he taught Cullen), and in 1832, at the age of nearly sixty, he was appointed to the presidency of Maynooth with the strong support of James Doyle, the influential and talented bishop of Kildare.

He served only briefly at Maynooth before being appointed, in December 1833, as archbishop of Cashel. A quiet and retiring man by nature, Slattery would find himself unable to take responsibility for the erection of a Catholic university when circumstances left him the only man in Ireland who might be able to do so.

Although not himself a bishop, Cullen was still one of the most powerful figures in the Irish church. He was agent to all the bishops, but some publicly claimed him as an ally, causing the others to suspect his loyalty (egged on by his colleague Nicholas Wiseman, rector of the English College). In the meantime the Propaganda was asking for his opinion on the national system. To make matters worse, his vice-rector and close friend had entered the debate with a published tirade against the schools. The existing evidence indicates that Cullen treated all sides fairly and acted with honour. His pragmatic approval of the schools seems to have been the most sensible course available, and was confirmed in the end by his actual examination of the schools themselves. He did not trust—and never would—the English, but he was willing to use them if they could do good for Ireland. He might not like it, but he would live with it.

The Propaganda's decision not to make a decision on the national schools ended the immediate controversy but by no means stilled the simmering divisions within the Irish church. Those bishops who approved of the schools could go on as before, and those who opposed them could likewise continue to withhold their support and that of their clergy. Neither side trusted or understood the other. The ease with which these latent divisions could reemerge was demonstrated when the government introduced, in 1844, a bill to regulate charitable bequests to religious organisations in Ireland. The previous system had insisted that all bequests must be made to an individual, not a (nonestablished) church. The new bill would create a charitable bequests board to regulate legacies, which would now be allowed to institutions of the Catholic Church, excepting religious orders. Once again, the details of the controversy are not relevant to our present topic, but a brief discussion of the issue will serve to illuminate the dissension still prevalent in the hierarchy and can cast an interesting light on the views of some of the primary actors in this debate and the ones that would follow.

Not surprisingly, Murray, Crolly, and many of the bishops who had supported the national schools also supported the Charitable Bequests Act, and for the same reasons: the bill was clearly an improvement on what had gone before; the government was doing the best it could given the situation; rejection would only play into the hands of Ireland's opponents and could lead to something even worse than the status quo. Also not surprisingly, MacHale, Higgins, and company were opposed: the government was presuming to meddle in church affairs; Protestants could sit in judgement on the bequests of faithful Catholics to their church; the religious orders were still prevented from receiving bequests; the English thought of it. As Higgins put it in a letter to Cullen, 'The Education question was the first wedge to [inflict] our body, and the enemy now puts another at its back.'[36]

Higgins spelled out the 'anti' case to Cullen, remarking that the great aim of the government, and the bill, was to 'undermine by degrees the just authority of the Holy See'. He wondered how could he 'or any orthodox Bishop admit the right in a heretical Government of issuing a commission to regulate purely religious bequests made by Catholics'. Intriguingly, Higgins also raised an issue that would later bulk large in criticism of Cullen's actions with regard to the Catholic University, pointing out that putting a bishop on such a committee 'must necessarily usurp the jurisdiction and right of his brother prelates!!!'.[37] As the existing system gave the individual Irish bishops almost total independence from each other and from the bench of bishops as a whole, Higgins was quite correct in noting that such a change as the bill envisioned would involve setting one or more bishop over others—at least in the limited area of charitable bequests. Indeed, almost any change to the Irish system would serve to decrease the power of individual bishops; it could hardly be increased. Because all power was held in Rome, as long as a bishop did not attract the Propaganda's attention he could essentially do as he liked without regard to anyone else in the Irish church. Higgins' worry about losing authority to another bishop in the matter of charitable bequests anticipates a fear that would drive many of the actions of MacHale and his allies in the 1850s.

Cullen involved himself in the opposition to the Charitable Bequests Act in a way he had not done during the debate over the national schools. Murray, who had agreed to sit on the bequests commission, wrote acidly to Cullen: 'I was hardly surprised at hearing that the new Charitable Donations and Bequests Act has found no favour at Rome.' This was because the Act, 'good or bad, . . . has not had fair play.' And, in a rare example of sarcasm, Murray told Cullen how 'much humbled I was to see a long letter from our Friend Dr. Kirby thundering with all his might against a clause which is not even in the act at all.'[38] Murray's anger at his opponents was clear, as can be seen when he urged Slattery not to miss a bishops' meeting on the issue so as not to 'leave the Irish Church at the mercy of a party which does not always confine its efforts within the limits of prudence'[39]—harsh words from that most prudent of men.

Cullen was not in a mood for compromise, telling Murray that 'while it may be said that the church gains something by the clauses of this bill', he could not see why 'any cath: principles sd. be sacrificed' nor why 'we' should 'acquiesce in, or approve of enactments contrary to the spirit of the church' that were of an 'evil tendency' and were 'calculated to produce discord among the Catholic body for mere temporal advantages'.[40] Cullen was not going to be asked by Murray to help the Propaganda better understand the issue this time.

If Cullen's opposition to the bill confirmed his unpopularity with Murray and Crolly, then the manner of his opposition provoked a rebuke from an unexpected source. That rebuke, and Cullen's reply, provide an interesting glimpse into both his role within the Irish church and his response to friendly criticism. William Walsh, bishop (later archbishop) of Halifax in Nova Scotia, had known Cullen in Rome and the two men had become friends. Until Walsh's death, he would be one of the few people outside his own family to whom Cullen would explain his thinking and confide his worries. Walsh wrote to Cullen in early 1845 to chastise him over his actions in opposition to the charitable bequests bill: 'Now, let me assure you from personal observation that the excitement got up against the Bequests Bill was in the worst possible taste.' Although the 'Bill was bad enough,' the 'shocking manner in which the Bishops and Clergy have been assailed—the furious appeals to the fear and passions of the people—the fever heat to which they were influenced—the tissue of shameless fabrications which was woven from day to day . . . these and many other sad features of the late and present agitation are such as every friend to religion and Ireland must bitterly deplore.' And, 'as I told you before the letters of my dear friend Tobias [Kirby] and your own supposed interference with the recent [debate] were most opportune for the designs of your defamers.'[41] Although Walsh softened the sting somewhat with some fulsome praise of Cullen's character, his letter remains one of the few occasions when Cullen would be so comprehensively rebuked by a friend.

In response, Cullen made what can only be described as an attempt at an act of perfect contrition. He told Walsh that he was 'exceedingly obliged for the good advice you gave' and was 'very far indeed from being annoyed.' Indeed, 'all I have reason to be annoyed with myself for is for having taken any part at all in the actual proceedings. Were I to live a century again in Rome, nothing would induce me to do such a thing again.' He went on to explain, 'In an excited moment I unfortunately let myself be led astray.' Cullen was clearly upset by Walsh's criticism and the part he himself had played in events. He told Walsh that he had 'well expiated' his mistakes 'by the keenest mental agony' and that he had 'spent entire weeks without sleep and I am now indeed in a very low state.' Considering what we know about Cullen's depression and his occasionally precarious mental health, it is almost certain that the attack he described was real, and was a result of his own recognition of his mistakes, perceived or real, in being too closely associated with the heated anti-Murray rhetoric which was flying about Rome and Ireland. As he told the bishop of Meath, John Cantwell, 'I was wrong in taking any part in the proceedings'.[42]

The point made by the exchange with Walsh, and by Cullen's moderate behaviour over the national schools, is that he was not wedded to the idea of opposing everything the government and its episcopal allies did in the same way that, say, MacHale was. He could be induced to take up an immoderate stance, but he was not comfortable there and would quickly withdraw, in great mental torment, when the nature of his position was pointed out to him, as it was in this case by Walsh. He was clearly opposed to the Charitable Bequests Act, but he was willing to distinguish between Murray the man and his support for the Act. That Cullen would become genuinely, enthusiastically, and unapologetically an opponent of the Queen's Colleges and its supporters shows how seriously he took that issue. His opposition, eventually growing into the kind of vituperation against Murray that he so eloquently repented of to Walsh, was not a simple extension of that offered over previous contentious questions. It was a clear break from his earlier behaviour and personal tendencies. Although Cullen promised Walsh that he would 'never take any public step again',[43] it was a promise that events would soon force him to break; the prospect of 'Godless' education brought Cullen to the barricades with all his being.

chapter two

'Godless' Education
for Ireland

THE QUEEN'S COLLEGES

THE 'GODLESS COLLEGES'—A PHRASE USED BY THE HIGH TORY
Sir Robert Inglis, later picked up by Irish opponents of the colleges—
were the result of the manifest inadequacy of university education in
Ireland.[1] The University of Dublin, with its single college, Trinity, was
the only university in the island and a bastion of the established church.
Founded by Elizabeth I, Trinity had been at least partially created to prevent the Irish attending foreign universities and there being 'infected
with poperie and other ill qualities.'[2] Although Trinity degrees were
opened to Catholics and dissenters from 1793 (long before Oxford and
Cambridge), it was not an option much availed of. College fellowships
and scholarships were only open to members of the Church of Ireland
and the curriculum remained influenced by the doctrines of that church.
As a result, Trinity incurred the disapproval of the Catholic hierarchy.[3]
There was no other real option for university education in Ireland. The
national Catholic seminary at Maynooth (founded in 1795) was just that,
a seminary. Although Maynooth had originally encompassed a lay element, by the 1840s it had long been entirely clerical and there was little

desire within the church to see a return of the laity.[4] The Presbyterians had the Belfast Academical Institute, but conflict between the orthodox majority in Ulster and the more Unitarian minority which dominated the institute made it unsuitable as a nascent Presbyterian university.[5]

Irish Presbyterians at least had the choice of sending their sons to the nearby and relatively convivial Scottish universities. Irish Catholics could not. Despite attempts by the Benedictine bishop Peter Augustine Baines to found a Catholic university college at Prior Park near Bath and the hopes of Nicholas Wiseman that the northern English seminary at Oscott might eventually become a university, in the 1840s there was no place in England where lay Catholics might gain a university education with ecclesiastical approval; Prior Park closed in 1856 (having given up its university pretensions in 1843) and Oscott never developed beyond a seminary and school. Nor were the ancient universities of Oxford and Cambridge open to Catholics (despite the presence of the occasional Catholic at Cambridge). The situation of the continent was little better. Other than in Belgium, where the hierarchy reestablished a university at Louvain in 1834, there was no specifically Catholic university in Europe (although Bologna and the Spanish universities were under church authority). France, for example, had only one university—a Napoleonic foundation with a distinctly anticlerical bent. It was not until 1850 that French Catholics were allowed to open their own primary and secondary schools; they were still prohibited from opening a university.[6]

In the autumn of 1844 Sir Robert Peel and his government determined to propose some sort of solution to the Irish university question. Options that were discussed included turning Maynooth into a dual seminary–lay university, adding new colleges to the University of Dublin, changing the exclusively established church nature of Trinity College, or affiliating both Maynooth and the Belfast Academical Institute (with possibly an entirely new entity based in Cork) to the University of Dublin.[7] The idea of turning Maynooth into a new state-funded university had little appeal to a government that was still less than enthusiastic towards Catholic claims and had seen enough controversy over Maynooth to wish to court any more; even if they had wished to pursue such a policy it is most unlikely that it could have made its way through Parliament given the level of protest over the regularisation of the Maynooth grant and the extension of funds for building. The inter-Presbyterian difficulties over the Academical Institute had led, in September 1844, to the General Assembly submitting a memorial to the Peel government requesting that it endow an entirely new (orthodox) Presbyterian college.[8] Nor was the idea of tampering with Trinity College likely to meet with much favour. Not only did the college have representation in Parliament, but it was also in effect the national seminary of the Church of Ireland. Adding new colleges to the University of Dublin (envisioned by the original statutes) was possible, but raised some of the same objections as changes to Trinity alone did. In the end the Cabinet voted unanimously on 22 November 1844 to tentatively approve the creation of entirely new colleges in Cork and Belfast and to leave Dublin untouched by the new scheme for Irish university education.[9]

The new institutions—to be called Queen's Colleges—were to be religiously neutral. This was despite the fact that, as Donal Kerr notes, Peel and his home secretary, Sir James Graham, would 'certainly have preferred a system based on religion.'[10] Peel himself admitted that he would not have recommended such a scheme for England or Scotland, telling the House of Commons that he could only justify his plans given the 'peculiar and unfortunate character of the religious differences' which existed in Ireland.[11] Given Ireland's religious complexities—and the increasingly bad name of sectarian education—the government felt that a university that did not fund the teaching of any theology, yet allowed for the private endowment of chairs by interested parties, would be the best solution to the Irish university question. No one church in Ireland would consent to 'its' students being taught the theology of another. Nor did the government believe that it could establish a separate university for each Irish denomination that might wish to have one. What the Peel government failed to take into consideration was the strength of opposition to the idea of secular education. Jerusalem was not yet ready to yield to Athens.

There was a precedent for the creation of a secular university in the United Kingdom, albeit a recent one. Before the foundation of University College in London in 1828 the only universities in England were the ancient establishments of Oxford and Cambridge. Long strongholds of the established church, subscription to the Thirty-nine Articles was required on matriculation at Oxford and on graduation at Cambridge. Scotland retained its own university system with ancient establishments at St Andrews, Glasgow, and Aberdeen, as well as a more recent one in Edinburgh. The Scottish universities retained their own religious character and traditions, as, of course, did Oxford and Cambridge.

Influenced by the utilitarian ideas of Jeremy Bentham and James Mill, University College was avowedly secular. Despite being granted a charter as London University in 1831, opposition from Oxbridge prevented it from gaining the power to grant degrees. At the same time an Anglican reaction against secular education was taking shape, resulting in the establishment of King's College in London in 1829 (it opened its doors in 1831) and the University of Durham in 1837. Both were exclusively Anglican in nature. King's, for example, required its staff and students to be members of the Church of England, a requirement that persisted until 1903. The two institutions competed in London until a compromise was reached in 1836. 'London University' reverted to University College and with King's College formed the University of London. The university was to be an examining and degree-granting body only, and its constituent colleges (at first limited to UCL and King's) were to retain their own religious (or otherwise) character; the university itself was totally secular. Later, the University of London would expand to include other colleges and would allow students from outside the federation to sit exams for London degrees.

The plan for the Queen's Colleges drew on the example of London but did not exactly copy it. There was no place within the degree-granting 'Queen's University' (envisioned by the Colleges Act and chartered in 1850) for a sectarian institution like King's London. The system was to be 'mixed' education. The idea was that students from all religious backgrounds would be educated together and religion itself would play no role in either the running of the college or its curriculum (although an interested denomination could establish a privately endowed chair of theology if it so wished). In effect, each of the Queen's Colleges was to be a UCL, not a King's. Secular education had proved controversial in the case of London; it would be even more controversial in Ireland.

Peel and the government were not unaware that such a plan might be met with opposition from the Roman Catholic hierarchy. Acting for the government, Graham instructed his secretary, William A'Court Heytesbury, to contact Crolly and Murray as the leading (and most sympathetic) bishops, as well as Anthony Blake, the lay Catholic commissioner for the national schools. It appears that Heytesbury did not execute his instructions exactly and only contacted Blake about the proposed colleges. Blake assured him that the hierarchy would be willing to accept the necessity of privately endowed divinity chairs, given the understanding that lectures could take place in college facilities and on college grounds. Yet, according to Kerr, it is unclear whether Blake in fact 'consulted any other Catholics and certainly the hierarchy as a whole did not delegate him to speak for them'.[12]

The reaction of some in the hierarchy would prove much more hostile than Blake had led Graham and the government to believe—although it is hard to imagine, in the wake of the controversy over the national schools and the one still raging over charitable bequests, how the government could have expected anything less than intense opposition to its plans. John MacHale weighed in almost immediately with a letter to Peel on the subject of the proposed colleges: 'I am anxious to apprize you before hand that you miscalculate much if you imagine that we shall ever suffer the education of the people of Ireland to be planned or conducted by those who seem to have taken upon themselves the exclusive office of the directors of the public mind, and to whom—so well have they till now accorded to your views—you seem anxious to entrust the guidance of the youth of Ireland, and the laws and regulations by which its academies, colleges, and universities are to be governed.'[13] In tone and content MacHale's letter was not all that different from his missive to Lord John Russell in 1838, only instead of national schools, the issue was now Queen's Colleges.

For once, Crolly and Murray found themselves in at least partial agreement with the Lion of the West. The original proposal, which lacked any protection for Catholic students from the threat of proselytisation, could hardly be acceptable to any but a small fraction of the bishops. Crolly called a special meeting of the hierarchy for 21 May 1845, telling Slattery that 'the Government plan of Academical Education appears to be pregnant with danger to the faith and morals of the youth of this country.'[14] The twenty-one bishops present unanimously adopted a resolution hostile to the colleges. Although they gave 'credit to Her Majesty's Government for their kind and generous intentions', they were 'compelled by a sense of duty' to declare that they could not give their 'approbation to the proposed system', as they deemed it would be 'dangerous to the faith and morals of the Catholic pupils.'[15]

This temperate objection would be backed up by a memorial to be presented to the government. That document expressed the desire of the hierarchy for the government to provide paid chaplains who would remain under episcopal control, and give the bishops a voice in the running of the colleges. The memorial also noted that Catholics could not attend lectures in just about any subject save law 'without exposing their faith and morals to imminent danger, unless a Roman Catholic professor will be appointed for each of those chairs.'[16] Such a concession could not be made without abandoning the government's policy of mixed education. That such a memorial could come from a meeting dominated by relative moderates on the education issue like Murray and Crolly goes some way to indicating the hurdles the Queen's Colleges would face.

Despite the initial rhetoric, it soon became obvious that at least some of the bishops were prepared to compromise with the government. By June, Murray was willing to privately assure the government that certain

concessions—primarily assurances about religious control of halls of residence and majority Catholic representation on any visitorial authority at
those colleges with Catholic majorities (Cork and Galway)—could persuade him and a majority of the bishops to support the bill.[17] This apparent willingness to make concessions was quickly opposed by MacHale
and his allies in Ireland, as well as by friends in Rome.

If Cullen had been pragmatic and conciliatory over the national
schools and was only just sleeping again after his ill-tempered attacks on
Murray during the charitable bequests controversy, on the question of
'Godless' education he was prepared to put his not inconsiderable power
at MacHale and the other opponents' disposal. Luckily for the historian,
Cullen was travelling in Ireland during much of 1845. His letters to
Kirby reveal his views most clearly. As early as 14 May, while Cullen was
still with his brother Thomas's family in Liverpool, he told Kirby that
'Peel's plan for academical education is now before the public' and that
not only was 'no religious instruction to be given' but that 'O'Connell
has denounced the whole system'.[18] Although he hoped that the bishops
would agree with O'Connell, he 'fear[ed] <u>not</u>.'[19] Cullen was pleased with
the May condemnation but was suspicious of the resolution of the bishops. As he told Kirby in June, 'I suppose you were glad to hear the bishops were unanimous about the education bill—In the beginning [they]
were most favourable to it, and I believe are so still.' That being the case,
'I suppose the government knows their views and will carry the bill.' He
correctly guessed what would happen: 'What I fear the Bishops will do
is, having declared the new system dangerous, they will accept office in
order to impede the dangerous tendencies of the bill—just as occurred in
the Bequests controversy.' 'However,' he optimistically concluded, 'I
have no reason to suspect this misfortune.'[20]

Perhaps emboldened by the probable support of the senior archbishops should some small changes be made, the government persevered and
the bill completed its passage through Parliament on 10 July. Cullen
quickly lashed out, telling Kirby, 'I believe the Bequests bill agitation
will [re-]commence' and, hopefully, that 'the colleges will be resisted by
the majority of the Bishops.' Perhaps still feeling guilty for his earlier
treatment of Murray, Cullen put the blame squarely on Crolly: 'the Primate is not to be relied upon in these matters . . . were it not for him Dr.
Murray wd. be easily managed.'[21] Over the summer Cullen became more
and more pessimistic, writing in August, 'I dare say some of the bishops
themselves will accept office as visitors of the new colleges.' If this were to
be the case, 'what confidence can the people have in them any longer—
they condemn the college bill as dangerous to faith and morals and then

they are in a hurry to recommend their friends for situations in those colleges, and they undertake to carry themselves the management of this scheme of godless education.'[22]

Cullen proved an accurate prophet as Murray, Crolly, and Patrick Kennedy, bishop of Killaloe (since 1836) duly became episcopal commissioners after receiving assurances that changes would be made along the lines Murray had sketched out. To make matters worse for Cullen, Catholics accepted the presidencies of both the Galway and Cork Colleges, and one, Joseph Kirwan at Galway, was even a priest. Crolly would also give cause for Cullen's assessment of him as the leading proponent of the colleges when he told a meeting in Armagh in August, intending to press the case for the northern college to be established in that town, that 'they [the bishops] discussed the provisions of the Bill; and, after mature deliberation, went to the Lord Lieutenant and represented their objections, and the amendments they deemed advisable. The Lord Lieutenant received the memorial, and forwarded the state of the case to the government, who made such amendments as were calculated to afford general satisfaction.'[23] Crolly's comments were widely seen to be unwise (as well as inaccurate—'general satisfaction' was manifestly not the condition of the Irish church concerning the colleges), and even such supporters as Murray distanced themselves from his campaign to gain the northern college for Armagh.[24] One of the episcopal commissioners, Patrick Kennedy, went so far as to describe Crolly's remarks as 'unguarded'.[25]

After the initial unanimity of the May bishops' meeting—never likely to last long in any event—the hierarchy quickly divided up into those for and those against the Queen's Colleges. In contrast to the controversy over the national schools, there would be no room for the pragmatic, middling view. Slattery, previously a supporter of Murray and Crolly, came out quickly and firmly against the colleges. He would remain an active ally of Cullen and MacHale on the question right through to the Synod of Thurles in 1850. The sea change in Slattery's alignment can be seen by the fact that letters from MacHale, never numerous and almost always regarding formal matters, suddenly became commonplace and quite open in nature after mid-1845. Conversely, Murray, heretofore a frequent correspondent, now wrote rarely, and then only to lament Slattery's continued opposition or to pass on official information.

Other former supporters of the national schools would join Slattery in vehement opposition to the proposed colleges, regardless of what changes might be made by the government to appease Murray and Crolly. Cullen was closely involved with this group, and was seen by them to be so involved. As Higgins reported to MacHale in September, 'Dr. Cullen passed a few days with me here. He is most indignant about the "Godless Scheme", and thinks it is the plain and imperative duty of the orthodox prelates to address a common document to the Irish clergy and people, strongly reprobating the Infidel Colleges. . . . He also thinks that we ought to accuse the three Episcopal commissioners before the pope, as bartering the principles and independence of our Church for worldly motives.'[26]

MacHale enthusiastically endorsed such a suggestion, telling Slattery, 'I should be most anxious that some of the Bishops opposed to the infidel scheme and the enslavement of our Church would in person proceed to lay bare the dangers with which we are threatened.'[27] The indications were that Rome would welcome such a move. Cullen reported to MacHale from Rome on the state of opinion at the Propaganda: 'I believe his Eminence [Cardinal Fransoni], and every one I could speak to regarding the new colleges, are decidedly opposed to them.'[28] He went on to say that Fransoni had needed to put pressure on Murray and Crolly because 'it is hard to make them take any step likely to bring on a collision course with the temporal authority.'[29] And, in fact, Fransoni did write to Crolly privately (although word quickly got out)[30] on 20 September, giving him what Donal Kerr notes can 'only be called a sharp rebuke.'[31]

In the meantime Slattery had been busy drafting a paper spelling out the case of those prelates opposed to the Queen's Colleges. He and MacHale forwarded it on to Rome via Cullen ('I am sure it will be productive of the beneficial results').[32] Kinsella, another national schools moderate, happily associated himself with the effort, telling Slattery that 'I am very glad indeed that you & Dr McHale have forwarded our opinions to Rome', and that he was 'sure they will be successful.'[33] Their letter attracted the signatures of eighteen bishops—a clear majority of the hierarchy. In the province of Dublin, Murray was unable to hold two of his three suffragans, and Crolly did not have the support of fully five of his eight. Although by no means all of those prelates who did sign remained opposed to the colleges, the rough division within the hierarchy remained the same.

By the end of 1845 the Propaganda had still not ruled on the colleges. Cullen now took control of the efforts to make sure that the ruling when it did come would leave no room for Godless education. He encouraged Slattery to write to Rome in an effort to further the cause. Cullen's request gives a good idea of the manner in which business was conducted at the Propaganda—and the disadvantage for those without a resident agent (as Murray and Crolly now found themselves). Cullen began by asking Slattery if he would have the 'kindness to write a letter to me on the subject [of the Queen's Colleges], which I could then show to some of the Cardinals [of the Sacred Congregation] and others interested in the question.' He then went on to more or less dictate the letter to the archbishop: 'It wd. be as well to point out the dangers of the proposed system and to show that there is no necessity of accepting it. The argument urged in favour of it is that the government might have made it much more unfavourable to the Catholics if they wished, that now they seem inclined to be reasonable, and that it is but just that the Bishops wd. aid in making the regulations as little objectionable as possible.'[34] He urged Slattery to 'write frequently' to Rome on the matter, as his letters would 'have a very good effect.' Cullen was also at roughly the same time urging Cantwell to write in a similar vein.[35] Almost all letters on the subject from sympathetic Irish bishops would be welcome, but Slattery would be particularly useful in the fight against the Queen's Colleges. He had little of the baggage that MacHale or, say, Higgins carried with Rome and as such would be more convincing. Indeed, Cullen went so far as to make this point to Slattery, telling him that MacHale's letters were often seen as being 'animated by political aims' and were frequently 'too violent.'[36]

The core of the opposition to the colleges would essentially form around six men: Cullen, MacHale, William Higgins, John Cantwell of Meath, Slattery, and the Dublin priest Peter Cooper, who would act as group spy on Murray and general ideological cheerleader. They would also, not incidentally, be the centre of the planning for the Catholic University before the Synod of Thurles. MacHale's and Higgins' opposition to the colleges was inevitable, and clearly understandable. Cantwell, too, had been an early opponent of the national schools and had joined Higgins in Rome during that controversy in an effort to secure and then preserve the Propaganda's condemnation of the system. Despite the passion and force of rhetoric that MacHale, Higgins, and Cantwell could muster, it was nevertheless the hitherto more moderate Slattery and Cullen who would serve as the most effective opponents of the colleges within the Irish church.

In an uncharacteristically vehement and frank letter to Cullen,[37] Slattery spelled out his views on the colleges. He began by noting that 'I am not & that I never have been a person of extreme opinions, or an advocate for extreme or violent measures' (a dig at MacHale), but, on the contrary, 'I love peace & retirement'. He was forced from his repose since 'I am indeed decidedly opposed to the Colleges because in the first place

I consider them to be by no means necessary for our middling classes,' who were already provided with adequate schools in Thurles, Clongowes, Carlow, and other places. He also denied that the colleges would be a 'boon to our people' as Murray and his allies 'asserted'. The costs of sending children to the colleges, which he felt many middle-class families might be unable or unwilling to meet, also caused him concern.

But the core of Slattery's objection to the Queen's Colleges was more than just pragmatic. As he wrote to Cullen, 'I regard them as dangerous in the highest degree to the morality & to the religious principles of the Catholic Youth who might resort to them.' Slattery would claim personal experience on this matter, as he himself had graduated from the University of Dublin. The experience had left a deep mark on him, and had permanently coloured his views on mixed education. 'God only knows', wrote Slattery, 'how I passed through the Ordeal & if I escaped at all unscathed it was his divine Grace alone that protected me'. As a result he was motivated by a 'feeling of charity for others' which 'should impel me to rescue them as far as I could from the imminent danger to which I know that their Faith & Morals would necessarily be exposed.' He concluded his letter with a rousing condemnation of the English government: 'I would implore him [the pope] not to suffer the Catholic Youth of ever faithful Ireland to be sacrificed to the views of a Protestant Government which still is, as it has always been, the faithless & unrelenting Enemy of his Spiritual Authority and of his Name.'[38] And, in a slightly later letter, Slattery's prose became even more florid, telling Cullen that, fourteen years ago to the day, he had been consecrated the 'Guardian of Faith & Morals amongst my People and if they were endangered it became my imperative duty as the Watchman of the Lord to sound the Trumpet to proclaim the danger: now this duty I cannot perhaps more faithfully discharge' than by again attacking the Queen's Colleges.[39]

Slattery was not exaggerating when he wrote that he was of a retiring nature. Not always well, and often unable to travel from Thurles (his archiepiscopal seat), he had hardly distinguished himself as an activist archbishop before 1845. He would again sink back into inactivity once the colleges were safely condemned and the Catholic University project seemed well underway. Nevertheless, between 1845 and 1850 he was Cullen's closest ally and an important moderate voice within the episcopal opposition to the Queen's Colleges.

The Irish bishops, meeting on 18 November 1845, had, as expected, condemned the Queen's Colleges and declared the government's offered changes to be inadequate. Unanimity, as always, escaped the prelates, and two reports, majority and minority, were produced by the meeting and sent onwards to Rome. The majority had to first win their case at the Propaganda before they could mount any serious attempt to block the colleges themselves. And, so too, those bishops in favour of the system had to convince what was bound to be a sceptical Sacred Congregation that the proposed colleges were not a threat to faith and morals.

Although rightly confident of a sympathetic hearing for their views, Cullen and his allies could not take Roman support for granted. It remained to be explained to the Propaganda why Cullen (and Slattery) could have been sanguine about national schools and yet so hostile to the Queen's Colleges. What had changed? Peter Cooper expressed the dilemma to Slattery, reminding him that 'when the National Education scheme was before the S. Congreg[ation] Rome came to the determination to condemn the system'. However, Murray's 'determined reply' had forced the Holy See to choose between tolerating the schools and 'necessitating the resignation of his diocese.' Cooper went on to point out that Cullen, 'up to that moment, a decided opponent of the scheme', when he reported on the schools for Rome, had 'said these extravagant words: "if this system go on all Ireland will become Catholic in 10 years".' Not surprisingly, Rome then 'issued the decree of toleration.'[40] Although Cooper's history might have been a bit off, he nevertheless put his finger on two fundamental concerns: would Murray resign if things went against him, and how exactly were the national schools different from the Queen's Colleges?

Murray's status was always a worry for the Propaganda. Although there was no question of him 'resigning' his see, it was always possible that he could be provoked into outright opposition to Rome. And, as will be seen, he showed a quite amazing degree of obstinacy in blocking, ignoring, or attacking any number of decisions made by Rome on both the Queen's Colleges and the Catholic University. Clearly, the Propaganda had to keep in mind that the most prominent and important of the Irish bishops—who was a great favourite of the British government[41] (Murray was offered but declined membership in the Irish privy council in 1846)— was at least potentially a rebel on the subject of university education.

The question of Cullen's views on education will be dealt with later, but suffice it to say here that the difference for him between national education and Godless education was clear. Under the national system, Catholic students were educated, for all practical purposes, by Catholic teachers under the supervision of the Catholic bishop, in an environment where the ethos was strictly Catholic. Yes, the government had supervisory authority, and, yes, textbooks could be chosen by non-Catholics. These concerns would bulk large in Cullen's later attitudes towards the national system, yet they were not enough to cause him to oppose that system in its entirety. He could not, however, accept an institution that both allowed Protestants to teach such subjects as history to Catholic students and also excluded the deity altogether. Cullen was not opposed to a 'modern' education (as it was understood in the mid-nineteenth century), but he was opposed to a secular one. For him such a system could only end in disaster and was not one that could provide a proper education at all. He shared this view with those in England who had opposed London University and UCL (and the later University of London), who had established King's College London, and who, like John Henry Newman, were fighting what they perceived to be the diminution of the exclusively Anglican character of Oxford and Cambridge.

Evidently, the Propaganda did not worry too deeply about Cullen's change in view because, as in 1840, they asked him to prepare a report on the safety of the proposed colleges. It was a tribute to Cullen's standing as the resident expert on Irish affairs in Rome that the Propaganda would choose such a noted opponent of the Queen's Colleges to report on those same colleges' safety for Catholics. As Macaulay notes, the 'invitation to Paul Cullen to submit a detailed analysis of the case to Propaganda offered him a golden opportunity of helping to down the Colleges, and he seized it with both hands.'[42] The death of Pope Gregory XVI on 9 June 1846 threw the entire question into doubt, however, as the machinery in Rome ground to a halt to await the new pope. As Cullen lamented to Slattery: 'the College question was to have been discussed this week— and now God knows when it can come out.'[43] In a slightly later letter to Slattery announcing the election of Giovanni Maria Mastai-Ferretti as Pope Pius IX, Cullen urged that 'it would be well for your Grace and the other bishops to write soon to the new Pope' as a 'good letter to him now would provide a powerful effect.'[44]

It was an indication of the importance that the Propaganda gave to the question that on 13 July, within a month of Pius's election, they tentatively decided to condemn the colleges.[45] That decision was confirmed by the new pontiff on 3 October. Both Crolly and Murray submitted, albeit reluctantly, to Rome's verdict; Cullen even ventured the opinion that the pope had 'reconciled all parties, and there will be no danger of revolutionary movements in future.'[46] Meanwhile, the colleges themselves continued to appoint staff and to prepare for opening. In practice, and despite the condemnation from Rome, those bishops who supported the colleges did little to block them or hide their personal support. They would only await a chance to reopen the question at the earliest opportunity.

Rome Suggests a University

Cullen's optimism quickly proved to be misplaced. The bishops' meeting held in the autumn of 1846 was just as divided as the one held the previous year. Although the debate was not directly related to the Queen's Colleges, it was—again—about education. The conflict over the national system had largely faded into the background since 1840, with each bishop supporting or obstructing the system within his own diocese as his conscience dictated. It always had the potential, however, to reemerge as a source of tension within the hierarchy. MacHale and his allies had never been reconciled to the system, but now changes introduced by the government managed to throw both Cullen and Slattery into doubt about the safety of the entire Irish educational system.

As originally designed, each national school to which the government had given money in its establishment (the normal procedure), had been 'owned' by local trustees—not the national board or the government. Not surprisingly, the trustees were almost inevitably, in Catholic schools, the local bishop or his nominees. Such an arrangement guaranteed that the church would always have the final say over what went on in those schools in which its young were educated. It was this safety net that the government was now, it appeared, taking steps to remove. As Slattery reported to Cullen, 'I have now before me an <u>Official Document</u>' changing the system of ownership. '[A]ll National Schools to be established henceforward & towards the erection of which the Government shall give aid <u>must be vested in the Government Board in its corporate capacity</u>.' This action could only be an 'open effort to take the National Education of the country out of our hands into their own' and would allow a 'hostile Board' to 'introduce whatever System of Education it pleased.'[47] Peter Cooper, who had met with both Slattery and MacHale regarding the proposed changes, made a similar point, telling Cullen: 'The practical effect of this regulation is to throw the education of the humbler classes completely into the hands of the Gov.t.' The results could only be bad for the church, as the 'Colleges Act aims at the same result in respect of the middle classes while already it possesses a perfect & injurious control through the Universities over the minds of our few aristocrats.'[48] The Queen's Colleges, it now seemed to their opponents, were simply one part of a larger English and Protestant conspiracy to control the entirety of Irish education.

These changes to the national system were, Slattery thought, an excellent argument against allowing the Queen's Colleges to have a trial; things would always be changed for the worse once episcopal approval—

even tentative approval—was secured by the government. MacHale would make exactly the same point to Cullen.[49] The former moderates were now forced to concede that MacHale had been right all along about the national schools. If anything, this realisation would increase their determination to stop the colleges with whatever means came to hand.

The annual bishops' meeting revealed the extent of the hierarchy's disagreements. As Edward Maginn,[50] the administrator of the Derry diocese, reported to Cullen, '[t]he introduction of the question of National Education produced a perfect hurricane.' The 'encroachments' of the government were condemned on a 9 to 4 vote, with a petition to Parliament asking for a 'separate system of education based on purely Catholic principles' passing by a similar margin. In a highly unusual move, Crolly refused even to be in the chair when the motion for the petition was discussed, leaving MacHale to chair the meeting. Crolly and his three supporters then entered a protest against the bishops' condemnation of the changes to the national system and the petition to Parliament.[51]

It was in the midst of the renewed controversy over the national schools and the continuing one over the Queen's Colleges that the idea of a Catholic university was first mooted. It seems the suggestion was totally Rome's, and did not originate in any way in Ireland. When the Propaganda reconfirmed its condemnation of the colleges in the early autumn of 1846, it also urged that a university should be established on the model of Louvain—a decision in which Cullen was involved.[52] The pope concurred, and the final rescript condemning the colleges enjoined the Irish bishops to 'procure the erection of such a Catholic Academy as the Prelates of Belgium have founded in the city of Louvain.'[53] It was not surprising that Pius would prove to be interested in a Catholic university for Ireland. As a bishop he had involved himself in attacks on the secular nature of the French university, and throughout his long pontificate (1846–78) he would prove a determined enemy of secular education.[54]

The rather tentative mention of a Catholic university in the 1846 rescript did not, at first, create much of a clamour for such an institution. The increasing pressure of the Great Famine obviously distracted the bishops' attention, as did the relative lack of action on the part of the pro-college bishops (although Murray had written Cullen to report that the government was willing to make changes in the colleges that would make them acceptable to Rome).[55] It was only in late 1847 that any real pressure began to get a Catholic university underway. The impetus, it seems, again came from Rome. In October the pope issued another rescript on Irish education, this time directly urging the establishment of a

Catholic university. As Maginn wrote to Cullen on 4 November, 'His Holiness has nobly done his part. It is for us to do ours.'[56]

Cullen was travelling in Ireland when the pope's rescript was issued. He welcomed the proposal for a Catholic university, telling Slattery that the 'decision of the Pope will, I hope, put an end to the Godless Colleges' and that if 'the Pope's recommendations be now attended to, religion will be saved in Ireland.'[57] And he reported to Kirby, with no apparent irony, that the 'condemnation of the colleges [again included in the 1847 rescript] was recd. with enthusiasm by all Ireland', and that the bishops had agreed to begin a collection for a university, with Cantwell promising £10,000.[58] Others would contribute 'as soon as the present distress shall be over.'[59]

Ambrose Macaulay has declared it a 'sad irony' that the call for erecting a Catholic university came in 1847—Black '47—when survival, not education, was the first priority for so many Irish Catholics.[60] Certainly the Famine made any effort to establish a university and to raise funds difficult. Cullen would tell Kirby that although 'I have been doing all I cd. to get something done, about the Catholic University', the 'distress is so great that scarcely any thing in the way of a collection can be set on foot.' Notwithstanding that, Cullen was 'sure if a beginning were made, many laymen wd. soon endow it.' After all, 'the thing must be followed up.'[61]

Others were less certain than Cullen that the middle of a famine was the best time to lay the foundations of a new university. Cantwell, whose promise of £10,000 was such an encouragement to Cullen, counselled delay in establishing the university, even though he noted that the government seemed able to 'command plenty of money to erect infidel Colleges [and] to squander on miscalled & ill conducted national schools . . . but when there is [a] question of a grant to mitigate the horrors of famine & pestilence the answer is that England is in difficulty & the Treasury would not afford such an outlay.'[62] Cantwell's allegation was not without foundation. The Queen's Colleges were each allocated £100,000 for buildings and £7,000 per annum in running costs. This was to maintain an establishment of twenty professors, a principal, registrar, bursar, and librarian at each college and to provide for forty-five junior scholarships per college valued at £30 a year (senior scholarships would come later).[63]

Despite English perfidy, Cantwell advised Cullen that '[u]nder the overwhelming burdens, which now press upon all classes of Roman Catholics in Ireland, it would be unwise to urge the erection of the Catholic University'. Cantwell was by no means giving up on the project, however, telling Cullen that 'in other times there would be no difficulty in securing ample means & when the present awful visitation is over, I have the greatest confidence that the united Prelates, Priests & people of Ireland will be successful in establishing what we all believe can alone frustrate the anti-catholic machinations of the enemies of our holy Faith.'[64] Slattery, too, was uncertain that a Catholic university could succeed. He told John O'Connell (Daniel's son), 'I fear it would be an impracticable project', mostly because he didn't feel that 'under existing circumstances' the entire hierarchy could raise the sums that were being promised, let alone what would be necessary.[65]

If the Famine were not enough of an obstacle, it quickly became apparent that Murray and Crolly were not prepared to support a Catholic university—whatever the pope might say. MacHale reported this fact to Slattery: 'To carry out the Pope's noble and benevolent views we talked already—a few of us—of the necessity of a National University—Catholic, and the two other Archbishops were consulted. They seemed to think that the infidel Colleges should be so modified so as not to fail to give . . . satisfaction.'[66] It is unfair to put too much emphasis on punctuation, but it is perhaps indicative of MacHale's priorities that he referred to the proposed university as a 'National University—Catholic,' that is, national first, Catholic second. It was a distinction that, whether he intended it in this letter, would bulk large in his later treatment of the university. As for Murray and his allies, it was clear that they were committed to the idea of the Queen's Colleges and would not support any institution that might prove a threat to them.

Just as Murray and Crolly were unwilling to support a competitor (which they honestly believed would fail anyway) to the Queen's Colleges, many of their opponents primarily conceived of the Catholic University as a means of destroying those colleges; very little thought was given as to just what a Catholic university should be. 'Louvain' seemed to be the obvious answer, but only Cullen appears to have given much thought as to what exactly that meant.[67] The attitude towards the Catholic University on the part of anti-college Catholics can be seen not only in such remarks as Cantwell's to Cullen, but also in a letter of John O'Connell's to Slattery, in which he told the archbishop that if a 'Catholic University project might be much advanced' then the 'real overthrow [might] thus be given to the English plotters against the Faith.'[68]

The erection of the Catholic University became an urgent matter to those opposed to the colleges in late 1847, regardless of famine. Anxious to gain Roman approval (or perhaps to simply keep stirring up the hierarchy), the new government under Lord John Russell proposed more concessions in the structure of the Queen's Colleges. Russell had been opposed to the original colleges act and was sympathetic to Catholic demands for denominational education. Political reality, however, dictated that the colleges be pursued.[69] Their opponents were not impressed, and it must be said that by this point nothing less than the government handing over the Cork and Galway Colleges in their entirety to the church would meet the approval of MacHale, Slattery, Cullen, and their allies. Murray and Crolly quickly forwarded the proposed changes to Rome, using them to claim that, as the situation had now changed, the pope's condemnation of the colleges should no longer be seen as binding; he had condemned, in their view, something which no longer existed.

With the proposed changes under consideration in Rome, it became imperative that a Catholic university be put in train immediately. Peter Cooper summed up the situation perfectly, telling Slattery that 'Dr. M[urray] & his friends' planned to claim that, as Ireland's youth would avail themselves to any University education offered, it was necessary to support the now acceptable Queen's Colleges, unless 'a Catholic University be established' for the youth of Ireland. Naturally, according to Cooper, a Catholic University 'they expect, will not be attempted, or [if] attempted will fail.' If this were the case, then Murray and his allies could claim that it was 'wisdom . . . to obtain a share in their [the colleges] administration & then endeavour to make them as harmless as may be.' This was precisely what Cullen had feared would happen when the colleges had first been proposed.

According to Cooper, Murray was not looking for 'an approbation on the part of Rome' for the colleges, but rather that Rome would 're-scind its prohibition to take a share in their management'. 'They expect in a word that Rome, seeing that nothing will be done towards the erection of a Catholic University will feel the necessity of allowing each bishop to act in the affairs according to his own discretion.' This was exactly what the Holy See had done in regards to the national schools in 1840. '[O]ur opponents', Slattery was told, 'rely upon our want of energy to realize the prospect which can alone deprive them of so plausible an argument—the project, I mean, of an University on Cath: principles.'[70]

Cullen certainly saw the threat as real. His concern was evident in a letter he sent to Slattery in late November: 'I trust an effort will be made to erect a catholic university as recommended by the Propaganda.' 'If something were not done in that direction', he worried, then 'the government plan will be carried out'. Cullen was optimistic such a university could work, as '[e]very one I met in Ireland was most anxious towards funding a university, and I am sure foreign countries would subscribe most freely.' 'Ireland will never be really safe in a religious point of view, until she should have a perfect system of Catholic education.'[71]

Cullen's fear of government success was not an unreasonable one. The situation at Rome in early 1848 was extremely volatile. Unrest was wracking the Papal States, and the pope's position was becoming more and more precarious. The situation took most of Cullen's attention, occasionally even to the exclusion of the university. As Pius had more pressing things on his mind than Irish education, it was unlikely that a quick condemnation of the proposed changes to the Queen's Colleges could be obtained. Nor could Rome simply ignore the wishes of the British government at such a time of crisis; Cullen's letters to Slattery are filled with accounts of English machinations and plots. With the situation so critical, MacHale and Higgins decided to travel to Rome to plead the anti-colleges case in person, carrying a petition signed by seventeen Irish bishops warning the pope 'time Anglos et dona ferentes'.[72] That they would travel at such a time, with unrest in Rome and famine at home (it was worst in MacHale's province, Tuam), gives an idea of just how important they felt the question of university education to be—and how serious the threat was believed to be.

The First Steps towards a Catholic University in Ireland

While MacHale and Higgins, aided by Cullen, pleaded their case in Rome, their allies in Ireland attempted to make a beginning with the university. In the spring of 1848 the bishops approved the establishment of a committee to determine how best to create a Catholic university of Ireland. Murray and his allies did not support such an idea, but they could not actually be seen to oppose it formally. So, as would happen later at Thurles, such measures to establish committees and the like would usually enjoy unanimous support among the hierarchy. As long as no concrete plan was proposed, Murray could lend his voice to calls for a Catholic university. It was only when he was asked actually to *do* anything for such a university that he became actively obstructive.

John O'Hanlon, a priest at Maynooth, reported on the establishment of a university committee to Cullen. He told him that 'on the occasion of the Anniversary Requiem for O'Connell' (the idea of the university as a memorial to O'Connell was being mooted at this time), a meeting was held and the 'following Gentlemen were appointed' to the committee. The members were to be Cantwell, James Maher, John Kearney, John

Miley, and O'Hanlon.[73] The membership was entirely clerical, which would not be the case when Cullen reestablished the University Committee after the Synod of Thurles. (Cantwell, O'Hanlon, and Maher would sit on that committee as well.)[74] Cullen would hardly have objected to the makeup of the committee. Cantwell, the only episcopal member, was a solid supporter of the Catholic University. James Maher, the parish priest of Carlow, was Cullen's uncle and an influential man in his own right. The wider Cullen family was tightly knit, and Cullen and Maher trusted each other and worked together closely. Miley was also aligned with Cullen, and went on to become the controversial president of the Irish College in Paris. He would remain close to Cullen and retain his support until events in Paris necessitated that Cullen agree to his ouster. But in 1848 the men were allies.

The meeting, O'Hanlon told Cullen, 'distinctly' saw its way forward and 'entertain[ed] not the slightest doubt of eventual success.' The delay in establishing the university was attributed to the 'awful condition of our people for the last two years absorbing as it must have done, all the care and attention of our Bishops.'[75] Maher, too, was confident, telling his nephew that 'our prospects are most cheering.' 'The project', he hoped, 'would put an end, at once to the intrigues of England in seeking by its modifications of the Godless Colleges Act, to get the education of the catholic people into its own hands'.[76] Not all members of the committee, however, were so sanguine. Miley reported to Cullen on a problem that was to plague the university until Murray's death in early 1852: 'My fear is that we cannot succeed unless it be located in Dublin—and that will be a matter of no small difficulty—1st on account of the part taken by his Grace Dr M[urray] with the Govt. & in the 2nd place, on account of Dr Cantwell's wish to have it in Meath'.[77] Cantwell would quickly drop his request (and no location in Meath was ever seriously considered), but the problem of a hostile archbishop of Dublin was not so easily surmounted.

In Rome, although political matters were getting more complicated by the day, Cullen nevertheless felt that the Holy See would not give in to English pressure over the Queen's Colleges. As he told Slattery, the 'Pope will not at all yield on the college question—He is quite decided that education ought to be Catholic.'[78] Since, according to Cullen, the amended statutes did not 'afford the slightest protection to religion', the English were simply trying to 'humbug the Pope.'[79] Although Pius might not be willing to accede to English pressure, it was still unlikely that Rome would make a quick determination. Indeed, the pope was forced from the city in November, and the cardinals of the Propaganda were forced to flee from the anticlerical fervour of the new Roman Republic. Being a British subject, Cullen enjoyed some protection and as a result found himself the temporary rector of Propaganda College. (The Propaganda College was attached to the Sacred Congregation and was charged with educating priests both for and from the mission territories. John Henry Newman studied at the college after his conversion in 1845.)

With no fresh condemnation forthcoming from Rome, and despite the hopes of the new university committee, little was done to establish the university. This was hardly surprising. Murray and Crolly were unlikely to lift a finger in its support; the status of the Queen's Colleges was still in doubt; Cullen was still in Rome; Rome was in chaos; the Famine still raged; and, of the two archbishops who supported the university, Slattery was too ill to manage such a project on his own and MacHale, never a builder, had to contend with a famine-ridden and poverty-stricken Tuam. Action was impossible. But delay, too, was dangerous to those who envisioned a Catholic university taking the place of the hated Godless colleges. In a letter to Slattery, Peter Cooper summed up this threat, remarking that the continued delay 'might be seized on by the friends of the Govt. & of the Colleges as proof positive how much deceived he [the pope] was in listening [to] the assurances of certain parties that Ireland could erect a University like Belgium.'[80]

In another letter to Slattery, Cooper suggested improvements to the university committee, which had more or less sunk without trace. He proposed that each bishop should name a member of the committee so 'that all may have a voice in what all will have an interest.' He also suggested that laymen sit on the committee, as they 'are cleverer far in worldly wisdom than we clerics are in general.' Although Cullen would prove hesitant about involving the entire hierarchy, he did include laymen when he came to reestablish the university committee as archbishop of Armagh. Cooper also expressed concern with MacHale's utility in the project of establishing the university: 'I will here observe that I deem it as very desirable that such a proceeding should originate with any one rather than Dr McHale', as his involvement would guarantee opposition.[81] Cooper had become, almost by default, the leading proponent of the Catholic University in Ireland. He wrote to all the parties, chiding, encouraging, and exhorting them to make a tangible beginning. But Cooper was merely a diocesan priest with a hostile bishop, and could do nothing on his own.

All hopes seemed pinned on another papal condemnation of the Queen's Colleges. In a letter to Cullen, Maher reported that as yet 'nothing had been done in favour of a Catholic University' and that the colleges were 'progressing rapidly.' 'Until the decision of the Holy See upon the college question be announced matters will remain as they are.' But, 'it is said in the event of a condemnation Dr Murray will enter warmly into the project of erecting a Catholic University.'[82] Maher could hardly have misread his man more completely.

Having overcome his previous concerns about the practicability of the university, Cantwell submitted a plan for beginning to Slattery. Telling him that a Catholic university was 'not so difficult as people at first sight imagine', Cantwell picked up Cooper's suggestion of having each bishop make an appointment to a committee charged with reporting on how to open the university (Cooper was busily writing on the subject to Cantwell, Cullen, Slattery, and, most likely, MacHale). That committee could, in Cantwell's view, then 'depute one or two of their body to visit Louvain' in order to learn what, exactly, a Catholic university was.[83]

In the meantime Rome had done its part to help Slattery and his supporters in their task, condemning for the third time (in October 1848) the Queen's Colleges and once again urging a Catholic university. When it reached Ireland, the rescript triggered a flurry of activity. James Keating, the bishop of Ferns and a suffragan of Murray's, wrote to Slattery to support the idea of a Catholic university, even if the 'present prospect of success appears gloomy indeed.'[84] Nevertheless, the pope had spoken and such a thing should thus be tried. He was not, however, happy with the suggestion that the bishops should nominate delegates to consider the question. Rather, he thought the entire hierarchy should meet to consider the matter. Charles MacNally, the bishop of Clogher, made the same point and argued that a synod was the only way to proceed.[85]

Neither suggestion could be expected to find much favour with at least some of the university's supporters (Cullen, for example, at first favoured a synod, then rapidly changed his mind).[86] As Cantwell remarked of Keating's letter (which Slattery had forwarded to him), it amounted to 'an anxious desire to carry out the recommendations of the Holy Father but forbids any one to move to that effect.' This was especially upsetting to Cantwell, as Keating knew 'that those who ought to originate such an effort will not dream of doing so.'[87] Allowing the matter to be referred to the bishops as a body would enable Murray and Crolly to obstruct any practical steps. A synod, likewise, would have to be chaired by Crolly—not a prospect that could appeal to Slattery or Cantwell. As Cooper told Cullen, 'the Archbishops & bishops in favour of the Godless Colleges adopt the very factious & very disedifying plan of passive resistance to the erection of the Catholic university';[88] ironically, when Cullen was forced, for similar reasons, to avoid vesting the governance of the university in the bishops as a body he would be heat-edly opposed by, amongst others, Cantwell.

With the two senior archbishops unwilling to help establish a Catholic university, the onus fell on Slattery and MacHale. MacHale had always been better at opposing things than building them, and with the colleges once again condemned in October 1848, it seems his sense of urgency about a Catholic university was diminished. And indeed, the Tuam provincial synod held in January 1849 neither took nor urged any concrete steps towards establishing a university. A document signed by MacHale and five of his six suffragans declared the Tuam prelates' willingness to 'offer their aid' towards any attempt to establish a Uni-versity.[89] They did not offer to establish such an institution them-selves. While it was perfectly understandable that Tuam could not, as a province, undertake such a project, it was less clear to observers like Cooper[90] why the Tuam synod felt it necessary to state that plans for a Catholic university must 'in the first instance be submitted, at the next general meeting, to the councils of the assembled Bishops of Ireland.'[91] Such a course of action would, given the level of dissension within the hi-erarchy, inevitably lead to nothing being done. As Cooper remarked to Slattery, the Tuam Synod 'did nothing. It only promised that if others wd. do anything, they ... wd. cooperate.' As if this were not bad enough, the synod 'condemns one kind of Education' even while it 'postpones Education of another kind.' As Cooper saw it, the Tuam synod thus consigned 'the People to ignorance or condemned them to disobedi-ence.'[92] Cullen, Cooper reported, was not impressed, and neither was Rome. In Cullen's view, Cooper wrote, Rome would be 'highly disap-pointed' with the synodical constitutions.[93]

The Tuam provincial synod was a sign of things to come for the Catholic University. If MacHale was unwilling in 1849 to even begin the university without referring it to the bishops as a whole, he would prove even less willing to leave the running of the university to Cullen and Newman in 1854. For all his fiery rhetoric, MacHale sincerely be-lieved that the Irish church as a whole must be in control of projects that effected the entire church; no bishop—and certainly no archbishop—should be set above another. It had been one of his objections to the char-itable bequests bill and it would be one of his objections to the way the Catholic University was run. Along with irascibility and an inability to compromise, this position was one of the few constants informing MacHale's behaviour.

Cullen had no illusions about referring the matter to the bishops' meeting, telling Slattery that it was 'too far off' and, anyway, 'there will be as little vision as ever' over the university. He instead suggested that a committee 'of priests and laymen' be established 'under the control of the Prelates' to begin work on the university.[94] Such a proposal was most unlikely to succeed. With MacHale declaring at Tuam that he at least preferred to consult the entire episcopate, it was left to Slattery to make some sort of beginning. Slattery, however, being from rural Thurles, was precisely the wrong man to attempt to erect a Catholic university against the opposition of Murray and Crolly in an Ireland still suffering from famine.

Peter Cooper summed up the problem, when he told Cullen that Slattery was 'an excellent man but too timid.' In a letter to Cullen, Slattery essentially begged off any responsibility for establishing the university on his own:

> I have [he wrote] only one thing to console me, in the arduous struggle we were engaged in I did my duty . . . and if there is not now in existence a Committee of sound minded Priests to carry into effect the recommendation of the Holy See regarding the University <u>the fault is not mine</u>, for want of co-operation I was obliged to abandon a practical prospect for that purpose [the proposal to establish a Committee to which each bishop would nominate a member] and I left it to wiser heads to carry out its execution—the Tuam Synod entertained the Question but came to no practical conclusion for its immediate solution; and there it lies without any step being taken to get the thing going.[95]

By early 1849 it seemed that a Catholic university in Ireland was simply not going to happen; circumstances had consistently conspired against it. It is important to emphasise the sheer ineffectiveness of the anti-college prelates in this period. That ineffectiveness is somewhat obscured by the fact that they succeeded, eventually, in much of what they set out to do: the Queen's Colleges were condemned three times by Rome and the Catholic University *was* established. But that had little to do with those bishops in Ireland. The condemnations were obtained from a Propaganda that, especially after the changes in the national schools, was little inclined towards any educational proposals that fell short of full church control. It is certainly true that the letters (and personal representations) of MacHale, Cantwell, and particularly Slattery did have an effect, but the bulk of the burden in pushing the anti-college case fell on the man on the scene: Paul Cullen. The pope first proposed a Catholic university in 1846, and it was taken seriously in Ireland from 1847 (when

Cullen, fortuitously on the spot, was able to chivvy the various bishops towards supporting it). Yet in February 1849, Slattery was complaining that nothing had been done to give it form.

It is true that circumstances were daunting. The opposition of Murray and Crolly meant that the university could neither be built in Dublin nor count on funds from that diocese. That fact alone was enough to put the project seriously in doubt (and would continue to do so until Murray's death in 1852). The Famine meant that little money was available from those dioceses which were inclined to support the project, and to make matters worse, the two pro-university archbishops ruled in the two provinces—Tuam and Cashel—hardest hit by the Famine.

Given the circumstances, it was impossible that the university could actually have been opened between 1847 and 1849. But no serious attempt was made to even lay the plans for an opening when circumstances might be more favourable. It was not that the various anti-college bishops lost interest in the university—they still needed it to combat the Queen's Colleges, to say nothing of carrying out the pope's wishes—but rather that they were ineffectual in doing anything tangible to establish it; the one attempt, the 1848 university committee, quickly foundered. It is likely that if William Crolly had not died of the Asiatic cholera on Good Friday 1849, nothing further would have been done to advance the project. Michael Slattery's remark to Cullen—'there it lies without any step being taken to get the thing going'—would then have become the epitaph of the Catholic University of Ireland.

chapter three

Enter the Ultramontane

EIGHTEEN FORTY-NINE WAS NOT A GOOD YEAR FOR PAUL CULLEN. IT opened with a death threat (signed 'I. Romani'),[1] and ended with an un-wanted elevation to the Irish episcopate. In the intervening months, events in Rome were hardly to the taste of the ultramontane Cullen.[2] Things were little better in Ireland. The Famine still raged, albeit with less ferocity than in previous years, and the Catholic University project appeared unlikely to move beyond fine words and pious hopes. Michael Slattery was unable to take matters in hand and John MacHale was unwilling to do so in a way that entertained any hope of success. It was hardly surprising that Peter Cooper would tell Slattery, 'I own I wish Dr. Cullen were one of the new bishops, if he were not requisite where he is.'[3] Cooper was right; at least in the short term, Cullen would be needed precisely where he was.

Despite the third Roman condemnation of the Queen's Colleges, Daniel Murray was still not ready to surrender his support for them. He argued that although Rome had prohibited *bishops* from taking any part in the colleges, it had not, in fact, prohibited *priests* from doing so. The threat of yet another appeal to Rome enraged the colleges' opponents. Uncharacteristically, Cullen chastised Slattery (who had asked for clari-fication on the question) for leaving everything to Rome: 'It is not to be expected that the Pope or the Propaganda should descend to details. Those who are on the spot must apply and enforce the principles which have been adopted.' Cullen informed Slattery that in Rome a 'new appeal will be considered as a foundation for the introduction of Jansensism into Ireland'.[4] 'I hope for the honor of Ireland ... that no Bishop will take upon himself to give an example which will certainly lead to the introduction of the most mischievous doctrines of that heresy'. Besides, what could be 'said in favor of the Colleges that has not been said already?'[5]

Murray seemed to be using the lack of progress on a Catholic university as a stick with which to beat the colleges' opponents. Cooper, who always kept a close eye on his superior, reported to Cullen: 'Dr Murray has written to the proper quarter [presumably the Propaganda]' to 'apprize' them that the basis on which they condemned the colleges was a 'suggestio falsi.' That suggestion was that a 'Cath: University was possible.' Cooper plaintively asked Cullen whether he could not find 'an opportunity of letting people know that it is his Grace [Murray] & they who think & act with him who create the impossibility'.[6] There was never any likelihood that Rome would change its mind on the colleges. However, the nature of the situation, with the pope exiled in Gaeta and the cardinals of the Propaganda scattered, meant that no quick response to Murray could be forthcoming. That being as it may, Murray did have a point: if the Catholic University could not be built, or successfully run in the event that it was, then the church would have to make some arrangements for higher education. Otherwise the young would attend whatever institution was available to them regardless of Roman opinion.

Crolly's death in April changed the entire nature of the debate, and the struggle to appoint his successor became the primary focus of activity within the Irish church. If a supporter of Murray and the colleges were to be appointed, then the Catholic University would be a dead letter. A new archbishop of Armagh and primate of All Ireland who opposed a Catholic university could guarantee that the project was never begun; the status quo was deadly to any idea of a new university. On the other hand, an anti-college archbishop who supported a Catholic university could tip the balance within the hierarchy in its favour and isolate the increasingly elderly Murray.

It appears that Cullen's name was not put forward for the position by anyone in Ireland, at least not initially. Nor does he seem to have at first figured in Rome's calculations. The normal procedure in Ireland for selecting a new bishop was to have the clergy of the vacant diocese assemble and vote on candidates. It was bad form for a candidate to be seen to be interested, but of course canvassing occurred. Once the election was held, the three names attracting the highest number of votes were submitted to Rome ranked by the level of their support. This *terna* would usually be accompanied by a recommendation, made by the bishops of the province in question, as to which candidate was the most suitable. It was then usually the case that the Propaganda would select a candidate for the pope's approval from this list. They were, however, under no obligation to do so. The three names on the Armagh *terna* were Joseph Dixon, the professor of Scripture at Maynooth (who would eventually succeed Cullen in Armagh), Michael Kiernan, the parish priest of Dundalk, and John O'Hanlon, also of Maynooth, who had been active in the 1848 attempt to form a Catholic university committee.

The provincial bishops were divided on the matter, with some backing Dixon and others O'Hanlon. Kiernan seems never to have been taken seriously. The division was largely along political lines, with MacHale's supporters backing O'Hanlon and Murray's supporting Dixon. O'Hanlon had long been a MacHale ally. As prefect of Dunboyne (Maynooth's fledgling house of graduate studies), he had led the faction within the college that had backed both O'Connell's drive for Repeal and MacHale's support for it.[7] As Cantwell told Cullen, 'O'Hanlon is the only hope & the only security for Ireland in her present difficulties'.[8] Higgins concurred in his own inimitable fashion, telling Cullen that '[a]ll those who deserve the name of Catholic in Ireland are ardently praying that Doctor O'Hanlon may be the new Primate; whilst the Heretics and place-hunting lukewarm Catholics will do anything to malign and misrepresent him'.[9] Of the seven voting bishops in Armagh (Maginn, in Derry, had died, and had not yet been replaced as administrator), four supported O'Hanlon and three Dixon. Ironically, upon being elevated to Armagh in 1852, Dixon would prove to be a loyal supporter of Cullen's and certainly no friend of the Queen's Colleges.

With such a close division amongst the bishops of Armagh, Rome consulted the three remaining archbishops. MacHale and Slattery backed O'Hanlon; Murray supported Dixon. In response to an inquiry from Cardinal Fransoni, Slattery also proposed an alternative candidate: Paul Cullen.[10] Probably in league with Slattery, MacHale, too, then told Rome that if the choice were not O'Hanlon it should be Cullen.[11] Unsurprisingly, such a suggestion was warmly welcomed by the Propaganda (with 'alacrity' as Donal Kerr puts it).[12] Despite Cullen's undoubted value in Rome, his promotion would allow the Propaganda to place one of its own in charge of the tempestuous Irish church. Certainly, in a letter to Kirby, Cardinal Fransoni took credit for Cullen's elevation.[13] The appointment was still not made hastily, however welcome the suggestion of Cullen was. It was not until late 1849 that Cullen himself seems to have been aware that he was a candidate. As he told Walsh of Halifax on 24 December, '[u]nfortunately the Bishops disagreed in their recommendations of a candidate [for Armagh] and the consequence is that the Pope is now threatening to send an Archbishop from the Irish College.' This was not a prospect Cullen welcomed, telling Walsh that 'God grant that he may not persevere in his intentions' and that it would be a 'great affliction to be sent to take so heavy a charge in difficult times.'[14] Cullen's remarks were likely more than just a *pro forma* expression of his unwillingness to take Armagh. He had avoided being appointed to a number of bishoprics in the past as well as positions in Ireland—such as president of Maynooth—that could have been expected to lead to preferment there.[15] This is not to say that Cullen was unambitious, but it is more than likely that he saw his future at Rome, not in Ireland. Whatever Cullen's wishes, Pius did persevere in his intention, and Cullen was consecrated at Rome in February 1850.

MacHale immediately wrote to congratulate Cullen, telling him, 'Seldom in my life have I received any letter which gave me more sincere pleasure than your last [announcing the appointment to Armagh]'.[16] Despite the subsequent falling out between the two men, there is little reason to doubt that MacHale was sincere in his welcome. After all, the rector of the Irish College had been an invaluable ally since the charitable bequests controversy in 1844 and had as yet displayed none of the centralising tendencies that MacHale would later come to deplore. Slattery and Murray also added their congratulations, although the latter managed to leave his until late February.[17] Cullen's appointment was not so welcome to the government. Clarendon informed the prime minister that Cullen was 'the most malignant enemy of the English and the English government in Ireland' and 'the devil incarnate'.[18] In the lord lieutenant's view, Cullen had been sent to Ireland to put down the Queen's Colleges because he and the pope feared 'the consequences of education and of looking in the light of reason on winking Virgins and Esatic *[sic]* Nuns and they make no secret of the necessity of teaching history not according to fact and acknowledged truths but according to the dogmas of the Catholic faith.'[19] As Donal Kerr has somewhat charitably noted, 'Clarendon's reaction was that of a nineteenth-century Liberal who perceived the Roman Church as opposed to the advance of civilisation.'[20] (As late as 1869 Clarendon was referring to Cullen as a 'viper' in official despatches.)[21]

CULLEN TAKES CHARGE

Cullen's appointment signalled a renewed attempt to erect a Catholic university. As MacHale told him, we 'are only waiting Your Grace's arrival to commence vigorously with establishing the Catholic University.'[22]

Patrick Leahy, the president of Thurles College and later the first vice-rector of the CUI and then archbishop of Cashel, told Kirby that, as the Catholic University was already mooted, 'Dr Cullen comes . . . just at the time when he is wanted most.'[23] Cullen was coming with more than just the power of one archbishop, albeit of the primatial see. He was given the title of apostolic delegate and was commissioned by the Holy See to convene, under his chairmanship, the first national synod Ireland had seen in centuries. This distinction granted Cullen what was at that time an unprecedented status within the Irish church. In the past, the primacy had carried with it little more than the right to chair episcopal meetings and a certain ceremonial dignity. Cullen's new title gave him a direct charge from the pope that was shared by no other Irish bishop. Nevertheless, it is important not to overestimate Cullen's power, either at this time or later. Outside of his own diocese he had no authority beyond the right to convene the synod and ensure the implementation of its decrees. This power was very real, but it had clearly defined limits. Beyond them, Cullen would have to rely on his vast but informal influence at the Propaganda.

There could be little doubt in Ireland of Cullen's support at Rome, so now all attention came to be focused on the upcoming synod. Although Cullen was appointed in December 1849, and consecrated in February of the following year, he did not arrive in Ireland until 5 May. In the interim, Murray and his supporters did all they could to assure a result favourable to their cause when the synod convened that summer.

In discussing a letter in which Murray made public his belief that the papal condemnation of the colleges extended only to bishops, Leahy told Kirby that the archbishop of Dublin, 'in his hurry to check the now daily increasing public feeling in favor of a Catholic University', was trying to prove that 'one great help towards the success of the undertaking is wanting, namely the unanimity of the Bishops.'[24] In March he informed Kirby that 'the present policy of the Government & of the Catholic Bishops disposed to favor the Queen's Colleges is to force on these institutions as rapidly as possible—in effect to run away with the question before a Catholic University c[ould] be established.'[25]

Cullen himself was optimistic about matters when he first reached Ireland, even telling Kirby that 'I have just heard that Dr Murray will probably join in the prospect of a C. University.'[26] Such optimism was rudely shattered when he arrived in the city of Armagh to take possession of the cathedral that Crolly had been building ('a miserable hole'). After the splendour of the Roman ceremonial, Cullen was appalled by what he found in Armagh. He complained to Kirby that, because of the provisions of the charitable bequests act, the bishop's palace and the diocesan seminary were legally in the possession of Crolly's heir, a fifteen-year-old boy.[27] Although the boy's family returned the house and seminary, they sold the furnishings of both. As if that were not bad enough, there was no archive, and Cullen was unable 'to learn even the names of the priests.' Ecclesiastical routine was no more acceptable; he told Kirby that the rite by which he took possession of the cathedral was the 'first regularly conducted ceremony that took place there since God knows when'.[28]

Already disillusioned by the state of his diocese, Cullen was quickly made aware that the hierarchy's divisions remained just as fierce and intractable as ever. William Delaney, the bishop of Cork, told Cullen that, although he would obey the pope's condemnation of the colleges, it was 'a most imprudent document.'[29] The other bishop with a college in his diocese,[30] Laurence O'Donnell of Galway, informed the new primate that he was reserving his judgement until the synod. Cullen dashed off a letter to Galway, informing O'Donnell that as 'the matter was already decided by Rome' the synod 'could not', therefore, 'alter or correct what was already decided by higher authority.' He also reminded the bishop 'that it was his duty to carry out the instructions received without delay.'[31] O'Donnell, apparently, did 'not condescend to answer.'[32]

Even some opponents of the Queen's Colleges were less than supportive of a Catholic university. Timothy Murphy, the bishop of Cloyne, was a staunch opponent of the Queen's Colleges, but he informed Cullen that if the Cork and Galway colleges might be obtained from the government without conditions then it might be possible to 'spare an impoverished people the overwhelming outlay and annual revenue which the erection and support of a "Catholic University" would necessarily entail.'[33] Although there was indeed a rumour at this time that the government might be willing to make over Cork and Galway, it seems to have been without foundation. Cullen had set his heart on a truly Catholic university instead.

Before he could begin his university, Cullen still had to contend with Murray. The elderly archbishop of Dublin now aligned himself even more closely with the government in an effort to save the Queen's Colleges. In the course of telling Kirby that the 'government is everything with some people', Cullen reported that Murray, with whom he had discussed the matter, was 'most decidedly in favor of the colleges, and says that he can not change his opinions.'[34] For his part, Slattery was certain he understood the reality of the situation and the close links that existed between Murray and the lord lieutenant, Lord Clarendon. He offered Cullen the prediction that 'when the question of a Catholic Uni-

versity is proposed [at the synod]' its opponents would at once claim that
the government had 'offered to make every concession to render the
Queen's Colleges acceptable to the Catholics of Ireland.'[35]

The synod opened on 22 August in Thurles, Slattery's seat, and a site
chosen both to be convenient to the ill archbishop of Cashel and to avoid
the influence Murray might be able to bring to bear in Dublin. Most of
August had been taken up with planning for the ceremonial, which was
held in a grand Roman style. Once the synod was formally convened,
Cullen placed nine propositions dealing with university education in Ireland before the assembled prelates. The first two propositions, regarding
the acceptance of the Propaganda's condemnation of the colleges and a
ban on episcopal participation in their governance, were passed unanimously. This hopeful start was not a result of any change of heart among
the colleges' supporters; rather it was acceptable only because Murray
still held to his interpretation of the anti-college rescripts as only being
binding on the bishops personally, and not on the clergy or the laity. It
would be those propositions dealing with a ban on clergy (as distinct
from the bishops) participating in the Queen's Colleges, and a warning
to the laity to avoid them, that provoked the most controversy. These six
propositions attracted varying levels of support, but the hierarchy was
divided by a margin of fifteen in favour and thirteen against any further
restrictions on the Queen's Colleges.[36]

Cullen was horrified by the level of support that the colleges still enjoyed. Murray, in particular, attracted his wrath: in a letter to Monsignor
Alessandro Barnabò at the Propaganda on 31 August, Cullen reported,
'The Archbishop of Dublin is so bound up with the Government that he
will never oppose any project that emanates from that Government, and
he always carries several other Bishops with him. I am still very shocked
at the way in which these several prelates have expressed themselves.'[37]
He told Kirby that 'Dr. Murray tramples on the rescripts of the Propaganda.'[38] Despite the conflict over the 'Godless' colleges, Cullen was able
to cajole Murray and his supporters into joining with all the other bishops in approving the establishment of a Catholic University of Ireland
(the ninth proposition put before the synod). Cullen's secretary, C. B.
Lyons, wrote triumphantly to Kirby on 5 September to tell him the
news: 'He [Cullen] fought a hard fight this morning for the establishing
of a Catholic University in Ireland. I am delighted to tell you that he has
succeeded.'[39]

That such a deeply divided synod could produce unanimous consent
on a Catholic university is, on the face of it, surprising. Part of the
answer must lie in the fact that Murray thought the whole project flawed

and useless; he expected it to fall under its own weight. Despite supporting the establishment of the university, and even agreeing to sit on the
university committee, it was clear that he had no intention of helping the
infant establishment in any material way. Those who supported the CUI,
like Cullen and Slattery, felt that Murray had gone into an almost immediate, albeit as yet discreet, opposition to the decrees of the synod. As
Slattery wrote to Cullen, 'I can't see what the next step for him [Murray]
and his party will be . . . either to yield at once or openly go into
schism.'[40] Less than a month later Slattery would write to Cullen again:
'It is quite clear the sooner the question is let at rest the better for the
University and for Religion . . . I am sure that many are holding back
[donations for the CUI] on that account as well as in consequence of the
cold water thrown on the project by opposition in high quarters.'[41]
There was no doubt in either man's mind who the source of the cold
water was.

Rome, too, was aware of Murray's obstructionism. In a letter known
to Cullen and Slattery, Cardinal Fransoni had already rebuked Murray
and Laurence O'Donnell, the bishop of Galway, who was still allowing
priests of his diocese to participate in the Queen's College there.[42] Rome
was undoubtedly pleased with the results of the synod; Kirby quickly
wrote to Cullen to tell him that the cardinals of the Propaganda (whose
meeting he had burst into to deliver the news) were 'all delighted beyond
measure' at the decision to create a Catholic university, and that the
pope, too, was 'very much pleased with the decree.'[43] Cullen could move
forward confident in his support at Rome. With no support forthcoming
from outside their own ranks, Murray and his friends were isolated. It
was now time to begin the university in earnest.

THE UNIVERSITY COMMITTEE

A university committee consisting of both priests and laymen was
quickly assembled. It met for the first time in Dublin under Cullen's
chairmanship, and with Murray present. The episcopal members were
the four archbishops, Cantwell, Francis Haly (Kildare), Nicolas Foran
(Waterford), Patrick MacNicholas (Achonry), and John Derry (Clonfert). The nonepiscopal members included such staunch supporters of
the university as Maher, O'Hanlon, Myles O'Reilly, Leahy, and Cooper
(the latter two serving as secretaries to the committee). Although
Murray's appointee, Dean Meyler (a long-time ally), also sat on the committee, neither he nor his sponsor made a habit of attendance after the

first meeting. At the 17 October meeting it was decided that a subcommittee should be formed to 'meet & act from time to time in Dublin for the transaction of business connected with the object of the committee.'[44] It was this subcommittee that would be the real power in the drive finally to give form to the university.

The subcommittee, also under Cullen's chairmanship, was given the task of soliciting donations from the clergy, issuing an address to the people of Ireland on the subject of the university, and preparing a 'programme of fundamental Regulations to be submitted as the basis of the construction of our University, as likewise of the different Faculties to be established in it.'[45] Fundraising, quite naturally, was the first order of business, and the various members of the committee began the process by looking in their own pockets. Cullen, Slattery, and MacHale each promised £100 (with Cullen promising a further £20 annually and the others a further £10), as did Cantwell and Foran. Other large donations included Patrick MacNicholas' £200 and £50 from O'Hanlon. Even Peter Cooper, hardly a wealthy man, gave £5, and Leahy £10. Cullen's family, too, was touched for donations, with his brothers Thomas and Michael each donating £100 to the university.[46] Neither Murray nor Meyler made any contribution at all. In total, donations at the first meeting came to £1717, plus a library with a value of £500. For a church just emerging from the Famine it was quite a respectable amount.[47] As Cantwell somewhat sanguinely told Cullen, the 'University project, all things considered, seems to take wonderfully well.'[48]

Cullen quickly set about raising funds as widely as possible, writing to a number of bishops to encourage the collection in their dioceses.[49] He also wrote letters (identical in every case) to the American bishops to introduce his agent and urge their support for a university which was 'most necessary for the preservation of the Faith in this poor and afflicted country': 'The undertaking is one of great magnitude and above our strength, but the Bishops of Ireland place the utmost confidence in the cooperation of their venerable Brethren in America, and trust with their assistance to be able to overcome every difficulty and to contribute to restore Ireland to the position which she occupied in other ages when she afforded to the nations of Christendom a safe retreat for learning and piety.'[50] Cullen even tried to convert monies raised on behalf of the Association of the Propagation of the Faith (donations for which Rome had granted indulgences) to the use of the university by 'begging' Monsignor Barnabò. And he was confident enough by October to tell Kirby that 'I expect we may do something about the university in a few months.'[51]

Others were not as confident. In November, only two months after the close of the synod, Patrick Leahy told Cullen that 'the grand aim of the Government & its supporters being to carry the Education Question before anything can be done against them, if a beginning of the University be not made soon it may as well not be attempted at all.'[52] Writing to Peter Cooper from Thurles, Slattery referred to the 'scandalous efforts that certain parties are making to uphold this vile government against the Holy See' and to 'drag through the mire Pope & Synod and all'.[53] And John Derry worried that 'any effective organisation of the collection [for the CUI]—amongst the laity, and perhaps I might add amongst the clergy—cannot be expected until the Synodical Statutes are returned confirmed by Rome.'[54] The receipts of the university committee for 1850–51 reveals the extent to which the project was being hindered by Murray's noncooperation (see table 3.1).

Surprisingly, Armagh, to which Cullen had only recently been appointed, had nearly doubled the total that the archdiocese of Dublin had offered to university funds. When it is remembered that Armagh was primarily an Ulster province, the least Catholic area of the island, and that Dublin was the centre of what Catholic power and wealth Ireland possessed, the contrast becomes even more stark. Perhaps even more surprising is the figure for Tuam, which at some £1,747 might not seem like much, even compared with Dublin's contribution, until it is remembered that this was the area in which the Famine had bitten deepest, and was still biting. And if a famine were not enough to depress contributions on its own, one of its largest dioceses, Galway, was headed by a bishop who was second only to Murray in his support for the Queen's Colleges. The poor support from Dublin should have provided the university's supporters with a warning: a Catholic university could not possibly survive without the support of the city's middle-class Catholic population. Even without Murray's deadening influence on collections, Dublin's lack of enthusiasm for the CUI was ominous.

Despite Murray's opposition and the disappointing Dublin returns, Cullen was reasonably happy with the fundraising. He told Slattery on 15 April (after the nationwide St Patrick's Day appeal) that the 'university collection is going on well. The thing now appears to be very practicable.'[55] And he also told Kirby that even 'in the diocese *[sic]* [that are] malevolent the collection is going on, and it will require great skills on the part of their Lordships to impede it.'[56] Fundraisers had been sent to both America and England (something even MacHale approved of: 'we ought to make common cause with the Catholics of England'),[57] and by the end of 1851 some $8,573 (£1,613.12.9) had been raised for the university in the

Table 3.1 Receipts for the Catholic University of Ireland, 1850–51 (in pounds) [a]

Archdiocese of Armagh		Archdiocese of Dublin		Archdiocese of Cashel		Archdiocese of Tuam	
Armagh	715.5.11[b]	Dublin	3,652.19.10	Cashel & Emly	993.12.0	Tuam	761.15.9
Derry	293.17.4	Kildare & Leighlin	764.2.6	Cork	130.16.2	Clonfert	273.4.6
Clogher	537.18.0	Ossory	461.2.1	Killaloe	307.16.10	Achonry	287.18.6
Raphoe	26.12.6	Ferns	624.14.10	Kerry	73.15.4	Elphin	244.13.1
Down & Connor	340.15.0			Limerick	41.12.6	Kilmacduagh	
Kilmore	148.1.8			Lismore	1113.8.6	& Kilfenora	23.0.0
Ardagh	159.1.0			Cloyne	661.7.5	Galway	65.12.0
Meath	3408.4.1			Ross	100.2.8	Killala	91.2.9
Dromore	78.2.8						
Total	12,164.18.2	Total	5,502.9.3	Total	3,425.1.5	Total	1747.6.7

Total in Ireland 22,840.5.5

[a] Source: Draft receipts, Cullen Papers, DDA, 45/3/9.
[b] The astonishing size of Armagh's contribution seems to have been realised by means of an anonymous £5,000 donation from James Hope-Scott. See Larkin, The Making of the Roman Catholic Church in Ireland, 432.

United States.[58] Indeed, the last total available for 1851 (in October) shows that the university committee had £26,076.3.8 on hand.[59] Cullen was now in a position to begin building an actual university.

Cullen was handed a further gift from a most unexpected source: the British government. Provoked by the reestablishment of the English hierarchy on 29 September 1850, and egged on by Clarendon, Lord John Russell delivered an extraordinary tirade against Roman Catholicism in early November. Taking the form of an open letter to the Anglican bishop of Durham, Russell condemned papal pretensions and famously described Catholic religious practices as 'the mummeries of superstition'. Such a statement was a surprise coming from the normally tolerant Russell. In common with his fellow Whigs he had long supported Catholic claims. Russell seems to have been enraged by a combination of the growth of Tractarianism in the Church of England and the intemperance of Nicholas Wiseman's pastoral announcing the reestablishment of the hierarchy. Whatever the motive (and he would become increasingly associated with anti-Catholic political moves as he aged), Russell's attack proved to be enormously popular with Protestant England.[60] Pressure quickly mounted to introduce legislation to counter the 'papal aggression'. The saga of the ecclesiastical titles bill need not detain us here.[61] We need only note that when a bill finally appeared its provisions were aimed directly at Ireland.

Bishops were forbidden to assume territorial titles in both England and Ireland, even though in the latter country the government had implicitly accepted the validity of the bishops' titles since the mid-1840s. Irish bishops would also be unable to append the name of their see on any document. Doing so would render it void. Even more seriously, any bequests made to a bishop using his title would be forfeit to the Crown. Although Russell would eventually be forced to drop those clauses of the bill that were especially offensive in Ireland, the attempt nevertheless played directly into Cullen's hands. He could now plausibly ask how any Catholic could possibly trust promises made on any subject by a government prepared to introduce penal legislation and whose premier referred to Catholic 'mummeries of superstition'. In future, Murray would find it much harder to drum up support for the Queen's Colleges.

On 26 June 1851, the university committee, in a motion made by Slattery and seconded by MacHale, requested that Cullen 'draw up a plan for organizing the University & report it to the Committee, associating with him whom he pleases for the purpose.'[62] It was now time to find a rector.

chapter four

Seduction

The Appointment of
John Henry Newman

THE QUESTION OF WHY, EXACTLY, JOHN HENRY NEWMAN WAS selected by the Irish hierarchy to run their new university is an important one. After all, if the dominant interpretation of the Cullen-Newman relationship is correct, if Cullen really did block and obstruct Newman at every turn, why then should he have chosen Newman in the first place? Historians have tended to congratulate Cullen for his selection of Newman, but, in the course of criticising his later behaviour towards Newman, have failed either to ask or answer this crucial question.

It seems that Cullen began to seriously consider the question of a rector in March 1851. The first surviving mention of Newman in connection with the university came from Robert Whitty, a former Oratorian, Wiseman's vicar-general, and a life-long friend of Newman's.[1] He wrote to Cullen on 12 April 1851 to suggest that Newman might usefully give some lectures on university education in Ireland. Whitty did not, however, suggest Newman as a possible rector, recommending instead Henry Edward Manning for that position.[2] Either Cullen had already been thinking of Newman as rector or Whitty's suggestion fell on exceptionally fertile ground; he wrote to Newman on 15 April asking for advice on the university and to Kirby on 16 April, telling him that '[n]ow we must see to get a good president—If Dr Newman could be persuaded to come, he would all at once give a name and fame to the good work.'[3] As early as March, Cullen had been contemplating introducing an English presence to the university, although not necessarily to the position of rector. In the course of discussing the appointment of a 'Rettore magnifico' of the university, Cullen wrote that the first rector must be a priest, but 'we hope that the vice Rector will be one of the University of Oxford converts and a layman.'[4] The English were necessary, Cullen thought, both to increase the university's reputation and to encourage financial donations from that quarter.[5]

Cullen had been acquainted with Newman since the latter's visit to Rome to prepare for ordination, and had been following his career since at least the early 1840s.[6] In 1847, Cullen, then still rector of the Irish College, had served (at Newman's request) as the official censor of his four Latin dissertations on Athanasius. That Newman should entrust these documents to Cullen speaks to a certain sympathy between the two men. Newman's *Essay on the Development of Christian Doctrine* had been met with some scepticism in Rome, and he had greatly feared it might be placed on the Index of Prohibited Books. He was anxious to do some work in Latin, as he was very conscious that the lack of a reading knowledge of English among such Roman theologians as Giovanni Perrone was contributing to the difficulties his work faced.[7] Newman enjoyed Cullen's hospitality at the Irish College[8] and in late 1848 asked Cullen's help at the Propaganda over problems between the Oratory and William Ullathorne, the bishop of Birmingham. In apologising for his troubling Cullen with the matter, Newman told him that, in asking for his help, he 'was tempted to avail myself of that kind interest which you showed in us when we were in Rome'.[9] Cullen replied promptly and promised to do what he could.[10] (Newman was unhappy with the results, remarking later that Cullen had 'almost snubbed me'.)[11]

Within a month and a half of his arrival in Armagh, Cullen had invited Newman to preach there. He told Newman that his 'presence in this part of the black north would do good.'[12] Although Newman declined the invitation, pleading commitments in Birmingham, he did send his fellow Oratorian, J. D. Dalgairns, whom Cullen had requested should Newman himself be unable to come.[13] In November 1850, Cullen remarked to Kirby in the course of discussing the prospects of the university that 'Mr Newman preaches excellently, and must do much good.'[14] Clearly, Newman was somebody whom Cullen thought could be useful in Ireland.

Whether or not Cullen's 15 April letter to Newman was provoked by Robert Whitty, it does show that Cullen already viewed Newman as a—possibly *the*—expert on educational matters. Cullen began by telling Newman that 'for the last few months several of the Irish bishops have been engaged in collecting funds for the purpose of establishing a Catholic University in Ireland.' The fundraising had been 'very successful', and therefore there could 'be little doubt . . . of the success of our undertaking' as 'it appears evident that the people are willing to supply the means to support such an institution.' Yet, having 'hitherto attended merely to pecuniary matters', the bishops must now 'proceed a step further.' Cullen then went to the point of his letter, telling Newman that 'the first thing to be done is select a fit and proper superior.' His advice 'would be of great importance', and Cullen asked if he would 'be able to recommend us any one that would give a character to the undertaking?'

Cullen went on to explain his reasons for setting up the university, noting that the 'Catholics in Ireland have been left without any means of education unless they frequent Protestant establishments.' 'It is now time to make some effort to have at least one college for the higher branches of science and literature.' He told Newman that he trusted 'you will not think I am too troublesome when I ask your advice in all this matter'. Should Newman 'have any intention of coming to Ireland', his presence at the university committee would be 'most welcome.' Cullen then extended an invitation, telling Newman that 'if you could spare time to give a few lectures on education you would be rendering good service to religion in Ireland.'[15]

Newman sent Cullen an initial response to this letter on 16 April. He noted that many of the 'leading men and authorities in the University would necessarily be priests—and England . . . has none to spare. I do not know how far the Professors would fall under the same rule—perhaps those who filled the chairs of Classics, History, Mathematics etc, need not be.'[16] He followed this up on 28 April with a list of eleven names, all converts, of whom nine were from Oxford and two from Cambridge. As to the matter of a president or rector, Newman told Cullen that 'there is no one strikes me who would fitly fulfil a place which involves the duties of government and oversight.'[17]

Newman, the best known of the Oxford converts and the English Catholic most in touch with university education, had essentially told Cullen that nobody in England was fit to head his university. Nor did Cullen receive any help on this matter from others in England; Cardinal Wiseman told him that he could think of no English priest 'equal to such an important office', although there were 'several admirable men among our converts, who would make excellent professors or tutors.'[18] That not even Wiseman proposed Newman for the rectorship is a further indication that his selection was entirely Cullen's own doing, albeit one conditioned by circumstances. It was only with difficulty that Cullen could choose an Irishman; he would quickly become caught up, even more immediately than a foreigner, in the internecine feuds of the hierarchy. An Irish rector would also be unlikely to have a substantial enough reputation to attract the first-rate faculty and students that Cullen desired.

THE SEDUCTION BEGINS

It was clear that Cullen had found his man; now he had to recruit him. He told Fransoni in June that if 'Mr. Newman could be appointed rector the matter would be secure, but I do not know whether he would be willing to accept such an appointment, or whether he may accept it without the permission of the Holy See, since he is a religious. If he cannot come perhaps we shall find some other person of great repute.'[19] Whether Newman would be willing, or even able, to accept Cullen's intended offer was a matter that had been concerning the archbishop. In his letter of 16 April to Kirby, Cullen had wondered 'would they let him come or tell him to come in Rome'? As 'I suppose he cd. not come without their authority', he instructed Kirby to consult with Barnabò on the subject.[20] Cullen, evidently anticipating a refusal, was contemplating trying to arrange for Newman to be ordered to Dublin. He was informed, however, by Bernard Smith (the new vice-rector of the Irish College) that with 'regard to Dr Newman Rome will give no orders; it will allow and give the necessary dispensations. But no more.'[21] Fransoni himself, on 23 July, wrote to Cullen in support of Newman's candidature.[22] Smith had earlier advised Cullen, 'ask Newman of his Eminence [Wiseman]' as it 'is the only way you can now try.'[23] Cullen, it seems, was not prepared to ask such a thing of Wiseman (perhaps he had hoped Wiseman would suggest Newman's name himself when asked about the university). Instead, he set about approaching Newman through his friends.

The idea of travelling to England to discuss the university seems to have originated with James O'Ferrall, a lay member of the university committee. He wrote to Cullen in early June to suggest that the archbishop 'go to London for a week . . . & confer with the Cardinal—Dr Newman[,] Mr Monsell and others who [are] desirous of aiding us, that it would do a great deal of good.'[24] Cullen duly crossed the Irish Sea, stopping first to visit his family in Liverpool, and then called on

Newman on the 8–9 July (a fact he at least made Slattery aware of, although not of his intention to ask Newman to be rector).[25] Despite his certain intention to offer Newman the rectorship, Cullen made no attempt to broach the subject during this visit. He did, however, discuss the university as such, and Newman reported to T. W. Allies that Cullen was on his way to London to 'talk about the University.'[26] It was in London that Cullen opened his campaign to gain Newman for the Catholic University of Ireland.

Cullen met with Henry Edward Manning, William Monsell, and J. R. Hope (later Hope-Scott) in London on 13 July. All three men were recent converts. Monsell, the MP for Limerick since 1847, had been received in 1850. Manning and Hope—two of Gladstone's closest friends—had only been received that same April. A twelve-page memorandum of the meeting exists in the Dublin diocesan archives, although it does not seem to have been noticed by any historians examining this question because of its being misdated to 1852.[27]

There can be little doubt that the meeting the document refers to, and the document itself, should date to 1851. Cullen wrote to Newman on 13 July 1851 to tell him that 'I have seen Dr. Manning, Mr. Hope, Mr. Monsell . . . and have spoken to them on the projected university. They have expressed a great desire to have a little conversation with you on the matter.'[28] (Note the 'they'—Cullen wished to imply that the idea had come from Newman's friends.) Newman replied to this letter on 15 July: 'Your letter dated Sunday has only just come. . . . I feel exceedingly the kindness of your wish that I should come up to London, and both in obedience to it and from my zeal in the matter to which it relates would wait on your Grace at once, could I possibly do so, as I am situated here. But really I cannot.' He went on to tell Cullen that he would most gladly 'make myself useful in so great an object as the Catholic University, but at this very moment I deeply regret, for I know what an important moment it is for the University, for I am literally tied here.'[29] And Hope, in a letter dated 12 July, told Newman, 'To-morrow I am to meet with the Primate of Ireland.'[30]

The memorandum is important not only for going some way to establishing why Cullen approached Newman but also for an understanding of what Cullen hoped for in his university. It begins by giving the purpose of the meeting and Cullen's visit, which was 'to consult persons of experience as to the best mode of proceeding to found the University.' Cullen set out the 'basis' 'of all teaching' in the university, which was to be the 'Catholic Religion.' 'Consistent with that main object', Cullen 'desired to see as extended a system of instruction in all the sciences as his means would admit.'[31]

The issue of the structure of the university was raised by Manning, who asked 'if his Grace had decided whether the students of the university were to live in colleges or were only to attend the lectures of the professors of the university.' Cullen quickly disclaimed any view on this point, and brought Newman's name into the conversation for the first time, telling Manning that 'his object was to elicit the opinion of persons of experience, such as Dr Newman, Dr Manning[,] Mr Hope and Mr Monsell.' It 'occurred' to Cullen that 'if Dr Newman, associated with Revd Mr Leahy of Thurles, would undertake to consider the subject and frame statutes' with the 'advice and concurrence' of those at the meeting, 'all those questions would be raised and decided by them.'[32]

The discussion then turned to such matters as the number of professors, the location of the university (with most present preferring a rural location such as Thurles), and the need to begin quickly before 'the present zeal had cooled.' Cullen, without committing himself, 'expressed himself much gratified with the turn the discussion had taken.' He observed that 'it appeared to him that if the aid [of Dr] Newman could be immediately obtained and if he could enjoy the advantage of communicating with him with the aid of the present company, that a decided step in advance would be made.' Manning felt 'sure that if His Grace would write to Dr Newman', Newman would come down to London for a meeting later that week. That being the case a 'general conversation then took place as to the subjects to be referred to Dr Newman.' According to the memorandum, the general opinion of the meeting was that 'he should be requested to consider the best means of establishing the University for the object stated by the Primate'. He should also consider the site for the new university and should 'frame a report for publication as the basis for all future proceedings.' It was then 'determined to postpone all further discussion until the arrival of Dr Newman.' Cullen told the group that he would invite Newman 'by that nights [sic] post',[33] something he did, telling Newman that 'it is a great liberty to trouble you to do so [come to London], but the zeal you have manifested in favour of the university encourages me to make the request. If you can come, you will confer a great favor upon me, and all those engaged in the good work.'[34]

The meeting, at least so far as the memorandum reveals, did not bring forward Newman's name as rector. All who participated seemed more than willing to consult and defer to Newman, but none mention him as a possible head of the university. It was Cullen who brought up his name in each case, and he seems to have been using the other participants as a way of getting to Newman. Historians such as McGrath have tended to follow Newman's own assumption that 'Hope . . . mentioned me to him [Cullen].'[35] McGrath goes so far as to say that 'Hope's arguments had, indeed, been so persuasive that, on his way back to Ireland, Dr. Cullen broke his journey at Birmingham on July 18th, and offered the Rectorship to Newman'.[36] This is an important misunderstanding of actual events. If Newman's appointment were a spur-of-the-moment matter provoked by Hope's advocacy, it would add plausibility to the idea that Cullen would quickly fall out with a choice he had not thought out. If, however, Hope had nothing to do with Cullen's choice, and that choice was long contemplated and planned for, then such an assumption must fail. As a letter he wrote to Bernard Smith on 12 July indicates, Cullen badly wanted Newman for the projected university: 'I very much want to put Newman at the head of the business. He has a very great name, much learning, and seems to be an excellent man in every respect.' Moreover, Cullen wrote with some optimism that 'Newman is so much esteemed in Ireland, that although English he will be very well received there.' Cullen even thought that other Englishmen—such as Allies—could be 'employed with advantage.'[37]

NEWMAN HESITATES, ACCEPTS, AND SETS TO WORK

As Cullen had feared, Newman did not immediately agree to the proposal. He instead offered to serve as 'Prefect of Studies' which, he recalled in 1870, would 'commit me less to an institution which had its seat in another country, and which on that account threatened, if I had the highest post in it, to embarrass my duties to the Birmingham Oratory.'[38] In section 1 of his university memorandum Newman recalled that those whom he had approached for advice, such as Hope and F. W. Faber, advised him to become rector (the implication being that they influenced the matter). In fact he had written to Cullen acceding to the idea that if he was to be anything at all it was best to be rector, on 23 July—a day before either Faber or Hope's advice reached him.[39] As he told his friend T. W. Allies, 'our Fathers have been clamouring for me to be Rector.'[40] In the meantime Cullen mounted something of a charm campaign, even sending Newman a donation as he was 'anxious to have a place among the benefactors of the oratory'.[41]

Although Newman would not formally accept the rectorship until November, and Cullen does not seem to have been easy about the matter until late September or early October, there can be little doubt that he intended to take the job from almost the moment Cullen had left him. It is also clear that Newman was grateful to Cullen for the offer; he dedicated the *Present Position of Catholics in England* to the archbishop that August. In the short term, it is true, he was engrossed in his lectures (even so, by 11 September he was telling Robert Ornsby, a friend and deputy editor of *The Tablet*, that he was unclear what power 'I shall have' to nominate professors);[42] he was also concerned about the absence from Birmingham such a post would imply. As he told Cullen in his letter of 23 July: 'What I should desire is, to do as much work for the University as possible with *as little absence as possible from this place.*'[43] As we shall see, the tragedy was that the two men had wildly differing ideas about how much absence from Dublin would be possible.

Even if he had not yet accepted the rectorship, Newman had promised Cullen that he would join a committee to consider the question of how to go about the establishment of the university and how that institution should be structured. The committee consisted of Newman, Patrick Leahy, and Myles O'Reilly, a lay member of the university committee. Cullen didn't fail to remind Newman of this promise, telling him on 12 August that 'Dr Leahy is ready now to go over to Birmingham to visit you and to consult with you on this important matter'. He hoped it would be 'convenient' to Newman 'to devote a little time to him'. Cullen also informed him that the university committee, which was 'exceedingly anxious to have something done', wished to retain Allies as secretary so as to save Newman 'from the trouble of writing and lighten your labour very much.'[44] Allies, a married Church of England priest who had recently converted and was without a private income, was in need of employment. Such an offer, which would ease his friend's plight, would be welcome to Newman.[45]

Leahy and O'Reilly arrived in Birmingham on 29 August, already armed with questions on the university 'which they had drawn up in Ireland.' After these initial consultations, Newman would wait until late September (apparently at Leahy's suggestion)[46] before travelling to Ireland to continue the discussions.[47] Throughout September, Cullen continued with his efforts to draw Newman ever more fully into the Catholic University. He reminded Newman on 15 September what a 'great good' he could 'effect by giving us a few lectures on education,' especially as it was 'necessary to put many persons' ideas right on the subject.'[48] He followed up this point with another, longer letter on the same subject on 20 September.[49]

Newman arrived in Ireland late on 30 September, and the next day made his way to Thurles, where he, Allies, and O'Reilly were to meet Leahy. The men quickly conducted their business, and Newman was able to write to Cullen on 3 October: 'We seem to have finished our work here, as far as we can do it'.[50] The 'Report of the Sub-committee on the Organization of the University' was submitted to Cullen, and by him to the university committee as a whole, who declined to judge it immediately, but instead asked for more time in which to consider it. This delay did not worry Cullen, who assured Newman that when the committee next met he would 'succeed in getting your views adopted'.[51] The university committee reconvened on 12 November, and a proposal, moved by Peter Cooper, that 'Dr. Newman should be appointed the first Rector of the University carried by acclamation.'[52] All three pro-university archbishops were present (as was Cantwell), and, according to Cooper, even MacHale spoke warmly of the appointment.[53] Cullen quickly wrote to Newman with the glad news, telling him, 'I trust you will accept the burden we are so desirous to press upon you.' He also added, in words that sound ironic in hindsight, 'I trust we shall do everything to conduct matters as you will desire.'[54] As Newman somewhat laconically noted in his memorandum: 'I accepted the post.'[55]

Cullen had been preparing the ground for the appointment since at least early October, and it is probable that Newman gave him a verbal assurance of his readiness to accept the post when he saw the archbishop in Drogheda on 4 and 5 October. Indeed, Newman's letters to Cullen after this meeting give every impression that he was planning to become rector.[56] Whether Newman had already told Cullen of his acceptance or not, the latter had clearly felt confident enough to canvass his name amongst the hierarchy even before seeing Newman in Drogheda—something he had not done before. The only warning note came from Bernard Smith in Rome. Although professing to be pleased with the prospective appointment, Smith warned Cullen that 'Dr Newman is viewed now in Rome with jelosy *[sic]* by some people.' This was as a result of his latest 'Conference' (presumably the lectures on the present position of Catholics) having been found to be not 'quite orthodox'. Smith summed up the problem: 'Dr N. is at the head of a new order, at least it may be judged so in England, he is now to be placed over a great University; which must form and mold the mind of all the Catholics wherever the English language is spoken.'[57] Smith never named these jealous people, and the letter itself reads rather as a warning from Smith to Cullen (who could hardly be comforted by discovering Newman was not 'quite orthodox'). Regardless of Smith's intent, Cullen persevered in his choice, and Smith, in a letter written once Newman had been publicly appointed, assured Cullen that 'Dr. Newman's nomination has given general satisfaction' in Rome.[58]

Reaction amongst the bishops to Newman's appointment seems to have been quite favourable. Cantwell wrote that he was 'delighted' at what

Cullen had told him 'in reference to Doctor Newman.'[59] Charles Mac-Nally of Clogher, in a 'humbling admission', thought there was 'at present no Irishman qualified for the presidency of the university'. He expected 'unanimity in the selection of Mr Newman'. MacNally was fulsome in his praise of Newman himself, telling Cullen that 'his [Newman's] high character must point him out to all as the person in every respect the most eligible. Indeed I cannot think of any one who could, for a moment, be put in competition with him.'[60] Even Murray, in the course of a long letter spelling out—once again—why he would not support the university, told Cullen that 'whenever the time shall arrive for attempting to carry into effect the university, Dublin would be the most suitable place wherein to fit it; and it would not[,] in my opinion, be easy to find an abler Man to preside over it, than Doctor Newman.'[61] Murray was not going to lift a finger to help the university, and would in fact do everything he could to hinder it, but he approved of Cullen's choice of both site and rector; it is unlikely Cullen was much relieved by this news.

The only possible obstacle within the hierarchy, then, was MacHale. Certainly the question of how the anglophobic archbishop of Tuam would react was troubling Cullen's friends in Rome; Smith, who had evidently overcome any doubts he might have had about Newman, told Kirby that 'I trust his Grace of Tuam will not prevent Dr N. from taking part in the University.'[62] Although MacHale would come to object to Newman's appointment by at least mid-1852, he nevertheless did not oppose it at the time. The fact that he was present at the university committee meeting which unanimously approved the appointment (he was never one to disagree quietly) and that no record of his disapproval exists in either Slattery's or Cullen's papers would seem to indicate that Newman was, at least initially, an acceptable choice to the Lion of the West.

Newman's appointment was a masterful operation, and showed Cullen's political skills at their best. He had carefully arranged everything before making his approach—one he made in the most politic manner available—and he then made sure that his quarry did not escape. He managed the neat trick of ensuring both that Rome would accept a man whose orthodoxy was sometimes in doubt and that such Irish bishops as MacHale would accept an Englishman being put in charge of their national university. Cullen wanted Newman, and he got him. As he told William Walsh, 'We elected Dr. Newman president in order to give a literary character to our project and to show that merit alone was to be taken account of in our selection.'[63] Newman was 'the most distinguished man we have, we can have Irishmen in abundance with him but he will give our institution a literary fame all at once.'[64]

chapter five

The Idea of a University, in Ireland

AT FIRST GLANCE, IT WOULD SEEM UNLIKELY THAT PAUL CULLEN and John Henry Newman could have much in common in the realm of educational theory. Through his *Idea of a University* Newman has come to be seen as one of the great, if not the greatest, theorists of higher education. By contrast, Cullen is seen as a more narrow, sectarian figure. Historians have not been kind to Cullen's views on education, especially in comparison to Newman's. In *The Convert Cardinals,* David Newsome is typical: saying 'Cullen never really understood the nature of a university'. Newsome then quotes a professor at the CUI during Newman's tenure to the effect that Cullen thought the university to be a kind of lay seminary.[1] Perhaps the neatest phrasing of the prevailing assumption is that of Edward McCarron and Richard Finnegan: 'Cullen sought to create a Catholic university to provide an Irish Catholic education, while Newman sought to provide a liberal arts education to Irish Catholics.'[2] None of Newman's biographers, or indeed historians of the Irish Catholic Church, have given much time to Cullen's ideas on university education.

In the realm of educational theory it would of course be foolish to class Cullen with Newman. Nevertheless, it is important to understand Cullen's views when examining the entire Catholic University project.

That Cullen wanted Newman as rector to draw support, both financial and otherwise, to the university is clear. Newman was possibly the only Catholic figure who had the experience and reputation necessary to make the project a success. Nonetheless, it is still unlikely that Cullen would be willing to turn over his cherished project to a man who differed substantially from him on matters of educational philosophy. It would be counterproductive to create an alternative to the 'Godless' Colleges if the Catholic University were to be no better in its approach to the education of Ireland's youth.

THE CATHOLIC ETHOS: CULLEN AND EDUCATION

At the time he was appointed archbishop of Armagh, Paul Cullen had spent almost his entire life in education. He entered the highly academic Carlow College as a thirteen-year-old in early 1817, leaving in 1820. Although offered a place at Maynooth, the young Cullen chose, on his uncle James Maher's advice, to attend the College of Propaganda Fide in Rome, leaving to commence his studies in October 1820. His eight years of theological study there were capped by an exceptionally well received public disputation held in the presence of Pope Leo XII. As Ciaran O'Carroll has remarked, 'Cullen's status as an outstanding Church figure in Rome was widely acknowledged' by 1830.[3] His reputation there was such that the Propaganda refused to allow him to return to Ireland to take up a teaching appointment at Carlow.[4] He was ordained in 1829 and was immediately appointed professor of Greek and Oriental Languages in the Propaganda College. He was also given charge of the Propaganda's polyglot press, which produced a number of scholarly texts during his tenure. He was personally involved in editing an edition of the Hebrew Bible for the press.[5] His success led, in 1832, to his being appointed rector of the Irish College.[6]

In the Irish church Carlow College was something of a powerhouse; Michael Slattery and William Kinsella were both professors there during Cullen's student days, and James Doyle (Cullen's bishop) had long been associated with the college. Cullen himself has left no memoirs of his education in Carlow, but the flavour of it can be gained from a letter his friend J. B. Taylor sent him in 1822, not long after Cullen had left Ireland. Taylor, who had been a classmate of Cullen's, had just been appointed a professor in the college and reported to Cullen on his schedule: 'I hear a class of prosody & Italian grammar in the morning, Livy & Juvenal . . . from 10 till 11[,] Greek grammar from 12 to 1[,] Homer from 1 to 2,

Cicero & Horace alternately from 2 to 3—I have six classes of Latin 4 of Greek 3 of French 1 of Italian—there is also a class of natural philosophy which Mr Kinsella has, and also one of geometry besides writing and arithmetic.'[7] Although there is no way of knowing either how well these subjects were taught by the clearly overworked staff or how much the students absorbed, it is obvious that a Carlow education was hardly out of line with the sort of education a student preparing for, say, Oxford might receive. Cullen must have done quite well to have been sent onwards to Rome. His Italian was perfect, and he was certainly competent in Latin, Greek, French, and Hebrew—more languages than Newman himself could command. Clearly, F. S. L. Lyons's reference to Cullen's 'peasant shrewdness' as against Newman's own worldly wisdom was grossly unfair.[8]

If Cullen was not a genius in Newman's league then he was most certainly a scholar and an educator, and was seen as such in Ireland and Rome. His name had been put forward by Daniel Murray for the presidency of Maynooth in 1834,[9] and in 1835 the pope vetoed an attempt to appoint Cullen president of Carlow College on the grounds he was too valuable in Rome.[10] When the turmoil of 1848–49 forced the Jesuits from the Propaganda College, Cullen was appointed pro-rector and managed to keep the college open through those troubled times. As rector of the Irish College, he had little real influence on the education per se of the students in his care. One of many national colleges in Rome, the Irish College was designed to serve as a hall of residence for students studying for the priesthood at the various Roman universities. It was responsible for the priestly formation of its students and their general welfare. Cullen was primarily in a pastoral role towards his students, but he must have been in very close contact with their education and the progress of their studies.

Cullen's interests were primarily theological, but he kept up a wide reading, often of works by authors who might be thought surprising for a man of his supposed narrowness. In 1838 William Meyler (an ally of Murray's and later an inactive member of the university committee) sent Cullen a number of Anglican texts, including works by Hooker and Berkeley. This was in response to Cullen's request for works by 'the Best English writers against Deists and Infidels'.[11] Meyler had previously sent Cullen and the Irish College works ranging from Dr Johnson and the complete Edmund Burke to *The Spectator*, *Guardian*, and *Tatler* (in eight volumes).[12] Although we have no way of knowing if Cullen himself read these works, it is unlikely that they were given wide circulation among the students (especially the Anglican books). Probably he, Kirby, and other senior members of the college were the intended recipients of Meyler's book parcels; Cullen was by no means isolated in Rome from wider intellectual concerns and currents.

As we have seen, the Propaganda turned to Cullen for counsel on the national schools, and his opinions were sought out during the initial debate over the safety of the Queen's Colleges. It was during that controversy that the idea of a Catholic university was first mooted. The question of what, precisely, a Catholic university should look like and what it should teach was, it seems, of little interest to the university's proponents—at least until after the Synod of Thurles. Louvain was assumed to be the appropriate template, and it duly became the model that was eventually used. Cullen appears to have been the only figure to examine Louvain itself before Newman, Leahy, and O'Reilly did so in 1851.

Preserved in the Irish College Archives in Rome is an undated memorandum written by Cullen on the subject of Louvain.[13] He began by setting out the history of the establishment of Belgium's Catholic university by that nation's hierarchy. According to Cullen, the established universities of Belgium were 'conducted in a spirit most hostile to the Catholic religion.' That being the case, the 'ecclesiastical authorities of Belgium were necessarily opposed to institutions founded for the purpose of injuring our holy faith'. Consequently, the Belgian bishops 'found it necessary to oppose a university to those already existing'. That university, which eventually became Louvain (it was founded at Malines), was a striking success and the government suppressed one of the offending universities.

In his memorandum Cullen dwelt on Louvain's students' success in independent national exams, success which he clearly felt to have been the result of a properly Catholic education. He commented favourably on the fact that Louvain did not receive any state aid, but rather was 'supported altogether by the Bishops, and the oblations of the faithful.' He also noted that there were few theology students or foreigners at Louvain, and that the 'professors are nearly all laymen'.[14] Rather than being a cause for concern, the lack of ecclesiastical students and a professoriate of laymen at Louvain were treated by Cullen as a component of its success.

Cullen's interest in Louvain was shared by Newman and the Thurles subcommittee established in 1851 by the Catholic University Committee to draw up plans for the CUI. Almost immediately after accepting Cullen's commission to join the committee (but before formally accepting his offer of the rectorship), Newman had written to such prominent figures in Catholic education as F. X. de Ram, the rector of Louvain, and Johann Joseph Iganz von Döllinger (Lord Acton's mentor).[15] He asked his informants to describe for him both existing and historical practice. Newman entered into a regular correspondence with de Ram and preserved in his personal archive not only the rector's responses to his questions but also the various pamphlets and reports on Louvain that de Ram sent to him.[16] Indeed, Newman seems to have asked himself—and de Ram—many of the same questions that Cullen had addressed some years earlier in his own investigation into Louvain. A number of undated notes in Newman's hand indicate those points that he wished clarified about Louvain: 'What was the first state of the University? Had the present Rector absolute power (under the Bishops)? Was the system provisional? What proportion of the students are lay? Are the Professors clergymen or laymen?'[17]

When in November 1851 the Thurles subcommittee submitted its report, Louvain was the dominant influence. Its recommendations on the appointment of the rector and vice-rector were '[f]ollowing the Encyclical Letter of the Belgian Bishops for erecting the University of Louvain', and decisions such as vesting the final authority for the university in the Irish bishops followed the Belgian model.[18] It was Louvain, not Oxford, which Newman had in mind when he drew up plans for a Catholic university. And it was Louvain, not a lay seminary, that Cullen had in mind when he invested his energy and authority in ensuring that such a university came into being.

Tracing Cullen's views on what the structure of the university should be is difficult; for all his learning he was not a man much given to philosophical musings. It is possible, however, to gain something of an idea from various sources that have survived. A number of undated, fragmentary notes on education—probably prepared for sermons or pastoral letters—are preserved in Dublin and can give a idea of the importance Cullen placed on a Catholic education and something of what he meant by one. 'The only hope for preservation of religion', wrote Cullen, 'is in the Catholic education of youth.' 'To banish God from the school [is to] train up youth without inculcating on their minds the principles of christian morality and the sublime doctrines of the gospel'. Failing to do so would 'bring back paganism and all its corruptions and souls innumerable will be lost'.[19]

One of his clearest statements came in the 'Address of the Catholic University Committee to the People of Ireland'.[20] Although sanctioned by all the bishops following the Synod of Thurles, the address was written by Cullen and can be seen as setting out his agenda for the university. In this address Cullen is explicit as to the problems of modernity: 'One of the greatest calamities of modern times is the separation of religion from science'. The Queen's Colleges were designed to separate the two, whereas Cullen believed that 'the perfection of knowledge is the union of both'.[21] To Cullen, it was impossible to have a scientific education (by which he meant any study of the temporal world, from history to geology) without it being informed by theological knowledge.

Nor could there be any conflict between the two, rightly understood: 'So far from there being any antagonism between religion and science, they are a mutual advantage, each reflecting light upon and facilitating the acquisition of the other.'[22] Cullen's Catholic University would be able to provide its students with the benefits of both religion and science, something a purely secular university would be manifestly unable to do. It was only a university like Louvain, or even Oxford or Cambridge, which could provide such an education, not the new secular creations such as University College London or the Queen's Colleges.

Secular education did not just imply giving an incomplete education to students, but rather had deeper consequences. The effects could be seen on the continent, where secular education had been in place for much longer than in Ireland: 'From science without religion has sprung that spurious philosophy which has overrun so many of the schools, and colleges, and universities of the Continent of Europe, and which the professors of Atheism, Pantheism, and every form of unbelief, make the groundwork of their impious systems.'[23] The danger was not just to the students' minds, but also to their faith. As Cullen wrote in one of the Dublin fragments, though 'catholics are so anxious for the progress of knowledge and have done so much to promote the civilization and enlightenment of mankind, it is not to be supposed that indiscriminately they approve every system of education invented by the fashion of the day or a desire of innovation.' After all, 'many of these educational systems are dangerous to faith and morals, and hostile to the eternal interests of the human soul'.[24]

Though undoubtedly believing that a true education was one informed by, if not saturated in, religious knowledge, Cullen perceived more serious civil implications than an ill-educated populace for a society that failed to educate its children properly. His long residence in Rome, including during the traumatic years 1848–49, led him to believe that the unrest was largely led by students of universities 'in which, according to the modern fashion, everything is taught but religion.'[25] In setting up a Catholic university in Ireland, Cullen hoped that 'the youth of Ireland shall . . . be saved from the taint of this mischievous philosophy by a thoroughly Catholic education.' This was to be one of the 'grand objects of a Catholic University'.[26]

It is difficult, at least with hindsight, to draw a credible link between the situation in Ireland in the early 1850s and that in Italy at the same time, and certainly with Italy as Cullen had known it in 1848–49. Young Italy—or rather that disparate set of groups that came together in Rome and elsewhere—was a vastly greater threat to order than was Young Ireland; there was never the remotest chance of a Roman-style Irish Republic being created in 1848, whatever William Smith O'Brien and his fellow rebels might have hoped. Cullen, however, was at least partially correct in identifying secular education—or at least secularism—as a common link in the programmes of both Young Ireland and Young Italy. To Cullen, such secularism, if left unchecked, necessarily led to the Roman Republic. That we now know there was little chance of such a thing happening in Ireland at this time is beside the point; Cullen reasonably thought it could, a belief that equally drove his campaigns *for* Catholic education and *against* Fenianism in the 1860s. Cullen knew that the United Kingdom was not Italy (for one thing, it was politically unified and free from foreign troops and meddling), but he was never sure that Italian evils could not take root in Irish soil.

It thus became a matter of paramount importance to found the Catholic University on what Cullen believed to be sound principles. His strong feelings can be seen in a pastoral letter to his Armagh clergy: 'Is it not the duty of ministers of religion . . . to obtain for their flocks the benefit of a good education, and to save them from the evils and dangers of a bad one? Who else but the pastors of the Church have the mission from Heaven to add the religious element to education? Who else have ever been able to confer this inestimable boon on humanity?'[27]

In a more tempered but no less heartfelt letter to Kirby, Cullen explained the seriousness of the whole project of a Catholic university: 'The future of Ireland depends on the education that we shall adopt now for the youth—without a University education will always be bad, because the youth always goes to the Protestant Universities, and there they are spoiled.'[28]

Cullen outlined the matter in a letter to an unknown correspondent with some heat and fluency: 'But you will ask, what are you to do with your children? How are you to provide a superior education for them?' His answer was, 'why not make an attempt to establish a really Catholic University in this country?' 'We are reproached with not having a Catholic literature in Ireland, we are taunted continually with our ignorance and the want of high literary and scientific institutions.' 'Such taunts', Cullen told his correspondent in terms that would have done MacHale proud, 'come with a very bad grace from those who utter them. They first confiscate the property of our forefathers, they sacked and pillaged our monasteries & colleges that were in bye-gone [sic] days nurseries of learning and piety, they extinguished our schools, they banished or put to death the men who could have preserved the torch of science amongst us—and to render the memory of these foul deeds more galling they now insult us with our poverty and ignorance.'[29]

After this attack on English behaviour towards Ireland, Cullen turned to the Irish themselves. He pointed out that, although 'we are poor' and 'overwhelmed with afflictions of every kind' there were nevertheless 'many wealthy and influential Catholics amongst us' who could, if they were 'really desirous to preserve a Catholic spirit in their children', 'come forward & give a helping hand in the great undertaking of establishing a Catholic university.' Such a university would 'foster & create a spirit of learning, [and] it would provide us with a Catholic literature'. What was more, Cullen wrote, 'Science and Literature would no longer be hostile to our holy Church'.[30]

Cullen's primary concern with the Catholic University was that it be just that—Catholic. As we shall see, it was not the content of the education that he was concerned about—nearly everybody in Ireland at the time agreed on a standard classical curriculum—but rather the environment in which that education would be gained. Cullen consistently expressed concern with any system in which Catholic students, of whatever level, were educated in a non-Catholic environment. These concerns remained constant long after Newman had left the Catholic University and it was clear to all observers that Cullen's grand hopes for that project had come to nought. The issue of regimental schools for Army orphans, which long occupied Cullen, is a case in point. In a letter to William Monsell, which was passed, almost certainly with Cullen's knowledge, to the then prime minister Lord Aberdeen, Cullen remarked that the secular environment of the schools would lead to trouble: 'The children grow up without any real religion: they are neither protestants nor catholics: in progress of time the schools will produce troublesome and dangerous subjects.'[31] In 1864 Cullen returned to the same subject, telling Monsell, 'I am persuaded that nothing will effectually protect the religion of our poor Catholic soldiers' orphans except the establishment of a separate school for them.'[32] And in 1872, in a discussion of further changes to the national schools, he again told Monsell that 'if men of every religious denomination, and some hostile to everything catholic, should succeed in vindicating to themselves the right of deciding certain questions arising between managers and teachers . . . [they] may seriously affect the interests of faith and morals.'[33] Cullen was concerned that, above all, the *ethos* of a school or university should be Catholic: 'In mixed schools catholic doctrines cannot be properly taught[.] In mixed schools catholic practices cannot be inculcated[.] In mix. sch. a catholic spirit cannot be cultivated and encouraged.'[34]

NEWMAN'S VIEW: THE UNIVERSITY AND THE 'QUEEN OF SCIENCES'

Newman shared his patron's emphasis on the need for a Catholic education to be truly Catholic; indeed, it would be strange if that most religious of men had not. Naturally, his Dublin lectures were heavily influenced by Cullen; the archbishop needed to sell his university—and its rector—to a still sceptical public. Before Newman had formally committed himself to the rectorship, Cullen outlined his view, in response to a request by Newman,[35] on what form such a course of lectures might take. In so doing, he informed Newman in plain language of his own ideas on education: 'What we want in Ireland is to persuade the people that education should be religious.' 'The whole tendency of our new systems is to make it believed that education may be conducted as to have nothing at all to do with religion. Moral philosophy, law, [and] history are proposed to be taught in this way.' Although Cullen thought such an idea 'absurd and impossible', he nevertheless told his prospective rector that it was 'necessary to instruct us a little upon this matter.' In order to do so, 'I suppose the whole question of education should be reviewed.' Cullen then suggested—'without order and merely to give some little idea of what we need'—a number of possible topics: 'the advantages of educating the people and the sort of education they ought to receive[,] mixed education—examination of the education given to Catholics in Trinity College and its effects. *[sic]* education in the Queen's Colleges, or education without any religion—the sort of education catholics ought to seek for'.[36]

Although Newman did not hold exactly to these topics in his initial six lectures (the only ones he gave publicly) of 1852, he nevertheless kept them in mind. All the available evidence suggests that Newman was in full agreement with Cullen on the issues of mixed education and the presence of God and the church in the curriculum. Without question, the order in which Newman gave his lectures, and even the emphasis he placed on certain questions, was influenced by political concerns; if he had not been founding a university in Ireland he would no doubt have approached matters differently. As he told Robert Ornsby ('in confidence'), the subjects for his discourses 'were suggested by high authority, and I think may please those whom I most wish to please if I begin with them.'[37] Nevertheless, one need not disagree with Ian Ker that the 'first three' discourses were 'written to episcopal order' in order to hold that the 1852 discourses reflected Newman's own long and closely held position on the subject of mixed and secular education.[38] It is impossible to support G. M. Young's view that in 'the first four [discourses] he [Newman] is in his cell, speaking, we may say, confessionally' and that only in the fifth discourse did Newman 'step into the daylight and speak to the world.'[39] It is a crucial error to try to separate the first three or four Dublin discourses from the rest of *The Idea of a University*. Newman was giving his lectures in Ireland and in an Irish context; his first task was to show why university education should be religious and not mixed or secular. Only with that task done, could he turn his attention to the nature of a university whose Catholicism both he and his audience now assumed.

Newman had turned his pen to the subject of secular education long before he would be called to do so again in Dublin. In the *Tamworth Reading Room*, originally published in the *Times* in 1841 under the signature of 'Catholicus', Newman stated his views on that matter quite clearly indeed. The *Tamworth Reading Room* grew out of a speech made by Sir Robert Peel on the occasion of the opening of a public library and reading room in Tamworth. Newman began by attacking Peel for promising that no works of 'controversial divinity' would be allowed into the library and that the library itself would be 'an edifice in which men of all political opinions and all religious feelings may unite in the furtherance of knowledge, without the asperities of party feeling.'[40] To Newman, the idea that such an institution could prove beneficial was nonsense.

In the course of considering Peel's view that 'in becoming wiser a man will become better' and 'will rise at once in the scale of intellectual and moral existence', Newman asked, 'how these wonderful moral effects are to be wrought under the instrumentality of the physical sciences'? He further wondered if 'the process' can 'be analyzed and drawn out, or does it act like a dose or a charm'?[41] Knowledge without religious understanding was, if not positively dangerous, at the very least worthless: 'In morals, as in physics, the stream cannot rise higher than its source. Christianity raises men from earth, for it comes from heaven; but human morality creeps, struts, or fret's upon the earth's level, without wings to rise.'[42]

The *Tamworth Reading Room* unambiguously showed Newman's interest in and appreciation of the dangers of secular education. His discourses in Dublin, largely directed against the same Sir Robert Peel's plans for the Queen's Colleges, had their roots not so much in Cullen's desire to attack 'Godless' education, although that certainly played a part, but in Newman's own preoccupations from before his conversion; he had been concerned about the risks of secular education long before he was made aware of the educational concerns of the Irish clergy. In 1834–35, while still at Oxford, Newman had taken the lead (along with E. B. Pusey and a few others) in opposing a bill to abolish religious tests at Oxford and Cambridge, securing wide support within the university. Newman had even gone so far as to oppose proposals to bring Oxford into line with the practice at Cambridge and allow subscription to the Thirty-nine Articles to be deferred to graduation, a move that would have allowed Catholics to attend the university, but not to receive their degrees.[43]

Newman delivered his lectures in Dublin between 10 May and 7 June 1852. In these first five discourses, he set out to explain not only why Ireland needed a Catholic university but also what such a university might look like. Newman was pleased by his first lecture, telling Ambrose St John that 'the room is very good for my purpose . . . It was just the room I have ever coveted, and never had.' His pleasure went beyond the room, and he noted to St John that there were some '13 Trinity fellows, Eight Jesuits; a great many clergy—and most intense attention.'[44] What his attentive audience—which also included Paul Cullen—would hear that night and in the following weeks was a crushing condemnation of mixed education and a plan for a truly liberal, Catholic education.

Newman's discourses would eventually be included in *The Idea of a University,* which is not a single book in any real sense of the word. The *Idea* is essentially of two distinct parts. The first consists of those discourses, some actually given and some not, written and published in Dublin in 1852. The second part is made up of occasional pieces that often appeared in the *Catholic University Gazette* and was first published in 1859. These later writings are of a primarily historical nature, being largely concerned with what various universities were and had been. It was only in 1873 that a book was issued with the title *The Idea of a University,* bringing the two halves together.[45] It is largely the 1852 discourses to which we must turn our attention and not the *Idea* in its entirety.

Newman had two primary tasks in his first lectures to the Catholics of Dublin. He had first to convince them that the Queen's Colleges were unsafe and second that a Catholic university was both a good substitute and a realistic one. He could not assume a sympathetic audience on either point; Dublin had not distinguished itself in donations to the university and Archbishop Murray was only some three months in his grave.

To achieve his aims Newman had to show his audience not only why a strictly secular education, as could be obtained in the Queen's Colleges, was false to the idea of a university, but also why a mixed education, even encompassing theology, as might be found by a Catholic student attending Trinity College, was unacceptable. In attempting to make these points, Newman advanced the doctrine that lies at the heart of his Dublin discourses (and thus *The Idea of a University*): that knowledge is a whole from which no piece can be excluded without fatally weakening what remained, and that theology is indispensable to a university education.

Newman began by explaining what precisely he thought a university to be. 'If its object were scientific and philosophical discovery, I do not see why a University should have students; if religious training, I do not see how it can be the seat of philosophy and science.' A Catholic university was to be neither purely research-based nor a seminary, but rather the seat of 'universal knowledge'. Such a university could not, however, in Newman's view 'fulfil its object duly without the Church's assistance'. The church was 'necessary for its *integrity*' as it would steady the university 'in the performance of that office.'[46]

The church might be necessary to the university, but why would the church establish a university? Why, asked Newman, would Pius IX want such a thing? 'Is he bound by office or by vow, to be the preacher of the theory of gravitation, or a martyr for electro-magnetism?' No: 'What he does, he does for the sake of religion'. When 'the Church founds a University', he continued, 'she is not cherishing talent, genius or knowledge, for their own sake, but for the sake of her children, with a view to their spiritual welfare, and their religious influence and usefulness, with the object of training them to fill their respective posts in life better, and making them more intelligent, capable, active members of society.' Although the purpose of an education for the student himself might be 'knowledge for knowledge's sake', for the church its benefit lay in the practical goods with which it endowed its recipients. As Newman put it: 'I conceive they [the Irish hierarchy] view it as prejudicial to the interests of Religion, that there should be an cultivation of mind bestowed upon Protestants, which is not given to their own youth also.'[47]

Newman began his first discourse by preparing his listeners for the source of many of his views on education: Protestants. In so doing, he made it clear why Trinity College could never be acceptable to Catholic students: 'It is far from impossible, then, at first sight, that on the subject before us, Protestants may have discerned the true line of action, and estimated its importance aright.' 'Here, then,' Newman continued, 'I con-

ceive I am right in saying that every sect of Protestants, which has retained the idea of religious truth and the necessity of faith, which has any
dogma to lose, makes that dogma the basis of its Education, secular as
well as religious, and is jealous of those attempts to establish schools of a
purely secular character.' These institutions, of which Trinity was one,
would thus be purely Protestant in nature. As such, although they were
unsafe for Catholics, they were at least true to their own faith. In an echo
of his campaign against the diminution of Anglican hegemony at
Oxford, Newman pointed out 'that there are a multitude of Protestants
who are advocates for Mixed Education to the fullest extent . . . but then,
first, they are those for the most part who have no creed or dogma whatever to defend, to sacrifice, to surrender, to compromise, to hold back, or
to "mix", when they call out for Mixed Education.'[48] Newman's audience were thus informed that Protestants who kept their faith would not
tolerate mixed education—only backsliders could favour that. Who,
then, were the Catholics of Ireland to countenance such a thing if sincere
Protestants did not?

Newman was certainly aware of the nature of the arguments made
by Catholics against the CUI and implicitly for the Queen's Colleges.
He put himself in these opponents' position:

> The more you think over the state of politics, the position of parties,
> the feelings of classes, and the experience of the past, the more
> chimerical does it seem to you to aim at anything beyond a Univer-
> sity of Mixed Instruction. Nay, even if the attempt should acciden-
> tally succeed, would not the mischief exceed the benefits of it? How
> great the sacrifice, in how many ways, by which it would be pre-
> ceded and followed!—how many wounds, open and secret, would it
> inflict on the body politic! And if it fails, which is to be expected,
> then a double mischief will ensue from its recognition of evils which
> it has been unable to remedy.[49]

Newman could only counter these objections with an appeal to the
authority of the pope that must have warmed the heart of the new archbishop of Dublin:

> Peter has spoken. Peter is no recluse, no abstracted student, no
> dreamer about the past, no doter upon the dead and gone, no projector
> of the visionary. Peter for eighteen hundred years has lived in the
> world; he has seen all fortunes, he has encountered all adversaries,
> he has shaped himself for all emergencies. If there ever was on earth

one who had an eye for the times, who has confined himself to the practicable, and has been happy in his anticipations, whose words have been deeds and whose commands prophecies, such is he in the history of ages who sits from generation to generation in the Chair of the Apostles.[50]

Ever the skilled rhetorician, Newman no doubt intended such fulsome papalism to appeal both to his audience's loyalty to the Holy See and, perhaps, to his ultramontane patron Cullen. Nevertheless, as his biographers have remarked, Newman in this period was intensely loyal to the person of the pope and held a view of Roman authority not far short of Cullen's own.[51] Newman was not in any doubt about the difficulties facing the project, but Rome had spoken, and so the university should be attempted.

Once he had done his best towards shaming his audience into supporting a Catholic university, Newman turned his attention towards explaining to them what such a university would be like, and why it would be more a university than the Queen's Colleges could ever hope to be. If Trinity College (and, by extension, Oxford and Cambridge) was unsafe because it was run by genuinely religious Protestants who would not compromise their necessarily anti- or non-Catholic dogma, then the Queen's Colleges were equally unsafe because they taught no dogma at all. Newman set out the dilemma of the secular university to his audience: 'I say, then, that if a University be, from the nature of the case, a place of instruction, where universal knowledge is professed, and if in a certain University, so called, the subject of religion is excluded, one of two conclusions is inevitable,—either, on the one hand, that the province of Religion is very barren of real knowledge, or, on the other, that in such a University one special and important branch of knowledge is omitted.'[52] Newman pushed the proponent of such a university into a corner where only the most atheistic of them might feel comfortable: 'I say, the advocate of such an institution must say *this*, or must say *that;* he must own, either that little or nothing is known about the Supreme Being, or that his seat of learning calls itself what it is not.'

Newman would go on to draw out what he saw as the logical conclusions of his opponents' theories. He had used this method in the past to great effect; as Stephen Thomas has pointed out in his *Newman and Heresy*, Newman often inferred conclusions from his opponents' principles that they themselves would never have dreamed of holding and would perhaps have objected to. In his discourses he used this approach in such a way as to discredit the Queen's Colleges with any Catholic audience: 'If, then, in an Institution which professes all knowledge, nothing is professed, nothing is taught about the Supreme Being, it is fair to infer that every individual of all those who advocate that Institution, supposing him consistent, distinctly holds that nothing is known for certain about the Supreme Being'. In a final dismissal of the principle of secular education, Newman noted that 'God and such a University cannot co-exist.'[53] Newman was assuming a consistency in his opponents that would be rare in any individual, let alone one dealing with the tangle of Irish education. Daniel Murray, to take only one example, would of course never have held that 'nothing is known for certain about the Supreme Being.' Nonetheless Newman's point must have been an effective one to a Catholic audience in early 1850s Dublin.

Of course Newman understood that a university must pick and choose its subjects; a dedication to universal knowledge did not mean that a university must teach, say, basket-weaving or morris dancing.[54] He could not, however, 'so construct my definition of the subject matter of University Knowledge, and so draw my boundary lines around it, to include therein the other sciences commonly studied at Universities, and to exclude the science of Religion.' 'Are we', Newman asked, 'to limit our idea of University Knowledge by the evidence of our senses? then we exclude history; by testimony? we exclude metaphysics; by abstract reasoning? we exclude physics.' After all, 'is not the being of a God reported to us by testimony, handed down by history, inferred by an inductive process, brought home to us by metaphysical necessity, urged on us by the suggestions of our conscience?'[55] His conclusion was uncompromising: 'Religious doctrine is knowledge, in as full a sense as Newton's doctrine is knowledge. Mixed Education, at least in a University, is simply unphilosophical. Theology has at least as good a right to claim a place there as astronomy.'[56]

Newman, no less than Cullen, emphasised the necessity of religious content within a university. The university certainly did not need to limit itself primarily or even largely to religious knowledge, but it could not ignore it. The conclusion to be drawn from Newman's 1852 discourses is that nothing other than a *Catholic* university could provide a proper education to Catholic youths. Any other would be unsafe; if run by sincere holders of another faith, it would necessarily teach that faith; if it were to take up a position of religious neutrality it was not only denying the possibility of theological knowledge but was, in so doing, destroying the proper role of the university as the purveyor of universal knowledge.

After establishing theology's necessary role within the university, Newman addressed the discomfort that Catholics supposedly felt with scientific knowledge. Once again he began by stating what he supposed to be his opponents' case: 'Nothing is more common in the world at large, than to consider the resistance, made on the part of religious men, especially Catholics, to the separation of Secular Education from Religion, as a plain token that there is some real contrariety between human science and Revelation.'[57]

He went on to remark that 'to the multitude who draw this inference, it matters not whether the protesting parties avow their belief in this contrariety or not; it is borne upon the many, as if it were self-evident, that religious men would not thus be jealous and alarmed about Science, did they not feel instinctively . . . that knowledge is their born enemy'. After all, 'truth is bold and unsuspicious; want of self-reliance is the mark of falsehood.' He answered this criticism at length, telling his audience that 'in order to have possession of truth at all, we must have the whole truth; that no one science, no two sciences, no one family of sciences, nay, not even all secular science, is the whole truth.' Rather, Newman held that 'revealed truth enters to a very great extent, into the province of science, philosophy, and literature, and that to put it on one side, in compliment to secular science, is simply, under colour of a compliment, to do science a great damage.' Obviously, 'not every science will be equally affected by the omission, pure mathematics will not suffer at all; chemistry will suffer less than politics, politics than history, ethics or metaphysics'. Nevertheless, 'the various branches of science are intimately connected with each other, and form one whole, which whole is impaired, and to an extent which is difficult to limit, by any considerable omission of knowledge, of whatever kind'.[58]

Newman was interested in showing that an explicitly religious, Catholic education was not narrow. Like Cullen, he wanted to educate Catholic youth in the most complete manner possible. His answer to the charge that Catholics were afraid of knowledge goes some way towards summing up his idea of a Catholic university in Dublin: 'It is not then that Catholics are afraid of human knowledge, but that they are proud of divine knowledge, and that they think the omission of any kind of knowledge whatever, human or divine, to be as far as it goes, not knowledge, but ignorance.'[59]

In a proposed introduction to discourse six, Newman set out a useful summary of his views on Catholic higher education. He sent a copy to Dr David Moriarty, a close friend and president of All Hallows Missionary College.[60] The first four points of his list of the things a Catholic university would be are worth quoting, since they give a good indication of what Newman had in mind:

1. The direct object of a University, as such, is to teach all knowledge.
2. The subject-matter of faith comes into the idea of 'all knowledge.'
3. Therefore a University *must*, cannot help, as such teaching the faith, and nothing else.
4. Therefore it does directly, *virtute Universeitatis suae [sic]*, teach and inculcate Catholic expression, feeling, fact, etc., and leaven all instruction with Catholicism.[61]

Moriarty largely concurred, telling Newman that 'in a University such as the Church would wish, all instruction should be leavened with Catholicism'.[62]

The implications of Newman's discourses seem quite clear. The proposed university, to be a university at all, must be strictly Catholic in tone. It must teach the faith and 'nothing else'. Such a university would not promote ignorance, but rather would truly fulfil the mission of the university as a place where universal knowledge was taught. Although historians have not always taken this line—V. A. McClelland has asserted that 'Newman's lectures not only failed to fulfil episcopal hopes but they set out to destroy the very basis of the bishops' arguments'[63]— the case for Newman and the Irish bishops being largely in agreement seems overwhelming.

Newman and Cullen found themselves on almost exactly the same wavelength. Neither man was happy with the separation of religion from science; each saw it as an artificial distinction that damaged both. The Catholic faith was the obvious and necessary basis of all instruction. If Cullen is to be accused of wanting a lay seminary,[64] Newman must face the same accusation. For although Newman's thoughts are more carefully and philosophically expressed than Cullen's, there is no evidence that Cullen disagreed with any of Newman's sentiments. Indeed, Newman appeared to agree with Cullen's views on the subject, which were already well-known from the bishops' address. Nevertheless, and despite some obvious glances at the gallery, Newman cannot be accused of playing to his crowd without actually believing all that he said. His history at Oxford and the *Tamworth Reading Room*, published some eleven years before he gave his Dublin lectures, clearly shows the roots of his thinking on the issue, albeit without the emphasis on a specifically Catholic faith.[65]

Cullen was pleased with the discourses. He told Bernard Smith in late May that 'Dr Newman's discourses go very well. The first was excellent, the second more metaphysical but more clearly against mixed education.'[66] To Kirby he remarked that the 'discourses of Newman are excellent' and suggested they be translated into Italian.[67] This is an important point. Italian was the language of the Propaganda and the Holy See; English was little understood at Rome. By causing Newman's lectures to be put into Italian, Cullen was both effectively recommending them and the views expressed in them to the Propaganda and ensuring the discourses a wide Roman audience. He also recommended the lectures to Cardinal Fransoni, praising Newman's treatment of mixed education and expressing confidence in its effect on public opinion.[68] Cullen and Newman agreed on the necessity of having a Catholic ethos in such an institution. The actual curriculum of the university did not raise any problems, as it was to be of a fairly conventional nature; the classics could mingle quite happily with scriptural exegesis.

A difference of opinion on educational philosophy between the narrow Cullen and the liberal Newman has often been seen as lying at the heart of the conflict between the two men. And that conflict, or better, relationship, has rightly been seen by historians as being at the centre of the entire Catholic University project. No historian, however, has ever offered any real proof for the assumption that Cullen was either personally narrow in his educational beliefs or disapproved of Newman's own views. Cullen was a well educated and widely read man deeply concerned with and experienced in educational matters. It is certainly true that he saw mixed or secular education as the primary threat in Ireland, but this view resulted from his closely held belief that secular learning was both incomplete and dangerous rather than from any fear of learning as such. He wanted, within the context of a university with a Catholic ethos, to give to those who would attend the best possible education that his means would allow. For Cullen, this context could be secured by ensuring that the atmosphere, practices, and faculty of the university were Catholic. By reposing final authority in the bishops (or archbishops), such an ethos could also be guaranteed for the future. As Desmond Bowen has correctly noted, Cullen 'was determined to make Irish Catholicism intellectually respectable through the brilliance of young graduates who would emerge from a model ultramontane university.'[69]

chapter six

Delay—
The University on Hold

WRITING IN AUGUST 1851, NEWMAN TOLD A FRIEND THAT 'WE shall commence in January, I suppose.'[1] He never expected that it would not be until November 1854 that the university would conduct its first classes. Written in 1870, Newman's university memorandum reveals the frustration he felt at this delay and at how he was treated during it. Even the most casual reader can be left in no doubt as to where Newman placed the blame for both the delay and his mistreatment: Paul Cullen. In the memorandum he recalled his feelings in early 1854 on these delays: 'I had now been appointed Rector for two years, and nothing had been done. If for the first of the two, the Achilli trial had kept me from Ireland, yet many things might have been done in Ireland, to smooth such difficulties, as were sure to beset me when I did come. For two years, Dr. Cullen had met my earnest applications for information or a settlement of particular points, or the expression of my views and wishes by silence or abrupt acts.'

To Newman, the spirit of the early days of the venture was gone: 'The éclat of the Synod of Thurles in 1850 and of the Pope's brief had passed away. My Lectures in Dublin in May 1852, which Dr. Cullen had sanctioned by his presence, were a flash in the pan.'[2] In using the memorandum as a reliable guide to events in the 1850s it must be remembered that, in 1870, Newman was again on the margins of the Catholic community and felt himself to be under-appreciated by Rome in general and the pope in particular; his never distant feelings of persecution were being given plenty of nourishment. (Newman was a noted 'inopportunist' on the question of papal infallibility, then the subject of the first Vatican Council, although he was not opposed to the doctrine as such.) As a result, it is necessary to allow for both hindsight and contemporary circumstances when using the memorandum. Having said that, Newman's recollections of the Catholic University are of a piece with his contemporary correspondence and can serve as a useful summary of that vast body of writing.

There were a number of complex and interlocking reasons for the delay in opening the university's doors, and a careful study of these will go at least some way towards elucidating Cullen's otherwise inexplicable actions. Delay was both inevitable and damaging, and Cullen was forced by circumstance to walk a very fine line in order to prevent his university from being stillborn.

MURRAY, ACHILLI, AND THE DUBLIN VACANCY

When Newman was appointed in late 1851, Daniel Murray was still archbishop of Dublin and an unwavering opponent of the Catholic University. Murray's opposition meant that since Dublin was the intended site of the university, nothing tangible could be put in train while the archbishop lived. As Murray explained to Cullen on 29 October 1851, he himself, 'in common with very many intelligent an[d] zealous Catholics', had 'from the beginning' considered the university 'unattainable for the intended purpose'. Murray had therefore decided to leave the 'project in the hands of other more influential Persons than myself'. He noted that an 'agitation has commenced in England against the Maynooth grant' (this was the time of the ecclesiastical titles bill and its attendant anti-Catholic feeling), and that the 'threatened University will be among the inflammable elements, which will be employed to excite to higher fury the animosity which [is] already raging against us and our Religion'. Murray was a passionate supporter of Maynooth and the threat he perceived to it 'tended not a little to agitate and embitter his closing days.'[3] Despite Cullen's assurances that Maynooth was not in danger, Murray informed him that he would 'deem it more safe' if he took 'no part in any exciting subject'—in other words, the Catholic University.[4] Of course, Murray went further than simply declining to help; as we have seen, he actively discouraged fundraising for the university and failed to attend university committee meetings held in his own archiepiscopal seat.

Cullen was unable to either convince or placate Murray. The archbishop told Cullen that his explanation of the need for the CUI had 'not proved to my mind that the proposed University should be considered as a necessary link to bind our Episcopal Body to the Holy See', and blithely asserted that the pope had 'wisely issued no order on the subject, and He would be still more disinclined to do so, were He aware of the heavy calamity which the fruitless attempt at such a measure would be likely to draw down upon our Church.'[5] Murray was unwilling to bend, and Cullen informed the secretary of the Propaganda, Barnabò, only a few days before Murray's death that the archbishop of Dublin was determined to use his influence among both bishops and laity to block the Catholic University.[6] Newman, certainly, was aware of the problem and remarked in his memorandum that 'the University could hardly have been commenced in Dublin during his [Murray's] life.'[7]

Fortuitously for the prospects of the Catholic University, Murray died on 26 February 1852, almost certainly of a stroke.[8] Both Cullen and Newman recognised the importance that Murray's death held for the University. Cullen wrote to Newman on 29 February to tell him of Murray's passing and observe that the 'greatest difficulty I felt in taking any new step, was the fear of coming in collision with the good archbishop, who tho' evidently wrong on the education question, was a man of many excellent qualities—Now this difficulty is removed, and in all probability we shall [have] the co-operation of the clergy and laity of Dublin the want of which chilled all our proceedings up to the present.'[9] For his part, Newman told Cullen that it 'rejoices me to find that matters are to commence in earnest about the University, though I feel a sort of reproach that I should rejoice, when the change is brought about by the death of so saintly and revered a man as the late Archbishop.'[10]

The path was now clear in Dublin, but matters could not progress until Murray's successor had been named. Although it was unlikely that Rome would appoint an opponent of the university in Murray's mould, Cullen's friends were prepared to take no chances and quickly moved to have him translated from Armagh. Kirby set himself up as the centre of an unofficial 'Cullen to Dublin' campaign, and gathered information on the best approach to be taken both in Rome and in Dublin. As Bernard Smith told him, 'Rome must be free, they cannot compromise themselves. Let things take their ordinary course; if the Priests of Dublin put Dr C in nomination they will have him.' As it happened, Rome clearly wanted that to occur; it was just, as Smith told Kirby, that it 'would be a great triumph for Rome to have Dr C called to Dublin by the <u>free choice</u> of the Priests.'[11] Ever willing to engage in intrigue, Peter Cooper informed Kirby that 'your information from Rome [on the best means of gaining Cullen for Dublin] came quite apropos & will do good service. I am taking all means quietly to spread it among the clergy here.'[12]

Naturally, Cullen could take no part in his friends' plotting, but then the matter was never really in doubt; Rome wanted Dublin to choose Cullen, and the Dublin priests were happy to oblige. The diocesan clergy placed Cullen head of the *terna* on 2 April, the pope confirmed their choice on 3 May, and the news reached Ireland in early June. Cullen summed up the situation in early April in a letter to William Walsh, telling the now archbishop of Halifax[13] that Murray's death had been 'a fatal stroke to all the plans of the government' who did 'not now know what to do'. He also told Walsh of his placement at the head of the Dublin *terna* and remarked, 'What will be the result I know not. For my part I am perfectly indifferent.'[14]

Cullen could not focus on the university before or even in the immediate aftermath of his appointment. While Newman was giving his lectures, Cullen not only had to supervise his own move from Armagh but also secure a successor of whom he could approve. In addition, he had to administer Armagh until his successor was appointed and also come to grips with Ireland's largest and most prosperous diocese. These reasons in and of themselves would have assured that any serious planning for the university could not possibly have begun until the very end of 1852 at the earliest.

Murray's wrecking tactics, the necessary delays incumbent on his death, and Cullen's move to Dublin were not the only problems facing the university. Shortly after he had agreed to become rector, Newman was faced with a libel suit that would consume the vast majority of his attention until early 1853. What time and energy that were not consumed by the Achilli affair were taken up with the running of a frequently fractious Oratory and the composition of his Dublin discourses.

On 5 July 1851, Newman, in his fifth lecture, 'The Present Position of Catholics in England', had attacked the morals and character of Giacinto Achilli, an apostate Italian Dominican who had been giving 'fantastic lectures of the horrors of the Roman Inquisition'[15] on behalf of the Evangelical Alliance. Achilli served Newman with a writ for criminal libel on 27 October. Although the prospect of a libel action had been brewing for some time, the formal serving of a writ came as a serious blow. Newman would now face a Protestant judge and jury over a religious matter during a time of intense hostility towards Catholics.

Cullen was well aware of the problems facing Newman over Achilli's charges. Before the suit was filed, he had offered to help raise funds in Ireland for Newman's defence should such a thing become necessary, and Newman had himself kept the archbishop abreast of developments in the case. He even went so far as to seek Cullen's advice as to whether he should settle the suit. After noting that the 'Judges are against me, and a Protestant bias pervades the whole Court', he told Cullen that his own lawyers were recommending that he 'submit' to avoid large expenses and, Newman was advised, a possible year's imprisonment.[16] In his reply Cullen recommended against retracting the charges as 'there is no doubt of their truth' and such a surrender would 'give him [Achilli] a triumph, and inflict a wound on the Catholic cause in this Empire'.[17] Cullen knew the danger his rector was in and supported him; besides, Newman's persecution in the cause of Catholic truth could only further endear him to the ultramontane Cullen.

Cullen allowed Newman to change the date of his lectures and the beginning of his service to the university in accordance with the demands of his trial (which finally began in June 1852). As Newman informed the archbishop on 4 February, 'I do not know how to promise to be in Dublin next month, as I hoped; for what I know legal proceedings may come then.'[18] He then suggested that he begin his lectures after Easter, an idea with which Cullen concurred.

Newman's biographers are clear on the intense stress that the Achilli matter generated. Sheridan Gilley quotes Richard Stanton to the effect that Newman was restless and excited about the trial and becoming more so.[19] And Wilfrid Ward notes that Newman at times was 'almost overwhelmed by anxiety and depression'.[20] Newman himself, writing to J. M. Capes, describes his feelings of confusion: 'If the devil raised a physical whirlwind, rolled me up in sand, whirled me round, and then transported me some thousands of miles, it would not be more strange.'[21]

The trial itself took place in June 1852, just after Newman had finished delivering his Dublin discourses. The jury ruled that Newman had failed to prove that all the things he had said about Achilli were true, but judgement was reserved until 22 November. An appeal for a new trial (which was rejected) postponed the final verdict until 31 January 1853. Cullen expressed his disappointment with the verdict and his fear that Newman would be jailed to Cardinal Fransoni at the Propaganda.[22] It was clear that the university was unlikely to begin while the resolution of the Achilli case was in doubt. The postponement of final sentence simply added to the delay. Even if all other circumstances were favourable, Cullen was unlikely to have called Newman to Dublin to begin the university only to find his rector cast into jail.

Newman escaped from the trial with a fine—promptly paid by his friends—and a lecture on the deterioration of his character. However, the matter consumed the majority of his attention, and jail had been a real possibility. The fact that he was able, under these circumstances, to compose and deliver his Dublin discourses, in many ways his most influential and enduring work, is little short of amazing. Newman himself acknowledged that the Achilli trial introduced an unfortunate element of delay into the university's proceedings. But, as he wrote in his 1870 memorandum, 'this loss of three years was a misfortune or a mistake; rather, partly the one, partly the other. Dr. Cullen had made a great effort, and thought it best to wait awhile after making it.'[23] In other words, the Achilli delay was unavoidable, but any subsequent delays could be laid at Cullen's door.

THE LION OF TUAM

The 'charges' of delay and discourtesy that Newman brings in his university memorandum, for that is precisely what they are, must be carefully examined. Newman was appointed rector at the very end of 1851 and yet almost three years separated his appointment and the opening of the university. The Achilli case was settled in January 1853, but it was not until 21 October 1853 that Newman was called to Ireland by the university committee. The university opened its doors to students slightly more than one year later—not an unreasonable amount of time in which to prepare such a large undertaking. The delay of which Newman bitterly complained was thus of no more than nine months duration. The question that must be addressed, then, is why, when the Murray and Achilli difficulties had been overcome, did the previously enthusiastic Cullen not only decline to begin the university but also engage in what can only be described as unprecedented discourtesy towards his chosen rector?

Ironically, Newman had himself initially backed Cullen's view that it was best to begin the university itself slowly and avoid expending all the available resources on flashy buildings and an immediate opening. In his memorandum he recounts how most of 'our friends', including MacHale, Leahy, and Cooper, were for such an approach, and noted that he and Cullen were in agreement about a more cautious start.[24] However, Newman drew a clear distinction between his own view, which was for 'beginning gradually, but any how for beginning, not for dawdling', and Cullen's.[25]

Despite his desire to begin the university in some way, somewhere, Newman himself ruled out the most obvious possibility. Perhaps encour-

aged by his college's financial problems, Patrick Leahy had offered the
university the use of Thurles College. Thurles had been mentioned as a
possible location for the Catholic University before, and Newman told a
friend in August 1851 that 'Thurles seems likely as a commencement, to
remove at a fixed time, say a year or two, to Dublin.'[26] Such a move would
have avoided the difficulty of starting in Dublin both while Murray lived
and in the period between his death and Cullen's arrival in the capital.
However, on seeing the place in October 1851 Newman reacted with
horror. He told Ambrose St John that 'this would never do for a site—a
large fine building but on a forlorn waste, without a tree, in a forlorn
country, and a squalid town.'[27] Despite Leahy's continued advocacy of
Thurles, Newman would never again consider it. In this too he was in
agreement with Cullen. The incoming archbishop of Dublin wanted the
university to be in his city. And for that, both men would have to wait.

According to Newman's memorandum, Cullen was 'timid, slow as
well as gradual in his choice of proceedings; he was for delay, after the
Roman fashion, and that from perplexity as well as from principle.'[28]
Newman was partially correct in his assessment of Cullen; he was quite
willing to use delay, in the time-honoured Roman fashion, when it suited
his purposes. Where Newman erred was in assuming that Cullen was temperamentally inclined towards procrastination. Cullen's long years of
effort in the cause of a Catholic university and the importance he placed on
Catholic education indicates that he must have had some reason other than
temperamental caution for his delaying tactics.

The most likely explanation for Cullen's actions lies in the internecine
feuds that still engulfed the Irish hierarchy. With the death of Murray and
his own translation to Dublin, Cullen was recognized as the most powerful man in the Irish church. His ascendancy, however, did not mean that
either Murray's now leaderless supporters would suddenly favour the
Catholic University or that John MacHale and his allies would prove any
more fond of compromise with Cullen than they had with Crolly and
Murray. As Cullen told Walsh in the spring of 1852, 'Dr. MacHale will be,
strange to say, the greatest obstacle, because he is fond of going a little too
far, and of having everything his own way.'[29] Newman too had quickly
identified MacHale as a potential problem. He worried about MacHale's
reaction to his 'introducing Oxford' in the Dublin discourses, telling
Robert Ornsby that 'it is the Archbishop of Tuam and his party I fear as
much as any'.[30]

MacHale's opposition, which was to dog the Catholic University of
Ireland throughout his long life, had roots that lay both in temperament
and in policy—with MacHale the two were often tangled impossibly

together. As with the question of the charitable bequests bill discussed earlier and his views on the establishment of the university in 1848–49, MacHale quickly came to object to what appeared to him to be a bishop or a group of bishops usurping the legitimate authority of their fellows. It is important to note that whatever Cullen might have thought, MacHale's opposition was not really Gallican in nature; he was willing, if not always happy, to accept a ruling from Rome that bound all the bishops. What he objected to was the setting of one bishop, even or especially an archbishop, over others *within* the national church. To MacHale, all the bishops of a given hierarchy had to act in concert on matters that concerned all of them. Under the doctrine of the apostolic succession, their authority as bishops came directly from Jesus Christ and not from any other bishop; any interference in the affairs of a bishop within his own diocese could only be an usurpation of his divine authority. Only Rome (or a synod whose actions had been sanctioned by Rome) could make decisions for an individual Irish bishop acting in his own diocese.

Although he had acquiesced in Newman's appointment, MacHale quickly made himself something of a nuisance on the university committee. As Cullen told Bernard Smith on 15 January 1852, it was 'almost impossible to do anything with the D. Leone di Giuda [MacHale]', and that while he was 'excellent for pulling down, or opposing error' he was 'still more effective in impeding anything good from being done.'[31] Even Canon Bourke, MacHale's friend and biographer, felt called upon to remark that as early as the 1830s the archbishop of Tuam had 'excelled in the power of pointing out what ought to be done, rather than taking an active, energetic part in carrying his enlightened views into effect.' Moreover, as MacHale 'advanced in years this unwillingness to co-operate . . . became a settled state of mental conviction.'[32] Whatever MacHale's genuine concerns about episcopal prerogatives, he was not the sort of man who could have ever played a constructive role in the Catholic University.

Matters came to a head when Cullen wrote to MacHale in early February (while Murray was still alive) in an effort to gain his signature for a petition requesting the pope to grant the university a formal brief. He would, Cullen informed MacHale, be 'drawing up a short petition' on the matter, and 'if your Grace concurs in the plan, I will send it to you'.[33] The next day Cullen sent MacHale a follow-up letter containing the actual petition, advising him that it was best to move immediately in Rome, before the new British government could intrigue against the university there.[34]

This apparently simple request met with a characteristically uncompromising response: 'Any petition to the Holy Father on the subject of the University should, I think, have the signatures of all the bishops, at least such as would wish to sign it'. MacHale went on to note that only sending the petition to 'the archbishops and the suffragans who are of the Committee would appear to encourage the notion of some member of the Committee, that they are a permanent body, to whom the bishops had transferred or delegated their trust.' According to MacHale, 'neither the bishops who consented to be of the Committee, or the others understood its formation in this sense.'[35] There can be little doubt that Cullen was the person on the committee whom MacHale thought was having 'notions'.

MacHale was worried that the 'wording of the petition' would 'limit the duty and powers of completing this affair [the university] to the Episcopal members of the Committee.' Nor, in MacHale's view, would the power lie exclusively with the bishops on the committee: 'we know well that several of the other members, lay and clerical, consider themselves equally entitled to vote on any great question as the episcopal members.' MacHale then went on to set out his thoughts on episcopal control of the proposed university: 'There should no longer be any doubt or ambiguity regarding the exclusive rights of the bishops to legislate and to make all appointments.' Because it would be 'ultimately injurious to the interests of the University' he refused to sign the petition until such time as 'the rights and suffrages of the bishops of Ireland are exclusively recognized.'[36] Cullen summed matters up to Kirby, telling him that MacHale thought it 'wd. be derogatory to the rights of the Bishops' to send a petition without the signature of all the bishops. Cullen informed Kirby that he was sending on the petition without MacHale's signature and expressed the opinion that MacHale was a 'poor man very anxious to have some grievance to fight with.'[37]

MacHale had drawn the battle lines. Cullen would not be able to take any independent action regarding the university without MacHale objecting and doing his best to block such an action. To make matters worse for Cullen, MacHale was making it known that he thought the university committee, which was based in Dublin and was more amenable to Cullen's influence than the hierarchy as a whole, was not an acceptable decision-making body. Only the entire Irish hierarchy could govern the university. Unfortunately, the hierarchy only met two or three times a year at most. They could not possibly act as an effective governing body. Nor, of course, would that body having 'the exclusive rights to make all appointments' be something that Cullen, let alone Newman, could accept.

MacHale was not alone among the bishops in expressing his objections to Cullen's plans. John Cantwell, still on the university committee, wrote to MacHale that same February, informing him 'that the bishops of Ireland possess exclusively the right to legislate for and govern the University cannot be a matter of doubt' after a 'distinct declaration' of the views of those who backed MacHale. He followed closely the archbishop of Tuam's line in holding that 'we of the Committee could never entertain the idea of assuming and exercising powers invading the rights of our brothers in the episcopacy.' Somewhat optimistically, Cantwell told MacHale that he was of the opinion that the 'Primate [Cullen] now adopts this view, and that he will act accordingly.'[38]

Cullen thought nothing of the sort. He backed the proposals of the Thurles subcommittee, chaired by Newman, which granted the bishops as a body the power of nomination and removal of the rector and vice-rector but left the archbishops 'acting in the name of the bishops' control over the nomination (on the advice of the rector) of professors and lecturers as well as such matters as salaries and the possible addition of academic chairs.[39] As we will see later, Cullen was consistent in his interest in asserting both the rights of the archbishops and the power of the rector; he would do his best to strengthen Newman's position against MacHale's demands for extensive episcopal control. The Thurles report and Cullen's support for it went some way towards provoking MacHale, Cantwell, and their supporters into believing that Cullen intended to usurp the rights of the Irish episcopate in favour of a committee of archbishops that he could manage more easily. In this case they were quite correct in their assessment of Cullen's aims.

Despite his undoubted support for the university, Cullen was in no position in 1852–53 to force an opening in the face of determined episcopal opposition. In *The Making of the Roman Catholic Church in Ireland, 1850–1860*, Emmett Larkin makes clear the extent of the opposition Cullen faced within the hierarchy in mid- to late 1852. He prints a chart showing that of the twenty-eight Irish bishops, only ten could be counted on to support Cullen. Of these, four were relatively recent appointments, and none was in the ecclesiastical province of Dublin. The majority of his strength lay in Cashel, although Archbishop Slattery himself could prove to be a hesitant ally at times. Cullen's ability to influence the appointment of Irish bishops would become an important tool in his effort to gain control of the Irish church, something he had largely succeeded in doing by 1860. In 1852–53, however, Cullen had not as yet had many opportunities to use this influence. Without a clear majority of the bishops backing him, Cullen was both unwilling and unable to make a start to the university. As Emmet Larkin has demonstrated in another context, Cullen was consistently concerned that the Irish hierarchy be publicly seen to be united on all-important questions.[40] Public dissension, which had plagued the church in the 1840s, was anathema and to be avoided if at all possible. If Cullen had pushed the university in 1852–53, public dissension on the part of MacHale and his allies would have been assured; success would not have been.

According to Larkin, MacHale could only muster seven solid supporters, all but two in the province of Tuam (the remainder were in Armagh). Of more importance were those bishops that had been followers of Murray. Larkin lists eleven bishops as still being, for lack of a better phrase, in the Murray camp.[41] Cullen could thus expect eighteen potential opponents to almost anything he might care to do regarding the university. MacHale and his supporters, while backing in principle a Catholic university, were making almost impossible demands regarding episcopal control. Those bishops who had supported Murray had never favoured, and in many cases actively opposed, the whole idea of the university. In this environment Cullen would be hard pressed to make the start of things that Newman expected.

NEWMAN, MACHALE, AND ENGLISH APPOINTMENTS

MacHale's opposition quickly began to involve more than his objections to the composition and power of Cullen's university committee. It was always something of a surprise that such an unbending patriot as MacHale was willing to tolerate the appointment of the English Newman. MacHale's patience began to wear thin when Cullen and Newman both together and separately threatened to introduce yet more Englishmen into Ireland. The final straw was the appointment of Henry William Wilberforce, a convert member of the famous English evangelical family, as secretary of the Catholic Defence Association. The association had been established by the Irish bishops in an effort to provide a focus for opposition to the continuing anti-Catholic agitation that had been provoked by Rome's reestablishment of the English hierarchy and Wiseman's intemperate pastoral 'From Without the Flaminian Gate'. The machinations that went into securing Wilberforce's selection by the general committee of the Catholic Defence Association need not detain us here, but it is clear that he was Cullen's chosen candidate for the post.[42]

When Wilberforce was selected on 17 December, on a vote of 24–16 against a 'Galway gentleman of no distinction',[43] those who had opposed him made their objections public. The primary ground for complaint against Wilberforce did not involve his qualifications for the post, but rather the simple fact that he was English. Seven Irish MPs sent a letter of protest to the *Freeman's Journal*, and two long-time Cullen allies, Maher and Cooper, entered the debate on the side of Wilberforce. Cullen himself tried to remain above matters, and neither Frederick Lucas, the editor of *The Tablet* and later a harsh Cullen critic, nor MacHale publicly entered the fray. Cullen summed matters up to Walsh by remarking that Wilberforce 'though an Englishman had at least great literary merits on his side'.[44] In a later letter to Walsh, he identified opposition to his English appointments with government fears of Catholic unity, telling him that government-inspired 'organs' had 'become so patriotic that they are continually crying out that we are going to Sell Ireland to the English Catholics and thus give up the rights of the Celt to the Saxon.'[45] Although open battle with MacHale over Wilberforce's appointment had been avoided (and Wilberforce retained his position), Cullen's support for a second Englishman for an important Irish post in two months had likely caused concern amongst MacHale and his supporters.

As it happened, Wilberforce was a close friend of Newman's. Newman was aware of the controversial nature of Wilberforce's appointment, telling Allies that although he 'had intended to go to Wilberforce' while delivering his Dublin lectures, he had 'been cautioned against it, lest it should encourage the notion of an English party.'[46] Newman was not in any doubt that his primary opposition now lay in Tuam. MacHale's opposition to the university committee was now entwined with his objections to further English appointments to Irish institutions.

However much Newman might have been aware of the archbishop of Tuam's objections, he was not prepared to sacrifice his assumed right to appoint whom he liked to the university. Cullen had certainly made Newman aware of the problems attendant upon making English appointments. In April 1852 he advised Newman not to appoint Allies (whom he had previously favoured) to a university post quite yet as 'we have a set of newspaper editors and others who are trying to excite prejudices against everything English; we must avoid giving them any motive to attack us for a little while longer.'[47] Newman himself had written to the archbishop on the same subject the previous October. In that letter Newman, in the course of discussing the appointment of the first professors, noted that he would 'naturally take my own friends', at least for the first two years. He did, of course, recognise that this might mean 'too much of an English and convert element' in the university. Although Newman acknowledged this 'great difficulty', he nonetheless told Cullen that he did not 'know

how to dispose of it.'[48] Newman, however, refused to make matters easier
for Cullen. As he told Allies on 27 April, shortly after Cullen had written
advising caution in Allies' own appointment: 'don't suppose that Irishmen are going to be put about me.' It was not that he objected 'to them distinctly . . . as Irishmen, but as persons whom I do not know, who were not
of the same school as myself, on whom I could not rely.'[49] A slightly earlier letter to Allies summed up Newman's views on the subject: 'I must
have men I know about me, and will.'[50]

Newman's relationship to the Irish as a nation is somewhat problem-
atic. Comments like the above to Allies imply a certain distaste for the
Irish. That impression can only be strengthened by numerous derogatory
references in Newman's letters to 'Paddies' or a letter of 1849 where
Newman contrasted Irish hygiene with that of the Scots: 'Your old Mary,
poor as she is, is, as a Scotch woman, the model of neatness—so that
poverty is not what makes the Irish such beasts.'[51] With a handful of
exceptions—David Moriarty of Kerry first among them—Newman made
remarkably few friends in Ireland and was clearly more comfortable with
fellow Englishmen than he was with the Irish among whom he lived (V. A.
McClelland has pointed out Newman's somewhat distant relationship
with his Irish students.)[52] In modern terms Newman unquestionably har-
boured 'racist' views towards the Irish. Modern sensibilities are not, however, at issue. Newman's opinion of the Irish was perfectly normal for an
Englishman of his time and background to hold and was in fact quite
moderate in that day and age. There is also no evidence extant to suggest
that Newman's views materially affected his behaviour in Ireland.

Nor, *pace* McClelland, is there any evidence that Newman went so
far as to favour non-Irish students over Irish students. Certainly Newman
seems to have been more *comfortable* with English students in Ireland,
just as he was more comfortable with Englishmen generally. But the natural preference of a man abroad for his fellow countrymen is a far cry
from favouritism or active racism. Nor was his discomfort limited to the
Irish—Newman was never notably comfortable with any foreigners
(Acton noted as early as 1858 that 'Newman's ignorance of things foreign
is deplorable'),[53] and he remained a proud and somewhat insular Englishman all his life. Nevertheless, he chose to go to Ireland, to work with and
for the Irish, and he kept what he conceived to be Irish interests very
much in view—however much he wanted the Catholic University to be
for the whole of the English-speaking world. Newman's attitude may
have made it more difficult for him to understand Cullen or MacHale or
their needs and desires, but it did not in any material way damage the
university project.

Whatever his feelings towards the Irish, Newman made his position on appointments clear to Cullen himself in July 1852. He told the archbishop that, 'as to Professors . . . I have no personal interest in their appointment,[54] and do not care who they are. . . . But it is different with those immediately about me, who are to help me and share in my responsibilities.' He must 'have perfect confidence in them, and power over them.'[55] The primary office he had in mind was that of vice-rector. Newman's first thought was of Henry Edward Manning, the future archbishop of Westminster. He apparently approached Manning about the position as early as October 1851.[56] As he was setting off for Rome and did not yet wish to decide his future, Manning declined the post. Considering that Newman's own Thurles report had vested the power to appoint the vice-rector in the body of bishops as a whole, it is somewhat surprising that he felt himself able to make such an offer (prior even to his being formally offered the rectorship) to Manning without consultation in Ireland. Although there is no evidence that he was ever aware of the prospect of Manning's appointment, it is certainly hard to imagine MacHale accepting him for the position of vice-rector in the wake of both the Newman and Wilberforce appointments.

The subject of the vice-rectorship would continue to be a sore point with Newman throughout his time in Dublin. He had made it quite clear to Cullen that only one of his friends would do for the post, and Newman's friends were invariably English. Newman's anger with Cullen's actions regarding the position was evidently still strong in 1870 when he came to record his memories of the period. He recounted how Cullen, after ignoring his letters on the subject for six weeks, 'simply informed me, as if my letters went for nothing, and with no reference to them, that a helper and associate such as I wanted, in a word, a Vice-Rector, had been provided for me in the person of Dr. Taylor, and he intimated a hope that I should consent to the arrangement.' Considering his oft-stated views on the subject, Newman was not surprisingly unimpressed: 'I [had] already given my opinion on this subject to Dr Cullen pretty plainly, viz. That I wished to choose the Vice-Rector myself. . . . The truth is that these Bishops are so accustomed to be absolute that they usurp the rights of others, and rough ride over their wishes'.[57] Cullen was most certainly riding rough over Newman's plans, but as it was in the power of the university committee (or, more correctly, the entire episcopate) to appoint a vice-rector, he was not infringing on Newman's rights as such. Taylor had been president of Carlow College, Cullen's own school,[58] and was, as Newman was told by his friends, a worthy and qualified man.[59] Taylor was styled as 'Secretary to the

University', and seems to have never been officially vice-rector. Newman felt his appointment, and the later (1854) appointment of Patrick Leahy as vice-rector, was made with the intention of making him 'the Archbishops' representative and as their security and safeguard against me, [rather] than as my own helper and backer up.'[60]

POLITICAL PRIESTS AND A LONG SILENCE

From October 1852 until early 1854, Cullen systematically ignored his rector. Newman recounted the situation in early 1853: 'I was now in the 16th month of my appointment and nothing was told me when I was to begin or what I was to do. I had written two letters to Dr. Cullen six months before, and two letters now—and could not get, I will not say information, but a reply from him.' Newman could 'understand he had great difficulties in moving: but I cannot understand his not plainly telling me so.' Cullen might have, he thought, 'written frankly to me: "you won't be wanted for a year to come at least, for we must have a synodal meeting of the Bishops: I really don't know when you will be wanted, and I cannot tell quite what your powers will be. I don't think you should have the appointment of the Vice Rector" &c. &c.' Cullen's failure to do so, Newman supposed, was due to 'what he had learned at Rome' which was 'to act, not to speak—to be peremptory in act, but to keep his own counsel; not to commit himself on paper; to treat me, not as an equal, but as one of his subjects.'[61]

The fact that Cullen did not write to Newman as he suggested lies at the heart of both Newman's anger and historians' subsequent assumption of a rift between the two men dating from roughly the summer of 1852. It is unclear, however, how likely it would have been that Cullen could write in such a way to Newman. Given Newman's oft-stated desire both to begin the university as soon as possible and his demand to name his own vice-rector, could Cullen be sure that Newman would not resign if told not only to stand-by indefinitely but that he could not, in fact, have his own choice for the appointment? We cannot know whether Newman would have resigned, but Cullen may have quite reasonably feared that he might. A resignation by Newman at this point in the creation of the Catholic University could quite easily have been fatal. Newman was essentially asking for Cullen to inform him of things that the archbishop simply did not dare to. It was much better, from Cullen's perspective, to string matters along 'in the Roman fashion' rather than to allow one side or the other to ruin his project irrevocably.

Cullen was right to fear for his university in 1852–53. MacHale's op-position to English appointments was exacerbated by the advent of the Tenants' Rights League and the Independent Irish Party. The Irish Ten-ants' Rights League was a coalition of groups that sought, in the wake of the Famine and in the face of continuing agricultural distress, to protect (in the case of northern members) or extend the 'Ulster custom', the famous 'three F's': fixed tenure, fair rent, and free sale. The league became active in politics, and the 1852 election saw more than forty MPs re-turned who were pledged to support its aims. Most of those MPs were associated with the Independent Irish Party (the 'Irish Brigade'). The party had developed in the aftermath of the ecclesiastical titles bill, and members were pledged to oppose all governments that failed to meet cer-tain demands. From August 1851 the Tenants' Rights League and the In-dependent Irish Party acted in concert. Although both organisations would later falter, in late 1852 they were at the height of their power and enjoyed the enthusiastic support of much of the Catholic community. Cullen himself had willingly associated himself with the demands of the league but was suspicious of the idea of independent opposition and the motives of many of its backers such as Gavan Duffy; the Roman Repub-lic was always in his mind and not always at the back of it. Archbishop MacHale enthusiastically backed both organisations.

Throughout the autumn and winter of 1852 and all of 1853 Cullen was deeply involved in the conflicts within the hierarchy over priests in-volving themselves in nationalist politics. The new Irish party had gained enough MPs at the recent election to be, in combination with other par-ties, a threat to the Russell government. In fact, they lent their votes on 20 December 1852 to the toppling of the ministry. Meanwhile, the British government had been doing its best to weaken the Irish party by seeking to divide Rome and the Irish clergy. To that end the government had been sending envoys to the Holy See to complain about clerical involve-ment in politics.[62]

The threat to the university was a real one, and Cullen was forced to take it very seriously indeed. MacHale, a great number of priests, and much of the wider nationalist community were in favour of the agitation, and Cullen, who was largely opposed to the intervention of priests in such secular matters,[63] was unlikely to pick further fights by imposing Newman's proposed English appointments to the university.[64] The Holy See was anxious not to anger the English. Although the pope had re-turned to Rome, the papal government could never be entirely confident that they might not in future need British help to preserve the papal states. France was much relied on and little trusted. Italian nationalism was not dead—as events would soon prove—and the papacy could not afford to unnecessarily alienate a power who might prove useful, and could very easily turn dangerous.

Cullen was caught in the middle. He was already suspect in some nationalist circles, and his opposition to clerical involvement in nationalist politics only served to make him more so. As Emmet Larkin has noted, 'the suspicion of a tendency towards West Britonism that had attached to Cullen . . . for his support of Wilberforce . . . and of Newman as Rector of the Catholic University came to be represented as something more insidious'.[65] Cullen could not afford to lose all credibility with Irish nationalists, and an open breech with MacHale over university appointments would have gone a long way towards achieving that result. Furthermore, such a rupture with MacHale would do more than damage Cullen's authority with the nationalists; it could also provoke MacHale to throw all his efforts into destroying the university before it had even been opened.

Cullen summed matters up to Kirby at the end of December 1853, telling him, 'We shall always be doomed to fight & I fear we shall continue to do so until Priests learn to mind their own business'.[66] Cullen could not move too swiftly on the Catholic University while the argument over priests in politics continued; Newman could not be allowed further to stir up conflict by appointing one of his Oxford friends as vice-rector. Although the dissension among the hierarchy over nationalism and the limits of clerical intervention in political questions would continue, it reached its height in the years 1852–54, and it was these two years that saw the height of Cullen's discourtesy towards Newman.

MacHale's interventions were not passing unnoticed. Bishop Murphy[67] told Cullen that information for various anti-CUI tracts and rumours that were then spreading in America 'were supplied from this side of the Atlantic—indeed I have learned during my late visit to Maynooth and Dublin that not a few of your Episcopal Bretheren participate in the same apprehension that the University will be too much of an <u>English Concern</u>'. Clearly, he had MacHale in mind. Murphy went on to tell Cullen that although he himself favoured Newman and did not object to English appointments—objections to which were simply the result of 'low partizan [*sic*] jealousies'—he nonetheless recommended the 'expediency of accommodating the Irish public humour by nominating a fair proportion of <u>qualified natives</u>.'[68] And Francis McGinnity, who had been appointed by the university committee in 1851 to raise money for the CUI in England,[69] wrote in November 1852 to tell Cullen that in England they 'seem to know more of the mischievous opposition of Dr. McHale than is known in Dublin.'[70]

In October 1853, even as the university committee was preparing to call Newman to Ireland, Cullen had to worry about a new problem: a possible alliance between Michael Slattery and John MacHale either to obstruct or to destroy the new university. MacHale had not attended a university committee meeting since 21 July 1852, and Cullen could not be anxious for his return, especially if he had a new ally.[71] 'It is curious', Cullen wrote to Kirby, 'that Dr. Slattery has wheeled round completely against everything done at Thurles. He and Dr McHale will unite against the University'. A meeting of the committee was to be held during the week, and Cullen (who could not attend as he was in Paris and in ill-health) was afraid that Slattery and MacHale 'will get up such a row as will destroy all that has been done. God help us and poor Ireland.'[72] Cullen had been worried about Slattery for some time, and the previously close correspondence between the two had dried up by the end of 1851. Cullen's infrequent letters to Slattery, though still friendly, were by no means intimate and were, in fact, largely dedicated to passing along official information.[73]

In the event, Slattery did not join with MacHale in blocking matters at the university committee, as neither man attended. This was fortunate, as in Cullen's absence the archbishop of Armagh, Joseph Dixon, was in the chair. Although totally in Cullen's pocket, Dixon was not a forceful man and was not particularly interested in the university, although he was by no means hostile to it.[74] It is hard to imagine that he could have stood up to a determined Slattery and MacHale and arranged for Newman to be called to Ireland to begin the university. Thankfully for him, he was not forced to. As Cullen remarked to Kirby, 'Dr Dixon and one other [bishop] attended so please God, we are likely to be left to ourselves. Dr Newman will come to Dublin immediately.'[75] Newman was in fact requested 'at his earliest convenience, to assume his functions as rector and to take such measures as may be necessary for the opening of the university.'[76] Newman, however, was far from pleased by his call to Ireland. He was, rather, 'disappointed, desponding and sore' that so little had been done and so much time wasted.[77]

Despite what Newman might have thought, Cullen was not entirely inactive during 1853. Early in the year, he arranged to purchase (for £3,400)[78] the magnificent Georgian house on St Stephen's Green—still in the possession of University College Dublin today and wonderfully restored as 'Newman House'—for a 'small beginning' to the university.[79] Even though Cullen informed Newman that the house could be 'sold on' later if it did not suit, the purchase of a building without consulting the rector confirmed Newman's belief in Cullen's high-handedness. Ironically,

MacHale, too, was less than pleased by the purchase of the Stephen's Green House; as Cullen remarked to Kirby, the 'Lion will send out shouts and be fiercely opposed [to the purchase], but what can be done?'[80] Nevertheless, buying the house seems to have been the only tangible thing for the university that Cullen could manage. The purchase shows that he was still interested in the project and doing what he could to advance it. The appointment of Taylor as secretary—Newman assumed, probably correctly, that he was to be vice-rector[81]—was also high-handed, but well within the rights of the university committee. It too can be seen as an attempt to keep things moving until something more tangible could be done. Taylor, as the university memorandum shows, kept Newman in close touch with events in Dublin; Newman was only cut off from communication with Cullen, never from the committee.

Cullen was not in any way disillusioned with his rector during the period 1852–54. There are no extant letters that criticise Newman or even hint at such criticism. If he was rude to Newman, it was for reasons of strategy, however ill-judged that strategy might have been. Given the level of opposition from MacHale and his allies it is hard to see Cullen's approach as anything other than a success; the university did in fact open with Newman in charge. He managed to walk the tightrope between Newman's oft-stated desire to make his own (English) appointments and MacHale's adamant opposition to any such nominations. Given the atmosphere of crisis over the political priests and the Tenants' Rights League, Cullen did well to keep Newman on board. He also prevented MacHale from switching from a damaging but relatively passive hostility to the university to an outright and public opposition that might have prevented the institution from ever opening its doors.

The opposition of MacHale was key to the delay, as it would be throughout the history of both the university in general and Newman's association with it in particular. As Cullen plaintively wrote to Kirby in January 1854, if 'you can devise any means of getting the university afloat without a battle with the lion [MacHale] you will be my hero.'[82] But, despite Newman's anger with Cullen, and Cullen's undoubted discourtesy towards Newman, the delay did not arise from any inherent problem in the relationship between the two men. As we will see in the next chapter, Cullen's correspondence with Newman picked up in 1854 almost where he left off in mid-1852. Although problems between them lay around a not too distant corner, it is clear that in 1854 Cullen still thought highly of his choice of rector. That June, he even went so far as to tell Bernard Smith that Newman was thoroughly Roman.[83] High praise indeed from that most Roman of men.

chapter seven

Opening the University

NEWMAN THE ALMOST-BISHOP

IN EARLY 1853 A RUMOUR REACHED IRELAND THAT CARDINAL WISEMAN, the archbishop of Westminster, had it in mind to have Newman consecrated a diocesan bishop within the English hierarchy. Such a move would have resulted in Newman having to give up any idea of heading the Catholic University of Ireland and to take up residence in whatever see he was assigned. Fortunately for Cullen, Newman himself had no interest in becoming a diocesan bishop. He told Cullen of Wiseman's intentions, assuming that it might be a reason to speed matters up in Ireland. He informed him that the proposed bishopric 'might only be a compliment . . . but if it be more, it simply destroys my work in Ireland.'[1] Newman would later hear, through Taylor, that Cullen had made it clear in Rome that his loss 'would be a great blow to the University.'[2] Although the matter was settled satisfactorily, the question of Newman's ecclesiastical status would later add to the misunderstandings between the two men.

If Wiseman's first attempt to elevate Newman was opposed by both Cullen and Newman himself, then his second attempt would meet with objections from only one of the men. The question of 'Newman and the missing mitre' (to use Vincent Blehl's phrase)[3] is well known and, since the publication of articles by Blehl and J. H. Whyte, well understood in its details.[4] Had it not been for Cullen's interventions in Rome—interventions he kept secret from Newman and his allies—Newman would have been consecrated sometime in 1854. The fact that Cullen did block the appointment, something considered and rejected by McGrath,[5] did not become apparent until the work of Whyte and Blehl appeared in 1960. At first glance, Cullen's successful opposition to Newman's appointment, coming as it did in 1854, gives additional weight to the view that Cullen was by this time in conflict with his chosen rector. It might, then, be useful to revisit the question of the missing mitre and to consider why Cullen thought it necessary to bring his influence to bear in Rome.

Upon finally being summoned by the university committee, Newman came quickly to the view that he needed some sort of official recognition or acknowledgement of his position as rector in order to gain support across the wide spectrum of Catholic Ireland for the university. This recognition should, Newman thought, be both more than was obtained in the committee's summons and should be granted to him personally. Newman's fear was that, without such a recognition, he would be seen to be acting on his 'own hook': 'I should be an Englishman, taking upon himself to teach the Paddies what education was, what a University, and how it was their duty to have one with me for a Rector.'[6] Newman took the matter so seriously that 'I could not go over to Dublin at all, unless I was distinctly called there by the Irish Episcopate, or in some formal and public way.'[7] He wrote to Cullen in late December 1853, setting out his desire for a formal installation. He was answered in mid-January not by Cullen, but by Taylor. Taylor counselled patience, advising Newman that it was necessary to obtain a papal brief before anything public could be done and that Cullen 'thinks it most probable that the issuing of the Brief whenever it do [*sic*] take place will be accompanied by some mark of distinction to yourself as its Rector.'[8] Taylor followed up with a second letter at the end of January suggesting that it seemed likely that the brief would soon be forthcoming.[9]

Cullen's response (by means of Taylor) promising an eventual recognition caused Newman to consider his entire position with the university. Newman's university journal (1854) and his memorandum (1870) make clear that he was seriously contemplating resignation if no official recognition was immediately forthcoming and was prepared to use the threat of such a resignation as a lever with which to gain it. He wrote to various friends, including Frederick Lucas, requesting advice on whether actually threatening resignation would serve his purpose. James Hope-Scott advised him that such a 'threat' might to 'the apathetic, reluctant majority appear a favorable opportunity for disposing at once of you and of the University'. Hope-Scott also pointed out that a resignation threat over such an issue 'might be so managed as to make you appear to be in the wrong.'[10] Newman seems to have heeded such sound advice and did not choose to threaten Cullen in this way.

Newman did have some reason to believe that Cullen had once at least understood the need for a public acknowledgement of his university position. In early 1853 Cullen had proposed to Newman, again via Taylor, that it might be possible to arrange for Newman to be appointed by each Irish bishop his vicar-general for the university. Although such a step had been taken at Louvain, the proposal seems to have failed to draw support. That MacHale, given his views on both Cullen's various English appointments and his consistent position on the rights of the episcopacy, would oppose such a plan can hardly be a surprise. Nor was it any more likely that those bishops who had supported Murray and the Queen's Colleges would wish to extend their support to the university by granting Newman such a position. Evidently, Cullen quickly realised the futility of the idea and quietly let the matter drop. Newman, however, did not forget the proposal and came to remind the archbishop of it nearly a year later when he made his own request for a public clarification of his status.[11]

It was in this atmosphere of frustration and contemplated resignation that Wiseman's second attempt to make Newman a bishop emerged. Unlike the previous plan to make Newman an English diocesan bishop, this time Wiseman had proposed in Rome that Newman be made a bishop *in partibus infidelium* with special responsibility for the Catholic University of Ireland. Such an appointment would give Newman all the recognition he might desire and would serve notice of Rome's support for both the university itself and Newman's role within it. In deciding how to respond to Wiseman's initiative, and the news that Pius IX was minded to support it, Cullen had to tread carefully.

Cullen's first recorded reaction to the prospect of Newman becoming the university's bishop came in a letter to Kirby on 16 January. He reported to the Irish College rector that Wiseman had written to him offering his assistance in getting the university started. Cullen was not anxious for such assistance and preferred that the 'business be settled by the Pope' instead of the English cardinal.[12] Cullen had long distrusted Wiseman (whom he accurately suspected of spreading damaging rumours about him as early as 1840). As rector of the Irish College, Cullen had set out (in a letter to Kirby, then vice-rector) his policy towards the Englishman, a policy he would maintain through the years: 'He [Wiseman] is very hostile to Irishmen. Still it will be well to pay him every respect.'[13] 'The Cardinal', Cullen continued in 1854, had also informed him that 'the Pope will make Dr. Newman a bishop if I propose it—I'd be very glad of it—but perhaps we had better first get things into proper order.'[14] Two weeks later Cullen again told Kirby that he would 'be glad of it' if Newman were to be made a bishop, but again counselled delay, remarking that 'it will be as well to wait until the university is opened.' He also noted that the 'Rector in Louvain is not a Bishop.'[15]

Cullen followed up his letters to Kirby (which were passed on, and likely designed to be passed on, to the Propaganda)[16] with one of his own to the Sacred Congregation. In this letter Cullen showed to effect the diplomatic skills he had learned during his time in Rome. It is a masterful letter and it likely doomed Newman's appointment. Cullen began by telling Barnabò, still secretary of the Propaganda, he 'should have the greatest pleasure in seeing a man so learned and saintly as Dr Newman raised to the highest dignities,' but that it 'would be better to wait a little until things are in better shape.' If it were thought 'expedient that Dr Newman be promoted, it is much better that the thing come from the Sacred Congregation than from Cardinal Wiseman', because 'there is much jealousy here of any interference by Englishmen of any kind in our affairs'. Cullen pointed out that if 'word got around that the English Cardinal was proposing plans for regulating our ecclesiastical affairs, it would ruin any project, no matter how good in itself.' 'This sentiment of nationality cannot be suppressed, and, indeed, it cannot arouse surprise, when one remembers how Ireland has always been treated by England—not only Protestant England but Catholic too.'[17] All that being the case, Cullen felt that 'it would not be desirable to expose Dr Newman for the moment to any suspicion which could give ground for ill-inclined people to excite animosity against him', and that, 'with a little delay', the appointment would 'come naturally, and there will be no opposition to it.'[18]

It is quite likely that Cullen was totally sincere in his sentiments about Newman's worthiness for promotion; nothing in the record suggests otherwise. The fact that Cullen told Kirby twice *in English* that he would be 'glad' if Newman were to become a bishop is significant. Letters to Kirby in Italian were quasi-official documents, designed to be shown around in Rome. If Cullen had made his comments in Italian, they then could rightly be seen as part of a campaign against Newman of which the letter to Barnabò was the culmination. However, as his remarks were in English, it is more likely that they reflect Cullen's personal views. What is clear is that he could not possibly recommend the promotion on the basis suggested by Wiseman. Regardless of whether the proposal was seen to come from Wiseman, the promotion of Newman to an equal standing with the Irish hierarchy, yet not holding an Irish see and remaining obviously English, could only enrage MacHale and his supporters; clearly they were the 'ill-inclined' people Cullen had in mind. Nor could the more moderate bishops, nor even Cullen himself, be much inclined to having a bishop as rector. It would, after all, be much harder (both in terms of form and in terms of publicity) to remove a bishop from the job should it become necessary. Cullen was extremely clever, however, in making these points only as against Wiseman being seen to initiate Newman's elevation. By suggesting that, if a promotion was to be made, it should come from the Propaganda, he was putting responsibility squarely on Barnabò and Fransoni. And, given the obvious strength of Cullen's objections, it was unlikely that either Barnabò or Fransoni would wish to take the risk of promoting Newman against the advice of the person most concerned.

For all his dissatisfaction with Cullen, Newman was unaware of the latter's plotting in Rome. Indeed, it seems likely that he never knew exactly how the appointment had failed to come about.[19] What he did know is that news of the proposed bishopric had been reported as fact and believed by many of his friends. In his university memorandum Newman recounts the quick spread of the news of his apparently imminent elevation. His own bishop, Bernard Ullathorne, addressed him as 'Rt. Rev.' in a public speech and as late as 8 June was addressing letters to Newman 'My dear Lord'. Others sent gifts, including a 'massive gold chain' from the duke of Norfolk. Newman even went so far as to represent himself, on a visit to Ireland that spring, as a designated bishop.[20]

Although it seems clear that Cullen did not block Newman's appointment out of malice, the question remains why he allowed Newman to remain under the apprehension that he was shortly to be made a bishop. Newman, and his friends, believed the matter settled until at least July 1854. From that point it was clear that Rome's intentions had changed but, as Newman recalled, not 'Dr Cullen, nor Dr Grant [bishop of Southwark], nor Dr Ullathorne, nor any one else, ever again say one single word on the subject; nor did they make any chance remark by which I have been able to form any idea why that elevation which was thought by Pope, Cardinal [Wiseman], and Archbishop [Cullen?] so expedient for the University, or at least so settled a point, which was so publicly announced, was suddenly and silently reversed.'[21] Cullen's only surviving remark on Newman's nearly six months as a presumed bishop-designate came in a letter to Kirby in early March. In it he informed his friend that Newman was in Dublin, and that 'Card. Wiseman has it is said written to him stating that he is made bishop.' 'It is', Cullen dryly remarked, 'all a gran pasticcio'.[22]

Newman clearly still believed himself to be only awaiting his consecration before becoming a bishop. Cullen must have been aware of this fact but chose not to inform Newman that he, Cullen, had effectively blocked the appointment. After all, Newman was actually in Ireland visiting with

Cullen while being treated by many as a bishop-in-waiting. Although the surviving sources do not make Cullen's thinking clear, a number of explanations for his behaviour are possible. One is that he had not yet been informed of the outcome of Wiseman's attempt to make Newman a bishop. We have no evidence of when, exactly, the decision to promote Newman was shelved in Rome, and it must not be assumed that Cullen, simply by writing a letter, however effective and clever, knew that he had succeeded in his aim of blocking the appointment. Cullen was enormously influential in Rome, and knew himself to be, but he could not presume success before matters had been formally decided. It is also more than possible that, by allowing Newman to continue under the illusion of his promotion, Cullen was thereby avoiding the difficult question of Newman's demand for a formal recognition as rector of the university. After all, the promotion to bishop was exactly the kind of recognition Newman had been demanding. As long as Newman thought he had received recognition from Rome, he was not pestering Cullen for a recognition in Ireland that Cullen did not then feel politically able to give. Simple human nature, too, must be considered a possible explanation for Cullen's behaviour in the spring and early summer of 1854; who would wish to tell a man one respected that he was being denied an appointment—and one that had been, through Wiseman's indiscretion, mooted so publicly at that—as a result of one's own intervention? Cullen could not have relished such a conversation (nor would he have been able to predict Newman's reaction). Far better, then, to let matters in Rome take their course and to allow Newman to continue to believe that he was soon to be a bishop.

The question of why Cullen felt unable to give Newman the recognition he had requested will form at least part of the basis of the next section. What seems clear is that, while Cullen certainly did all he could to block Newman's elevation to the episcopate and allowed his rector to labour under the misapprehension that he was to be a bishop, he did not do either of these things out of any dissatisfaction with Newman. In the first half of 1854 Cullen was faced with the serious threat that MacHale's opposition to the university might just prevent it from ever opening its doors. It was this opposition that made it impolitic for Cullen to accede to Newman's elevation.

THE STRUGGLE TO OPEN THE UNIVERSITY

Although Newman was unhappy, in early 1854 it appeared that the Catholic University of Ireland was finally taking shape. Newman had now been formally called to Dublin. And Wiseman's attempt to have

Newman made a bishop had, almost providentially, allowed Cullen to at least temporarily avoid having to gain from the divided Irish hierarchy a public recognition for the rector of the Catholic University.

The primary problem that confronted Cullen was precisely how he was to gain the final approval of the Irish bishops for the university and its statutes. Although unquestionably the most influential Irish prelate, neither Cullen's status as archbishop of Dublin nor his position as apostolic delegate gave him the authority to open a *national* institution such as the CUI without the consent of his brother bishops; nor could he independently decree what its regulations were to be. In fact, it was only in 1853 that the *Dublin* provincial synod deputed Cullen to act on their behalf on university matters. The university was being funded by the donations of the faithful of each of the dioceses of Ireland (if in wildly varying amounts), and each bishop believed that he himself should have at least some say in how the university should be run, and when (or even if) it should be opened. It was not merely the obstructionist MacHale who was unwilling to hand his powers over the university to the archbishop of Dublin. In trying to overcome this problem and enable the university to open in the autumn of 1854, Cullen was forced to bring his influence in Rome to bear and, in so doing, even further alienated those bishops who were not committed to either the university or to Cullen personally.

Cullen set out the problems that would plague him throughout much of 1854 (and even later) in a letter to Kirby in December 1853. Written in Italian, this long letter was almost certainly designed to be passed on, either in whole or in part, to officials in the Sacred Congregation. Informing Kirby that 'Mr Newman promises to come to Ireland in the month of January', Cullen observed that it was therefore necessary 'to make something like a start to the University.' Such a start would not be easy, although were 'it possible to act in harmony, we would not be short of means.' Such harmony was not, however, to be found amongst the Irish hierarchy. 'I fear', Cullen wrote, 'that even in this business Monsignor MacHale will spread discord.' The archbishop of Tuam did not, it seemed, 'want to act in concert with the <u>committee</u> which was appointed at Thurles'. And, to make matters worse, 'if we do something without him, he makes the people believe that we are all hostile to the advantages of Ireland, that we want to introduce an English spirit, and similar other things.' Cullen also knew that MacHale would have important backers in any campaign to vilify him: 'Almost all the newspapers which we have here are ready to spread these rumours.'[23]

'I am beginning to think', Cullen wrote, 'that in order to succeed we must hold an assembly of all the bishops' as 'the importance of this business [of opening the university] demands that we do something decisive'.

Such a meeting would, he felt, give him an advantage over MacHale, as he accurately pointed out that the archbishop of Tuam was not a 'man who can propose or discuss a business.' Rather, he 'is good only to attack somebody else's projects, and to make a fuss before the public.' The 'difficulty' came in 'how to hold a canonical assembly of the bishops.'

Cullen did not feel that he could simply call a bishops' meeting to discuss the matter, as he knew all too well what the result of such a meeting would likely be. As he told Kirby, if the bishops 'assemble as they used to do a few years ago, the matter will end in an uproar, and nobody feels himself bound by the decisions which have been adopted.' It is difficult to disagree with Cullen's assessment of the likely outcome of such a meeting. The bishops had not been united at their annual meetings since at least the controversy over the national schools in the late 1830s, if in fact they had ever been. Under canon law, a decision taken at such a meeting, no matter what the majority, was only an advisement and was not binding in the diocese of any particular bishop. Only a rescript from the Propaganda, a papal bull, or a synod whose deliberations had been ratified by Rome could force a recalcitrant prelate into line.

A full, public, national synod or council, as Cullen informed Kirby, was not a solution, 'because there is no business which requires it'; Cullen needed more than the question of the Catholic University to justify the convening of a national synod of the sort that he had called at Thurles in 1850. He proposed a middle course that Kirby could take, unofficially, to the Propaganda: 'Were it possible to obtain from Rome the authority to assemble without the formalities of a council, but under the Presidency of some superior authority, the thing would be easy. We could act with order, and refer the decisions adopted to Rome in order to obtain their sanction.' Such a course would serve to isolate MacHale, as he did not, in Cullen's opinion, have the support of the majority of the bishops and thus 'could not do anything.' Nor did Cullen leave Kirby (and the Propaganda) in any doubt as to who the 'superior authority' he had suggested might be, although he did offer the pliant Dixon, archbishop of Armagh, as an alternative to himself. If he or Dixon were given the authority to pursue such a course and 'to preside over the assembly to be held privately', Cullen was optimistic that he could obtain an 'excellent result'.[24]

Cullen was confident that such an approach would allow him to publicly set the university on course (even if the meeting was private, its conclusions need not be) and give Newman the formal, public, call that he desired. He continued throughout the winter of 1854 to push this solution on the Propaganda. As he told Kirby in late January, it 'is difficult to hold a proper meeting of all the bishops and it is difficult not to hold one, lest all the bishops who side with us should be dissatisfied or think themselves passed over.'[25] He knew, too, that if the Propaganda was not minded to allow such an irregular meeting it might be necessary to involve the pope directly, over the heads of the Irish hierarchy, to obtain the necessary authority to open the university; 'If we can have first a meeting of the Bishops, it will be better', but if not 'the Pope's brief will be necessary for opening.'[26]

Time was not on Cullen's side. As he informed Kirby, he feared that 'it will be difficult to get the bishops together in Lent'. To that end he urged the Irish College rector to 'let me know at all events as soon as possible the . . . result of their [Propaganda's] deliberations.' After all, 'Dr Newman is here', they had the Stephen's Green house, 'so all we want is to begin in [some] satisfactory way.'[27] By March, Cullen had still not heard from the Propaganda about his plan. 'I suppose they have given up the business.' 'Perhaps', he thought, 'it is all for the better. If any instructions come now I fear it will be difficult to get anything done as Lent is advancing'.[28] With the Propaganda seemingly unlikely to accept his proposal for a meeting of the hierarchy, Cullen informed Kirby that he himself intended to visit Rome following Lent. In the meantime, he told his friend, 'Dr Newman is in town' but he 'is not quite satisfied as he is not regularly installed, nor can anything be done without seeing the Bishops.'[29] In fact, Propaganda had decided to follow Cullen's advice, and Pius IX issued a brief, dated 20 March, which formally appointed Newman as rector and required the Irish bishops to meet in synod, along the lines Cullen had suggested, within three months.[30]

Because of a late Easter and the Armagh provincial synod, Cullen was unable to convene his synod in Dublin until the third week of May 1854.[31] In the meantime, Newman had been in Ireland since early February to finally begin the process of making the university ready for an autumn opening. Under the impression that he had the necessary authority and recognition (in the form of his proposed bishopric), Newman travelled extensively in Ireland and began to make appointments to the university. He was able to see Cullen on 13 February and toured the Stephen's Green House with him. He also gained the archbishop's approval to approach the other Irish bishops about the university.[32] Indeed, he saw quite a lot of Cullen, noting in his diary that he dined with the archbishop on at least three occasions—and was taken separately on a tour of local schools by him—during the slightly more than a month he was in Ireland.[33] And, for much of that period, Cullen himself was either away or Newman was touring the country. If Newman had been ignored by Cullen during the previous year, he was certainly not so treated during his first extended visit to Ireland.

Newman pursued a hectic schedule during his trip. He wrote to Ambrose St John in mid-February: 'Next Sunday I am at Carlow—On Wednesday 22nd at Cork—Sunday 26th at Limerick—Ash Wednesday at Belfast.' In Dublin, too, he was busy. Although the 'first week I was here was simply lost, the Archbishop being away', Newman had since 'engaged one Lecturer, and almost another' and had also 'laid the foundations of a quasi Oratory' and 'thrown lawyers, architects, painters, paperers, and upholsterers into the University house, with a view of preparing for our Autumn opening.'[34] Despite all this activity in Dublin, his trip to the provinces did not fill Newman with hope. He was received everywhere with kindness ('I may say most truly and thankfully, that, many as are the varieties of opinion in Ireland, on one point it seems quite agreed, to be kind to me'),[35] but his travels brought home to Newman the extent of the divisions within the Irish church. As he reported back to the Oratorians in Birmingham, the 'dissentions [sic] in Ireland are awful—as many and sub divided and cross divided as dissenters in England. I have nothing to rely on but God, the Pope, and myself, and as yet I have not any sort of misgiving—but I do not know what encouragement I see.'[36]

Newman's meetings with the Irish bishops had mixed success. He found Archbishop Slattery 'a most pleasing, taking man—mild, gentle, tender and broken', but on meeting the bishop of Cork, William Delany, Newman remarked that he would 'rather be pawed by the lion [MacHale].' The Lion of Tuam bulked large in Newman's thoughts during this trip. He warned the Oratorian fathers never to let slip a word of what he said about MacHale, noting that '*if he thinks I think* he does not like me, he at once will set himself against me.'[37] If he was in any doubt about how little support for the university would be forthcoming from the divided hierarchy, this visit should have enlightened him.

Cullen, meanwhile, was preparing for the synod. It opened on 18 May and closed two days later. From the beginning MacHale opposed everything Cullen proposed, even down to a joint letter thanking the pope for his advice and promising to follow it.[38] After a heated debate over the as yet unsettled matter of political priests, the meeting turned to the university question, but a lack of time prevented the assembled prelates from dwelling too long on it. On the 20 May, Cullen managed to steer through the synod resolutions approving the establishment of the university on the model of Louvain, adopting the majority of that institution's statutes. At the urging of MacHale and his ally John Derry, the bishop of Clonfert, the adopted regulations continually emphasised the ability of the Irish hierarchy as a whole to change them at will. In his report to Cardinal Fransoni, Cullen noted that their insistence on such phrasing was 'with the object to give them an opportunity to change the whole plan immediately on being able to obtain a sufficient number of votes to do it.' Cullen also remarked ('tartly' in Emmet Larkin's phrase) that 'these two Prelates, though very involved in preserving to themselves the right of governing the university, have not demonstrated an equal zeal in the collecting of funds to establish it.'[39] Although Mac-Hale and Derry had not been active in university fundraising for some years, it was somewhat unfair to compare, as Cullen did, the returns of poverty-stricken and depopulated Tuam with prosperous Dublin.

MacHale was also able to force through a regulation that required the rector of the Catholic University to make an annual report to the assembled bishops. Cullen, as he told Fransoni, felt unable to oppose this plan for the very good reason that he could not answer the question of how, then, 'will the Rector render an account of the state of the University?'[40] Such an annual meeting would cause a return, in Cullen's view, to the bad old days before he was appointed to Armagh, when 'for the last twenty years' the bishops had 'never parted without quarrels, without tearing each other to pieces in the newspapers'. 'It is', Cullen informed the cardinal, 'impossible that such an assembly could meet without renewing similar scenes.' The 'Bishops are divided into four provinces, and those of one province do not wish to be guided by the others.' To make matters worse, it would 'be difficult to control him [MacHale] in a meeting where all are equal, and the more moderate would withdraw in order not to be involved in quarrels with him.'[41] The problem Cullen faced was the same as when he was contemplating the calling of the bishops together to approve the university's statutes; he could not rely on a non-canonical annual meeting of the bishops to behave as he wished (especially with MacHale present), but he could hardly ask the Propaganda to authorise a synod every year solely to hear the rector's report.

Cullen's solution was once again to appeal to Rome. In his letter to Fransoni, he set out his proposals:

> I venture to suggest with all humility, that it would be necessary for the Holy Father to bring to perfection by his authority the work that has been begun under his instructions, otherwise some Bishops will seek to change every year what has been done, and thus nothing permanent will be accomplished. I believe that it would be possible to avoid these evils if the Holy Father condescended to fix some princi-

ples for our conduct in the reply which he will make after having examined the decrees and acts of the present meeting. He would be able to sanction the fundamental rules that we have borrowed from Louvain for five or seven years, in order to be able to see by experience how they work out. In order also to facilitate the governing of the University it might be entrusted to the four Archbishops for the same period of time, nominating however someone among them to decide when the votes were equal. In our decrees there is one that give[s] such power to the four Archbishops for some time—I wished to extend it longer and the Archbishop of Armagh agreed with me— but the Archbishop of Tuam was opposed because he saw that in calmly treating matters among four persons, he would not have had field enough to exercise his energetic spirit.[42]

Cullen followed up this long letter to Fransoni with another on the subject of the university's statutes to his unofficial representative to the Sacred Congregation, Kirby. In it Cullen moved to augment the power of the rector of the Catholic University against any outside influence. At Maynooth 'the Rector cannot do any thing, he cannot make the least possible move.' As a result 'things will always remain as they are.' Cullen thought it better if the appointment of professors and the like were not left to a board but rather to the rector personally. 'I know it is a great power to be placed in the hands of the Rector—but let him be a man worthy of it—if not let him be removed.' Once again looking to the model of Louvain, Cullen remarked that in 'Belgium it has succeeded well.'[43] Cullen was putting a great deal of trust in the office of rector and in the man he had chosen to fill it.

The Propaganda accepted Cullen's proposed changes in their totality. Bishops meetings were to be held either every five (the norm) or three years (exceptionally), depending on the circumstances. In those years that there was not a general meeting, the four archbishops would meet during the university's convocation and receive the rector's report and make any necessary decisions regarding the university. In addition, Cullen was assured of getting his way in the committee of archbishops as any tie was to be decided by the apostolic delegate—himself. With Dixon's assured support, Cullen could carry his view in the face of any opposition. As Cullen had desired, the university's rules were to be confirmed for six years. As Emmet Larkin has noted, the decision of the Propaganda was 'nothing less than an unqualified vote of confidence in Cullen.'[44]

Despite this signal victory, Cullen could not rest easy after the synod. Although the Propaganda had moved at what was for Rome lightning speed, their recommendations were not formally submitted to the pope until 6 August. They did not reach Ireland until after Cullen had left for Rome to attend the consistory to advise on the definition of the dogma of the Immaculate Conception in late September.[45] Despite his triumph, Cullen's success came at a price. By appealing to Rome, and in being backed so fulsomely, he had once again demonstrated his power in the Irish church. MacHale and his allies had every reason to believe that their fears of Cullen's centralising and usurping tendencies were being fulfilled. Not only was Cullen using his influence in Rome to pack the hierarchy, but he had also arranged matters so that he appeared to be in total control of the Catholic University. Many bishops, and not only those who would normally be classed as allies of MacHale, were unclear why they should continue to support a supposedly national institution from which they had been excluded from any influence. Given the impossibility of running the university by means of annual meetings of all the bishops, it is hard to see how Cullen could have acted other than he did. Nevertheless, he sacrificed a great deal of the university's remaining support among the bishops and confirmed many in their suspicions that he wished to dominate and control the entire Irish church.

The practical effect of this alienation of episcopal affection towards the university can be seen by comparing, by diocese or province, funds raised for the university in 1851–52 and 1854. On a provincial basis, in 1851–52 Armagh raised, under Cullen, some £12,164. In 1854, under Dixon, the total was £3,514. Tuam, the poorest province, contributed £1,747 in 1851–52 and a mere £358 in 1854. Cashel too showed a decline, albeit a relatively small one, dropping from £3,424 to £2,424. Even Dublin, now under Cullen, raised less money in 1854—£4,329—than the £5,502 donated under Murray in 1851–52. Another indication of the change in mood among the bishops can be seen when it is considered that, in 1851–52, not a single diocese failed to make at least some contribution towards the university. In 1854 four of the twenty-eight Irish dioceses failed to make any contribution whatsoever. Although two of these—Kerry and Clonfert—were poor and had contributed little to the original collection, the other two, Cashel and Waterford, had both previously been major givers. Waterford dropped from £1,113 to nothing and Cashel, Archbishop Slattery's see, from £993 to nothing.[46]

The dissatisfaction with Cullen's centralising of university affairs can be seen in a letter written by its vice-rector, Patrick Leahy. Leahy had long been interested in educational matters and had been an early advocate of the Catholic University. He was born to a middle-class family at Fennor, near Thurles, on 31 May 1806. He was educated in Clonmel (partially in a Protestant school) and read for the highly classical Trinity entrance exam. Leahy did not matriculate but instead took up a place at Maynooth in 1826. He was ordained in 1833 and was on the original staff at Thurles College when it opened in 1837. At Thurles he held the chair of moral theology from 1842 and was appointed president in 1847.[47] He had sat with Newman, T. W. Allies, and Myles O'Reilly on the committee established to draw up preliminary statutes for a Catholic university in Ireland. Despite the fact that Leahy retained Cullen's respect and trust, he was not in any sense 'entirely Cullen's man' (as E. R. Norman put it).[48] He had long been close to the archbishop of Cashel and, as Slattery's health declined, had often been delegated to act for him. He was widely tipped to succeed the ailing Slattery when the latter died, as in fact he did in 1857. As archbishop of Cashel he would largely ally himself with Cullen, but he retained his independence in a way that, say, Dixon did not.

Sometime in 1854, likely late in that year, Leahy set down on paper his thoughts about Cullen's management of the university. Pulling no punches, the letter shows clearly that Cullen's actions had alienated many more than those, like MacHale, who were temperamentally inclined to oppose anything the archbishop of Dublin might propose. Although Leahy does not seem to have sent the letter,[49] it nonetheless is an important piece of evidence about the state of the opposition Cullen faced in 1854.

Leahy began by remarking that it 'is now certain that Dr Cullen has taken the whole thing into his own hands, & thrown overboard the whole Episcopacy of Ireland.' Even the university committee, in Leahy's view, had been cast aside. Leahy then addressed the consequences of Cullen's usurpation of the rights of the Irish hierarchy: 'The project of the University may now indeed be looked upon even by the most sanguine as impossible or at least so long as the state of things continues. It could not & it ought not succeed without the cooperation of the Prelates, which, as things are, can not be hoped for. They are called on to cooperate, and yet will not be allowed to cooperate, for all is taken into the hands of one Prelate, and even the form of holding meetings of the Committee is no longer observed.'[50]

The just dissatisfaction of the bishops with being asked to support the university while being excluded from its governance could only be exacerbated by 'their seeing one person, but lately come among them & having but little experience of things here, set at nought the feelings and the opinions and the authority of his Bretheren in the Episcopacy.' To Leahy such behaviour, 'no matter of what personal consideration', was a 'great evil in our ecclesiastical *status*, calling for immediate removal.' Such was the seriousness with which Leahy viewed the actions Cullen had taken that he wrote that 'if the project of the University gives rise to such an evil, it becomes itself an evil instead of a blessing.'[51]

There can be little wonder that the normally prudent Leahy thought better of sending this letter to Slattery. Its tone and message were so sharp that even MacHale might have hesitated. Although we do not know exactly what action of Cullen's provoked such a tirade, it is most likely that Leahy was upset by Rome's amendments to the decrees of the May synod dealing with the regulations of the Catholic University. Those amendments, made at Cullen's suggestion, did indeed remove the university from the authority of the wider episcopate in Ireland and instead vested it in the hands of the four archbishops. And, of course, Leahy and others knew as well as Cullen that the granting of a tie-breaking vote to the apostolic delegate meant that Cullen could control the archbishops' committee even in the face of opposition from MacHale and Slattery. The bishops explicitly and the archbishops implicitly had been removed from any direct influence over the future of the university.

The lessons of the preceding years had taught Cullen that the bishops as a body were incapable of taking action in the face of dissension; and, as long as MacHale lived, dissension was a given. Essentially, Cullen made a trade. By centralising power in his own hands, Cullen did indeed alienate many bishops (as Leahy suggested he would) from the university and damaged its ability to raise funds almost beyond repair. On the other hand, he was able to open the university, with the statutes and rector he desired, in November 1854. It is difficult to imagine that such a thing might have happened without Cullen exercising his power in Rome and, in so doing, breaking the power of the Irish episcopal body. Cullen was, not for the first or last time, faced with an almost impossible situation and made the best of it. The final judgement must be that Cullen did, in the end, succeed in his aim: to open the Catholic University of Ireland.

NEWMAN SETS TO WORK

While Cullen was embroiled with his machinations to formally establish the university and prepare the way for its opening, Newman too had been busy. Almost as soon as he had been called to Ireland by the university committee in October 1853, he began to make appointments. His university journal, which he kept throughout late 1853 and all of 1854 opens with the offer of a tutorship at £100 per annum to Thomas Scratton (who would become the secretary to the university). On 5 November he offered his friend Robert Ornsby both a tutorship and a lectureship, both at £100 per year. And on 23 November he had offered Henry Wilberforce, whose appointment as secretary to the Catholic Defence Association had caused Cullen such trouble, both a lectureship and a tutorship, but advised him instead to become the editor of the proposed *Catholic University Gazette*, a position Wilberforce accepted (but seems never to have actually filled).[52] Newman's initial plan was to offer four tutorships and a number of lectureships, and to not, as yet, begin appointing professors.

By early 1854, with his supposed bishopric in hand, Newman was ready to come to Ireland and begin to lay the ground for the university. He began the process of converting the University House on Stephen's Green to university requirements. His tour of Ireland, although not a striking success, gave him a chance to survey the country and get an idea as to what was needed on a practical level in the new university. If further progress awaited the May meeting of the bishops, Newman was nevertheless often in Ireland, spending not only most of February, but a large part of April and May in Dublin on university business. He continued to make appointments, despite the fact that he could not give a definite start date. The letters of Peter le Page Renouf give a flavour of the confusion that surrounded Newman's personnel decisions. On 16 May 1854, Renouf informed his brother that he had been offered a 'professorship' in the university. The offer was attractive, as it doubled the pay Renouf received as a tutor to a noble French family and allowed him 'over four months holiday in the year to go and see you.'[53] By mid-April, Renouf was telling his parents that 'it appears that my professional duties will not begin till the month of October at least.' Nor was he clear what, exactly, he was to do: 'It is not absolutely certain as yet, what my province may be, whether literature, history or philosophy.'[54] Despite the fact that Renouf went on to become a prominent Egyptologist and president of the Society for Biblical Archaeology, in 1854 he was appointed lecturer in French literature in the Catholic University of Ireland.

In addition to staffing the university, Newman saw to publicising it. The first issue of the *Catholic University Gazette* appeared, with a substantial piece by Newman, on 1 June, and he was formally installed as rector (by Cullen) during a High Mass on 4 June. Certainly, Cullen encouraged Newman's activities and his presence in Ireland. Their regular meetings and Cullen's anxiety to make a beginning are evidence enough of that. In April he wrote to Newman in order to inform him of the date of the forthcoming synod. Cullen told Newman that it 'wd be necessary to have every measure connected with the university matured before that time in order to ensure success.'[55]

It was in May too that an old source of grievance raised its head again: the matter of who was to be vice-rector of the CUI. At the Dublin Synod, it was decided to appoint Patrick Leahy to the job without consulting Newman on the matter.[56] Although not in any way disliked by Newman, Leahy was not exactly welcomed by him either. Newman still viewed the position as being if not directly within his gift, then at least subject to his influence. The anger that he had felt at Taylor's appointment returned on the imposition of Leahy. Recalling events in 1870, Newman remarked that, once again, he had been 'disregarded'.[57] Nor, again, was there anything practical Newman could do to block the appointment, especially of so well qualified and well connected a man as Leahy.

Leahy himself moved quickly to promise full support to the rector. He wrote to Newman on 22 May to announce his appointment, promising that he would work 'with & under you with perfect harmony & entire subordination to you as the Head of our University.'[58] Leahy soon settled into his role, keeping Newman informed of events in Ireland when the latter was in Birmingham. Leahy also assumed responsibility for the necessary repairs to the Stephen's Green building and began the process of recruiting students.[59] It was through Leahy that Newman gained his information on his powers of appointment as decided by the May synod. Writing on 26 May, Leahy advised Newman that although the entire episcopate was to have the power of appointment of professors—on the recommendation of the rector—in the short term the names of those proposed should be submitted by Newman to the four archbishops for their approval.[60]

Cullen, too, was quick to advise Newman on the results of the Dublin Synod. The university's statutes were by and large what he himself had suggested in 1851. Cullen did, however, insert a note of warning into his letter, telling Newman, 'It is better to try to gain every one by degrees and therefore we should be cautious not to publish any thing that might be interpreted in a wrong sense'. Cullen even added, hopefully, that 'I think we are all on a fair way united'.[61] Once again Cullen was advising his rector to make haste slowly and carefully.

Cullen's correspondence with Newman, so desultory in 1853, sprang back to life as the opening of the university grew imminent. The two men had been in close although not constant contact during each of Newman's visits to Ireland in the spring and summer of 1854, and Cullen clearly wished to maintain that contact while he was in Rome late that year. His letters during this period tend to be long and friendly, and it is clear that Cullen was deeply interested in and committed to the university. Although Cullen was continually offering Newman advice and suggesting various courses of action, the tone of the letters was advisory and even somewhat anxious; there was no attempt to force Newman to pursue any particular course of action.

Cullen had left Ireland for Rome in September, and during the trip and upon his arrival wrote to Newman on the subject of the university, now scheduled for a November opening. Reporting to Newman that he had heard complaints of Scratton's management style as secretary to the university ('I do not know what grounds for them'), Cullen advised that he 'call Dr Leahy and Revd Mr Flannery [a Cullen ally appointed, without Newman's consent, to be dean of the university] to you once or twice a week, and as they are well versed in the management of temporal affairs, they wd be of great assistance to you.'[62] Cullen did not, however, require Newman to do any such thing and seemed most interested in smoothing his path. His concern to assist Newman in his administrative duties was not totally unreasonable. Scratton, in whose hands Newman left nearly the entire day-to-day running of the university, does not seem to have been an effective administrator. By 1859 Thomas Arnold (professor of English literature and no friend of Cullen's) told his wife that he did not believe that Scratton was possessed of a strong enough personality for the position and wondered how 'Newman ever came to appoint him'.[63]

Writing two days later, in a long letter marked 'private', Cullen again discussed his desire to begin the university on a small scale. 'I recollect', Cullen told Newman, 'that about two or more years ago Mr Scott Hope [Hope-Scott] in a conversation I had with him insisted very much on the necessity of making every one understand that every thing done about the university in the beginning was only a preparation for a university, & that the real university was still at a distance.' Hope-Scott, Cullen recalled, gave as his reason for this course of action the fact that, in such a case, the 'people might not be disappointed by the smallness of the beginning.' Cullen clearly agreed with such an approach, telling Newman, 'I think it wd be prudent for us to act in the same way, and if you cd supply professors in a temporary way for the first year, or get the one professor to act for another perhaps it wd be better'. Cullen even suggested that 'Dr Leahy for example might teach something connected with the classics this year.'[64] Cullen was consistent in his desire that the university be begun on a manageable and sustainable scale, but once again he did not impose this view on Newman.

While Cullen was en route to Rome, Newman had been putting the finishing touches on his proposed appointments to the CUI. Not surprisingly, he largely appointed those who were either personally known to him or were recommended by friends. His appointments thus had a strong Oxbridge, English, and convert flavour to them. Long time friends like T. W. Allies and Robert Ornsby made wholly expected appearances. Of the fifteen names that Newman submitted for the archbishops' consideration, seven were English and had their professional origins in Oxford or Cambridge.[65] Of the fifteen appointments, there were to be six professors and nine lecturers (a far cry from Newman's original intention to have only four lectureships); a far cry also from Cullen's suggested small beginnings with a short-term faculty. The professorships were to be in dogmatic theology, exegetics (to be held by Leahy),[66] archaeology and Irish history, classical literature (Ornsby's position), mathematics, and civil engineering. There were to be lectureships in political economy, poetry, the philosophy of history (Allies), geography, logic, ancient history, English literature, French literature, and a dual position for Italian and Spanish. As Newman explained in a letter to MacHale, the appointments in the 'School of Art' were the most pressing, those in the 'Schools of Theology, Law, and Medicine' 'certainly may wait'.[67] With these first appointees, Newman would begin his university.

Newman's list of appointments was ambitious for a university that did not, as yet, have any students and had not opened its doors. The breadth of the faculty was impressive and was indicative of Newman's desire to make the Catholic University a place where all the academic disciplines were to be studied, theology holding its place with the rest. Although he had advised a more tentative beginning, Cullen gave Newman's list of appointees his unequivocal support: 'I place so much confidence in your judgement and prudence that I cannot hesitate one moment to give my sanction to their appointment.' This vote of support came with a promise from Cullen that 'I shall be always ready to give you every possible assistance in my powers.'[68] Dixon, too, expressed his rather disinterested approval, telling Newman the 'list is most acceptable to me, as indeed any list should be, which meets with your approval.'[69] Certainly the catholicity of the faculty (who were anyway required to make a profession of faith) could not trouble any bishop: Peter le Page Renouf described his 'new vocation' as 'a call from God to do upon a large scale what every one is bound to do in his degree, to advance the spiritual Kingdom of His Son, with reference to myself and all who come under my influence, that Christ may dwell in our hearts by faith, and that we may be rooted and grounded in his Love'—and this in a letter to his parents![70]

To no one's surprise, MacHale was less supportive. Even without the substantial English presence on the proposed faculty to provoke him, MacHale was in no mood to take his defeat over the May synod gently and come to support the university. His willingness to allow Newman to place his name on the university books was about as far as he had been willing to go; active support, or even quiet acquiescence, was out of the question.[71] Newman's solicitation of the archbishop's support for the university's faculty was met by silence, and MacHale's later letters indicate that he was by no means pleased with being consulted on appointments only, as he saw it, out of courtesy. Archbishop Slattery in Cashel, too, does not seem to have bothered to reply to Newman's letter (although Cullen, in a letter to Kirby, implied that he approved of the list, as indeed he might with his protégé Leahy as both vice-rector and professor).[72] With the university now seen to be fully in Cullen's hands, Newman's appointments passed with little comment from the rest of the Irish hierarchy.

With his faculty approved without cavil by both Cullen and Dixon, and with MacHale and Slattery silent, Newman was able to set about finding students for the newly appointed professors and lecturers to teach. It quickly became apparent that this would be no easy task. In mid-September, Leahy advised Newman that they had as yet only three confirmed students. As a result, in October the sessional fee was dropped from £50 to £40.[73] The vice-rector was hopeful, and was keen to ensure that the university's students were drawn from throughout Ireland. Leahy was especially interested in gaining students from those areas that already had a Queen's College: 'The more students from Cork the better. Every student from Cork may be set down as won from the enemy's camp.'[74] For his part, Newman was doing his best to recruit students from English and (to a lesser extent) continental Catholic circles.

Cullen, too, knew that students were unlikely to be numerous at first; in its first year Louvain enrolled only eighty-six students. As he reported to Kirby, there 'will not be a good attendance' when the university opened in November. Nevertheless, 'there will be some.' He also informed his friend, 'We have made several appointments for the classes—3 Archbishops agreed to all.' 'I believe', continued Cullen, 'that Dr McHale is not inclined to do much.'[75]

Despite the pessimism over student enrolment, the Catholic University of Ireland was formally opened by Newman on 3 November 1854. Cullen, writing from Rome, was delighted: 'It was very gratifying to hear that there were so many students. I hope God will continue to bless, and prosper your undertaking. Every one here is most anxious about your success. The Pope and Cardinals make continual inquiries about you—I was not, up to the present, able to give any information, but now they will be delighted with the intelligence conveyed in your letter.' Cullen also informed Newman that Pius IX had granted the university the power to confer pontifical degrees.[76] Cullen's pleasure over the number of students could only be the result of extremely low expectations on that front. According to the Catholic University student register, only thirty-eight students matriculated between 3 November 1854 and 14 June 1855. Although many more would attend evening courses (particularly those in theology) without entering upon a full university course, numbers were nonetheless not great. In fact, those thirty-eight students were to prove the largest one-year registration in the history of the Catholic University, and the battle to attract students would remain the university's foremost practical problem throughout its existence.[77]

The students that did come in that first year were not particularly diverse. St Laurence's School in Dublin (which shared a building with Newman's Harcourt Street residence) sent ten students, Newman's own Oratory school seven, the Jesuits' elite Clongowes Woods eleven, and one student each came from Thurles and the elite English Catholic schools Stonyhurst and Downside. The latter two could not be expected to provide much in the way of students as they were both committed to preparing their pupils for University of London exams (as was Leahy's Thurles College). Various other institutions accounted for the balance of the first year's intake (including private tutors—Renouf's former employer insisted his sons accompany their old tutor to Dublin).[78] The emphasis among the student body was on the sons of the Irish and English elite, who were largely attracted by Newman. Most of those students had already been as well, and as classically, educated as was possible in the United Kingdom of the day.

Despite the relatively poor student enrolment, the university had finally opened. A plan that was first mooted in 1846 and had been the source of almost neverending conflict within the Irish church had finally come to fruition. Despite the delay, the continued opposition of MacHale, the sometimes hostile indifference of much of the rest of the hierarchy, and the disappointing student numbers, the university was nonetheless open. By guiding his project to this point Paul Cullen had taken the university as far as he could, and he left it in the hands of his chosen rector. It was now up to Newman to see what could be made of it.

chapter eight

Rupture, Failure, and Departure

ONCE THE CATHOLIC UNIVERSITY OPENED, IT DID NOT TAKE long for practical problems to emerge, problems that would haunt the university for the remainder of its days. The all-important relationship between Newman and Paul Cullen foundered over the issues of Newman's residence in Dublin, style of university discipline, and choice of friends and appointees. For his part, Newman became increasingly frustrated with the university and with Ireland. Meanwhile, Cullen, despite increasing dissatisfaction with his rector, did everything in his power to retain Newman, seeing in him the only hope of preserving the project. Indeed, the stress of trying both to persuade Newman to remain and to plan for the future of the university if he did not would drive Cullen to a serious nervous breakdown in the summer of 1858.

While the tension between the two principal figures increased, student numbers did not and the university, despite a flourishing medical school, began to look as if it might fail for a lack of interest on the part of the Irish people. Fundraising, so successful in the heady days following the Synod of Thurles, plummeted as the Irish bishops, stripped of any authority over the university, failed to exert themselves to support it. The government, too, played its part in the effective failure of the Catholic University, denying it the charter that might, perhaps, have attracted the students necessary to build the sort of institution Cullen and Newman had dreamed of. The story of the Catholic University of Ireland between its opening and Newman's departure is largely one of frustration and failure.

FIRST TENSIONS: NEWMAN, LUCAS, AND YOUNG IRELAND

Despite the difficulties that lay in the near future, Cullen did not immediately lose faith in either his rector or the university. The seeds of their conflict, however, became evident quite soon after the CUI's November opening. Cullen, still in Rome for the proclamation of the Immaculate Conception, wrote to Newman on 20 December to discuss the university. It is ironic that the letter that paved the way for the break between the two men was also the longest and most confiding that Cullen had ever written to Newman.

Cullen began by reporting the events in Rome surrounding the proclamation to Newman and suggested that he might wish to commission (or write himself) some poetry commemorating the event. In a personal touch rarely to be found in a letter to any but his family or Kirby, Cullen even told Newman of 'an old Irish litany and a very beautiful one' that he had always liked.[1] He then went on to tell Newman of the activities of Frederick Lucas, Gavan Duffy, and their allies. Lucas was in Rome in an effort to get the Holy See to overrule Cullen on the involvement of the church in nationalist politics. After criticising Lucas and his friends, Cullen went on to tell Newman, 'I know many of Lucas' adherents in Ireland are anxious to assail yourself—but I am confident that you will be supported by every one that has the interest of religion at heart.'[2] Cullen then took Newman as far into his confidence as he ever would, informing him that 'Dr McHale has made every effort here to prevent the confirmation of those regulations [establishing the CUI] or to get it withdrawn.' 'He says now', Cullen wrote, 'that he will have nothing to do with the university'. Although this was 'so much the better', Cullen still feared that MacHale 'will excite a storm against it.' He even went so far as to advise Newman not to share this information with his vice-rector, Leahy, 'lest Dr Slattery be displeased.'[3]

The warm tone and confiding nature of his letter to Newman make Cullen's next communication seem much less like a warning on the subject of Young Irelandism than it otherwise might have done. Writing on 12 January 1855, Cullen, after again complaining of the activities of Lucas, Duffy, and 'some Priests' in Rome, remarked that they 'seem quite determined to make the world believe that I wish to sell the Irish church, and that the price is to be a charter for the university.' 'You will be surprised perhaps to learn', he continued, 'that your authority is quoted to prove that I am really become a slave of the government'. 'Tho' in the deluge of lies which has been let loose on the country nothing can surprise us.' Cullen disclaimed any belief that such charges against Newman might be true, writing, 'Of course I did not attach the least importance to vague rumours.' In this climate of conflict, however, Cullen did not hesitate to caution Newman, telling him, 'I trust you will make every exertion to keep the university free from all young Irelandism'.[4]

It seems likely that in early 1855 Cullen was confident that Newman had kept the Catholic University free of any such taint. Members of the faculty supposedly sympathetic to Young Ireland such as Eugene O'Curry (professor of archaeology and Irish history) and John O'Hagan (lecturer in political economy) were, as Peadar MacSuibhne has pointed out, seen as quite safe by Cullen; O'Hagan remained a close associate of the archbishop's and eventually drew up his will; O'Curry was a frequent visitor to Cullen's residence.[5] And, of course, Cullen had fulsomely approved of Newman's appointments only some three months earlier. It was not until early 1855, shortly after Newman received his letter, that an appointment would be made to the university of a man whose undoubted Young Ireland sympathies made him anathema to Cullen.

The acceptance, on 1 March, by John Pigot of an offer to lecture on the law of real property marked a turning point in Newman's appointments. According to Fergal McGrath, Pigot had been 'one of the poets of the Young Ireland movement', and was also known for the composition of nationalist songs.[6] David Moriarty, the recently consecrated bishop of Kerry and Newman's closest friend in the Irish church, advised Newman to set aside Cullen's mistrust 'of those he calls Young Irelanders'. He also specifically defended Pigot, telling Newman that he 'is a truly estimable young man . . . [who] withdrew from his political party in '47 and never, that I remember, took part in politics since.'[7] Despite Moriarty's suggestion that Pigot was now apolitical,[8] Newman remembered in 1870 that he 'talked like a republican' and that he 'was a fanatic even then'.[9]

Cullen made no effort to conceal his distaste at the prospect of Pigot's appointment. According to Newman's university memorandum, Cullen enlisted the aid of William Walsh, the archbishop of Halifax and his close friend, to 'dissuade me by telling me things against Mr. Pigot.' Newman, however, was unmoved and did not see that, because of Pigot's

politics or the 'wild things' he might have done or said, he 'should separate myself from him.'[10] Newman had sought Pigot's advice on the university at least as early as mid-1854.[11] He knew both the man's politics
(he warned Pigot against bringing politics into the university, but told
him he had no objection to his holding the opinions that he did)[12] and
Cullen's intense hostility towards them. Indeed, in his memorandum he
noted how Cullen, in the course of opposing Pigot, 'always compared
Young Ireland to Young Italy—and with the most intense expression of
words and countenance assured me they never came right—never—he
knew them from his experience in Rome.'[13]

Newman was quite correct in his assessment of Cullen's views on
Young Ireland and his association of that movement with Young Italy.
Indeed, Cullen's experience in 1848–49 lie at the heart of his reaction to
Irish nationalism, both in the 1850s and later. Cullen's earliest information about Young Ireland came while he was still in Rome. Michael Slat-
tery, writing to Cullen in 1846,[14] dismissed them as 'a bad set, in Religion
they are Latitudinarian, & in politics revolutionary'.[15] Neither their secularism nor their revolutionary inclinations appealed, nor did the Young
Ireland leadership's (especially Gavan Duffy's) support for the Queen's
Colleges endear them to Cullen. Edward Maginn, the administrator of
the Derry diocese, made the comparison between Young Ireland and
Young Italy to Cullen, remarking that the 'Devil was busy with it
[Young Italy] and in it' and that '[o]ur own "Young Ireland" was not less
mad than they.' Nor, according to Maginn, was Young Ireland any less
'demoniacal' than Young Italy, and had, in their failed rising, 'rushed
headlong into the pit that was dug for them; regardless of all counsel &
what is worse dragged our ill fated country after them.'[16] Cullen himself
wrote similar things, telling his brother during the height of the troubles
in Rome that the 'same wd. have happened in Ireland had the young Irelanders got the upper hand for a month.'[17]

Events in Rome solidified Cullen's distaste of any and all secular revo-
lutionaries. To him, Mazzini's Roman Republic was a period of unheard
of outrages against the church, and he witnessed a great deal of it from his
post as rector of the Irish College. His opinion of the unrest that gripped
the Italian peninsula was that 'there is a very bad mob through Italy' who
'seem determined to put down all ecclesiastical authority.'[18] Things
quickly became much more serious than the desire of a few radicals to
overthrow the temporal power of the church. Cullen's letters in 1848–49
are full of accounts of atrocities against priests, nuns, and brothers. He
remained in Rome when the pope and curia fled, and he claimed to have
either witnessed or spoken to witnesses of many murders and outrages.

In the Irish College he concealed a cardinal, some Jesuits, and various other ecclesiastical dignitaries from the forces of the Republic. At one point the college itself was fired upon.[19] Cullen even kept a personal 'Memorandum of Republican Atrocities', a typical entry for which reads: 'Murders—Several in Ancona/in Rome 2 Dominican P[arish] P[riest]'s / about 13 other priests. . . . The day of the entry [of the] French a priest killed—torn in pieces, and the savages washed their hands in his blood.'[20]

To Cullen, the events of 1848–49 were a turning point. As we have seen, he laid the blame squarely on the secular, revolutionary ideas of Young Italy and the other radicals (ideas, he thought, that had grown up as a result of secular education). If the overthrow of the pope and the murder of priests was where secular nationalism led, then Cullen wanted no part of it. Young Ireland was simply too close to Young Italy in Cullen's mind ever to gain his support, or even his toleration. In the 1860s, Cullen's dislike of Young Ireland was transferred, with no diminution in its ferocity, to the Fenians.

Cullen's antipathy to secular nationalism does not, however, imply that he was not himself a nationalist and of a nationalist family. Cullen's uncle (and namesake) was shot in the wake of the 1798 rising, and his father, Hugh, was imprisoned in 1803 after Robert Emmet's rising but acquitted by a court-martial.[21] Cullen was Irish, conscious of the fact, and very proud of it. A single stanza from a poem of his, probably written in the 1830s while he was rector of the Irish College, gives an idea of his attitude towards Ireland and her troubled history:

> And slavery trailing the chains ee'n of ages
> Has not frightened thee yet from the Emerald Isle
> Tho' contemned by the bigot and laughed at by sages
> Thou hast never deposed for a moment that smile
> Which consoles us mid grief, mid oppression and sorrow
> For our evening's adversity allays every pain
> Which mildly proclaims that some glorious morrow
> Will rise oe'r the genius of Erin again.[22]

Nor was Cullen in any doubt as to the source of Ireland's misery and oppression. Cullen never learned to like the English as a nation, despite friendships with some individuals and his brothers' long residence in Liverpool. Although as an archbishop he always masked his distaste with diplomatic tact (unlike, say, MacHale), Cullen's early letters are full of wonder at and contempt for the English and especially for their approach to poverty. In a letter he wrote to Kirby during a visit to his family in Liverpool in 1842, Cullen noted the destitution of the people but remarked that 'you see no beggars on the streets, as the policemen are charged to remove all such nuisances, but the eyes of the rich should be offended by such sights.' He went on to quote, quite favourably, a writer who had asserted that the 'English are the most uncharitable people on the face of the earth.'[23] His opinion of English charity only deepened during the Famine, and in a letter to his nephew Hugh, Cullen remarked, 'only our rulers are such Turks, or worse than Turks, they would not let so many thousands die of pure starvation.'[24]

Paul Cullen was both anti-English in a pragmatic and nonviolent way and a nationalist of the O'Connellite sort. What he could not accept, however, was the secular, revolutionary nationalism offered by Young Ireland and the like. English rule in Ireland was wrong, but a violent revolt on behalf of the principles of Young Ireland (or, later, Fenianism) could only result in the horrors of the Roman Republic being visited on Ireland and on its national church. Cullen linked the two quite clearly in a letter, written in 1852, to Monsignor Barnabò at the Propaganda. Referring to the opposition his policies faced, both from the English government and, more particularly, his Irish opponents (whom Cullen lumped together under the category of 'Young Ireland' whether or not they were members of that rather nebulous grouping), Cullen remarked that, if 'your Excellency wishes to form an idea of the manner in which they treat the Catholics in these countries [Britain and Ireland] it is sufficient to recall to your memory the happy days of the republic of Rome.' This was true, wrote Cullen, as all the 'same arts, all the same stratagems are being adopted daily by the enemies of religion against us. The spirit of Mazzini has spread to these kingdoms.'[25]

After he was appointed archbishop of Armagh, and especially after he was translated to Dublin, Cullen came to associate all opposition to him and his policies originating within the Catholic community with Young Irelandism. He attributed opposition to Newman's appointment as rector, in 1851, to 'a few young Irelanders who have been steadfast friends of the Queen's Colleges and enemies of the Catholic University from the beginning.'[26] And, in 1855, he told Monsell that 'the system of so called independent opposition wd. be likely to produce the evils occasioned in Italy by Mazzini's principles.'[27]

That Newman, aware at least to a degree of the archbishop's views on the matter, would nevertheless persevere in his desire to appoint Pigot is remarkable (the fact that Pigot never actually taught students is irrelevant—there were no law students to teach). What is more remarkable still is that Cullen did not, after Newman had refused his entreaties and those of Archbishop Walsh, intervene to block the appointment. Given the strength of his views on the matter, Cullen's restraint was extraordinary. A more serious disagreement than the appointment of Pigot to the Catholic University would soon, however, arise between the two men. At issue was the continued friendship between Newman and Frederick Lucas, the editor of *The Tablet* and one of Cullen's fiercest critics.

Lucas had long been a thorn in Cullen's side. A convert and an Englishman, he had moved his publication to Dublin and given himself wholly to the cause of Irish nationalism. Lucas saw himself as a good Catholic and the church as his natural ally in the cause of Irish nationhood. To that end he had long courted Cullen's support, both in Rome while he was rector of the Irish College (even going so far as to request Cullen arrange some sort of papal recognition of *The Tablet* in an effort to increase subscriptions)[28] and upon Cullen's return to Ireland. Relations began to sour between the two men as Lucas became more and more involved in nationalist politics. He was elected an MP for Meath in 1852 on a platform of support for the Independent Irish party and the goals of the Tenant League. As Cullen remarked in late 1853 to Kirby, 'Lucas appears to be going astray' and 'wishes to coerce all priests and bishops to join the tenant league.'[29] Still, by early 1854 Cullen had not quite lost faith in Lucas, again telling Kirby that, although, 'I think that he is very much disposed to quarrel with me', he would nonetheless 'flatter him as far as possible'. It was, Cullen thought, a 'pity' that Lucas should 'go wrong as he is good and clever—but the young Irelanders have got him in their hands.'[30]

Lucas quickly made Cullen's continued toleration of him difficult and then impossible. His already close association with MacHale became even closer, and the two men (one explicitly and one implicitly) set out to paint Cullen as antinationalist and pro-English. By May, Cullen, who was regularly being called a 'Whig' by Lucas, told Kirby that Lucas was now 'altogether in the Lion's hands.'[31] Matters came to a head when the May synod in Dublin, called formally to establish the Catholic University, also addressed the question of the involvement of priests in political questions. It is sufficient to note here that MacHale, Lucas, Duffy, and their allies were not happy with Cullen's success in preventing the wholesale enlistment of any sympathetic clergy in the nationalist cause. In an effort to gain a change in the decrees of the synod, they chose to take their case directly to the Holy See.

In Rome, Lucas placed himself in direct opposition to Cullen, who was also in the Eternal City. His activities there roused the archbishop to something like fury. A letter Cullen wrote to Francis Haly, the bishop of

Kildare and Leighlin, gives an account of the activities of the archbishop of Tuam and the editor of *The Tablet* in Rome: 'Mr Lucas is here. A more impudent proceeding I never witnessed. After insulting the bishops of Ireland and joining with Moore and Duffy in exciting suspicions against the H. See, he comes meekly to ask to have all his proceedings confirmed. . . . Dr MacHale I suppose is his great hope in Rome, but his Grace has displayed so much bad feeling and violence even here that he is not likely to be able to throw much influence into Lucas' cause.'[32]

That Lucas had allied himself completely with MacHale and against Cullen is made clear from his own record of his time in Rome. His journal (which took the form of letters to Gavan Duffy) sets out his strategy, which was to control 'popular feeling' so that Rome, in 'a case where they feel they half understand [and in] which they must be guided by some one' might come round to their view. 'Dr Cullen', Lucas continued, 'is, or has been, *in possession,* and will remain so until his inability to manage affairs fortunately be demonstrated.'[33] Lucas's strategy, then, was to demonstrate to Rome that Cullen was unfit for the trust placed in him, and he set to his task with a will.

The alliance of MacHale, Lucas, and Duffy was the most serious internal threat Cullen had faced since coming to Ireland. And it was with Lucas, perhaps his most virulent critic, that Newman was known to be associated. Rumours of Newman's sympathy with Lucas's attacks combined with the appointment of an obvious Young Irelander like Pigot cannot have made Cullen confident in his rector's continued reliability.

For his part, Newman refused to be separated from his friendship with Lucas; 'I never of course would give up Lucas as a friend.'[34] Although Newman admitted to differing with him politically, he thought Lucas 'an honest good man' and held Cullen's 'treatment of him at Rome' to be 'too painful for me to talk of.' Newman was under no illusion as to exactly how Cullen viewed his relationship with Lucas, recording that as 'soon as the Archbishop thought I was on what may be called speaking terms with him, he grew cold towards me, then warned me against him, and I of course would not be warned.'[35] Newman told Cullen as much in a letter of 24 January. He assured the archbishop, no doubt accurately, that he had not 'said any thing in favor of Mr Lucas against your Grace'. As to Lucas himself, 'I know him and respect him highly', but he assured Cullen, 'I think he is simply mazed and wild, when he speaks of your Grace having done this or that, *if* (as people say) he says it.' Newman also assured Cullen that he had taken the point over appointing Young Irelanders to the university: 'I feel deeply that we shall be ruined, if we let *politics* in.'[36] It is doubtful if Cullen was much comforted by these words.

It should also be noted that not letting 'politics' into the university is slightly different from not allowing Young Irelanders into the university; the Pigot appointment was, after all, imminent.

Although Newman's letters to Lucas have not survived, it is clear from the university journal and the university memorandum that Lucas was a close confidant who often advised Newman how to navigate the ever-tricky shoals of Irish ecclesiastical politics. Indeed, in his university memorandum Newman clearly states that he aimed to take Lucas's advice (proffered in late 1853) that he should not attach himself too closely to Cullen or any one ecclesiastical party and should endeavour to court MacHale, Cantwell, Derry, and their allies.[37]

It is over the issue of his friendship with Lucas and his knowing appointment of Young Irelanders that a charge often levelled against Newman, that of naïveté, is most appropriate. Newman claimed that he wished to remain neutral in the Irish hierarchy's internal battles, but it is difficult to credit that he truly believed that he could be successful. As he himself noted, 'Dr MacHale was rude from the first',[38] and his letters for the period are full of references to his frustration with the Lion of Tuam. Newman had been wooed by Cullen, appointed by Cullen, and fought for by Cullen; the archbishop of Dublin had made every effort to extend the rector's power and to protect him from the excessive attentions of the rest of the Irish episcopate. To Irish eyes, Newman was inextricably linked with Cullen, just as the Catholic University itself was. No other ecclesiastical party was taking any interest (except a hostile one) in the university, and for Newman to aspire to 'neutrality' was simply ludicrous. It is possible that Newman's own bitterness at the archbishop's shabby treatment of him in 1853 had caused him to forget how closely linked they were and who, exactly, his patron was. It is not even the case that Newman's links to Lucas and others of his party saved the university from public criticism. Peter le Page Renouf remarked in January 1856, 'we are beginning to be attacked violently', which, he thought, was 'an additional sign of life' for the university. Nevertheless, 'of <u>course</u> the attacks come from our <u>friends,</u> from those who were most enthusiastic.' 'They find', Renouf wrote, 'that the professors confine themselves strictly to <u>education,</u> & do no intend to make the university a tool for political agitation.' Since the university could not be turned to 'their purposes' these former friends 'are becoming rabid enemies.'[39]

For Newman then to retain such friendships as that with Lucas—who was doing his best to paint the archbishop as an English toady—and to appoint men like Pigot could only have been interpreted by Cullen as a calculated snub. That Newman most likely meant it in no such way (malice aforethought formed no part of his character) would have gone little way to assuaging Cullen's anger. After all, *his* appointee to *his* university was refusing to cease association with his harshest critic and, moreover, was persisting in the appointment of men whose views Cullen sincerely believed to threaten the very existence of the church in Ireland. It is a credit to Cullen that he did not force Newman either to forgo the appointment of Pigot or insist on the severance of his relations with Lucas;[40] the cooling that Newman detected in their relationship was the least that could be expected under the circumstances. By way of contrast, it is perhaps useful to imagine the reaction of the ever-sensitive Newman if a subordinate or friend of his had publicly continued relations with as harsh a critic of himself as Lucas was of Cullen. Nevertheless, and despite the new coolness, Cullen continued to back his rector and to give him and the university every support he could. Early 1855 did, however, mark a turning point. After that time, relations between the two men would continue on a downward slope for the remainder of Newman's tenure at the CUI.

THE PROBLEMS MOUNT

Despite the increasing coolness in relations between Cullen and Newman, the two maintained a certain level of contact and cordiality. Cullen arranged for Newman to be allowed to keep the Blessed Sacrament in his own personal chapel in Harcourt Street and Newman promised to say a mass once a week for Cullen until the archbishop returned from Rome.[41] Newman also made every effort to keep Cullen informed as to what was going on with the university and to seek his advice or approval when necessary.

The university itself was settling down to a routine as the academic year wore on, and Newman continued to add to the faculty at an impressive rate. In a letter to Cullen in late February, he announced his desire to appoint professors in chemistry, natural philosophy, and physiology for the medical school. He also announced his intention to appoint John Hungerford Pollen, who was later to be responsible for the magnificent university church, to the chair of fine arts.[42] He later appointed another convert, Aubrey DeVere, to lecture in English literature.

For his part, Cullen seems to have returned to his earlier strategy of ignoring Newman's letters. Certainly, he did not communicate with the rector, despite a number of direct questions Newman posed in various letters, from 12 January (in which he reported the rumours of Newman's

support for Lucas and received the reply discussed above) until he returned to Dublin in mid-July. As a result of Cullen's silence, Newman
was forced to make his desired appointments provisionally (as he informed Cullen on 5 July),[43] as he was unable to make them permanent
without the archbishops' sanction. An idea of the frustration this could
cause is evident in a letter of DeVere's, in which he remarked that he was
still working hard to prepare his lecturers 'on the <u>chance</u> of being useful;
though I infer from your [Monsell's] note that my time will probably
be thrown away.'[44] Even though DeVere was, eventually, provisionally
appointed to his lectureship and did in fact give his lectures, it is not
difficult to imagine the effect such delays had on his morale, and on
Newman's.

Newman continued to write to Cullen on university business
throughout the summer of 1855. In those letters Newman discussed
topics ranging from the difficulties pertaining to the establishment of the
school of theology (always dear to Cullen's heart)[45] to the necessity to
announce, at least provisionally, the appointees to the chairs in surgery,
anatomy, and pathology.[46] Cullen maintained his silence in the face of
such letters, a silence that was not quite deafening but was nonetheless
substantial and had serious effects on the university.[47]

While largely maintaining his silence towards Newman, Cullen was
by no means silent about him. On 28 July, while reporting favourably to
Barnabò on the university's prospects, Cullen noted that the 'only point
on which I have heard some complaint is that Father Newman shows a
certain ignorance of practical affairs'. As a result of such ignorance he
had 'permitted the introduction of things which could be very inconve-
nient as the years go by.' Evidently, the prospect of Newman becoming a
bishop had reemerged, as Cullen informed Barnabò that, as a result of
these flaws of Newman's, 'I should be very glad if he were not yet made
a bishop, and I hope that no step will be taken until the affairs of the university are well launched.'[48] Cullen also pointed out that a bishop would
have a great deal of difficulty in attending to the 'details and minutiae
that must be dealt with while the university is being established.'[49] To
Kirby, Cullen (writing in Italian) was blunter: 'I fear that Father Newman
has made a mess of matters relating to the University', as he 'does not
know Ireland and has not consulted anybody about the things he had
done.'[50]

In a letter to Kirby on the same subject about a month later, Cullen
remarked, 'It wd. be very unfortunate if in Rome they were to make Dr
Newman a bishop and have him over the university—we wd. not then be
able to get on at all.'[51] Cullen also expanded on his hint to Barnabò about

the sort of 'things' Newman was introducing to the university of which he did not approve. As he forthrightly told Kirby, 'I do not think that Dr Newman is managing things well.' Newman had 'the idea of Oxford so much before his mind, that he appears to forget how dangerous its practices are.' Examples of such Oxonian dangers being replicated at the CUI included allowing 'the students out at any time they wished' and excessive expenditures. 'This will', Cullen wrote, 'give a triumph to our opponents but I will not attempt to defend him.'[52]

During the summer and early autumn of 1855 Newman, who was back in Birmingham and increasingly frustrated with Cullen's unwillingness to communicate, turned to William Monsell for his help with the matter. He told Monsell that he was sending him a 'specimen of Dr Cullen's way' and noted that he had written to Cullen 'six weeks ago to know whether we had got from the Pope the power of granting degrees' but had heard no reply.[53] He had then been forced to send Robert Ornsby to the archbishop with the same question, and Ornsby had only managed to elicit the information that Cullen did not know but would examine the question and see.[54] Monsell offered a somewhat implausible explanation for Cullen's actions, telling Newman that 'in Ireland one often meets with people of his [Cullen's] class, kind & considerate after their fashion, but moving in a sphere completely different from ours & therefore acting in a [way] if we acted we should shew a want of consideration & respect for others'. He then offered an anecdote about Irish priests who fail to reply to dinner invitations yet come anyway. Despite this rather unhelpful assessment of Cullen's character, Monsell nonetheless promised to try to provoke a letter from Cullen to Newman.[55]

Monsell must have succeeded in his aim, as the day after he wrote to Newman Cullen wrote to his rector for the first time in months. Cullen began gently enough, begging 'a thousand pardons for so long a delay' and blaming it on a desire to gather enough information to answer Newman's queries. However, he quickly raised, at least obliquely, those issues that had been troubling him. In asking Newman to prepare 'a minute account of everything' concerning the university for the bishops, Cullen added that 'I hear many complaints about the expenditure of money, and some disciplinary matters'. Although he was sure that 'by a little explanation every thing will be made clear', Cullen cannot have left Newman in any doubt where his concerns lay.[56]

Student discipline and financial rectitude were the two practical issues on which Cullen and Newman most differed. Although an educator himself, Cullen had only had responsibility for a seminary—something rather different in nature from Newman's experiences as an Oxford tutor. The disciplinary regime at the Irish College during Cullen's tenure was stern but nevertheless in keeping with the standards of a seminary in that day and age. Cullen remained above the fray as much as possible, leaving discipline in the hands of Kirby, his vice-rector. Kirby was a born disciplinarian and on more than one occasion students in the college wrote to their bishop or bishops to complain of ill treatment. Student concerns ranged from the withholding of private letters[57] to poor food and the provision of clothing that was 'so bad as to attract the attention of the Romans as they [the students] pass in the street'.[58] Although the Irish bishops consistently cleared the leadership of the Irish College of such charges,[59] there can be little doubt that the environment was strict and demanding.

What Cullen seems to have most objected to in Newman's administration of the Catholic University was his liberality (as Cullen saw such things) towards the students and his willingness to discipline by means of influence and exhortation rather than by rules and regulations.[60] Nor were matters of discipline and expense always separate; Cullen, in early 1856, complained to Kirby that 'Dr Newman expended a very large sum on billiards.'[61] 'I suppose such things are done in Oxford but here it is really too bad for us to throw away the money of the poor on such trifles.'[62] That Newman was pursuing some liberal, Oxford model to the detriment of his students' moral character was a persistent theme of Cullen's. 'Dr Newman has the Oxford system in view. He wishes to leave young men to themselves. This will not do in Ireland[.] The people do not wish to have their children exposed to corruption, they wish to have them under discipline.'[63] And again, 'He appears to think the Oxford system perfect. The students must have great liberty, go hunt etc play billiards smoke cigars, and study just as they like. I think this is not a catholic system—but perhaps it is better to say nothing.'[64]

To a large degree, Newman did have the Oxford system in view on the question of student discipline and moral formation. Or rather, he had in view the Oxford system as he would have wished it to be and had campaigned for it to be. As a young fellow and tutor (from 1826) at Oriel, Newman had been a driving force behind reforms in that college's tutorial system. Instead of all students being assigned at random to a tutor, the tutor himself would be able to select and personally teach a small group of the more gifted or industrious pupils. The 'pass-men' (largely students who had no intellectual pretensions) would be herded together into large groups and taught there. As Dwight Culler has perceptively pointed out, Newman did not have in mind 'those who were less able so much as those who were wilfully idle, and if they were sacrificed one can only say that it was a sacrifice to which they submitted with some alacrity.'[65] The small groups of 'reading-men' would be under the influence of a single tutor for their entire college career. He would take responsibility for both their educational *and* pastoral well-being. In this way, Newman thought, moral (which was inseparable from religious) and educational formation could be achieved in tandem.

Unfortunately, Newman and his tutorial allies Robert Wilberforce and Richard Hurrell Froude had failed to secure the support of Oriel's provost, and their plan failed. Although they did not resign as tutors, Provost Hawkins ensured that Newman, Wilberforce, and Froude were not assigned any more students to teach. Undaunted, Newman would try again at Oxford. He took as his model E. B. Pusey's decision, in 1836, to take some three or four young graduates into his home and give them the run of his substantial library. Because of his wife's poor health, Pusey's experiment came to an end in 1838. However, in that same year Newman purchased a house in St Aldate's and sought to carry on the idea. Residents were given housing and the opportunity to assist with the various academic projects (such as the 'library of the Fathers') of Newman or Pusey. And, of course, in such an intimate environment they could be influenced by Newman. The experiment was not a success, as a college fellowship would always be a more attractive proposition, and a promising young man marked with Tractarianism (as any inmate of St Aldate's would be)[66] was increasingly finding himself at a disadvantage in fellowship elections. Newman's house closed in 1840. The Oriel reforms and the St Aldate's experiment (and Newman's preconversion community at Littlemore) give ample proof to his long-standing belief that discipline and moral supervision was best undertaken in small groups and not in the university as such.

It was a view that Newman would carry with him to Dublin without apology. His insistence that the residents of the Catholic University should be divided up into small groups—which he hoped eventually might become Colleges on the Oxbridge model—was simply another manifestation of that principle. Newman's own 'House' at Harcourt Street was a direct descendant of his earlier attempts at community. So in a sense Cullen was right about Newman's ideas on discipline; Newman had certainly taken his models from his time at Oxford but not from the practice of that university.

Although the question of university discipline divided Cullen and Newman, and further alienated Cullen from Newman, it had little practical effect on the way in which the university was run. Cullen continued to fulminate to Kirby over the issue, and periodically dropped heavy hints to Newman, but he made no effort to intervene directly either on his own account or by manipulating the archbishops' committee. At no time did Cullen instruct Newman to change anything that he was doing in the matter of university discipline. Cullen might have disagreed with Newman's methods, but he seems to have recognised the rector's right to run the university in his own way.

Financial questions, too, served to put further distance between the two men. Cullen had always been for a slow, cautious beginning to the university, as much to preserve resources as anything else. In his *Making of the Roman Catholic Church in Ireland, 1850–1860*, Emmet Larkin has carefully analysed the various, and often conflicting, sources of information about the university's finances in this period and has painted a grim picture. Larkin estimates that by the spring of 1858 some £76,000 had been raised for the university, of which £54,000 had been raised in 1851–52 in the initial collections following the Synod of Thurles. Cullen's collections in 1854, as the bishops began to lose interest as they lost authority, had realised another £11,000. The remaining £11,000 was accounted for by some £6,000 in interest on the monies previously raised and an additional £5,000 in donations. The university, according to Larkin, had already expended something on the order of £36,000 on buildings, faculty, and the like. That left it with a relatively healthy endowment of approximately £40,000. With the low student numbers, however, tuition income and interest on the endowment combined to bring in only some £6,000 per annum. Costs, however, were on the order of £9,000 per year. With a not insignificant deficit of £3,000 a year and no sign that any large amounts could again be raised by appeal, it is hardly surprising that Cullen thought billiards an unnecessary luxury or that he wished Newman to be more careful in the number of appointments he made to the university.[67]

For his part, Newman was not pleased with Cullen's behaviour on financial matters either. Newman had long advocated the establishment of a predominantly lay committee to oversee the university's finances. He felt that the mechanism by which university funds were spent and accounted for was disorganised and did not allow for proper oversight or accountability. He also feared that it might lay him, 'a foreigner', open to 'imputations', perhaps years later, as to how he had spent the money under his control. In Newman's view a committee made up of laymen 'would put an end to this' and 'would conciliate the laity and would interest them in the University more than anything else.' The laity 'were treated', Newman recalled, 'like good little boys—were told to shut their eyes and open their mouths, and take what we give to them—and this they did not relish.'[68] In an effort to gain such a committee, Newman 'in vain repeatedly assailed

Dr. Cullen on the necessity of a Finance Committee—& this was a great source of suspicion, of irritation to him.'[69]

Cullen's views on such a committee are not recorded. It is not difficult to imagine that he might oppose an entirely lay committee (although he was happy enough to encompass a lay element on the university committee), but we do not know why or even if he did. None of his letters to Kirby or to the Propaganda bring up a lay finance committee, and his complaints about Newman on matters of money do not include this issue. Such an entity did make at least a brief appearance in 1853–54 as a subcommittee of the Catholic University committee. Its members were Cullen, Michael Errington, More O'Ferrall, Myles O'Reilly, and Taylor. The subcommittee seems to have met either never (except perhaps once in September 1855)[70] or very infrequently. Certainly Patrick Leahy, who had replaced Taylor on the subcommittee in October 1853, either forgot or never knew he was even a member.[71] At any rate, the subcommittee played no real role in university finances and Cullen did not back it.

After Monsell had finally broken through Cullen's wall of silence, letters came a bit more freely to Newman. Cullen wrote again on 16 September to encourage him in the matter of theological training in the university[72] and brought up directly to Newman for the first time the question of his residence in Dublin, telling him that 'if you were here it would [be] easy to come to a better understanding about every thing.' 'During your absence in the beginning', Cullen continued, 'and before things are settled, it is impossible to know what should be done.'[73] A more strongly worded letter followed on 24 September. In it he told Newman 'that there are great complaints here [Newman was in Birmingham] that no one is doing any thing for the university, and no one is charged to give information about what is to be done next year.' When 'those concerned are asked, they say they have no instructions. I fear that if things are left in this state, we cannot expect any success. I beg and implore of you to take some steps to set things right.'[74]

Unsurprisingly, Newman was not impressed with such exhortations. In 1872 he recorded his reaction to the first of these letters (his remarks are equally applicable to all of Cullen's September letters). Not all of Newman's charges were fair,[75] but it is hard to argue with a number of his points: 'If he [Cullen] wanted information', Newman recalled, 'how could he hope to gain it in the depth of the Long Vacation except from me, yet of me he had asked no questions.' Equally fair was Newman's comment that he did not need Cullen's reminder to prepare a report for the bishops, as he *knew* that Report was coming—and it did appear at the proper time to the length of 52 octavo pages'. And as for the question of his residence, or rather lack of residence, in Dublin, Newman only re-marked, 'How could he expect me to be at Dublin in the Vacation, when I had duties at Birmingham?'[76]

Clearly, Cullen could have gained any information he wished about the university by the simple expedient of writing to Newman himself. Almost desperate for contact with Cullen, Newman would have un-doubtedly provided the archbishop with any information he might have required. It is also difficult to see Cullen's reminder about a report to the bishops as anything other than nagging, as there was never any question that Newman might somehow ignore his duty to produce such a report. What is not so easy to defend was Newman's view on the necessity of his residence in Dublin.

RESIDENCE AND RESIGNATIONS

The conflict between his commitments as rector of the Catholic Univer-sity of Ireland and superior of the Oratory of St Philip Neri in Bir-mingham in many ways overshadowed Newman's years in Dublin. Never able or willing to commit his time and energy totally to one or the other, he instead tried to do what were effectively two full-time and highly de-manding jobs. Cullen without question saw the issue of Newman's resi-dence in Dublin as the most serious problem with the university itself. Questions of discipline, finance, and even the appointment of faculty with Young Ireland sympathies could be overlooked or finessed, but a full-time rector was, to Cullen, an absolute necessity. Newman was cer-tainly aware of Cullen's views on the matter; the archbishop's letter of 16 September (discussed above) was not the only mention of the subject in the autumn of 1855. Word was reaching Newman of Cullen's concern from other sources as well. Edmund O'Reilly, the professor of theology at the CUI, wrote on 12 October to advise Newman 'in confidence that Dr Cullen seems uneasy at your absence and anxious for your return.'[77]

Cullen himself made his position clear that December, when, com-menting on Newman's visit to Rome on Oratory business, he told Tobias Kirby that '[h]is absence is of course a loss to the University' and that Newman was 'so much devoted to his own congregation and to En-gland.'[78] In January 1856, Cullen told Kirby that 'about the time of my return [from Rome, in July 1855] he [Newman] went to England and re-mained there till near the beginning of November.'[79] Newman's university memorandum makes clear the extent of his absences and the unques-tionably large amount of time he dedicated to the affairs of the Oratory.

Cullen was not overestimating the time Newman spent away from Dublin.

Cullen was not the only one worried about Newman's absences. Renouf, writing on 22 January, noted that 'Newman is away on his own business until next month'. As a result, Renouf had 'the care of this house [Newman's Harcourt Street residence] as well as my own lectures to look after.'[80] Unsurprisingly, Newman's reappearance in late February caused Renouf to remark that his 'return has relieved me of a great deal of a[nx]iety.'[81] In only the second full year of the university's operation, Newman had absented himself from it for nearly two months at the beginning of the second term.

By the end of 1856 the problem of Newman's residency was becoming acute. Following the pattern he had set in 1855, Newman 'was not here since the beginning of last June', Cullen told Kirby. 'He spends at least 7 months in England'.[82] Cullen could not see how the university was to be run on such a basis. In the normal course of things, the vice-rector could perhaps have been expected to act on the rector's behalf when pressing Oratory business called Newman away to Birmingham. Unfortunately, Patrick Leahy was, if anything, even more of an absentee than Newman himself. In September 1855, Leahy, long the ailing Slattery's protégé, was appointed his vicar-general and parish priest of Cashel and became the acknowledged heir apparent to the archdiocese of Cashel.[83] Christopher O'Dwyer has neatly summed up the situation in late 1855: 'Leahy held important positions in three different centres, Thurles, Cashel and Dublin. It was impossible for him to fulfil the duties of all three satisfactorily.'[84] With such responsibilities, it seemed unlikely that Leahy could continue to be as active an administrator of the CUI as he had previously been; certainly Leahy himself, in informing Newman of his new position, thought it probable that he should have to quit the university altogether.[85]

As it happened, Leahy did not decide that it was necessary to leave his position as vice-rector in order to take up his new positions in Cashel (although he did finally sever his relationship with Thurles College in December 1855).[86] Instead, he seems to have formed the intention of resigning his new responsibilities and devoting himself fully to the university, telling Newman in March 1856 that 'it is my intention to remain permanently attached to the University & therefore disengage myself altogether' from Cashel. He did, however, have something of a problem in carrying through his aim: 'I am in a difficulty between my duties in the University which, of course, cannot be neglected & my duties here.' 'In his present health', Leahy wrote, 'I cannot make known to Dr Slattery my [intention] to resign my Parish & Vicar-Generalship.'[87] The upshot was that Leahy was going to have to attempt to split his time between his conflicting obligations.

Already unhappy with Newman's erratic residence in Dublin, Cullen was not best pleased to discover that now the vice-rector, too, would not be devoting his full attention to the university. As he remarked to Kirby in November 1856, 'Everything wd. go well if the superiors [Newman and Leahy] wd. mind their business.' 'Dr Newman', Kirby learned, 'goes to England, and gives no directions to Dr Leahy.' And Leahy, for his part, 'spends his time in Cashel where he is P[arish]P[riest].'[88] Cullen spelled out the situation in depth to Kirby near the end of 1856. His letter sheds valuable light not only on his attitude towards both Newman and Leahy—and the entire vexed issue of residence—but also on the state the CUI found itself in only two years after opening its doors. The letter, which was provoked by Leahy requesting that the Propaganda grant him leave to be absent from his parish to attend to university business, deserves to be quoted extensively:

> Dr Leahy is P[arish] P[riest] of Cashel, Dean of the diocese, Vic[ar]. general also. If he get[s] leave to absent himself, the affairs of his parish and diocese will go badly, because Dr Slattery is sick, and for the transaction of business depends almost entirely on Dr Leahy. On the other side if Dr Leahy be not here, the university will be neglected. He is Vice-Rector and professor of scripture, and can not fulfil his duties unless he reside[s] [in Dublin]. . . . Let him resign one or the other position. This wd. be my advice. . . . I know Dr Leahy does not wish to give up his connection with Cashel, because Dr Slattery is likely to last but a short time, and of course his present position as Dean and V[icar] G[eneral] and P[arish] P[riest] give him influence at an election. Yet is a bad thing to establish precedents of an evil tendency.

> Dr Newman is pretty much like Dr Leahy. He has been absent since the 15th of last July altogether with the exception of 3 weeks. Last year I think he did not spend 3 months in Ireland. Dr Leahy was only for 3 or 4 days in Dublin since last July. Things cannot go on well in this way, so at least Dr Leahy ought to be made to reside or resign.[89]

It didn't help matters that on 8 September 1856 Leahy was thrown from his gig and badly hurt. He recuperated in Thurles and managed only one visit to the university between his accident and January 1857.[90] Even when Leahy was in Dublin, he chose to stay in outlying Dalkey—hardly a convenient spot from which to work in St Stephen's Green.[91]

Newman's position was analogous to Leahy's. He had never ceased to think of himself as both rector of the Catholic University and superior of the Birmingham Oratory. Nor can there be any doubt as to which he held to be the more important responsibility: the university, as Newman's memorandum frequently reminds us, was only a temporary task; the Oratory was his life. Thomas Arnold (whom Newman appointed professor of English literature in 1856) caught the depth of Newman's attachment to Birmingham when he told a friend in 1857 that Newman 'never seems quite at his ease in Ireland; his monastery at Birmingham, with its unbroken quiet, and little society but that of his books, is evidently the point where his affections are centered, and to which when away from it, he seems ever gravitating.'[92] When he was first approached about being rector in 1851, Newman had warned Cullen that he was concerned with the effect such an appointment might have on his work in Birmingham: 'What I should desire is, to do as much work for the University as possible with *as little absence as possible from this place.*'[93]

Cullen, as Newman accurately assumed, 'thought, that, with the exception of a fair annual holiday, I ought to be at my post all through the year.' 'He did not', Newman recalled, 'recognise I had duties elsewhere. He thought I ought to give them up.'[94] Newman was of the opinion that Cullen believed that either the 'superior attractions of the Rectorship' would lead to his resignation as superior of the Birmingham Oratory or that a Dublin Oratory could be built either in place of, or as a satellite of, Birmingham.[95] Indeed, as late as May 1856, Cullen rather plaintively told Kirby that if 'an Irish oratory can be established, I will be very happy.'[96] Newman certainly wished for such an establishment in Dublin (and even took some small steps towards such an end), but no permanent foundation was attempted and Newman was quickly drawn back into the increasingly bitter politics of the English Oratory.

The primary cause of trouble in Birmingham was the request made to the Propaganda by F. W. Faber's London Oratory to vary the English Oratorian Rule against the hearing of nuns' confessions. This seemingly trivial variation caused a furore, more because the London house failed to inform Birmingham of its intentions than because of London's desire for such a change. Newman, who had adapted the Oratorian Rule to English conditions, was furious with what he perceived to be Faber's lack of courtesy. He was also concerned that Rome might perceive the London request as having come from the English Oratory as a whole and thus grant a variation of the Rule to both Birmingham and London; Newman wished to retain the prohibition against hearing the confessions of nuns. The disagreement quickly degenerated into a battle of wills between the two houses and relations became increasingly strained. Matters reached such a point that in December 1855 Newman felt it necessary to travel to Rome, in the company of Ambrose St John, to plead his case and attempt to have the two Oratories declared separate entities—as was already the case with the Congregation on the continent. He remained in Rome until February 1856 dealing with the matter, and the dispute festered on for some time.[97]

Whatever the rights and wrongs of the conflict between the Birmingham and London houses, it is clear that Newman felt Oratory business to have a pressing demand on his time; Dublin would have to be fitted in as and when it could be. Newman, at the time and later, was unrepentant about his need to spend so much time in Birmingham (or in Rome on Oratory business) during his university tenure. As he recalled in 1870, 'I do not say that he [Cullen] was not right in wishing for a Rector who had no duties elsewhere; but, if that were his judgement, he ought not to have asked me to be Rector'.[98] Newman's remark is truthful but disingenuous. Obviously, if a full-time rector were wanted, Cullen could have approached somebody other than Newman. By the same token, however, Newman could have (and, on the logic, perhaps should have) refused to accept the position, knowing that it demanded and deserved more time than he could offer to it. Nowhere does Newman seem to acknowledge that a new and by no means strong institution like the Catholic University could not possibly be run by a rector and vice-rector who were only ever in passing residence; rarely has the office of university rector (or president, or whatever the title) been a part-time position. Although Newman gave his all for the university while in Dublin, he could not make up for the simple fact that he was not often there.

Newman's and Leahy's erratic residence was not the only problem facing Cullen and the university in 1856–57. MacHale, after his defeat in May 1854, had not gone quiet or become reconciled to the university or Cullen's control of it. As Cullen remarked to Kirby in late 1855, 'Dr McHale is also ready I believe to give a good growl'.[99] MacHale had reacted poorly to Newman's circular letter to the four archbishops announcing the appointment of various chairs within the new medical school. Newman, at that time (August 1855) largely cut off from communication with Cullen, simply announced the appointments in expectation of the archbishops' approval. MacHale replied with a pertinent question, asking Newman whether 'in forwarding to the archbishops the list . . . you consider it only as a communication of courtesy, or whether it is meant to submit it to their approval?'[100] Newman replied that he was merely acting in accordance with the decrees of the May synod in giving the right of appointment to the Irish episcopate and merely thought it 'seemed respectful' as the bishops as a body had not met to inform the archbishops.[101] Despite its erroneous assignment of the power of appointment to the entire body of Irish bishops (long MacHale's desire),[102] this answer did nothing to placate MacHale. He would remain an enemy of the CUI to the end of his days.

MacHale's animosity had tangible effects, despite Cullen's ability to control the archbishops' committee. As Cullen told Kirby at the end of 1856, 'Dr McHale's opposition has done a great deal of mischief, because he obliges me to leave every thing in the hands of others in order not to provoke attacks from the Lion.'[103] As a trustee of the university, by virtue of his long inactive membership on the university committee, MacHale was, or Newman believed him to be, occasionally required to endorse various cheques (such as from collections) on the university's behalf. Although at first willing to perform such a function, he eventually declined to do even that—informing Newman of the fact via John MacEvilly, soon to be bishop of Galway.[104] Newman's continuing attempts to involve members of the university committee in university finances met with no little annoyance on the part of MacHale and his allies. John Derry, the bishop of Clonfert, wrote to MacHale in May 1856 expressing his support for that part of the British constitution that placed 'expenditure under the control of those whom the payers of taxes appoint to watch it'. In Derry's view the Catholic University was not following such a course, and he remarked that, 'surely, there has been as much latitude already taken, rather than given, in respect to its administration, as could well be endured'.[105] Ironically, MacHale and his allies shared Cullen's concerns about the amount of money being spent on the university. As Cantwell told MacHale in 1857, 'Rome should be informed of such monstrous expenditure by an institution conferring such little benefit.'[106]

Cullen was very much aware of this continued opposition by a small but significant portion of the Irish hierarchy. Although Rome's amendments to the university's statutes had left the supervision of the CUI in the hands of the four archbishops, it nevertheless allowed for periodic meetings of the bishops. The first of these meetings since the opening of the university was scheduled for the early summer of 1856. It would be there that MacHale, Cantwell, and their remaining supporters could muster an attack on the university and, through it, on their real target: Cullen. Newman, now largely cut off from the sympathy of the archbishop of Dublin, would be forced to face alone a meeting that would associate him inextricably with Cullen and where he might be seen as a fit subject of attack as a result.

The risks the bishops' meeting posed were well understood by Cullen. 'I suppose', he wrote to Kirby, 'we shall have a great deal of trouble.' Newman would be 'assailed left and right' and the 'lion wd. root up the whole business very probably if he were allowed.' Cullen knew he would have to put aside his own problems with Newman and back the rector: 'I do not approve of many things done by Dr. N[ewman] yet in general he must be supported.' After all, the 'University will certainly succeed if it be only let alone. Of course everything is not as one wd. wish, but yet the whole thing is going on, and will by degrees assume a proper shape.'[107] Cullen himself warned Newman, not entirely sympathetically, of the reception he might expect: 'I fear some one or two prelates may not appear kind—but you must bear a cross as well as every one else.'[108]

The assembled Irish hierarchy met in Dublin on 20 June to discuss various matters of mutual concern, including Maynooth and the problems then facing the Irish College in Paris. The week started poorly, with both MacHale and Derry snubbing a dinner for the bishops hosted by Cullen. The university was not dealt with until the twenty-sixth of the month, once all other issues had been dealt with. Cullen's secretary, C. B. Lyons, described the meeting for Kirby. 'Dr Newman was called before their Lordships and spoke for about an hour.' He was greeted courteously, and, on entering the room 'all the Bishops, except two or three, rose up and most graciously bowed to him.' It seems he spoke well, and 'so much pleased' the assembled prelates with his report on the university that, 'on retiring, all, including Dr. MacHale, stood up and bowed.'[109] Newman, who had prepared himself for an onslaught from MacHale, was surprised when the archbishop of Tuam 'kept a dead silence' and Derry limited himself to a few courteous questions.[110]

Despite Newman's triumph, the meeting itself did little to resolve the dissension within the hierarchy. MacHale, however, was revealed to be a leader with almost no followers, causing Cullen gleefully to comment, 'Everything terminated most happily—Poor Dr McH[ale] had no party to support him—his followers were scarcely more then Dr Derry and sometimes one or two others.'[111] On a practical level the only decision taken of any consequence for the university was formally to delegate, in Cantwell's words, to the 'archbishops and the Rector until our next meeting the entire management of the University'[112]—something that Rome had already effectively commanded in late 1854.

Cullen had every right to be relieved after the bishops' meeting. There was no prospect that MacHale would give up his opposition, but both the university and its rector had passed the trial with flying colours and he himself had further consolidated his position as the single most powerful man in the Irish church. The successful termination of the meeting must also have come as an enormous mental relief for Cullen. Throughout 1856 he had been plagued by ill health. In January he had complained of insomnia in a letter to Kirby,[113] and, later that same month, of being 'laid up with rheumatism'. 'I am becoming', Cullen wrote, 'good for nothing, and I am afraid of my own shadow. I have lost all courage about every thing.'[114]

The state of Cullen's health was closely linked to the state of his mind. Throughout his life, he would feel the most acute mental anguish under pressure (see, for example, his letter to Walsh at the time of the charitable bequests controversy in 1844). This stress, bordering occasionally on despair, would often manifest itself in bouts of insomnia. The meeting of the bishops was the occasion for another serious period of depression and sleeplessness. As Lyons reported to Kirby near the end of the meeting, 'another week such as the past would send him to his grave'. Besides the 'fatigue in preparing for the meetings and sitting so long at them', such was Cullen's 'anxiety of mind, that he had no sleep for the last 8 or 9 nights.'[115] Cullen's illness appears to have been reasonably common knowledge in Dublin; certainly Newman was aware of the situation, telling Ambrose St John, 'Poor Dr Cullen gets no sleep at night. It is very serious.'[116] Newman, of course, was no stranger to mental breakdowns; to the surprise of all he had taken a third in his Oxford examinations as a result of an almost total collapse brought on by stress and overwork. Although Cullen would recover quickly after the meeting, the precarious state of his health and nerves would lead, in the summer of 1858, to a much more serious episode.

Things were not all bad, however, with the university itself during this period. In addition to the successful bishops meeting, the medical school on Cecilia Street was proving to be a stunning success, as it would continue to be throughout the university's history. As Cullen told Kirby in November 1856, the medical school expected 'to have about 80 pupils' when it opened later that month.[117] Such an intake was all the more impressive considering that the main university had only enrolled some twenty-five students in the 1855–56 academic year and twenty-eight the following year.[118] Cullen was no less impressed with the faculty Newman had chosen, telling Kirby, 'The professors are excellent, all good Catholics and Irish.' Later in the same letter, he referred to the medical school as the 'best in Dublin.'[119]

Traditionally, a university consisted of at least three of four faculties: arts, law, theology, and medicine. From the beginning Newman intended that the Catholic University should come to include all of them. After arts (which began with the university), the next faculty to be fully created was medicine. There was a clear need for a Catholic medical school in Dublin (Newman noted in his 1855–56 report to the bishops that of III doctors 'in situations of trust and authority' in Dublin only twelve were Catholics),[120] but it was by no means obvious that a medical school would be the university's first substantial expansion. Circumstances, however, proved favourable, and a ready-made facility came on to the market in late 1854. A medical school had been established in Cecilia Street in 1837 and had received the necessary recognition from the Royal College of Surgeons of Ireland. In Ireland at that time it was not necessary to attend a university (chartered or otherwise) to become a doctor. Rather, it was necessary to attend an approved course of lectures at an approved institution. This allowed the successful student to enter his name on the medical register and to be eligible for professional examinations.

Although the Cecilia Street school had flourished in its early years, by 1854 it was up for sale. Through an intermediary (Andrew Ellis, later professor of surgery), Newman arranged to purchase the building and its contents for £1,500. The school formally opened in November 1855 with thirty-six students. At first there was no guarantee that the vital recognition that had been given to the Cecilia Street school would be extended to the Catholic University medical school. Competition was fierce; there were a number of other 'private' medical schools in Dublin as well as successful faculties at each of the Queen's Colleges. Nevertheless, in mid-1856 the Royal College of Surgeons extended its recognition to the new school. From then on, its success was assured and the medical school of the Catholic University went from strength to strength— even while the university itself teetered on the brink of collapse.[121]

The rest of the university was to prove something of a disappointment to Cullen as 1856 wore on. As he told Kirby, 'the other classes are not going on so well' as was the school of medicine. Cullen then gave vent to an extraordinarily intemperate attack on the English and on Newman. In terms that would have done MacHale proud, he told Kirby that it had been 'a mistake to let Englishmen have anything to do in the concern.' Indulging a favourite complaint that England had contributed little financially to the university, Cullen wrote that the English 'wd. be happy to take all the advantages and management of it—but they will give no money.' Nor did he think that English professors could 'succeed here' as it was 'useless to try to serve two masters.'[122] In his frustration Cullen was effectively declaring that, on the issue of nationality, MacHale had been right all along. Not, of course, that he would ever admit such a thing in so many words.

Nor did Newman escape Cullen's condemnation of the English. Noting that Newman had spent some seven months in England in 1856, Cullen wrote that there 'his English minions of the Tablet are writing that I am ruining the university, going to sell it to the government etc.' 'It wd. be well', Cullen concluded, 'for the university if he were made Bishop in England.'[123] Cullen was furious with *The Tablet*, which despite Lucas's premature death continued to pursue the archbishop of Dublin with ever-mounting passion. A typical letter, signed 'Catholicus', rehashed many of the old charges against Cullen and even introduced a few new ones. 'Catholicus' went so far as to allege that, as '[a]ll Dr Cullen's friends are rich graziers', the archbishop, when he travelled in rural Ireland, 'sees nothing but rich land and still richer kin: he does not see the exterminator at work, and hence he believes Ireland to be a very paradise.'[124] Linking Cullen and his family to the landlord class (a charge that would be made many times in future years) was not only unfair and damaging but also inaccurate; it was little wonder that Cullen was incensed.

Cullen's frustration with Newman continued to grow during 1856, even as it became clear that Newman intended to resign the rectorship sometime in 1857. Cullen's complaints ranged from the fair—residency, expenditure, the short lease (in Newman's own name) of Pollen's exquisite university church[125]—to the debatable question of university discipline, to the patently unfair association of Newman with *The Tablet* and its attacks on him. Indeed, his first reaction to the rumours that Newman actually intended to put into effect his long-expressed intention to resign[126] was one of relief, despite the fact that he knew Newman's name 'does us good.'[127] As he told Kirby on 13 December 1856: 'Dr Newman says himself that he will remain here only one year longer, as he cannot neglect the affairs of the oratory.' 'If he goes of his own accord,' Cullen wrote, 'we shall have the merit of having called him, and at the same time we shall be able to get somebody to reside here, and to work for us not for the oratory or England.'[128] And, as late as February 1857, Cullen still hoped that Newman 'will resign next summer so that we may have some one here on the spot.' 'It is hopeless', he told Kirby, 'to go on without a head.'[129]

THE FIRST RESIGNATION AND THE IRISH REACTION

Newman's frustration with his circumstances combined with the continuing press of Oratory business caused him to consider his options. As Fergal McGrath has remarked, Newman's correspondence after he returned to

Dublin on 24 October 1856, and even before, 'is overshadowed by the prospect of his inevitable resignation'.[130] As he told Wilberforce on 21 October, 'my work I trust is getting to an end' on behalf of the university.[131]

Newman had a strong sense of having spent enough time in the cause of the Catholic University. To Wilberforce he explained that 'my third and last year of residence is beginning, which will make my sixth of active exertion'. 'Six years', Newman wrote, 'is a long time in any man's life and a serious portion of a man's who is between 50 and 60.'[132] That describing his time in Dublin as 'residence' was a debatable use of the word and that he had hardly been called upon actively to exert himself (except in small bursts) on behalf of the university until early 1854 is beside the point: Newman was determined to go. 'I cannot conceive that I shall be formally told to go on—and to any thing but a formal order I shall be insensible.' He did, however, leave open a small hole, writing that '[i]f I am driven into a corner, from the urgency of those who wish me to stay, I shall insist on quasi non-residence'.[133]

Newman thought he had enemies all around him in late 1856, and his mood was quite close to despair; at one point in late October he compared himself to Job.[134] As he told Wilberforce on 25 October (the day after he returned to Dublin), 'I never was so surrounded with troubles as I am now.' Those troubles included an extensive debt of some £6000, contracted under his own name, on the University Church and a smaller debt of £300 for his own Dublin students' residence. Moreover, 'No one helps me at all—Except Dr Dixon and Dr Moriarty, no one seems to say a good word for me.' 'And', he added, 'I much fear that in England I have secret enemies.'[135] 'The only way I can get all these things off my mind, is by taking them as coming directly from the Evil Spirit—and forgetting all human instruments.' He longed to get back to Birmingham and leave his cares in Dublin behind. 'I am wanted', he told Wilberforce, 'at Birmingham more than I can express. At the age of 56, as I shall be next year, I may demand to return to that home to which the Holy Father has by his brief consigned me for life.'[136] As he told Ambrose St John, 'I think my friends will look very black here at the notion of my leaving, but, please God, I will carry it out.'[137]

As he contemplated his resignation, all Newman's old bitterness over how he had been treated came welling up to the surface. In a letter to Laurence Forde, the professor of canon law and a Cullen ally, Newman laid out his grievances:

> I was first applied to with a view to my presiding over the University and brought over in 1851; yet full three years past [*sic*] before I

was called over to commence my duties here. During that three years, in spite of my continual remonstrances, I was kept in such continual suspense, that for months my portmanteau remained packed in my room, ready for a start which never took place. Since I came here, I scarcely have got a question answered or a request complied with, without a series of efforts which might have sufficed for ten times the work done. I have asked for persons to advise with, and, instead of getting them, have been only accused of acting without advice. I have earnestly desired to have nothing to do with money for my operations, have a cheque returned on me by one person in authority [MacHale], and a notice from another [Slattery] that he would not sign any more. I have been forced to build a Church at my own risk, and then not been able to gain a loan from the University for a portion of its expenses. And all this when I have been urgently wanted by my House in England which I have left for no object of my own.[138]

With all this ill-use in the past, Newman felt, as he told St John, that he was now only coming to Dublin to 'be repelled by Dr McHale and worn away by Dr Cullen.'[139] It can be little wonder that he yearned to lay down the cares of university affairs and return to Birmingham.

Newman was not disinterested, in 1856–57 or later, about the fate of 'his' university. As he considered his forthcoming resignation, his prime concern was for who might succeed him as rector. His own favourite was David Moriarty, his one real friend among the Irish bishops.[140] As he somewhat cryptically told Flanagan, 'if we do not get a strong buffer (Dr M.) [Moriarty] the engine (Dr C.) [Cullen] will recoil on the train, (the University)'.[141] Newman wrote to Moriarty directly, putting his case and, in the process, adumbrating some of his own grievances:

If I longed a year ago for some one like yourself to be Rector, much more do I desire it now. I very much fear some collision in time to come, between bodies so distinct as the Hierarchy and the University, when the latter has come into shape, unless the Rector is a connecting link between the two—and this can only be, when he is both a Bishop and an Irishman. You alone can amalgamate the various elements of the University—you alone can render them duly subordinate to the Bishops. For myself, even were I Bishop and Irishman, I have not the talent of ruling. I never had—I never ruled—I never have been in a position of authority before—I can begin things—and I never aspired to do more. The time is come, even independent of my having determined it years ago, over and above my increasing years, over and above the extreme needs of my Congregation here, (which will go near to be ruined, if I am much longer absent) it is, for the reason I have mentioned, the time for me to retire, because I have done my work, and cannot do the work which lies before me.[142]

Moriarty quickly disclaimed any idea of becoming rector. He advanced a number of more or less plausible reasons why he could not take the job, ranging from his desire that Newman remain, to his preference for an English rector ('there is a momentum in the Englishman which is as sure to conquer now as in the days of Strongbow, and Irishmen will more easily unite in submission to what is English'),[143] to his own inexperience and unsuitability. Significantly, he also told Newman that he was unlikely to be able to 'get on in Dublin.' 'With the Angel of that Church [Cullen] I agree in theological opinions and in views of Ecclesiastical policy, but not in the estimate he forms of many of the men around us, and as he appears rather intolerant I fear he would not tolerate my latitudinarian ways';[144] quite a sensible view given Moriarty's backing of the Pigot appointment. In any event, Cullen would not have approved of Moriarty as rector; of Dixon's suggestion of him for the post in July 1857, Cullen remarked to Kirby, 'Were he not such a young Irelander he wd. do admirably well.'[145]

Newman held off formally announcing his intention to resign until early April 1857. Before leaving for England for most of the month, he wrote to each of the bishops and archbishops of Ireland to declare his intent and explain his reasons. To Cullen, Newman wrote that the 'time is now approaching for the resignation of the high office which the Bishops of Ireland have so condescendingly committed to me.' His resignation was to be effective as of 14 November that same year, 'when the six years will be more than completed since I began to devote my thoughts and exertions to the service of the University, and the term of absence from my Congregation will have arrived for which I have asked permission.' 'My most urgent reasons for this step are,' Cullen learned, 'the fatigue which I experience from my frequent passages between Dublin and Birmingham, the duty of the Rector to show himself in public more than my strength will allow, for the good of the University' and for the good of the Oratory.[146] The other Irish prelates received similar letters.

Almost immediately, Newman was pressed by various members of the Irish church to reconsider; MacHale and his allies, however, remained pointedly silent. The bishop of Elphin, George Browne, told Newman that he still hoped 'that the Archbishop of Dublin & other Prelates may devise some means of averting the separation.' 'Your loss to the University will be irremediable.'[147] John Leahy in Dromore agreed, telling Newman, 'Your name is in itself a mainstay to the University and if you leave it I fear it will at once sink in public estimation.'[148] Indeed, the damage Newman's departure would do to the Catholic University was a common theme of those bishops who wrote to him. Dominic O'Brien, the recently appointed bishop of Waterford,[149] told Newman that so 'dreadful a blow to a young & struggling institution was not expected.' 'Perhaps there is yet time to avert it, and you may be induced to relent and defer your intended resignation to some other time.'[150] Patrick Leahy, busy in Cashel after Archbishop Slattery's death, wrote to tell Newman that 'Your separation from the University in its present infant state would be most injurious, if not fatal, to its best interests.'[151] But Moriarty, writing from Kerry, offered Newman a glimmer of hope for the future if he were to consent to stay on in Dublin: 'I suppose Dr Leahy will be ArBp of Cashel.' 'He ought to know the wants of the University & your difficulties, and his position would enable him to give you that help . . . which we should have, but have not received from the Episcopal body.'[152]

In the meantime Newman had his own letter of resignation augmented with one from the Oratory compelling him to return. '[W]e hereby unanimously determine', the Birmingham Fathers wrote, 'in General Congregation assembled, that his [Newman's] leave of absence shall end, and that in virtue of obedience to St Philip he must return to us.'[153] As he told St John, 'The Decree will strengthen my hands uncommonly.'[154] By making his resignation into a question of obedience, Newman complicated the situation dramatically. Now, if Cullen, Leahy, or another archbishop wished him to stay, they had to negotiate with the Oratory as a body. Of course Newman, whatever decrees the Fathers might issue, controlled the Oratory, and it is impossible to believe that he could not have arranged their approval to stay on in Dublin if he so wished. As a negotiating tactic, however, the Oratory's letter of recall was invaluable.

As for Cullen, he made no immediate move towards changing Newman's mind. He appears not to have written to Newman in Birmingham; on 18 April Newman told Wilberforce that 'Dr Cullen writeth not—nor of course McHale.'[155] He instead chose to make his appeal personally, calling on Newman at Harcourt Street on 12 May. Newman's report of the meeting to Ambrose St John makes interesting reading and shows exactly how seriously Cullen now took the impending departure of his rector.

'The poor Archbishop', Newman wrote, 'is just gone—I say "poor", because he was evidently so nervous and distressed, as to melt me internally, though I was very still or very much moved, both at once perhaps, during the short interview.' Cullen first 'begged me to stop, for everyone said I must—for three years more, so as to make six from the opening of the University.' Unimpressed with the archbishop's arithmetic, Newman 'reminded him how I had urged him to begin sooner, for I had lost my first years in waiting.' 'Also,' he told St John, 'that I told him a year ago what was to be.' Cullen went on to suggest that the Propaganda could arrange a dispensation from residence at Birmingham, but Newman told him that that 'the whole Oratory would go off to Rome to present in person an expostulation, rather than let such dispensation pass sub silentio.' Blocked, Cullen then allowed that 'some arrangement perhaps might be made, by which I should be more time at Birmingham—and a Vice Rector who might reside always [at Dublin].' 'Lastly', Newman wrote, 'he said that perhaps some of the Bishops, perhaps an Archbishop, might write to the Birmingham Congregation.' Newman replied that he was sure the Oratorian Fathers would be grateful for such a letter. 'All this took place', Newman informed St John, 'with pauses of silence on my part and his'.[156] It must have been an extraordinary interview.

Leahy, now the archbishop designate of Cashel, had called on Newman earlier that same day to plead for him to reconsider. Newman simply brandished the letter from Birmingham ordering his return; he told Ambrose St John that 'your Decree has done me incalculable service.' Leahy then suggested, as Cullen would, that an archbishop or archbishops should write to the Oratory. Newman gave him little hope (although Leahy himself never entirely gave up on persuading Newman to stay),[157] and the idea of his being a partially resident rector was not, according to Newman's account of the meeting, raised by either man.[158]

Cullen, at least, seems to have come away from the meeting believing that he had failed to persuade Newman to stay on as rector. As he told Kirby on 21 May, 'Dr Newman persists on going away.' 'I tried to persuade him to remain but in vain.' He then reported Newman's fear that 'his order in England is going to pieces' and allowed that 'you see there are good grounds for his going.' 'Besides he is a little piccato [piqued] because I did not purchase the [university] church or get some one to purchase it for him.'[159]

With Newman seemingly intent on his departure, Cullen turned to the question of who might replace him. 'It will be difficult', he told Kirby, 'to get a new Rector—I dare say it wd. be better to get one of the Archbishops to assume the name.' Cullen then reminded Kirby that he himself, on the suggestion of Archbishop Hughes of New York, had in 1851 considered becoming rector.[160] He had only been dissuaded because he thought 'Dr Murray might take it ill.' However, if 'either Dr Leahy or Dr Dixon wd now take the title and give the sanction of their name I wd. be perfectly satisfied.' Cullen did not imagine that such an archiepiscopal rector could be a day-to-day head of the university, but rather supposed he 'visit once a month and see how things go on.' Failing such an appointment, Cullen thought that 'one of the Archbishops sd. be appointed Cancelliere [chancellor] and retain some power over all the superiors and professors.'[161]

In a letter to Kirby some two weeks later, he again brought up Archbishop Hughes's comments in 1851 on the subject of the rectorship. Apparently, the archbishop of New York had believed that 'we committed a great mistake in appointing Dr Newman' and that 'one of the Bishops or Archbishops sd have been at least nominally at the head—in this way more support and greater subscriptions would be had.' With hindsight, Cullen agreed with Hughes: 'I have no doubt that we ought now to correct that mistake.' He confided to his friend that 'Dr Leahy having been vice rector might now in case of a vacancy become Rector.' 'It wd.', Cullen wrote, 'be only a nominal thing, and he could look in once a month.' It was in this way, Cullen thought, that 'the departure of Dr Newman wd. not be felt.'[162]

Patrick Leahy was thinking along the same lines as Cullen. In a letter of 25 May, he urged Cullen himself to assume the rectorship by virtue of his being apostolic delegate, archbishop of Dublin, and '[b]ecause you will always be on the spot.' If, however, Cullen was unwilling, Leahy would accept the job if Cullen 'thought it would tend in any way to the advantage of the University . . . that I should be Rector'. He would return to the university, though, 'only on condition that you should be the recognised Head of the University by assuming the office of Chancellor'. Leahy was even willing, 'if you were Rector', to remain as vice-rector and manage the university during Cullen's absences from Dublin.[163] These plans never reached fruition, as both men renewed their efforts to retain Newman's services.

When they separately visited Newman on 12 May, both Leahy and Cullen had mentioned the possibility of an official appeal by at least some of the archbishops to the Birmingham Oratory for Newman to continue in some fashion as rector. It is apparent from his letters to Kirby that Cullen was not entirely enthusiastic about such a course. After Newman had rejected his own plea to remain, Cullen was less than keen to try again. Nor was he impressed by some aspects of the campaign to urge Newman's continued tenure. When such talk emanated from English sources, as it often did, it especially roused Cullen's ire. 'I think', Cullen wrote to Kirby, 'the English are doing everything in their power to excite a great business about Dr Newman.' They were even 'talking of petitioning the Pope etc to make him remain here.' Of course, Cullen himself had contemplated such an action, but it bothered him that 'people that never gave a shilling to the university are now all zeal for Dr Newman's remaining.' Apparently, these Englishmen believed that 'no one in Ireland can do anything etc etc.' Frustrated with such people, Cullen even threatened to write 'a little expose to the cardinal [presumably Barnabò, who had succeeded Fransoni as cardinal prefect of the Propaganda], so that he may see that all that glitters is not gold.' Of course, 'Dr Newman himself is very good and very talented, but his way of management can scarcely bring us to any good.'[164]

Despite his disappointment with Newman's management of the university (not to mention the vexed question of his residence in Dublin), Cullen nevertheless resolved to try once more to secure his continued service. By July 1857 he seems to have come to believe that there was at least a hope that Newman might change his mind. Writing to Kirby, he noted that Newman 'appears very sore',[165] but he nonetheless thought that 'Dr Newman does not intend to go.' Newman's reason, Cullen speculated, was that 'he heard, I think, that I complained of his being absent so often, and he wishes to have his absence approved of by the bishops.'[166] Such approval would be implicit in any agreement that allowed Newman to remain as a part-time rector. As Newman never seems to have felt any guilt about the time he spent in Birmingham and away from Dublin, it is unlikely that Cullen was correct in his assessment of Newman's motives. However, Cullen was correct in believing that Newman might be willing to stay on as rector, at least temporarily, if he were formally allowed to limit his residence in Dublin as he saw fit.

In an effort to resolve the question of the rectorship, three of the four archbishops met in Dublin on 22 July. MacHale's absence was felt ('what can be done if he will not act with us'? Cullen asked), as it eliminated the possibility, however faint, that the archbishops could come to some sort of unanimous decision about the university. Dixon, Leahy, and Cullen did agree, however, to 'write to the Oratory to beg that Dr Newman wd continue'. They also offered to 'purchase his church—and to take it ourselves', an important concession to Newman himself.[167] If, however, Newman were to refuse to continue on as rector, the archbishops agreed to meet again in late August to appoint a new one.

Newman had himself been dropping broad hints for some time that he could be persuaded to stay in Dublin if the circumstances were right. Writing to Leahy on the subject of Leahy's replacement as vice-rector, Newman referred to the possibility that 'at length an arrangement were made which contemplated my continuance here with less residence'.[168] He was anxious for the archbishops to write to Birmingham; he told Dixon that he had heard that Leahy had proposed 'six weeks or two months ago to write to the Oratory on the subject' of his continued residence and strongly implied he would welcome such a letter. Newman was aware of the strength of his position. On 23 July he told Thomas Arnold (the convert son of Dr Arnold of Rugby and the brother of Matthew Arnold), whose appointment as professor of English literature Cullen had opposed on grounds of cost,[169] that 'I don't think that there is the least doubt of your election—not only because I have not heard a word against it—but because they seem to want me, and I positively will have not a word to say to them unless you have the Professorship.'[170] His letters for this period make it clear that Newman was perfectly prepared to remain in post, but only if the archbishops asked him (via the Oratory), and only if he were allowed to be a nonresident rector.

The content of the archbishops' letter, when it finally appeared, came as something of a disappointment to Newman. He was pleased with the offer (made in a separate letter of Leahy's on 20 July) to purchase the university church, but he was less pleased with their failure to mention the possibility of his being a nonresident rector in the letter to the Oratory.[171] As he explained to James Hope-Scott: 'the three Archbishops write to ask to have me *as hitherto*—and do not hint at non-residence'. This was, Newman wrote, 'simply impossible.' 'We [the Oratory] do not oppose the continuance of my Rectorship,' he continued, 'but my residence in Dublin.'[172]

The response of the Oratory, drafted by Newman personally,[173] was to respectfully decline the archbishops' request, citing the damage that the Oratory would suffer should Newman continue on in Dublin as he was.[174] He was anxious that some compromise be reached, however, and hinted as much in a separate letter to Leahy.[175] He told the archbishop of Cashel that he was surprised by the failure of the archbishops' letter to suggest 'some middle plan' as he had confidently expected. He closed his letter to Leahy with another hint of his openness to such a plan: 'Had some measure of compromise been proposed, I should have sent you some point of detail about the University. . . . This, alas, is unnecessary now.'[176] Leahy believed that such a compromise might prove acceptable. He told Cullen that were 'Dr Newman such [a partially resident rector], you would have all the conveniences, whatever they may be, of his exercising supreme control over everything, and you could have some of the compensatory advantages of his presence.'[177]

Presumably with Cullen's approval, Leahy wrote back to disclaim any intention on the part of the archbishops to preclude the possibility of a limited residence. He told Newman that his own impression of the letter was 'that we simply asked the Fathers to consent to your continuing to fill the office of Rector of the University without saying whether you would be expected to devote as much time to it as heretofore, or what time, or upon what conditions.' He went on to tell Newman that the archbishops had not considered the issue because they were unaware that Newman might entertain such an option.[178] On receipt of this letter, Newman made his offer explicit to Leahy, telling the archbishop that he thought the Oratory could tolerate his absence in Dublin for some nine weeks per academic year for two such years.[179]

After consulting Cullen and Dixon, Leahy replied that the archbishops 'will gladly try for One Session [year] the "middle plan" suggested in your Letter to me, releasing you from permanent residence in the University and from residence for any longer time than you have indicated.' If the experiment proved successful it could be extended for another year.[180] As sweeteners, Leahy informed Newman that the archbishops had accepted his terms for the purchase of the university church, and, in a second letter, that they had tentatively accepted the appointments of Arnold and Denis Florence MacCarthy (as professor of architecture) to the CUI faculty.[181] Newman had won an almost total victory. He could continue as rector in name and thus help protect the university from the damage he knew his departure would cause; yet he could also give his nearly full attention to Birmingham and the troubled state of the Oratory. He even gained the purchase of the university church and the appointment of Arnold and MacCarthy, two things that Cullen had long either delayed or refused to contemplate.

On the other hand, Cullen gained very little from this agreement with Newman. Long unhappy with Newman's erratic residence and free-spending habits, he had capitulated on both counts. What he gained was a reprieve from having to select a new rector. He knew how difficult that would be, and how much value Newman's name gave to the university; as long as Newman appeared as its rector, the Catholic University of Ireland was a serious concern. If he left, nobody knew what it might be. Cullen, then, in the timeless Roman fashion postponed the inevitable and bought time for his cherished university. It was not a compromise that could last long, and the deal quickly unraveled. In the end, the 'middle plan' only postponed Newman's departure by slightly over a year.

THE LAST YEAR

With Newman's all-but-total departure from university affairs, 1858 saw the end of the Catholic University of Ireland as a growing, vital entity. Newman's name, and the attention it attracted, served as an assurance to a sceptical public that the CUI was more than merely a small struggling college in a glorious house on St Stephen's Green, more than an eminent and oversized faculty teaching ever fewer students (except of medicine). All concerned knew that the university was in crisis, but no one seems to have been able to find a way to resolve that crisis. Newman's final year as rector, the academic year 1857–58, brought into ever clearer focus the conflicts and controversies that had dogged the Catholic University from its inception.

As he had gained permission to do, Newman was seldom in Ireland. His intention, on proposing and tentatively accepting the 'middle plan', had been that a new vice-rector, replacing Leahy, would assume his own day-to-day responsibilities. He made this quite clear in his negotiations with the archbishops in August 1857. He told Leahy that the feasibility of him becoming a nonresident rector 'would depend nearly entirely upon the selection made by your Graces of the Vice Rector, which, if the Rector is not to be in continual residence, is the cardinal point of the whole arrangement.'[182] Newman reinforced this point again upon being informed by Leahy that the archbishops were willing to accept his proposals as to his own status. 'I wish to urge upon your Graces', Newman wrote, 'that the success of the attempt depends on the person to be selected for the Vice Rector.' 'It must be one in whom both the Professors and the Rector can place confidence, else I shall despair of being able to make the arrangement work.'[183]

Unsurprisingly, and as it always had before, the issue of who should be vice-rector proved to be contentious. Hints of the problem came in a letter from Leahy to Newman in mid-September. The archbishop of Cashel asked whether Newman had any objection to Laurence Forde, the professor of canon law and a priest, as vice-rector (Forde had already served as acting vice-rector when Leahy was ill).[184] If he did have an objection to Forde, Leahy asked Newman to suggest to the archbishops 'the names of two or three Irish Priests, residing in Ireland, from amongst whom they may choose a Vice-Rector.'[185] Leahy's insistence on a clerical vice-rector would prove the sticking point.

At first, Newman complied with Leahy's request and submitted only clerical names to the archbishops. He omitted any mention of Forde, thus implicitly announcing his objection to the appointment.[186]

Newman was not pleased to be forced to limit his suggestions to priests. In a memorandum drawn up on 17 September 1857, Newman observed that he would have preferred to nominate someone already a professor or official of the university, but was precluded from doing so by the terms of Leahy's request.[187] The October meeting of the archbishops passed without a nomination being made, and Newman complained to Leahy that he could not even appoint a pro–vice-rector of his own choice, being limited by the archbishops to the four clerical university officials. And, as Fergal McGrath has pointed out, one of these had refused, one was away, and the other two were in Newman's opinion unqualified.[188]

Newman had a candidate of his own in mind, and he was not a priest. Edward Butler had been one of Newman's original appointees to the university as professor of mathematics and had been elected dean of the Faculty of Philosophy and Letters by the members of that faculty in late 1856.[189] Newman had first proposed Butler for the post of vice-rector to Cullen shortly after Leahy's resignation in the spring of 1857. Although Newman's letter to Cullen on the subject does not appear to have survived, Cullen later informed Kirby that 'Dr Newman wrote a long letter urging the necessity of having a lay Vice R[ector] he proposes a Mr Butler. Were this done, the clergy wd. not subscribe.' Newman 'appears to wish to make everything secular.' Cullen had no intention of appointing of lay vice-rector, and told Kirby, 'I will never consent to such a thing.'[190]

Unfortunately, Cullen never made his categorical opposition to a lay vice-rector clear to either Newman or Butler. In mid-November 1857, Butler was advised by Newman that it 'is our wisdom to make Dr Cullen our friend, to stick by him, and please him, not caring what any one else says.' Newman knew that he himself was unable to do much good with Cullen, as he believed that Cullen was incapable of intimacy or trust with an Englishman. Nevertheless, Newman informed Butler, 'I am sure he likes you' and that Butler would be well advised to cultivate that liking in order to secure both his appointment and his success as vice-rector. In a spectacular misreading of Cullen's character, Newman even told Butler that the archbishop 'will respect a layman more than a priest.'[191] Cullen did nothing to dissuade either man from their impression that he was at least open to persuasion. In a letter to Newman in early December, Butler reported that he had come away from a meeting with the archbishop with the impression that 'he has not his mind made up on the point of a lay or clerical Vice-Rector.'[192]

In fact, Cullen had never changed his view. Nor, it must be said, was there any support for the notion of a lay vice-rector among the other archbishops (excluding, as always, MacHale, who was not participating). Although he disagreed with Cullen on some issues of university governance, Leahy was unwilling to appoint a layman to the post; Dixon would simply, and as always, do as he was told. Depending as it did on the (ever-dwindling) contributions solicited by the clergy, the university needed to remain, and visibly remain, under clerical control. That being the case, there was never any real prospect of Butler being appointed, a fact he came to accept by early January 1858.[193]

Newman entered 1858 with a mounting sense of futility. Although he was hardly in residence at Dublin, he was kept in close touch by his correspondents and was continually consulted about university business by Thomas Scratton and Butler. His frustration with the archbishops' failure to appoint a vice-rector led to him informing Leahy in early February that he would no longer accept his salary as rector.[194] And his letters indicate that he was once again considering immediate resignation from the university.[195] It was not until May 1858 that the archbishops informed Newman of the reasons for the delay in appointing a vice-rector. Leahy told him that 'months ago' the archbishops had appointed Dr Matthew Kelly, the professor of ecclesiastical history at Maynooth, as vice-rector, but he had declined, changed his mind, and then declined again. Kelly had been Cullen's choice for the vacant presidency at Maynooth. However, to Cullen's fury the lay trustees on the Maynooth board had preferred Charles Russell for the post.[196] Edmund O'Reilly, too, was appointed by the archbishops, but declined. 'It is very difficult', Leahy wrote, 'to get a fit person.'[197]

Meanwhile, the university was in an even worse state than it had been in the 1856–57 academic year. At least in that period Newman was semi-resident in Dublin and Leahy was able to make occasional appearances. Now, however, Newman was by agreement almost totally nonresident and there was no vice-rector at all. Discipline began to break down (something Newman himself acknowledged),[198] and Cullen was confirmed in his fears about student behaviour in such a 'lax' environment. With Newman only in Dublin for some thirty-three days during the 1857–58 academic year—29 October 1857 to 18 November 1857 and 24 October 1858 to 4 November 1858[199]—it was impossible, despite frequent letters across the Irish sea, for him to remain in anything like control of the university.

Cullen and Leahy, the only two prelates who retained any real interest in the university, were well aware that things had reached a crisis point. They were unable to locate an acceptable vice-rector; MacHale continued his opposition to anything and everything emanating from Dublin; collections had almost totally dried up while expenses remained high; student numbers, except in the medical school, were low and getting lower; and it was clear that Newman's tenure, even in its present greatly attenuated form, was drawing to a close. Cullen could see no way to improve matters. Indeed, his acute fears for the university pushed him, in the summer of 1858, into an almost total mental and physical collapse.

In his letters to Kirby that summer Cullen's fears for the university and its future are painfully clear. Since 1847 Cullen had pushed and prodded the Irish hierarchy to establish a Catholic university. On his appointment to Armagh he had himself done everything in his power to bring it about in the face of intense opposition. It was, in a very real sense, his project and his alone. He had invested years of interest and energy, not to mention a great deal of prestige, in assuring its success. Now it seemed the entire thing might fail. Cullen blamed Newman and MacHale for their part in the bringing the CUI to its present condition, but he nevertheless also blamed himself.

Even at his most despairing, Cullen never placed anything like total responsibility on Newman. As he told Kirby on 28 June, 'Dr Newman appointed a great number of professors and very good ones'. Despite this fact, though, 'the opposition [of MacHale and his allies] has stopped the contributions & I am full of fear for the future.'[200] This fear manifested itself in Cullen's usual complaint in times of stress: insomnia. Although previous episodes of ill health had been serious enough, Cullen's condition in the summer of 1858 was exceptionally poor. His secretary, C. B. Lyons, told Kirby that he had never known Cullen 'to be so ill in all my life' and reported that his doctor had forbidden his attendance at the meeting of the Maynooth board 'as it would be dangerous to his life!' Cullen had been suffering from 'sleepless nights—loss of appetite—diarrhoea—all three complaints brought on by excessive weakness.'[201] By late July, James Murray, another of Cullen's secretaries (and the nephew of the former archbishop), told Kirby that Cullen was 'extremely delicate and that he is in a precarious state' and that if he did not change his work habits 'he cannot possibly last long.'[202] Cullen himself knew the severity of his situation, telling Leahy that the 'Doctors tell me I must give up business for some months, or that I shall not be able to recover.' He was also concerned that his judgement might become impaired and, highly uncharacteristically, he asked Leahy 'as a merciful favour to correct me or admonish me, if you see me at any time taking a false step or going astray.' 'I am so weak', Cullen explained, 'that any little thing might put me wrong.'[203]

Cullen set off for his family in Liverpool in an attempt to regain his health. While in England, he wrote two extraordinary letters to Kirby setting out both his fears for the university and the extent of his own mental collapse. On 24 July he explained to his friend what had been troubling him: 'My complaint is nervousness or an excitement of the nervous system.' The want of sleep 'was near destroying me. I looked upon everything in despair.' 'The two things that disturbed me most were the Irish College in Paris and the Catholic University.'[204]

Cullen then proceeded to set out his thoughts in detail. This letter is the closest Cullen ever got to a complete explanation of his feelings on the entire university question:

> Regarding the University Dr Newman has left it to the mercy of God for the last year and more, and I fear it will go down. We have expended an immense sum, and we see nothing done. [A]s it was that I put forward Dr Newman and did everything to support him, all the blame will be thrown on me. The loss of so much money and the failure in this undertaking will be all put on my poor shoulders. To be sure everybody thought Dr Newman wd accomplish wonders as well as I did, but now others will say that I am guilty of all. Perhaps however through the mercy of God, and the intercession of the B[lessed] and immaculate mother of God, things may not turn out so badly as I fear, and we may yet get some one to put things on a proper footing. Dr Newman nominated a great body of professors and good ones, but he did not get students except in the medical school, so that there is an enormous expense for the professors, and very little done. This was a great mistake, and what remedy for it now—seeing that the students are not attending, the people will not subscribe, and so we shall be placed in a great difficulty. . . . See what a miserable thing man is, how easily he is disturbed. What a reed agitated by the winds! Dr McHale will have a great triumph, he always opposed Dr Newman's appointment, and now it appears he was right. I was wrong in the whole case—we must take all in punishment of our sins.[205]

In his second letter to Kirby from Liverpool, written a week and a half after the first, Cullen returned again to the subject of the university, Newman's legacy, and the consequences of its, as Cullen saw it, imminent failure.

> I am beginning to get better—but I have suffered a g[rea]t. deal in mind and body. Why do you not write a line to tell me what to do. . . . As to the University I fear a complete breakdown. God help us. I

will be very much compromised as I wrote so much in its cause, and collected such sums of money. The donors may cry out against me. May God and his holy Mother avert the crisis.

I write to the Card. [Barnabò][206] asking him to tell us to hold a general meeting of the bishops. I fear such a meeting will not do any good, but if it be not held, the university can not go on, as the money is failing, and the bishops only can get it. I have got into a bad position and I fear that I shall have to suffer, and to lose the little influence I have heretofore enjoyed. Prayer alone can get me out of this difficulty.[207]

Despite the somewhat unpleasant note of self-pity in these letters (perhaps understandable in a man suffering a nervous breakdown), Cullen was largely accurate in his assessment of the situation. The university *was* failing, money *was* running out, and student numbers *were* dwindling. Without the active support of the bishops, which he had sacrificed in 1854, Cullen could not hope to begin again the process of raising money. Yet he could not return the governance of the university to the episcopal body for the very good reason that they were no more capable of assuming it than they had been in 1854. William Monsell expressed Cullen's dilemma on this point in a letter to Newman in early November 1858: 'until the bishops & clergy are interested' in the university, 'no hearty national movement can be made in its favour'. They would not, however, 'become really interested in it so long as Dr Cullen is considered to be the sole . . . director of its movements and policy'. But, he added, 'on the other hand how could its government be in the hands of the whole episcopal body?'[208] To make matters more complicated, Leahy still believed, as he had in 1854, that the university should be under the authority of all the bishops and, as he told Newman, had 'again and again . . . urged this upon Dr Cullen.'[209]

Cullen was also correct in assuming that he would be blamed for the university's failure—the historiography of the subject has borne out that fear amply—as he was inextricably associated with it in the public mind. More than his fears for a possible loss of his own influence, Cullen lamented the death of his project and the consequences of that failure. As he told Kirby on 9 August, it would 'be a bad thing to see such an institution fall, tho' it has not done much, it's [*sic*] fall wd be a triumph for protestantism and infidelity and bad catholicity.'[210]

As Cullen recovered, Newman's time as rector of the Catholic University of Ireland was finally drawing to an end. In late September 1858,

Cullen had, for the first time in many months, written (or, rather, dictated) a letter to Newman. Commenting on the recently submitted report of the dean and faculty of science, which appeared to call for an increase in the number of professors, Cullen pointed out that there were already enough professors for the few students and that such an expense could not be justified given the university's precarious finances. 'For my part I think it will be necessary to curtail the expenses very considerably to prevent us from getting into debt.'[211] Such unwelcome news was quickly followed by a letter from Leahy, in which the archbishop of Cashel told him that 'Dr Cullen before leaving Dublin wrote to me on the necessity of your residing in the University as before, or at least for some time, some considerable time, each session.' Leahy expressed his agreement with Cullen, telling Newman, 'I believe your presence for a much longer time than you gave last year necessary to the success of the University.'[212]

Newman was having nothing to do with any such proposal, and he gently reminded Leahy more than once in early October that he was awaiting his replacement as rector.[213] Not even the long overdue appointment of a vice-rector (the changeable Dr Kelly, who promptly died) could change Newman's mind. Certainly Leahy's tactless suggestion that Newman should leave Birmingham in favour of a Dublin Oratory, as Birmingham 'dwindles . . . to a small thing in comparison with the Catholic University', did nothing to alter his view.[214] Final resignation seemed inevitable, and Newman told Robert Ornsby that he was 'in great anxiety about University matters.' Cullen 'has told me to reduce the number of Professors' and the archbishops had 'peremptorily (and abruptly) told me to come into residence.' Since Newman believed that to be 'impossible', he told Ornsby that, 'I suppose, my resignation is imminent.'[215]

Faced with Newman's requests to be relieved from the rectorship, Leahy and Cullen found themselves in a quandary. As Leahy told Cullen, 'It appears necessary to do one or either of two things—to get him [Newman] through the influence of the Authorities in Rome, or of the Pope, if need be, to reside some considerable time each Session for a couple of years to come when the University may have got out of its present critical situation—or, to provide a new Rector.' For his part, Leahy would 'much rather retain Dr Newman, if retain him we can.' 'The prestige of his name is great,' Leahy wrote, and 'his separation from the University would, I fear, inflict upon it a heavy, if not a fatal blow.'[216] Although he still desired to retain Newman's services, Leahy allowed his own frustrations with the rector to show in another letter to Cullen:

'There will always be difficulties with him on account of his rather angular character'. Were it not for the damage Newman's departure would cause to the university, Leahy wrote, 'I would say, "accept his resignation and look out for a new Rector."'[217] Continuing on as they had during the 1857–58 academic year was out of the question, but Newman's final departure could only seriously, and perhaps fatally, damage the university.

As the archbishops were unwilling—hardly unreasonably—to continue with Newman as a nonresident rector, Newman himself knew that the game was up. On 11 October he told Ornsby, 'It is simply impossible that I can remain Rector.'[218] Newman clearly blamed Cullen for circumstances having reached this point. As he told Ornsby on 17 October,

> You must give up the notion of my continuing at Dublin. Dr Cullen has no notion at all of treating me with any confidence. He grants me nothing—and I am resolute that I will have all I want, and more than I have yet asked for. He has treated me from the first like a scrub, and *you will see he never will do otherwise.* I have wished to organise a method of collection by which we should have money enough—he never has done any thing but take my letters, crumple them up, put them in the fire, and write me no answer. And so with every thing else.[219]

Newman followed up this complaint in a letter to Monsell, telling him that 'Dr Cullen is the only one of whom I have cause to complain—Drs D[ixon] and L[eahy] do but record his decisions. He has been, and is, ruining us.' 'He will do nothing, let us do nothing; he will give no answers to questions, or imply he grants and then pull you up when you have acted.' 'He is perfectly impracticable.'[220]

John Henry Newman formally and finally resigned the rectorship of the Catholic University of Ireland on 12 November 1858. In his letter of resignation he told the Irish archbishops that, as he had been required by them to return to residence in Dublin and was unable to do so, 'one course alone is in honor left to me.' 'I hereby resign into your Graces' hands the high office, the duties of which have occupied my mind now for seven full years: and begging you to pardon all my shortcomings in fulfilling them, during the time for which I have had so distinguished an honor.'[221] Slightly over four years since the Catholic University had opened its doors to students, Newman was leaving Dublin for good.

Cullen and Leahy reconciled themselves, after some short while, to Newman's departure. Writing from Rome in early 1859, Cullen closed the matter, telling Leahy, 'I fear there wd. be no use for asking them here to order Dr. Newman to remain with us.' 'His going away creates a difficulty, but we may as well grapple with it at once.' He then suggested Bartholomew Woodlock, the president of All Hallows Missionary College, as Newman's replacement.[222] However, Woodlock would not be appointed rector of the Catholic University of Ireland until April 1861. Between Newman's resignation and Woodlock's appointment the university would experience a near fatal drift.

chapter nine

New Beginnings, Old Problems

THE STORY OF THE CATHOLIC UNIVERSITY OF IRELAND DOES not end with Newman's departure. Just as it was important to consider the history of the university before Newman came, it is equally important to examine that history after he left. Only by putting both the university and Newman's tenure at it in their proper context can we hope to understand the project as a whole. It is not my intention, however, to trace the entire course of the Catholic University from the time of Newman's departure. It is not clear, in fact, what exactly that course might be.

University College Dublin traces its own origins to the Catholic University. That the link is somewhat tenuous has done nothing to dispel UCD's enthusiasm. For example, UCD has a 'Newman House' (the CUI's former buildings on Stephen's Green), its Arts building is the Newman building, and it awards Newman fellowships. In 1954 UCD celebrated a 'joint' centenary with the CUI (which still existed on paper, with the archbishop of Dublin as rector and the papal nuncio chancellor).[1] In fact, the Catholic University of Ireland did not merge seamlessly into UCD but rather continued in name but not reality into the 1950s. A portion of its actual premises around St Stephen's Green became University College and passed to Jesuit control in 1883. Its students became eligible for degrees of the new Royal University from 1880. Eventually,

University College became part of the new University College Dublin, itself a constituent college of the National University of Ireland.[2] With such a genealogy, there is no obvious endpoint for a study of the Catholic University of Ireland.

The decision, then, to terminate this book in the winter of 1865–66 is somewhat arbitrary. At that time the Irish hierarchy—particularly Paul Cullen—and Bartholomew Woodlock admitted that the Catholic University need not, and likely would not, continue as a university in the sense that both they and Newman had meant the term. The continuing campaign for a charter and the university's own dire circumstances caused Cullen and Woodlock to accept the idea that the Catholic University of Ireland could become a mere college within some sort of larger, degree-granting university, which is more or less what happened in 1880 with the creation of the Royal University of Ireland. The Catholic University continued to call itself a university, but after the changes of 1865–66, it was no such thing.

After 1866 the university fell into an almost total stupor. Despite Woodlock's continuing purchases around Stephen's Green, there was little or no activity within the institution itself in the later 1860s or the entire 1870s, despite continued fundraising. By 1873 W. K. Sullivan, the professor of chemistry, told William Monsell that the 'University is all but defunct.'[3] In 1879 only three new students enrolled there.

An examination of the period between 1859 and early 1866 is important for a number of reasons. It allows us to gain a picture of how the university functioned after Newman's departure and the situation that departure left it in. The early years of Woodlock's rectorship, particularly 1861–62, saw a resurgence in the university that made it look, for a time, like the whole project might just succeed after all. Finally, it provides a useful corrective to the notion that the Catholic University of Ireland was, in some proprietary way, Newman's own.

THE INTERREGNUM

The final resignation of John Henry Newman on 12 November 1858 left the Catholic University of Ireland—and its sponsors—in an almost impossible position. Although Newman's resignation was not formally accepted by the bishops until August 1859, he ceased to have anything to do with the university almost immediately. There was no rector, no vice-rector, and no prospect of either in the immediate future. The bishops' choice for vice-rector, Matthew Kelly, fell ill in October 1858 and died soon after. He never assumed his duties. Newman filled the gap with the university chaplain W. H. Anderdon, whom he appointed pro–vice-rector on his own authority and on his way out the door (although he did obtain the consent of Leahy and Dixon—Cullen was in Rome).[4] Although amiable and well regarded by the students, Anderdon had no particular qualifications for the post and, to make matters worse, was English.[5]

Still, at least the university now had some kind of authority, however tenuous. Thomas Arnold expressed his relief to Newman, telling him in November that ever 'since Anderdon's provisional appointment, the benefit of it has been felt'.[6] Kelly's death and Anderdon's perceived unsuitability left the archbishops with a problem. For once, they acted with speed. A net was cast for any Irish cleric who was remotely qualified, uncontroversial, and unable to think up a good enough reason not to do the job. Their attention fell on a Dr James Gartlan, the rector of the moribund Irish College at Salamanca. Gartlan had been vacationing in Ireland and seems to have been more or less press-ganged into the post. Not enjoying good health, Gartlan saw himself as merely holding the job on a temporary basis and looked forward to his return to Spain.

Of Gartlan's tenure, Fergal McGrath has justly remarked that, despite being unprepared, Gartlan did have 'considerable ability, and acquitted himself, on the whole, with credit in what was undoubtedly a difficult situation.'[7] That it was a difficult situation is without question. Nevertheless, despite the upheaval caused by Newman's final departure, Kelly's death, and Gartlan's sudden appointment, the business of the university did continue. Classes were conducted as normal, and Newman's faculty remained in place. Students, of course, were no more numerous than before. Newman's own St Mary's House (which Anderdon had taken over) was forced to close in 1859, despite an offer by Thomas Arnold to keep it open.[8]

Cullen was in no doubt as to the severity of the situation. However, neither he nor the four archbishops as a group had the power to appoint a new rector. That power remained with the bishops of Ireland. With the backing of Leahy and Dixon, Cullen determined to convene the bishops to discuss the education question (not just the university, but also the national schools and intermediate education). He sought Rome's approval to hold the meeting canonically and to preside himself as apostolic delegate. Barnabò approved, and Cullen announced the meeting to the bishops on 5 July 1859. The assembled prelates—including MacHale—met in Dublin on 2 August. On the third day they discussed the future of the Catholic University. The next day they formally accepted Newman's resignation and agreed that the university should be supported, have a new rector, and that new rules should be drawn up for its governance. A decision on the new rector and the new regulations was postponed until late October.[9] John MacHale, of course, opposed everything.

Cullen had won an almost total victory. MacHale, as Emmet Larkin notes, 'had been reduced to a party of one'.[10] Through his influence at Rome, Cullen had finally succeeded in moulding the Irish hierarchy to his taste. MacHale's isolation, first evident in 1856–57, was now complete. Cullen could never entirely ignore the archbishop of Tuam, but without episcopal allies MacHale could no longer mount a serious threat to Cullen's policies in the Irish church. MacHale could, however, make a public fuss and thus deny Cullen the united front he so desired. It was the threat of public dissension—playing as it did on Cullen's wish for unity—that now became MacHale's only remaining weapon.

The bishops reconvened on 19 October, again canonically and again with Cullen in the chair. In Italian, Cullen briefly summarised the results of the meeting for Kirby: 'Nothing other than the Catholic University was dealt with. The things done by Father Newman were examined, it was determined to restrict expenditure, and then to make a general collection in order to maintain the institution.'[11] Never one to let such a thing as the opposition of his colleagues get him down, MacHale did his best to disrupt the meeting. He urged a root-and-branch condemnation of Newman and all his doings and opposed any plan to mount a fresh collection. Eventually, he was persuaded to sign an address supporting the university.

MacHale was perhaps slightly mollified by various changes made to the government of the university. Cullen was appointed chancellor, and MacHale himself was made vice-chancellor. These offices had no real power, and Emmet Larkin is surely right in remarking that MacHale's appointment 'was mere window dressing and was undoubtedly designed to contain him by incorporating him.'[12] More substantively, Cullen now conceded something that MacHale had claimed to want all along: episcopal control of the university. It was to be governed by an episcopal board consisting of each archbishop and two bishops from each of the four provinces. On the face of it, this was a staggering concession for Cullen. In 1854 he had risked the university's financial future by excluding the bishops from any such control. By late 1859, however, his position within the Irish church was much stronger. He could count on the members of the episcopal board (saving always MacHale) being broadly sympathetic to his goals, or at least not actively hostile. Returning control of the university to at least a committee of the bishops might also increase the interest of the entire hierarchy in fundraising. It should have been a victory for MacHale. Others who had advocated a return to episcopal supervision, such as Patrick Leahy, were satisfied with the change. And even John Derry, MacHale's closest ally, announced his intention to sit on the committee and to do his best to make it work (although not to the point of allowing collections for the university in Clonfert).[13] In reality, the episcopal board was a defeat for MacHale. Cullen would never have returned power to the bishops if by doing so he increased MacHale's power; that Cullen was willing to do so was a clear indication of the new balance of power within the hierarchy. MacHale might once very well have held a principled objection to Cullen's centralising tendencies and his willingness to overlook or usurp the traditional prerogatives of the Irish bishops. By 1859, however, it was clear that his frantic hatred of Cullen and his policies had blinded him to what was a very real concession on Cullen's part to those very principles that MacHale had long espoused.

In practice the episcopal board was as much Cullen's creature as the archbishops' committee had been. He attended every meeting and chaired all but two. MacHale never attended.[14] Those bishops who were not minded to support the university (nearly half of the twelve members) simply didn't attend board meetings. What Cullen was not able to obtain at the October meeting was a rector. Despite his preference for Woodlock, Cullen was not immediately able to secure his brethren's approval. For the time being, Gartlan would remain in place. The failure to appoint Woodlock in late 1859 is an important reminder of the limits of Cullen's power. For ten years he had been the most powerful man in the Irish church. By 1859 he had overseen the appointment of two archbishops, thirteen bishops, and three coadjutor bishops who succeeded after 1859. If some appointments (such as Leahy's) had been inevitable with or without Cullen's influence, nonetheless, most were made by the Propaganda on Cullen's recommendation. In August and October 1859, Cullen knew himself to have finally vanquished both MacHale and the remaining bishops who had supported Archbishop Murray on educational questions. Yet despite this, Woodlock did not become rector until April 1861.

The failure of the bishops to appoint a rector only perpetuated the dangerous drift following Newman's departure. In December 1859 Thomas Arnold told Sir John Acton that it 'seems really to be the intention of the Bishops to appoint *no* Rector, to keep as Vice Rector an old unwieldy man of infirm health, who steadily declines to decide anything or to take responsibility even in the most trifling matters'. Arnold was no more impressed with what he took to be the decision 'to commit the executive as well as legislative conduct of the institution to a Board of twelve Bishops, meeting about once in six weeks!' Arnold was wrong in assuming the bishops wished to take executive powers away from Gartlan (or later Woodlock), but he was correct both in identifying a trend towards greater episcopal control and in his emphasis on the need for a Rector: 'An active Rector might yet save the sinking ship.'[15]

Arnold was also right about Gartlan's health. By January 1861 he was too ill to return to Dublin for the new term and remained in Dundalk. His condition was so poor that he was unable to write and had to use an amanuensis.[16] An idea of the state the university had fallen into in 1860–61 can be seen in a letter from James Kavanagh, the newly appointed professor of mathematics, to Michael Flannery, formerly dean of the university and the recently appointed bishop of Killaloe. Kavanagh wrote in an effort to secure payment of his full stipend of £300 per annum. To justify his salary, Kavanagh described in detail the number of students in the university at this time. From his appointment in November 1859 to mid-June 1860, Kavanagh noted that 'only 27 students have been resident in the University, but less than that number at any one time'. Of those, Kavanagh had taught some seventeen. Beyond the handful of resident students, Kavanagh further estimated that there were ten externs (not living in a university house) and 187 attending evening classes for a total of 224 students (of whom he had taught 170).[17] Residential numbers had been low enough in Newman's day. Now they were positively anemic.

The lack of either a rector or sufficient students was compounded by continuing problems with the annual collection. Despite their partial return to authority over the university, the bishops seemed no more interested in supporting it. Between October 1859 and March 1861 only £4,899.12.2 was raised for the Catholic University (all but £29 from the diocesan collections). Sixteen dioceses failed to make any contribution at all, including Cork and Down & Connor (which included Belfast). In Tuam province, only Elphin and Galway contributed (a hefty £501 from Elphin). MacHale, of course, ensured that nothing came from Tuam itself. Even membership on the episcopal board proved no indicator of enthusiasm for the university collection. Although three of the four archbishops held reasonably successful collections, only three of the eight bishops on the board did (James Walshe of Kildare & Leighlin, Laurence Gillooly of Elphin, and Michael Flannery of Killaloe). The final provincial totals were: Armagh: £567.0.10; Dublin: £2,210.2.9; Cashel: £1,518.6.10; Tuam: £574.18.8.[18] Judging by the returns, the unanimous support for the university secured in August and October 1859 did not extend, in the case of many prelates, to financial support.

Cullen railed against this episcopal parsimony, telling Kirby that 'there seems to be a curse on our common undertakings—if the University had been taken up by Dublin alone, I am sure it wd. have prospered.

Now it is withering—the protection given by the meetings of the Bishops only helps to pull it down.'[19] He called a meeting of the hierarchy (which still retained the power to appoint a rector) for 23 April 1861. The assembled prelates were to consider various questions, including poor law reform, changes in the marriage laws, and that old favourite, the national schools. The Catholic University, however, would once again take centre stage. Despite Cullen's by now almost habitual anxiety before such events, the bishops' meeting passed off peacefully and productively. This unwonted calm was no doubt directly attributable to MacHale's failure to attend (watching from afar, Newman called MacHale's absence a 'bird of good omen').[20] At the meeting Cullen was able to secure the appointment of Woodlock as the new rector of the Catholic University of Ireland. According to Cullen's formal report to Barnabò at the Propaganda, the appointment was proposed by Dixon. Apparently, 'almost all the Bishops approved of the proposal' to appoint Woodlock. The only exception was Newman's old friend David Moriarty, who made the truly bizarre suggestion that Thomas MacHale—the archbishop's nephew and protégé—be appointed rector. What Moriarty was thinking we can only guess. He was at the time at loggerheads with Cullen over the national schools—he was minded to accept some government proposals relating to them to which Cullen was opposed—and so might have been inclined to make mischief. Even so, it is difficult to believe that as intelligent a man as Moriarty could have possibly thought that Thomas MacHale would make a suitable rector. Cullen was surely correct when he told Barnabò that if MacHale had been appointed 'the University would be undoubtedly crushed.'[21]

Woodlock's nomination sailed through with no other opposition. James Gartlan immediately resigned as vice-rector on the grounds that he was not needed. He was not replaced, and the office of vice-rector itself was formally suppressed by the episcopal board as an economy measure in 1863.[22] Newman welcomed the appointment, although he noted somewhat ominously in a letter to Renouf that '*youths* must come before you are all right.'[23] On 25 April 1861, Woodlock found himself in charge of Arnold's 'sinking ship', a ship that had been left to drift without a rector for nearly three years.

THE WOODLOCK YEARS

Bartholomew Woodlock was born in Dublin on 30 March 1819 and was educated by the Jesuits (including a spell at Clongowes Wood). He had originally intended to study for the priesthood at the Irish College in Rome, but it was full in 1836 and Tobias Kirby referred him instead to the Roman Seminary. He was ordained for Dublin in the Lateran on 18 December 1841. On his return to Ireland he joined with a Rev. John Hand in founding All Hallows College in Drumcondra, north Dublin. All Hallows was created to educate Irish priests for the overseas missions. Despite many predictions of failure (including one from Cullen), the college flourished. David Moriarty took over the presidency in 1846 (rendering his opposition to Woodlock even more inexplicable). Under Moriarty, Woodlock was professor of dogmatic theology, Italian, and sacred ceremonies, and he had responsibility for the day-to-day care of the students. On Moriarty's departure to Kerry, Woodlock was elected president by the clerical staff. His tenure at All Halllows seems to have been a great success, and during his seven years as president enrollment doubled to more than two hundred students.[24] Woodlock's value to All Hallows was so great that Barnabò put pressure on him to retain some link with the place after his appointment as rector of the CUI. In obedience to the Propaganda's wishes, Woodlock gave up the rooms he had just taken in the university and returned to his quarters in Drumcondra, where he remained until his appointment as bishop of Ardagh in 1879.[25]

Woodlock enjoyed a close working relationship with Cullen (he had been a vicar-general in the Dublin diocese since the mid-1850s) and was able to use his archiepiscopal support to good purpose. The relatively relaxed nature of their relationship can be seen in a letter of Woodlock's to Cullen. In the course of discussing who should preach at his inauguration, Woodlock wondered somewhat mischievously, 'Shall I ask Dr Moriarty? Or what, if I tried to get Dr MacHale!!'[26] For his part, Cullen wrote open, occasionally chatty and sometimes startlingly frank letters to Woodlock. Although, as we shall see, Cullen was not adverse to playing politics at his rector's expense, there was never the kind of trouble between Woodlock and Cullen that there had been between Newman and Cullen after 1855. As he had with Newman, Cullen continued to leave the affairs of the university to its rector. After appointing Woodlock, Cullen only involved himself in the wider political questions of the university's future and its finances.

The university calendar for 1861 gives a good picture of the university at the time of Woodlock's appointment. It had twenty-seven professors and lecturers (one dual appointment) in all faculties including medicine. There were a further six honorary professors. Newman's faculty remained largely intact, and the core of the teaching staff that was in place by 1858 was still there in 1861.[27] We have already seen how few students there were. Now that he was in charge, Woodlock had to address two long-standing and pressing difficulties. First, he needed to attract more students and, second, he desperately needed to put the university's financial house in order and ensure a stable and predictable source of income.

Woodlock recognised that it would not be possible to obtain any substantial number of students in Ireland without first creating schools that they could attend before coming up to the university. The 1861 census revealed that in Ireland only some 1,242 Catholics were receiving a 'collegiate' education that might suit them for university entrance.[28] The quality of this education no doubt varied widely, and at any rate, those schools had not to date provided many students to the university.

Newman, too, had addressed the problem of student supply during his time in charge. In 1856 he had appointed a committee consisting of Michael Flannery, Edward Butler, and D. B. Dunne to consider the problem. They submitted a proposal to the rector that called for the affiliation of Irish schools to the Catholic University with a view to 'extending the strength & influences of the University, and of developing and improving the character of the Catholic educational establishments'. Their recommendations included opening CUI qualifications to ecclesiastical students in seminaries and colleges (and any lay students in such institutions) and the establishment of burses tied to certain schools that would be tenable at the university. However, holders of such burses would have to become resident members of the university and all exams for affiliated students in approved institutions were to be held in Dublin.[29] By 1858–59 'extern' students could sit exams in the CUI and take its qualifications.[30] Newman's committee seems to have taken the view that it was necessary to build up links with the various existing intermediate schools and, where necessary, improve their standards. It was hoped that in the long run these links would provide the Catholic University with a steady stream of well-prepared Irish students. There were, however, a number of problems with the affiliate system. One was that a number of institutions simply refused to affiliate—often because they were already preparing their students for degrees from the University of London. The Jesuits, for example, declined in 1857 to affiliate St Francis Xavier's School in Belvedere, Dublin, to the CUI.[31] An even larger problem was that no matter how many affiliated students the university might obtain, it seemed to have no effect on the number actually becoming resident within the university.

On assuming the rectorship, Woodlock decided to pursue a slightly different approach. He retained and even attempted to expand the affiliate system. The 1861–62 session was, in fact, the high-water mark for affiliates, with 210 of the 250 matriculated students in the university being taught a CUI-suggested curriculum in an affiliated school. After 1862, however, the number of affiliates dropped off and never climbed higher than the 71 who matriculated in 1865–66.[32]

In addition to the affiliates, Woodlock also sought to address the problem of poor *resident* enrollment in Dublin. He obtained from the episcopal board permission to open 'Catholic University Schools' designed to feed students directly into the university. They would be under the rector's supervision and could, at least initially, expect to call on university funds to establish and support themselves. Woodlock had demonstrated an appreciation of the virtues of feeder schools before coming to the Catholic University. In 1857, while still president of All Hallows, he had established a preparatory school for the college at Belmont House in Stillorgan.[33] As rector of the Catholic University, Woodlock pursued the same strategy.

As he explained the plan to Bishop Moriarty of Kerry, the 'object of these University schools should be to prepare students for the University'. Although ecclesiastical students should 'not be excluded', the main target would be 'aspirants to the Univ., and through it to the learned professions & and to the numberless respectable positions open to educated men', positions, Woodlock thought, that were unfortunately 'generally occupied by Protestants'. The schools would be based on the model of the old English 'high schools' (he had ancient establishments like Winchester and Westminster in mind here) and would provide a 'first-rate classical, scientific & commercial education'. The local bishop would be the school patron (and would have the power to demand the dismissal of staff), but the schools would be run from the university itself.[34]

Woodlock had Cullen's full support, as well as that of at least some other bishops. The first university school—in Waterford—came about almost entirely as a result of the local bishop's efforts. And Patrick Dorrian, the bishop of Down & Connor, told Woodlock that not only would his proposed schools 'be the making of the University' but that they were indeed 'the best idea that has come out yet.' In Dorrian's view, the Catholic University schools could do more than simply provide students to the university; they could also provide 'a first rate education to that large class of Catholics who want, not Degrees in a University, but a first-rate safe commercial education.'[35]

The first of the Catholic University schools opened in the city of Waterford on 24 September 1862. It took over the location of the recently defunct Waterford Corporation School. It was a sign of Woodlock's own confidence that he appointed the first rector on the advice of John Henry

Newman. Unsurprisingly, Newman recommended an English convert (and Merton man), George Erskine.[36] In 1863 Erskine moved to the newly opened CU school in Dublin. His replacement was another convert, this time a Scot, Robert Campbell. The Waterford school was followed closely by another in Ennis, which accepted its first students (some thirty) on 29 September. As in Waterford, the school was opened on local initiative. Whereas in Waterford the bishop was the driving force, in Ennis it was the parish priest (and vicar-general for Killaloe).

The third and final CU school opened in Dublin in September 1863. Woodlock had not originally intended there to be a school in Leinster, but when the opportunity arose he accepted it. The Dublin school was effectively the old St Laurence's school that had figured so heavily in CUI admissions during Newman's tenure. Founded by Daniel Murray in 1850 (though it did not open until 1852), it was based in Harcourt Street. Its first president, Dr James Quinn, had invited Newman to take up residence there when he first came to Dublin. Between 1855 and 1861 St Laurence's had sent thirty-five students to the Catholic University, easily the largest total from any school. Quinn, himself a product of the Cullen-era Irish College, left Ireland to become bishop of Brisbane in 1859. It seemed natural enough that the now financially troubled school, the control of which had passed to Quinn's younger brother, should formalise its long association with the Catholic University. By the time St Laurence's became available, however, the CUI was already experiencing increasing financial difficulties and the transfer, first mooted in late 1862, was delayed until 1863.[37]

The Catholic University schools proved to be a signal failure. During their time under CUI management the three schools sent only thirty-four students to the university. Only eighteen of them became resident students. One school—Ennis—never sent any students at all. The schools cost the university some £2,900 in all, at a cost of slightly over £161 per resident student. Hardly value for money. Faced with these losses, the episcopal board was forced by late 1863 to conclude that the Catholic University schools were not 'financially advisable'. The schools were to be made self-sufficient as soon as possible. Waterford ceased to be under CUI management in 1868. The Ennis school was transferred to the control of its headmaster in 1863 and it became the Killaloe diocesan college in 1879. The former St Laurence's in Dublin passed through various hands before being taken over (and moved) by the Marist fathers in 1867. It still exists today as the Catholic University School.[38]

In addition to creating a network of feeder schools, Woodlock also conceived an ambitious plan to expand the university's physical plant. Despite additional purchases made during Newman's time, the Catholic

University main building on St Stephen's Green was entirely inadequate to the needs of what Woodlock hoped would be a growing institution filled with students from his new university schools. His plan was to build from scratch a new campus at a site in Drumcondra not far from his home in All Hallows College. An architect was retained and the land was purchased out of the university's endowment. The necessity of using endowment funds allowed MacHale an unexpected opportunity to make trouble. Naturally, he availed himself of it.

Woodlock felt himself obligated to gain MacHale's signature as a trustee of the funded capital (a position dating back to the original university committee) in order to use some of that capital for his building project. In theory MacHale should have been in favour of Woodlock's plans. As we have seen, in 1851 he had advocated, against Newman and Cullen, spending the majority of the university's funds on a grand, purpose-built campus. Ten years later, he seems to have changed his mind. Woodlock wrote to MacHale several times in the autumn of 1861 seeking either his support in releasing the necessary funds or his resignation as a trustee. MacHale refused point-blank to do the latter and announced himself to be highly reluctant to do the former. In his letter to Woodlock we can gain both a final picture of MacHale's objections—not all of them unreasonable—to the university and a convenient summary of his many grievances:

> An immense staff of officers and professors has been, for some years, quartered on that infant establishment, with enormous salaries, with whose appointment the Bishops of Ireland, nay some of the Trustees themselves, had so little to do, that to speak for myself, I was not even consulted on their qualifications. Irish Clergymen, who had labored hard and impaired their health in collecting funds for the University in foreign lands, were overlooked, though as well qualified for places, as some who were named to its many offices; and persons who did nothing, and had nothing to do, were, at the same time, receiving large salaries, whence it was difficult to gainsay the observation that the payment of Sinecure Gentlemen, was deemed more important than their performance of any duties: whence the indisputable conclusion that comparing the annual amount of moneys expended with the fruits to be shown, there are few institutions on which such vast sums have been expended with such little advantage.[39]

Despite MacHale's objections, Woodlock was able to obtain the necessary land in Drumcondra.

Conscious of the need to demonstrate the university's new vitality to the public, Woodlock conceived a grand ceremony to mark the acquisition of the new site and the symbolic laying of the cornerstone of the university building. The ceremony, held on 20 July 1862, was preceded by an enormous procession from the pro-cathedral in Marlborough Street up to Drumcondra. An estimated one hundred thousand people either watched the ceremony or lined the parade route. Some historians have seen the whole affair as Cullen's riposte to the massive funeral accorded to the Young Irelander Terence Bellew MacManus some nine months earlier.[40] That being as it may, the whole event was nevertheless a clear sign of the renewed vitality of the Catholic University during Woodlock's first two years as rector. Although unable himself to attend because of illness, Cullen declared the ceremony and procession 'the greatest and grandest ever witnessed in Ireland.'[41]

Unfortunately for Woodlock and Cullen, the Drumcondra plan was never fully realised. Soon after the July 1862 ceremony, it was announced that a new railroad line would pass over a portion of the site, rendering the whole of it unsuitable for the university's purposes. Woodlock first sought to have the proposed routing changed, and when he failed, sought to enter into negotiations to sell all or part of the proposed campus. By the time it was clear that Drumcondra was no longer suitable, the affairs of the Catholic University had again become too fragile to consider moving from St Stephen's Green. After all the publicity and high hopes, the planned new home of the Catholic University of Ireland eventually became a Redemptorist monastery. Without ever hosting a single student, the site wound up costing the university some £10,000 that it could ill afford.[42]

The combined losses on the Drumcondra plan and the unproductive Catholic University schools more than offset the gains made by the increased vigor of the university collection under Woodlock. The rector had devised a plan that sought to spread the financial burden fairly across Ireland. He calculated that the university needed to spend some £8,000 per year. He divided its income in to two sources: interest on its endowment and a 'National Tribute'. Under Woodlock's plan the endowment was to provide £1,000 per annum. The rest had to come from the people of Ireland. According to Woodlock, to raise this sum it was only necessary for each of the twenty-eight Irish dioceses to contribute some £250. If it was felt to be unsuitable to assign the same goal to each diocese, then the target could be expressed a different way. Woodlock calculated that each of the 2,485 parochial clergy in Ireland needed only to 'secure' by 'his local influence the small sum of £2 16s. 4d.'[43] However the funds were obtained, it was hoped that a regular national collection with clear diocesan and parish goals could secure for the university the stable income it so desperately needed. Astonishingly, Woodlock nearly achieved his goals by the 1862 collection (the first one fully conducted under his scheme). Whereas between 1859 and 1861 fully sixteen dioceses had failed to make any contribution to university funds, in 1862 every diocese save Cork and Tuam made at least some contribution. The total raised came to a highly encouraging £6,437.14.5.[44]

Despite this good news, the university had clearly reached a point where hard choices had to be made. Either it had to close or it had to dramatically curtail its spending. As we have seen, Cullen had long complained about Newman's spending habits. As almost his last act as rector, Newman had in November 1858 drawn up a budget for the university to be presented to the bishops. He estimated that the university would need to continue spending some £6,800 per year. This figure was arrived at by assuming a fixed burden of £5,000 for academic salaries and £1,260 for the university officers, occasional lectures, servants, and bills. Newman also allocated £600 for scholarships, burses, and prizes. He hoped to meet the academic salaries entirely from the university collection (£5,000). Six hundred pounds was to be raised from fees on the optimistic assumption that the university could attract sixty students paying £10 net each. Interest on the endowment and £600 of deficit spending 'to be made up by the trustees' would account for the remainder of the budget.[45] Given the paucity of students and the anemic collections in 1858, such a budget was only loosely connected to reality.

Matters did not change dramatically during Gartlan's tenure. In 1860 two lay auditors refused to continue examining the university's accounts on the grounds of extravagance. Michael Errington and Charles Bianconi—both long-time advocates and friends of the university—had been retained, probably by Newman,[46] to audit the university's books on a half-yearly basis. Errington wrote to the vice-rector (Bianconi added his name) to inform him that 'in going through the University Accounts on previous occasions, I became convinced that greater economy was requisite.' That being the case, and as the 'University has not obtained that amount of support & popularity, which was hoped for', it was necessary to rein in spending as increasing public criticism of the university would 'sooner or later' direct attention to its accounts.[47] Neither Bianconi nor Errington felt they could defend those accounts publicly, and neither man wished to be associated with them.

Now, in the face of the failure of the CU schools and the Drumcondra plan, the episcopal board was forced to examine the finances of the

Catholic University and recommend drastic changes. The board established a finance committee consisting of Cullen, Patrick Dorrian (the coadjutor bishop of Down and Connor), Laurence Gillooly of Elphin, and the bishop of Kildare and Leighlin, James Walshe. Cullen's three colleagues on the committee were close allies and could be counted on to support whatever Cullen's own conclusions might be. The finance committee reported on 18 September 1863 and the picture they painted was bleak. Between January 1850 and July 1863 the Catholic University's total receipts were £115,000. It had spent some £69,950 and still held slightly over £35,000 in a combination of government stock and property. Between January 1856 and July 1863 the university had spent on average £8,300 per year (substantially more than Newman had estimated and slightly more than Woodlock had). In that same period average annual receipts were only £5,300, leaving an annual deficit of £3,000.[48]

The situation was clearly unsustainable. The committee (and thus Cullen) was especially concerned with the continuing operating deficit. They observed that this 'amount Deficit, which has already involved the university in a debt of £1000, should in a few years, if allowed to continue, swallow up the entire funded property of the University and infallibly lead it to bankruptcy and ruin.'[49] Spending had to be reduced, and the committee spelled out where the axe should fall. They recommended cutting the budget back to average annual receipts—a reduction of £3,000 per annum. To achieve this the committee proposed to close two of the university houses and to make the few resident students pay the full economic cost of their room and board. Academic staff were to receive their commons in place of a proposed £50 pay rise and all the servants except two porters were to be sacked. The medical school and the Catholic University schools were to be made self-sufficient. The university journal *Atlantis* was to be discontinued and there were to be no further outlays for a future museum or for the library (bar an annual £50 for new books).

The size of the academic staff was also affected. It was proposed that only one professor should be retained to teach ancient and modern history, geography, and English language.[50] Such a consolidation would result in a net loss of three chairs. Further, the professor of natural philosophy would take on lectures in geology and there would be no replacements for the vacant chairs in Irish language and antiquities, civil engineering, and botany (although outside lecturers might be retained for single lectures). It was hoped the changes would realise savings on salaries alone of £2,130. In all, the committee recommended making £3,600 per annum in cuts. It was proposed that some of the annual savings (above the £3,000 needed to balance the books) would be combined with some endowment monies and put to retiring all university debts—including the remaining £2,400 owed to Newman for the university church. In the future the endowment was not to be used to cover day-to-day running costs, and any capital improvements were to be funded by special collections.[51] Although not all of the committee's proposals were put into effect (the *Atlantis*, for example, continued to appear, albeit erratically), it was inevitable that the vast majority would be. After all, Cullen dominated both the finance committee and the episcopal board.

It is hard not to see the report of the finance committee in September 1863 as the death of the Catholic University of Ireland. That its empty body lingered on life-support for many years after is almost beside the point. Cullen's cuts made it impossible for the university to exist as the sort of institution that both he and Newman had desired it to be. Instead of the hoped-for Catholic university for the English-speaking world, the Dublin institution was reduced to sacking staff and closing facilities. Given the situation spelled out by the finance committee, however, it was clearly impossible that the university could carry on as it had under Newman and Gartlan. The failure of the CU schools and the Drumcondra plan only made this more clear. Even Woodlock's impressive work to increase the annual collection was not enough to offset the lack of students and the resulting excess of faculty and facility. The annual collection, too, quickly dropped off after 1863. By 1865 Woodlock was forced to report to the episcopal board that the university's

> financial position is also most unsatisfactory. It is at present burthened with a debt of about four thousand pounds; its annual collection is made most irregularly, and although all the bishops of Ireland assumed (in 1859) a yearly obligation of about £5,000 for one item (salaries) alone, many parishes and even diocese, feel no difficulty in exempting themselves from their share of the common responsibility. In the year 1864, four dioceses made no collection at all, and five others contributed but very small sums. . . . The position of the University is, therefore, most unsatisfactory, its very existence is precarious, unless the confidence of the clergy and people be restored to it by its receiving legal recognition.[52]

Woodlock's final point—that the university could perhaps be saved by 'its receiving legal recognition'—hints at an issue that we have not yet addressed. As Woodlock and the bishops knew by 1865 (and likely much earlier), only a charter could save the Catholic University of Ireland.

THE CHARTER

We have already seen the tremendous difficulties under which the Catholic University and its rectors laboured. Episcopal dissension, erratic funding, and, above all, insufficient students all contributed to its relative failure. However, all of these problems could probably have been overcome if it were not for one thing: the university had no charter and was not empowered to award degrees. The experience of the medical school proves the point; prospective doctors did not need to attend a chartered, degree-granting institution, and the medical school flourished even while the rest of the university languished. The inability to grant degrees was a burden that the infant establishment proved unable to bear. It could not attract students to an institution that could offer them nothing tangible to advance their careers; the university even found it difficult to control its students without the ability to threaten the ultimate sanction of withholding degrees.

In 1851 Newman and his colleagues on the Thurles subcommittee did not consider the question of the legality of awarding degrees. They were content to discuss then, and for some years more, the requirements for the traditional qualifications of bachelor, master, and doctor. Newman recognised early on the importance of state recognition of the university's degrees but was unsure how to obtain it. In his report to the bishops for the 1854–55 academic year, he noted that the rector had the power 'under sanction of the Holy See, to confer any Academical Degrees whatever.' To that extent the university 'exists and needs nothing for its completion'. Nevertheless, Newman noted that 'it is difficult to find an instance in the history of Universities, though such may occur, in which Academical Degrees were not accompanied by state recognition and civil privileges'. In 1855 Newman thought that the problems caused by the lack of a charter could be surmounted by convincing the Irish people that there was in fact no problem at all. 'It is plain that public opinion, and individual impression, must be regarded and treated as facts; and that if the absence of legal sanction to our degrees is judged an evil, it is so far forth an evil, whatever be the value of the judgment.' It was also true, Newman wrote, that 'in proportion as public opinion changes, the evil so far vanishes.' The trick, then, was, while not denying a charter would be useful, to ignore the lack of one so far as possible in the 'expectation that, if the opinion has no solid basis, it will in course of time disappear of its own accord, dying as it has arisen, without our having anything to do with it.'[53]

In the university's first year, this was perhaps a reasonable hope, but problems soon arose. Far from merely denying state recognition of the university's degrees, it seemed that the lack of a charter actually precluded the university from awarding any degree at all. In his 1854–55 report Newman was still referring to the degrees of bachelor, master, and doctor (although he contemplated a two-year qualification, later called 'scholar', from the beginning). In 1856 Newman received legal advice from his friend Edward Badeley, a leading Tractarian lawyer who had converted in 1852. Badeley advised that 'Degrees are to be regarded as titles of Honour, & that, as such, they can only be conferred by authority derived either from the Crown, or from an act of Parliament, or by some ancient prescriptive right, which may be presumed to have emanated from some Charter.' That being the case, Badeley wrote, 'the act of conferring Degrees, without such authority, may be treated as a violation of the law.'[54] In 1864 Woodlock sought advice on the same topic from his lawyer nephew and met with much the same response.[55]

Cullen seems to have fully committed himself to obtaining a charter somewhat late in the day. He was certainly assumed by his opponents, however, to be actively engaged in attempts to secure a charter from the very beginning. As his letter to Newman in early 1855 indicates, Cullen believed that Frederick Lucas and his allies were spreading the rumour that he intended to 'sell the Irish church, and that the price is to be a charter for the university.' Cullen does not seem to have fully committed himself to obtaining a charter until 1858. In May of that year he told Monsell that the archbishops were 'anxious to obtain a charter for the Catholic University' and asked him to take the matter to Lord Derby, the then prime minister. '[A]ll the bishops of Ireland', Cullen wrote, 'with the exception of Dr MacHale, and one or two others will join in a petition to her Majesty for a charter, if you having consulted Lord Derby should [tell] us to do so.'[56] In a second letter to Monsell that same day, Cullen remarked that it 'is a loss not to have a charter.' The problem as always was MacHale, and Cullen believed he would oppose a petition as 'he does not appear anxious to secure the success of the University.' Despite MacHale's obstructionism, they nevertheless needed to try: 'Had we a charter the number of students wd. soon increase.'[57]

Newman and Cullen were not the only ones concerned with the university who recognised the need for a charter. J. M. Capes, the editor of *The Rambler* and a friend of Newman's, put the case starkly in an article published in September 1857. After discussing the university's continuing problems with money, Capes declared that a 'charter for conferring degrees, then, the University must have.' He did not underestimate the problems in gaining such a charter and noted that 'it may be doubted' that the government would grant one to a Catholic institution unaffiliated with any other educational institution in Ireland, such as the Queen's University (the degree-granting body for the Queen's Colleges).[58] The faculty of the university, too, knew a charter to be necessary. They were unable, however, to put much of a plan into effect. The minutes for the 2 April 1857 meeting of the Council of the Faculty of Philosophy and Letters records that 'some desultory conversation followed about taking the Archbishops' opinion concerning an application for a charter: but no definite plan could be arranged.'[59]

Individual faculty members too took an interest in the question of a charter. Henry Hennessy told the episcopal board in the early 1860s that he had 'observed that very few students regarded the degrees or certificates of the University as possessing the slightest value, and several have respectfully complained to me of their inferior position compared to students in other universities.'[60] Thomas Arnold actively lobbied the Derby government for a charter. In January 1859 he told Newman that he had seen Lord Stanley (Derby's son) in order to 'speak to him about the charter.' Stanley was polite, but noncommittal. At any rate, it is unlikely that the Irish bishops would have appreciated Arnold's case for a charter: 'if the Government recognized it [the university], they would, so to speak, take a powerful weapon, or what might be easily made such, out of the hands of the enemies of England and imperial interests—secure Dublin and so on'.[61]

Arnold was right to target the Conservative government. There is evidence that as early as 1859 Disraeli at least had considered granting the CUI a charter, but he fell from office before he was able to make any move in that direction.[62] Under Lord Derby and Benjamin Disraeli, the Conservatives were better able than the Liberals to make concessions to Catholics. This might seem somewhat paradoxical given the many fire-eating ultra Protestants who inhabited the Tory back benches (and not infrequently the front bench). Certainly the Conservatives would happily ally themselves to almost any anti-Catholic legislation proposed by a Liberal government (although sometimes against Disraeli's wishes); nothing else was expected of them. However, political reality dictated that an inevitably minority Conservative government could only survive by dividing its opposition. Wooing Irish members could prove a very effective way of doing just that. Moreover, the Tories were not burdened, as the Liberals were, with a substantial component of the party which opposed *all* state-sponsored religious education; it was Sir Robert Inglis who had first called the Queen's Colleges 'Godless'.

On the level of personalities the Conservatives also made a good target for those seeking a charter for the CUI. It was not unknown for both

Derby and Disraeli to make anti-Catholic comments (Derby's 1865 comparison of Catholics to 'dogs that ought to be muzzled' was particularly unfortunate),[63] but neither man seems to have been bigoted to the point that it affected his pragmatism. Indeed, Disraeli had quite good things to say about the 'Old Faith' in *Sybil, Coningsby,* and *Tancred;* even *Lothair* is not as unambiguous an attack on Catholicism as it has often been made out to be (although Manning and Cullen, the latter briefly, are harshly treated). For his part, Derby had, as chief secretary in 1831, helped to establish the practically denominational national schools. In 1839 he told the House of Commons that 'Religion should be interwoven with all systems of education, controlling and regulating the whole mind and habits and principles of the persons receiving instruction.'[64] Derby had also backed Disraeli's tentative moves in 1852 to gain the support of Irish members with concessions on tenant rights—despite the fact that in Robert Blake's opinion Derby, like all other former chief secretaries, 'detested the native Irish.'[65] Certainly Disraeli was frustrated by his negotiations with Cullen in 1867–68 (hence the attack on Cullen in *Lothair,* where he was called 'Churchill'),[66] and he broke off those negotiations when they could no longer serve his purposes. But the point remains that he was willing and able to deliver a charter if he thought one useful to himself and his party.[67] That was more than the Liberals could do.

The Liberal party (as it was slowly becoming)—whether under Palmerston, Russell, or Gladstone—faced a much more complex situation. Whereas Derby and Disraeli could at least potentially grant concessions acceptable to Catholics on educational matters, the Liberals could not. In this period the Liberals were more a conglomeration of interest groups than a disciplined political party. Almost no group within the party would support Catholic claims to a specifically Catholic university. The influential Nonconformist element was opposed both to state-sponsored religious education (on the very good grounds that in England that usually meant Anglican education), and to Roman Catholicism (on religious grounds).[68] The Peelites and the more 'advanced' Liberals (insofar as they were not Nonconformists) might be amenable to addressing Catholic grievances but were in many cases suspicious of jettisoning the principle of 'mixed' education. Although Gladstone personally was sympathetic to Irish demands for a charter (and was known by Woodlock and Cullen to be), he was not able to carry his party in any acceptable agreement either before or after he assumed the leadership. Henry Bruce—a Liberal MP for Merthyr Tydvill in Wales who was heavily involved in the 1865 charter negotiations—spelled out the realities of the Liberal party for Woodlock in early 1866: 'The Scotch M.P.s are of two classes: one the ultra-liberals, who will make a stand against Gov't on this question, if they get it in their heads, that mixed or as they call it <u>liberal</u> Education is in danger: the second the bigots, who will oppose it, if they see it is favorable to Catholics. The ultra-liberals of England will join in the opposition for the reasons alleged by the first class: the "opposition Party" will join just to annoy the party in power.'[69]

Despite the difficulties of gaining concessions from the Liberals, Cullen was never as willing to openly support the Conservatives as, say, Wiseman had been. There were far too many ultra-Protestants on the Tory benches for his taste. He was hardly any more likely, however, to welcome a government headed by either Palmerston or Lord John Russell. Palmerston was not noted for his sympathy to the Catholic faith, and Russell could never in any Catholic's eyes escape from his 'mummeries of superstition' remark and the ecclesiastical titles bill. By late 1859 Cullen was distinctly pessimistic on the chances of gaining a charter. He told The O'Donoghue (at that time the leading Irish Catholic parliamentary figure), 'I fear we shall get little from the Whigs yet we cannot desire the advent of the Tories to power, since they place us at the mercy of Orangemen. . . . The Scotch and Presbyterian liberals are just as hostile to us as Whiteside and Lord Naas,[70] so it is necessary for us to steer between the two parties and to get as much as we can expect from enemies.'[71] Cullen knew that it was most unlikely that any possible British government would be minded to grant a charter for the university merely on the merits of the Catholic case.

The resignation of the Derby government in April 1859, and its subsequent electoral defeat made a charter even less likely. Worse still was Palmerston's appointment of Sir Robert Peel (son of the more famous father) as chief secretary in July 1861. Peel has been described by Emmet Larkin as 'at one and the same time an evangelical Protestant and an enthusiastic supporter of the policies of Garibalidi and the late count Cavour in Italy.'[72] Peel was militantly anti-Catholic to the point that he was known, as his father had been, as 'Orange Peel'. Although of no particular ability and temperamentally unstable, he nonetheless gained a measure of popularity by baiting Cullen and the Irish hierarchy. He initiated a campaign to extend scholarships at the Queen's Colleges and even proposed opening a new college in Dublin. A clearer provocation is difficult to imagine, and Cullen launched a vitriolic attack on Peel in the *Freeman's Journal* of 9 November. Peel responded in kind. As Lord Stanley put it in his journal, 'Dr Cullen having attacked him in the ordinary style of the Catholic priests, that is, very violently, he has retorted in the same strain'. (Stanley himself—no bigot—thought that Peel had

had the better of the exchange.) He noted that the 'Protestants are loud in their rejoicings: the Catholics equally loud in censure. Ireland is thoroughly stirred up.'[73] Peel remained as chief secretary until 1865, and as long as he was in office (and Palmerston was prime minister) there was little or no chance of a charter.

There were some desultory attempts to gain a charter during this period, but none ever came close to success. In the same month as Peel's appointment, Woodlock informed Monsell that the best model for a charter was that of the University of London. After all, 'that Institution is a free University, with whose establishment the Government had nothing to do, so also is ours: that as the former has received a charter, so also can we demand it.'[74] The fact that London had a charter and that, in 1856, a charter had been granted to the Catholic seminary at Laval, Quebec, seemed to imply a precedent of which the CUI could take advantage. That precedent, however, was more imagined than real. Quebec was far away and London, whatever else it might be, was certainly not Catholic. Ireland was too close and Catholicism too unpopular for Parliament to be swayed by logical argument or appeals to precedent. By mid-1862 Woodlock had informed Cullen that he had been advised by Irish MPs that united parliamentary action would prove futile.[75] In June 1863 Woodlock reported that both More O'Ferrall and William Monsell held out little hope of obtaining a charter and had instead focused their attentions on a plan to create a Catholic hall at either Oxford or Cambridge.[76]

Despite the difficulties, Woodlock never entirely gave up hope of securing a charter even while Peel remained chief secretary. Throughout 1862 he urged the various Irish corporations and towns to send memorials to the government urging the granting of a charter. He also initiated a petition drive. Although Woodlock met with some success in gaining support in Ireland, the campaign proved ineffective; the memorials and petitions were simply ignored by Palmerston and Peel.

In addition to his attempts to apply public pressure on the government, Woodlock also sought to make the university itself more palatable to it. His solution was to introduce a lay element into its management. Woodlock's intention was to make the university less objectionable to both ultra-Protestants and voluntarist Liberals by reducing the visible and total clerical control first recommended by Newman and the Thurles subcommittee in 1851. The change need not, in Woodlock's view, threaten the Catholicity of the institution. As More O'Ferrall told him in February 1862: 'If they [the bishops] retain formally in their own hands all that pertains to the security of faith and the means of doing so, they may safely share all other power with the laity.'[77] There were precedents. From the beginning Maynooth had been administered by a board consisting of both clerics and laity. There too questions of faith and morals had been left to the sole discretion of the episcopal members of the board. As Maynooth was a seminary, almost all matters that might come to the attention of the board could be classed as questions of faith and morals and were thus left to the bishops. Cullen, however, was never comfortable with Maynooth and it is at least possible that the lay trustees' refusal to support his candidate for president of the college in 1857 may have contributed to his unwillingness to allow laymen into the management of the CUI a few years later.[78]

Woodlock's idea was that increasing lay involvement would serve to both increase lay interest and financial support and, perhaps, make it easier to gain a charter. After all, Maynooth had such a board and held both a charter (although it was not empowered to grant degrees) and was financially supported by the British government. His proposal was to add twelve laymen and the rector to the episcopal board and make the resulting body the one that would seek a charter from the government. In the first instance the lay members would be elected by the entire bench of bishops (not just those that sat on the board). Each year four of the lay members would depart—although they could be reelected—and their replacements would be elected by a majority vote of the entire board, including the laymen.[79] Under Woodlock's plan the laity would quickly come to dominate the episcopal board. He had no intention, however, of giving them control over religious questions, a sphere that he defined very broadly indeed. The episcopal members of the board would 'alone be the judges in all cases regarding faith or morals, that they have a right to veto any appointment before it is made, & to exclude any book, without giving any reason for doing so: that they have the right to represent to the Board the teaching of any Professor or other teacher, as contrary to the doctrine or discipline of the Church, and the Board be thereupon obliged to suspend or dismiss such Professor or other teacher.' The entire body of bishops would also retain the right to appoint and remove the rector.[80] All in all, the plan was one with which Newman would have happily associated himself.

Perhaps with recent events in Maynooth in mind, Cullen had no intention of lending his support to such a plan. He did not tell Woodlock this, though, and let him believe that he was prepared to at least tentatively support the plan when the bishops met to consider it. There seems to have been as little enthusiasm among the bishops for a lay-dominated board as there had been for a lay vice-rector. MacHale predictably opposed the plan on the familiar grounds that it would usurp the power of the bishops. He also expressed the view that laymen couldn't be trusted not to support England. Cullen expressed his own opinion to Kirby: 'I think it is not of any great importance to have the laymen in question. They do without laymen in Belgium. We have scarcely any great laymen, who could help to keep up the University and it is in the body of the people that we must rely.'[81]

Cullen placed the blame for the bishops' rejection of the plan (during their meeting in August 1863) on MacHale. Emmet Larkin has pointed out that this was yet another example of Cullen's political skills. He informed Rome that laymen wished to be on the board only because of the troubled state of the university. But, according to Cullen, the university was in such a condition because of MacHale. As Larkin noted, Cullen's report to the Propaganda allowed 'him to blame both the failure of the University and the demand for power sharing by the laity on MacHale, but even more important, it allowed him to continue to mask from Woodlock his own more crucial opposition to laymen on the board of the University.'[82] Cullen knew perfectly well that MacHale would oppose the plan, as in fact did most of the other bishops. Given that he could blame MacHale for its failure, he evidently did not see any reason why he should pick a fight with his rector. Certainly he could not afford the possibility of Woodlock resigning. It had taken nearly three years from Newman's resignation to appoint him.

The August 1863 bishops' meeting did introduce a smaller lay element—of eight—but left the board fully under episcopal control. Cullen had again found himself in a difficult situation. Neither he nor most of his fellow bishops could support what they saw as lay domination of the university (however extensive the reserved episcopal powers); the steady decline in collections from 1863 could only accelerate if laymen took over. However, the university required the support of the Irish Catholic laity to survive and, perhaps, grow. It also desperately needed a charter. And even if Palmerston and Peel were to leave office it was impossible to visualise a situation in which a British government would be willing or able to grant a charter directly to a corporation consisting largely or exclusively of Irish Catholic bishops. Not for the first or last time, Cullen tried to have it both ways. He introduced a small lay element in the hopes that it would both satisfy lay demands and pass parliamentary scrutiny. But he refused to countenance a lay-dominated board that could never have commanded the support of a majority of the bishops and would likely have resulted in the collapse of university fundraising. His compromise was a failure. Precious few laymen of station would willingly join a body subservient to the bishops; nor would the presence of eight laymen do much to quiet parliamentary objections to a charter.

Despite these various initiatives, there was little or no progress towards actually obtaining a charter between the fall of the Derby government in 1859 and slightly before the death of Palmerston on 16 November 1865. Although Palmerston's death (and Peel's departure) cleared the ground, there had already before that event been contacts between Woodlock and senior members of the Liberal government. In June, Woodlock informed Cullen that the home secretary, Sir George Grey, Gladstone, and Edward Cardwell (a once and future chief secretary) were in favour of some sort of charter. He was optimistic that they might be granted one on the Belgian model.[83] After a private meeting with Gladstone (who declared himself to be 'heart & soul with us'), Woodlock thought it likely that the CUI would be chartered as a college—much as Maynooth was—and that there would be a subsequent commission charged with reforming the Queen's University to meet Catholic demands. Woodlock still preferred the Belgian model and through The O'Donoghue again pressed this course on the government.[84]

By 19 June, Woodlock was able to report what he believed to be a victory in cabinet and urged Cullen to make the CUI ready for its new status: 'if we want to be recognized as able to teach, we must show, that we have the machinery ready.' Woodlock wanted Cullen to create various chairs, but not to name the incumbents to them just yet.[85] The next day Woodlock more fully informed Cullen of the situation:

> Sir George Grey is decidedly in our favour, and will do everything he can do without a special Act of Parliament. Of this he has apprised Mr Monsell. This evening I think they will declare their willingness to modify the Queen's University so as to meet our wishes & to give us a fair representation upon it. They will recognize our right to educate Catholics, and will give us a Charter of incorporation, if it can be done without an Act of Parliament. . . . I do not know how far they will <u>declare</u> all this to-night; for L. Palmerston was <u>dead against</u> us in the Council & the thing was carried against him. They are also afraid of the bigoted party in this country.[86]

The problem was that the government was unwilling or unable to propose anything that Cullen and the majority of the bishops would find acceptable. And without the bishops—and especially Cullen—there was no point in doing a deal. William Monsell made this point to Woodlock when he wrote to ask the rector to see if there were any of the proposed solutions that Cullen might support: 'there is no use in reading any he does not sanction.'[87] With Palmerston still alive and Peel still chief secretary, there was little chance of finding a compromise acceptable to all sides. Less than two weeks after Palmerston's death, Grey invited the four Irish archbishops to London to discuss university education. It seemed possible that something positive might be done—even if Lord John (now Earl) Russell was again prime minister. Cullen was initially quite hopeful. He told Kirby that at their meeting Sir George Grey had given the archbishops 'good hopes that something will be done for us.'[88]

Cullen's confidence soon faltered. By late December he told Kirby that the 'question now is, shall we get anything from the government?' He thought not, and, if not, 'it is probable that our University will fall.'[89] Grey replied to the bishops' proposals (submitted in the form of a memorial) in January. He proposed that the charter of the Queen's University be modified to conform to the model of the University of London. Students would be able to receive its degrees so long as they passed its examinations. The Catholic University could, Grey proposed, be granted a charter of incorporation as a college but not as a university. Moreover, although the Catholic archbishops might be visitors, if 'it is to receive a Charter from the Crown [its governing body] should not be entirely composed of Ecclesiastics but should contain a considerable proportion of laymen.'[90] Unsurprisingly, such proposals met with overwhelming episcopal opposition, although Cullen deferred final judgement until the proposed charter actually appeared. He clearly held out little hope, and he told Kirby on 2 February that the 'government will do no good. They put us to a great deal of trouble, but after all we get nothing.'[91]

Woodlock was not as pessimistic as was Cullen. He informed the archbishop of Dublin on 13 February that the proposed charter would create a new entity called the 'Queen's Irish University'. Two Catholic bishops (chosen by the bench of bishops) would sit by right on its senate along with between six and eight lay Catholics (as well as Woodlock himself and Charles Russell of Maynooth).[92] Protestants, however, would retain a majority on the senate. If a majority lay element on the Catholic University board had proved unacceptable to Cullen and the hierarchy in 1863 it was hardly likely that they would agree to this proposal, let alone with Protestants added to the mix. If Cullen and the hierarchy were consistent, so too was Woodlock. He had favoured lay control since at least 1862 and he did so now. His letters to Cullen always recommended taking nearly anything on offer. Even when Manning (now archbishop of Westminster) informed him in late February 1866 that the government was likely to fall and that a better deal could be obtained from Derby, Woodlock still urged the acceptance of the ministry's proposals with a view to using them as a starting point for further negotiations.[93] Woodlock's reasoning was clear: it was better to take something now and ask for more later—especially as the university itself was in such a 'precarious position'.[94]

For his part, Cullen was unprepared to accept the possible salvation of the university at the price of effectively turning the higher education of Irish Catholics over to a body, the senate of the Queen's Irish University, which would not be under Catholic, let alone episcopal, control. Nor was he willing to cede control of the university to a board dominated by laymen. What both he and Woodlock did come to accept in 1865–66, however, was that the Catholic University of Ireland could no longer continue as an independent university in the fullest sense of that word. Both men were willing to see the university affiliated with some sort of new degree-granting institution. Although they differed on what form that institution must take, they implicitly agreed that the Catholic University as a university was dead. Woodlock summed up the state of affairs that would exist if no suitable charter were obtained: 'if our [University] gets no Charter and obtains no position before the country, it will, I fear, be dragged down to a level with the lowest school in the country, be turned into an <u>academy in Stephen's Green,</u>—not as good for teaching boys and forcing them to learn as many others—and, in fact, be effectually "snuffed out"'.[95] In 1867 W. K. Sullivan, the professor of chemistry, even suggested—perhaps only half-seriously—that the CUI could be transferred to New York and 'instead of American students crowding its halls in Ireland, & drinking in the traditions of its past, as Dr. Newman dreamed, Irish students would crowd the halls of its American institutions'.[96]

Negotiations continued over the next several years. In 1868, with a Conservative government in power, efforts became particularly intense, and Cullen at least seems to have believed that both a charter and a government endowment were within his grasp. Although willing to take a charter without an endowment (which might cause the government to demand too much control over the university's governance), Cullen preferred to get both together, albeit on his own terms. Leahy was despatched to London to meet Disraeli, and Cullen told him that 'very probably you wd. succeed in inducing him to grant the endowment as well as the charter.'[97] Unfortunately for Cullen and the university, Gladstone, now the leader of the Liberal party, declared himself in favour of disestablishing the Irish church—not something, of course, that Cullen would disapprove of. As the Conservatives were only interested in granting a charter to the CUI in order to secure Irish parliamentary support for their minority government, Gladstone's announcement spelled an end to both the government and the chance at a charter. The Tories could only remain in office so long as the opposition was divided. Irish disestablishment was something that nearly all shades of Liberal opinion could agree on. Certainly Irish Catholic members would back any government promising such a thing. Back in office, Gladstone made a further attempt at a charter in 1873, but Cullen opposed it as unacceptable with fatal consequences for the both the bill and the government.[98] He dismissed Gladstone's efforts as upholding mixed education and remarked to Monsell that it was a pity that 'when Mr. Gladstone took up this matter, he did not adopt a more liberal course.'[99]

Despite these failures, the Catholic University continued its precarious existence. It was not until 1880—two years after Cullen's death—that an agreement acceptable to all parties was arrived at. A new entity—the Royal University of Ireland—was created and was empowered to award degrees to all students who were able to pass its examinations. An endowment of sorts was created for the Catholic University in that a large proportion of the fellows (examiners) of the Royal University were to be drawn from it. The stipend attached to a fellowship relieved the CUI (really now University College) of at least part of the burden of academic salaries. In fact, the 1880 settlement closely resembled, except for the fellowships, what had been offered in 1865–66. In fact, the negotiations of 1865–66 marked the end of the Catholic University of Ireland as a viable concern. Thereafter the university was kept alive more as a cause than as a reality. To be sure, there were various plans to revivify it, notably the idea to join it with Maynooth in a 'St Patrick's University', but nothing ever took hold. Technically, the history of the Catholic University of Ireland can be said to run from Rome's first mention of the idea in 1846 through to the 1950s when its last 'rector' was appointed. In reality, the story of the Catholic University as an institute of higher learning closes in the winter of 1865–66.

The last words on the state of the university in 1865 (even before the charter negotiations failed) belong to Bartholomew Woodlock: 'No one doubts that the present position of this University is most unsatisfactory. The small and not increasing number of its students, the want of motives for study or sanction for discipline, by withholding degrees, as in other Universities, the estrangement of Catholics of position, both those aspiring to professions and others, all show that something is needed to secure the efficiency, nay, the very existence of the University.'[100] That 'something' never came.

chapter ten

An Actual, Existing University

THE STRUCTURE, STUDY, AND LIFE OF THE UNIVERSITY

IN NOVEMBER 1851 JOHN HENRY NEWMAN, PATRICK LEAHY, AND THE Thurles subcommittee recommended that the Catholic University of Ireland should consist of the traditional four faculties of arts, law, medicine, and theology. It was decided, however, to closely examine only the plans for the arts faculty, as it was the only one likely to be ready when the university first opened (whenever that might be). The arts were to be divided into two 'branches', letters and science. At Thurles these were defined as consisting of, in letters: 'Latin; Greek; the Semitic and Modern Languages; History, Ancient and Modern, both National and Ecclesiastical; Archaeology, Christian and Profane; English Literature, and Criticism.' Science was defined as the fields of: 'Logic, Metaphysics, Ethics, including Economy and Politics; Philosophy of Religion; Mathematics; Natural Philosophy; Chemistry; Natural History; Mineralogy and Geology'. Nor was science to be limited to these specific disciplines, as the list terminated with an 'etc., etc.'. In addition to the letters and sciences, it was envisioned that there should be a school of engineering subsidiary to the faculty of arts. It was also decided that the BA course should be four years, with an undefined number of further years for the MA.[1]

The Thurles report also set out the obligations of the faculty as to the profession of the Catholic religion, both personally and in their teaching. All 'Officers and Professors of the University' would be required to make a profession of faith, and in their teaching would be 'bound' not 'to teach anything contrary to Religion'. Moreover, professors were to 'take advantage of the occasion the subjects they treat of may offer, to point out that Religion is the basis of Science, and to inculcate the love of Religion and its duties.'² Although there could be no doubt that both teachers and teaching were to be explicitly Catholic, it should be noted that the phrase 'subjects they treat may offer' did allow a certain latitude for deciding just when a particular subject offered such an opportunity. Newman would later (1856) expand on this requirement in a letter to his faculty. He held that, so far as formal instruction went, the 'subject of religion in the school of Philosophy and Letters' would be treated 'simply as a branch of knowledge'.³ He wished the students to learn about the history of both scripture and the church. Naturally, this history would be taught from a specifically Catholic viewpoint and would 'encourage in our students an intelligent apprehension of the relations . . . between the Church and society at large; for instance, the difference between the Church and a religious sect; between the Church and the civil power; what the Church claims of necessity, what it cannot dispense with, what it can; what it can grant, what it cannot.'⁴

Although three years passed between the submission of the Thurles report to the university committee and the opening of the university itself, the substance of that report was nonetheless kept in view by Newman. Details certainly changed, but the essence (to use a favourite word of Newman's) of the plan remained; if not exactly the same, then remarkably similar. Newman's lectures of 1852—the heart of the *Idea of a University*—largely dealt with his vision of a university as such, its ends and its purpose, and particularly with the necessity of incorporating theological study within it. He was not for the most part concerned with spelling out to his audience the exact form and practices that would be assumed by the new university.

After Thurles, the next substantial statement of goals and practices came in a submission by Newman to the May 1854 synod in Dublin. Newman's memorandum set out for the assembled hierarchy what exactly the new university would be like (it was only some five months away from opening). To that end, he listed what he believed to be the objects for which the Catholic University was to be established. In general it was to 'provide for Catholic Education (in a large sense of the word "education") in various respects, in which at present we have to depend upon Protestant institutions and Protestant writings.' Newman then noted ten specific objects of the new university. They give a good idea both of what Newman planned for the Catholic University and what the bishops believed themselves to be getting.

1. To provide means of finishing the education of young men of rank, fortune or expectations, with a view of putting them on a level with Protestants of the same description.
2. To provide a professional education for students of law and medicine, and a liberal education for youths destined to mercantile and similar pursuits, as far as their time will admit it.
3. To develop the talents of promising youths in the lower classes of the community.
4. To form a school of theology and canon law suited to the needs of a class of students who may be required to carry on those sciences beyond the point of attainment ordinarily sufficient for parochial duty.
5. To provide a series of sound and philosophical defences of Catholicity and Revelation, in answer to the infidel tracts and arguments which threaten to be our most serious opponents in the era now commencing.
6. To create a national Catholic literature.
7. To provide school books, and generally books of instruction, for the Catholics of the United Kingdom, and of the British Empire, and of the United States.
8. To raise the standard, and systematize the teaching, and encourage the efforts, of the schools already so ably and zealously conducted throughout the country.
9. To give a Catholic tone to society in the great towns.
10. To respond to the growing importance of Ireland, arising from its geographical position, as the medium of intercourse between East and West, and the centre of the Catholicism of the English tongue, with Great Britain, Malta (perhaps Turkey or Egypt), and India, on one side of it, and North America, and Australia, on the other.[5]

With these objects in mind, Newman explained to the bishops how the university would be staffed. Newman expressed his preference for an eminent professoriate, observing that 'students . . . are to be gained specifically and pre-eminently by means of the celebrity of the Professors.' That being the case, the professors should be appointed before students were found for them to teach.[6] Newman presciently recognised that there might be some objection to hiring a large number of professors before there was anything for them to do. He suggested to the bishops that it might be of value to establish 'institutions, which will have their value intrinsically, whether students are present or not.' Examples of such institutions were the medical staff of a hospital, an observatory, or an 'archaeological department' which would concern itself with the 'language, remains, MSS., etc., of ancient Ireland, with a special reference to Catholicity.'[7] To modern ears Newman's proposals sound very close indeed to research institutes.

Near the end of his tenure in Dublin Newman created the *Atlantis*, a journal specifically designed to showcase the academic work of the university's faculty. As Newman put it in a letter to James Hope-Scott, it was to be 'a dry professional production which will show that we are at work and doing something.' In perhaps the neatest summary of the purposes of an academic journal yet written, Newman told Hope-Scott that the 'Professors will write: 1. To puff themselves to the world; and 2. to be *doing* something lest their Professorships should be taken away.'[8] The *Atlantis* continued in half-yearly parts until 1870 and contained substantial articles, some contributed by Newman, on various subjects of literary and scientific interest (science predominated).

Newman's academic appointments fell into two broad categories, which we can more or less call working and decorative. In the latter category fell such men as Aubrey DeVere, John Hungerford Pollen, and T. W. Allies. Their purpose was to give one or more courses of public lectures and to lend their names to the university (in Allies' case there was a further desire on Newman's part to supplement his income). They were not expected to handle the day-to-day tasks of lecturing the students or assessing their progress. Newman's idea was that retaining famous names to lecture in the university and bear the title of professor or lecturer would obtain for the institution a standing and intellectual credibility that it could not otherwise hope to achieve. In a sense these 'decorative' appointments were somewhat analogous to the eminent professor in a modern research university who descends periodically to give a series of lectures before returning to his laboratory or library. Oxford's professor of poetry is perhaps the most obvious example of the type, one that would have been well known to Newman (his friend John Keble had long held the post).

Obviously, no university could sustain itself only by retaining the services of eminent but nonresident and nonteaching professors. Setting aside appointments in the medical school, Newman retained a core of twelve teaching faculty. By 1859 (the year after Newman left) this group

had coalesced to include: Edward Butler, W. G. Penny, Peter le Page
Renouf, J. B. Robertson, Henry Hennessy, a Signor Marani, the Abbé
Schürr, Robert Ornsby, D. B. Dunne, James Stewart, Thomas Arnold,
and W. K. Sullivan. Respectively, these men taught: maths; catechism; ancient history and French; modern history, geography and international
law; natural philosophy (including physics); Italian and Spanish; French
and German; classics; logic and ethics; classics (including Latin composition); English literature; and chemistry.[9] Obviously, there was some va-
riety both to the make-up of this group (Eugene O'Curry, although
remaining a professor, seems to have dropped his teaching responsibilities sometime after 1856) and to what each individual taught, but
there was a surprising consistency to the core teaching group both
before and after Newman's departure as rector.

This group was not in any way intellectually second-rate or without
their own research interests. Renouf became a prominent Egyptologist
and published heavily in the subject. He was appointed keeper of Egyp-
tian and Assyrian antiquities at the British museum in 1885 and was
knighted in 1891. His collected works run to several volumes.[10] Henry
Hennessy was elected a fellow of the Royal Society in 1858 and published on such varied topics as the best way to teach science and the need
for a uniform international system of weights, measures, and coinage.[11]
Thomas Arnold published extensively throughout his career, producing
among other things a translation of *Beowulf* and editions of Dryden and
Pope.[12] Robert Ornsby published an edition of the Greek New Testament,[13] and J. B. Robertson published both his lectures on modern history delivered in the Catholic University and a series of lectures on
Edmund Burke.[14]

Perhaps the most prominent member of the teaching staff was
Eugene O'Curry. He had been an early member of the ordnance survey
and had long worked on cataloguing the Gaelic manuscripts held by the
Royal Irish Academy, British Museum, and Trinity College, Dublin. By
the time he was appointed to the Catholic University, O'Curry was already a member of the Royal Irish Academy and had an unparalleled
knowledge of early Irish history. His lectures to the Catholic University
were published in 1861 as *Lectures on the Manuscript Materials of Ancient Irish History* (another volume of lectures appeared posthumously
in 1872). The university authorities—and Paul Cullen personally—had
long urged O'Curry to publish his work.[15] After O'Curry's death in
1862, Bartholomew Woodlock made a sustained (and eventually successful) effort with the support of the hierarchy to obtain his manuscript collection for the university.[16] Those manuscripts eventually appeared in six

volumes as the *Ancient Laws of Ireland*. By 1864 Woodlock had made the acquisition and publication of O'Curry's manuscripts a central plank in his appeal to American Catholics for further funds for the university.[17]

After he had obtained an academic staff for the new university, Newman turned his attention to its internal institutions. As a 'means of securing Catholic unity' within the university, Newman proposed that the students be assigned to live together in small communities under the supervision of a dean (who would also be a priest). Some of the more advanced students in the community would tutor the more junior ones.[18] Newman hoped that in time these houses would develop into colleges on the Oxbridge model. In his 1854–55 report to the bishops Newman expanded on his idea. The university 'Houses' were 'instituted in order to [ensure] the enforcement of discipline upon young men, who are at a very anxious time of life, and come to us under very anxious circumstances.' The communities were to be kept small, as '[p]ersonal influence requires personal acquaintance'.[19] It was Oriel and St Aldate's all over again. Students would live and be taught in small communities under the supervision of a priest. It was there, and not in the university as such, that moral formation was to be pursued. In his Harcourt Street House (which he called St Mary's), Newman put this plan into practice himself.

It is important to emphasise this point: Newman's Dublin lectures clearly show that he was not interested in the university *as such* inculcating Catholic morality and practice. That was not its function. That is not to say, however, that he did not believe that such a thing was needed for the young men who attended the university. The place for that would be within the university houses, where the students would live, study, and play. They would also pray there and be under clerical supervision. The houses were designed to be small enough that the all-important personal influence could be exercised. The matter is best seen as a division of labour: the university would see to the education of its students (including in theology); the houses (and later the hoped-for colleges) were designed to ensure the morality and Catholicity of the university's students. The practice would be similar in some ways to the Roman practice of national colleges and larger, multinational pontifical universities; one looked after the students' moral and religious formation, the other his academic education.

Although the Catholic University of Ireland was largely unable to expand beyond the faculties of arts and medicine, that does not mean that Newman and the Irish bishops did not wish it to. The first of Newman's annual reports to the bishops acknowledged that it was 'essential' to open the arts faculty immediately, but its activities were necessarily 'the work of a College'. As the bishops were founding a university, Newman advised them (as he had in May 1854) that hiring eminent professors and establishing intrinsically useful institutions was the best means of beginning.[20] By the time he came to make his report in October 1855, Newman was able to point to some progress towards the building of a university as such. The most obvious expansion in the first year was the medical school. In addition to a second faculty, Newman had also arranged for a substantial purchase of chemical apparatus—before even the appointment of a professor of chemistry. With Newman's blessing, the professor of natural philosophy (Henry Hennessy) had outfitted his labs with equipment from Paris, and Newman believed that he had 'good reason for anticipating that an Institution in Physical Science will have been created, which has no parallel at present in the United Kingdom.'[21] The bishops were also informed that Newman had himself taken the lease of ground next to university house for a university church. The library, too, was growing satisfactorily and was the beneficiary of a number of donations (including, ironically enough, the personal library of the late Archbishop Murray). Newman was forced to report, however, that he had made no progress towards founding a theological school or university press, although he hoped to make progress towards both in the near future.[22]

By his second report, delivered on 31 October 1856, Newman was able to describe the administrative and academic organisation of the university, which he modeled after Louvain. Since, he told the bishops, Louvain had been a 'great success', 'I had evidently nothing more to do than, in accepting what was already provided for me, to adapt it, in certain of its details, to our own peculiar circumstances'.[23] Two bodies were created to govern academic affairs, a rectorial council and an academic senate. As at Louvain, the council consisted of the rector, vice-rector, and the deans of the faculties. In a modification of his own, Newman also added three professors from the faculty of philosophy and letters on the grounds that it was the dominant faculty of the university. The council was charged with advising the rector and with assisting him in the drafting of academic regulations.[24]

The academic senate was created with the express purpose of approving the regulations and statutes drawn up by the rectorial council and approved by the bishops. It was to be the final authority (under the bishops) in the university. In the composition of the senate Newman deviated quite significantly from Louvain. He was concerned to create a body that could not be dominated by an 'oligarchy' of resident professors. To that end he created 'Fellows of the University' who were members of the senate but not resident in the university and could serve as a 'check upon the power of the Senate, such as the Senate is itself upon any tendency to arbitrary spirit of the part of the Rulers and Officials of the University.' Of course, Newman noted that the 'Senate, as well as every other function and department of the University, is ultimately responsible to your Lordships'.[25] Newman's concern to avoid 'oligarchy' and provide a check on the power of university officers no doubt grew out of his own frequent conflicts with the authorities in Oxford.

Practical achievements during the year included the foundation of a number of burses in the school of letters for those who eventually wished to attend the medical school. In creating these burses Newman was addressing a concern that the medical school and its students had little to do with the university as a whole. The fifty-three students in the medical school from October 1856 were 'almost entirely' not matriculated members of the Catholic University and had not passed through the faculty of arts and letters. Eventually, Newman hoped that most (never all) medical students would first pursue a two-year arts course before enrolling in the medical school.[26] Newman was also able to report the opening of a fourth residential house and the dedication (in Cullen's presence) of the university church. No mention was made of a formal opening of either the faculty of law or theology. By his 1857 report Newman felt able to declare that the two faculties of arts and medicine were fully and satisfactorily underway.[27] He even turned his attention to such future needs as a hospital and a museum (there was already a nucleus of a collection for the latter).[28] As we have seen, however, after 1857 Newman was already well on his way to separating himself permanently from the university, and further material progress had to await Woodlock's appointment in 1861.

The students could pursue a number of options at the university. Young men would, Newman thought, normally enter at about the age of sixteen (he himself had matriculated at Oxford while only fifteen) and would be resident there. Once a student had matriculated, he would pursue a two-year course in 'classics, the elements of mathematics and logic, ancient history, etc.' At the end of that course there was an examination which, if passed, would earn him an 'initial degree'. Under Irish circumstances the university must, Newman wrote, expect to lose 'the majority of our students' at this point. These years would not be wasted, as Newman observed that 'those who are destined for business will nevertheless have gained a certain amount of liberal education, without any unreasonable postponement of the time when they are to enter on the duties of their particular calling.' Those students who did not leave at eighteen could expect to follow two more years of study in 'modern history, political economy, law, metaphysics, etc.' which would conclude with an examination and the awarding of the bachelor of arts degree (thus keeping intact the Thurles scheme of a four-year BA). Three additional years of study were now required for the MA or the doctorate in law, medicine, or theology.[29] Although the university was forced to alter the names of its qualifications because of the lack of a charter, the basic scheme remained the same throughout Newman's tenure and beyond.

The Catholic University of Ireland opened on 3 November 1854 with 'no pomp and circumstance to set off the event; no crowds assembled to behold a spectacle.'[30] That same day Leahy, Ornsby (now professor of classical literature) and D. B. Dunne (the lecturer in logic) conducted the entrance examinations. According to the *Catholic University Gazette*, the examination consisted of 'Latin composition and of questions submitted to the candidates on paper; after which a further trial was given to each student separately, by questions asked and answered *vivâ voce*'. 'Above twenty' passed the exam and became students of the university—including Daniel O'Connell, grandson of the 'Liberator'.[31] Two days later Newman held a *'soirée'* for students and staff where he was introduced to each of the students and gave them a short talk about university education. On 6 November the first lectures were held and on 9 November Newman gave his inaugural lecture (followed by Leahy and the other professors in turn).[32]

In January 1855 the university expected its students to attend, on Monday, Wednesday, and Friday, lectures on both Euclid and Euripides (not together); on Monday they heard Robert Ornsby discuss the *Odes* of Horace; and on Mondays and Wednesdays they received lectures on ancient history. On Friday the new students were introduced to ancient geography. Evening lectures, which met at nine every weeknight, alternated between Irish ('The Irish Language and Literature'), geography ('The Geography of the First Ages of Mankind'), holy scripture ('Inspiration, Canon, and Interpretation, and Uses of Scripture'), classical literature ('Seneca and the Roman School of Stoic Philosophy'), poetry ('Spanish Poetry'), and Italian ('Dante's *Inferno*').[33]

Engineering students followed a practical course that included discussions on fluid bodies; heat; machine theory; the equilibrium of structures; material strength; the application of the laws of sound in the construction of public buildings; the laws of reflection and refraction of light; mining and tunnelling, electro-magnetism; and technical drawing. It was Newman's intention that, as the university developed, students in such courses as engineering would first be exposed to two years of classical education in the faculty of philosophy and letters. Scripture and religion certainly played a part in the Catholic University's curriculum—lectures on dog-

matic theology averaged thirty students (by no means all of them matriculated students) and Cullen established a £30 prize for the best essay on a
theological subject—but it was by no means the dominant element.[34] As
for the theology faculty itself, it had professors, but not students and no
real form either in Newman's day or after.

Classics were the primary component of the university's curriculum.
Certainly, those hoping to gain an exhibition to the Catholic University
from an Irish school had to be well versed in the classical canon. In 1856
(only the University's second full year of operation) a prospective exhi-
bitioner had to be prepared to be examined on: '*Oedipus Rex*, Xenephon's
Memorabilia, and Herodotus I; Horace, 3 books of *Odes*, Cicero's
Catalinarians, Virgil's *Georgics*, 2 books'. Prospective scholars had to be
conversant in: 'Aeschylus *Agamemnon*, Demosthenes *Philippics* I. II.
Thucydides I. Horace *Ars Poetica*, Cicero *de Oratore* I. Tacitus *Agri-
cola*.'[35] All texts would be in their original language.

Samples of the type of question that could be asked in an exhibition
exam were printed in the *Catholic University Gazette*. Included in the
classics examination, for instance, was 'Constrast the national character
formed by the institutions of Lycurgus with that of the Athenian people.'[36]
There was also a mathematics exhibition for those whose interest in the
classics did not extend to the finer points of Greek grammar or Roman
history. A sample question for this examination was: 'Give an algebraic solution of the 11th Prop[osition] of the second Book of Euclid. Explain the
negative result. Show how the value of x is to be constructed.'[37] Newman
did elsewhere caution the prospective student 'not to be frightened at the
apparently high standard which has been adopted' for exhibitions on the
grounds that 'what is *desirable* and to be *aimed at*' is different from what
might actually be achieved.[38] Nevertheless, such exam questions neatly
reveal both the emphasis and the rigour of the new university.

As intimidating as the exhibition exam was, the prescribed course
for the university as a whole was little easier. Adopted in 1856, the regulations for examinations provide a useful window into the studies pursued
by students at the Catholic University of Ireland. Entrance examinations
were simply used to determine 'whether a candidate for admission is in a
condition to profit by the course of study' that he would pursue if admitted. In Newman's view the university required an assurance that a
prospective student was 'already well grounded in the elements' of those
fields to be pursued there.[39]

Serious exams began after two years of residence. Newman created
the qualification of 'Scholar' to meet the needs of Irish students who
were unable, for whatever reason, to pursue more than two years of uni-

versity study in the arts. Those who wished to continue with their studies were also required to sit this examination. To become a scholar, the student had to offer himself for examination in three of four subjects. These were '1. The text and matter of one Greek book' from a list of acceptable titles. '2. The text and matter from one Latin book', again from a set list. Section three—the only one required of all candidates—was divided into seven parts: philosophy, criticism, geography, chronology, mathematics, logic, and physical science. There were set texts in each of these fields upon which the student could expect to be examined. Finally, the student could choose to be examined in 'one modern language and literature.' As if this were not enough, all were required to be 'prepared with an exact knowledge of the matters contained in some longer Catechism and in the four Gospels, and with a general knowledge of ancient history, geography, chronology, and the principles of composition'.[40]

It was envisioned that after the successful completion of the scholars' exam the student would face a number of choices. He could leave the university with a credential, join one of the professional faculties (theology, law, medicine), or remain in the school of letters and pursue the 'Licentiate in Letters' (the BA equivalent). If he chose the last option, he then had either to select the faculty of science or to remain in the arts. Those who remained in the arts could expect increasingly rigorous demands. As Newman put it, the school of letters 'now addresses none but those who voluntarily attend its classes as an end; and its peculiar studies gain accordingly, and the character of its Examination is materially affected.'[41] The licentiate examination was divided into two parts, one to be held at the end of the third year and one at the end of the fourth. Students would also be assessed as to whether they had passed satisfactorily or meritoriously. By passing the first portion of the exam, a student received the title of 'Inceptor', which he retained until passing the final examination at the end of his fourth year.

All students, whether shooting for satisfactory or meritorious status, took examinations under four broad headings: Christian knowledge, philosophy, literature, and history. The amount of knowledge required varied, however, with the student's ambition. To achieve a pass it was required to sit examinations as follows:

1. Knowledge of the Four Gospels and Acts of the Apostles; of the history of the Old Testament; and of an extended catechism.
2. Logic; six books of Euclid; algebra to quadratics.
3. One Greek and one Latin historian or orator; i.e., a sufficient portion of their works.

4. One out of the six tercenaries of profane history since the Christian era; (1) from A.D. 1 to 300; (2) 300–600; (3) 600–900; (4) 900–1200; (5) 1200–1500; (6) 1500–1800.

Sections one and two and the Latin historian from section three were examined at the end of year three; the Greek historian and section four, at the end of the fourth year. Those who wished to achieve honours had to sit in addition in the fourth year an examination consisting of the same four heads and twenty-seven possible subheads. At least one subject from each major category was required for honours. As candidates were given marks for each paper attempted, some students no doubt sat more than the minimum four papers.[42]

In addition to these formal exams, the university also held 'Collections' at the end of each term. These proceedings—exam is not the right word—were designed to check a student's 'progress and behaviour'. John Augustus O'Shea recalled the experiences of 'one student' (obviously himself) at collections. 'He was called into a spacious hall with the Rector [at this time still Newman], the Deans of Houses and Faculties, and the entire professorial staff seated at a table at one extremity.' The student sat down, and his dean of house read out a report of his 'conduct and attendance at chapels.' Each professor was then asked to comment on the student's progress. O'Shea reports that in his case the professors were by and large gentle with him—although he claims that James Stewart (the professor of Greek and Latin) told the meeting that although O'Shea was 'not devoid of brains' he was nevertheless 'idle, and let his brains lie fallow.' O'Shea's recollections are too colourful to be entirely accurate, but they give a wonderful picture of what a student must have faced.[43]

Newman's plans for other faculties beyond medicine never materialised (although there were at least some students pursuing studies in engineering, and professors were appointed in law and theology). Those students who passed the scholars' exam thus had no real choice beyond leaving, transferring to the medical school (an option little availed of), or continuing in the arts. Nor did the faculty of science, despite having professors and some experimental equipment, ever really take shape. To that extent Newman's scheme of study does not describe anything that actually occurred, but it is still useful to consider on two grounds: first, Newman's plans give an excellent idea of what he intended for the university and, two, it accurately describes the course of study pursued and the examinations sat by actual students in the arts.

Even within the limits on the university imposed by circumstance, and despite the heavy focus on the classics, Newman by no means limited the CUI to the kind of narrow classical curriculum that, say, Oxford was still largely following. The medical school was obviously vocational in nature, and the engineering curriculum discussed above was designed with professional needs in mind. And, in late 1856, Newman ordered the faculty of philosophy and letters to ascertain what sort of knowledge was needed by a student wishing to become a member of the Royal Artillery, Home Civil Service, or a civil engineer, and to pass the various entrance exams.[44] By 1858 such practical courses were being offered to prospective students.[45] If anything, the Catholic University was intended to be more practical in nature than its Dublin competitor, Trinity College.

A student at Trinity College in the mid-1850s would be expected in his first year to study Euclid, Demosthenes (*Philippics* and *Olynthiac Orations*), Cicero (*Against Catiline*), algebra, trigonometry (up to the 'Solution of Plane Triangles'), Herodotus, and Livy. The course offerings in the final two years included, for physics: Hart's *Mechanics* and *Hydrostatistics*, Lloyd's *Optics*; for Greek: Euripides' *Medea*, Sophocles' *Oedipus Tyrannus*, Aeschylus's *Prometheus Vinctus*; for Latin: Terence's *Adelphi*, Juvenal's *Satires* (iii, viii, x, xiii), Horace's *Odes* (Books III and IV); for classics: Aristotle's *Ethics* (Books I and II), Cicero *de Officiis* (Book I), Thucydidies (Book VII), Tacitus *Annals* (Book I); for ethics: Stewart's *Outlines of Moral Philosophy*, Butler's *Analogy*, and Paley's *Evidences*. Also offered were works in the fields of logic, experimental and mathematical physics, and astronomy. Divinity students—Trinity was the primary Church of Ireland seminary—would naturally follow a different course of study. With the exception of those works in the ethics course (Butler and Paley particularly) which were Anglican in nature, there could be nothing in *what* Trinity taught its undergraduates that could disturb either a Catholic parent or prelate. Indeed, although the exact books to be studied might differ from those taught in the Catholic University, the difference was inconsequential. It could only be *how* those works were taught and the atmosphere in which they were taught that made a Trinity education unsafe to Catholics.[46]

The content of the education provided in the Queen's Colleges, again, differed little from either Trinity or the CUI. Queen's College Cork, for example, in its 1854–55 session, insisted that its first-year students take three terms each of Greek and Latin, one term of English language, and three terms each of modern languages and mathematics. The second year required a term of logic, three terms of both chemistry and the principles of zoology and botany, and three terms of either higher mathematics or Greek and Latin. The third and final year of the BA course demanded three terms of natural philosophy, two terms of English history and literature, one of physical geography, and two either of metaphysics or jurisprudence and political economy (one term each).

Although the classics were not as heavily emphasised as they were at Trinity or the CUI, Cork nonetheless placed them at the heart of its scholarship examinations for literary subjects (science scholarships were purely technical in nature). The only non-classical component was a demand for original essays on subjects of the examiner's choosing in the field of the English language (literature). Any ambitious Cork student who was not a scientist would have done well to look to his classical learning.[47]

As with Trinity College, the material taught at the Queen's Colleges could not, by and large, be the subject of any objections from concerned Catholics. Rather, the objection came on two points: the lack of religious teaching in any part of the curriculum, and the fact that such potentially contentious topics as history and natural philosophy could be taught by Protestants to Catholic youths. Considering that only some seven of the initial sixty professorial appointees in the Queen's Colleges were Catholics, this was not an unreasonable concern.[48] All three Irish institutions of higher learning in the early 1850s were in broad agreement as to what should be the subject of university instruction. True, Trinity College and the Catholic University insisted on religious knowledge being a component of that instruction where the Queen's Colleges excluded it, but then neither put it at the centre of their actual curriculum either. The difference lay in the ethos of each place: Trinity was establishment Protestant, the Catholic University Roman Catholic, and the Queen's Colleges secular.

As for the students of the Catholic University, we know relatively little about them. The Catholic University Register (preserved in the archives of University College Dublin) gives us only the names of the student and his father, the place of birth, and year of matriculation in the university. We do know that they were not particularly diverse geographically: of the one hundred and sixty-two students who matriculated in the period 1854–60, no fewer than forty-four were born in Dublin. Besides Dublin, only Cork, Limerick, and Tipperary sent more than five students in the same period.[49] We can safely assume, too, that those who did attend came from the upper middle class and the Catholic elite—in other words, those who could afford to send their sons to an intermediate school. During Newman's tenure as rector there was also a smattering of European aristocracy drawn by his name. That element did not outlast Newman himself, and he seems to have used them as what Thomas Arnold called 'decoy ducks' to spread the fame of the university and attract students.[50] On the whole the academic standard of the students seems to have been relatively low. Certainly Newman felt called upon to report to the bishops in 1857 that, in spite of real advances, most students 'scarcely possess the qualifications necessary for any real and substantial improvement.' Particularly worrying was a 'serious lack of grounding in the learned languages, in history, and in the sciences'.[51] This appears to have remained a problem after Newman's departure; in 1862, J. B. Robertson complained that 'Professor Renouf says that the first-year's men are incapable of following his lectures' and that 'the students know nothing of foreign and little of English History.'[52] This difficulty can largely be ascribed to the poor state of Irish intermediate schools. At Maynooth, for example, the 1853–54 commission drew attention to the low academic standards of entering students and placed the blame primarily on the intermediate schools.[53] Not that many existed. An 1848 investigation carried out for the Propaganda estimated that there was provision for some fifteen hundred Catholic students 'at the most' at the secondary level across Ireland.[54]

Despite what Newman saw as the low standard of the students (and their small numbers), the Catholic University did produce a number of famous graduates during his tenure. William Walsh, later archbishop of Dublin and the first chancellor of the National University of Ireland; the nationalist politician John Dillon; and the writer John Augustus O'Shea are among the more prominent names.[55] It also produced a lord mayor of Dublin, an unofficial British representative to the Holy See, and a solicitor general for Ireland.[56] Less creditably, the future cuckold Captain O'Shea was also briefly a student. (In later years University College, the CUI's successor, had James Joyce as a student and Gerard Manley Hopkins as a professor.)[57]

There are very few memoirs of university life left by students between 1854 and 1865. The best one is probably that of John Augustus O'Shea, who deals with the university in his *Roundabout Recollections*. Between O'Shea's memoir and other sources it is possible to give something of an idea of what life was like for the students beyond the cold facts of lecture tables and exam questions. The *Catholic University Gazette* tells us that it was Newman's intention that a student's day would consist of mass at eight, breakfast at nine, lectures from ten until two, and dinner at five. After dinner, hours would be up to the dean of each house.[58] We know from O'Shea that the students had wine parties, rowed, played billiards with the professors, and even had the use of a cricket pitch in Rathmines.[59]

Unsurprisingly, Newman's nascent college system provoked the usual rivalries. According to O'Shea, 'St. Mary's [Newman's Harcourt Street House] was the swell house, a sort of fellow-commoner's preserve.'[60] St Mary's men looked down on men from St Patrick's (O'Shea's house and the largest), who in turn 'looked down upon the fellows at Dr.

Quinn's, which we patronizingly regarded as a mere upper school'.[61] This rivalry was confirmed by a student in St Mary's who remembered that we 'were rather scoffed at, being the aristocracy of the new University.'[62] Students competed in interhouse sporting events (including the quintessentially Oxbridge rowing), wore mortarboard and gown, and could even 'sport their oak' (the double door system still to be found in the older Oxbridge colleges). There was the grandly titled Literary, Historical and Aesthetical Society, which, despite not being allowed to discuss contemporary affairs (after 1800), seems nonetheless to have been quite lively. Newman remained its honorary president until 1863. And, at least in St Mary's, the students were 'allowed to come and go according to our fancy', although leave was required to miss dinner or be out at night.[63]

Some critics (V. A. McClelland is by far the worst offender) have gone out of their way to criticise Newman for both the aristocratic tone of his house and what they perceive to have been his demands for total control over student life.[64] On the first point, it is unquestionable that Newman kept, as it were, the better class of student for himself. However, those students had only come to the university because of Newman and would not tarry long after he left; St Mary's House closed in 1859. Perhaps there was an element of snobbery in it too—unquestionably some of the English professors looked down on the Irish—but that seems to be of little matter.[65] Certainly nobody reading O'Shea's memoirs can come away with the impression that the other students either were, or felt themselves to be, hard done by. As for Newman's close management of student life in St Mary's, it was all of a piece with his belief in the necessity of personal influence and pastoral supervision. It was also not unusual for that day and place, and it should be remembered that Cullen was at this very time criticising the rector for being too *lenient*. It should also be recalled that at Oxford Newman was never overly sympathetic to the idle aristocrat or the fellow-commoner. At Oriel, for example, he had unsuccessfully opposed (against his own provost) the practice by which fellow-commoners dined by right with the fellows on high table.[66]

All in all, the picture that emerges of the Catholic University of Ireland is one of a place where a small number of students lived a fairly agreeable and not untypical university life. The academic work was difficult and demanding (and many were evidently not properly prepared for it), but there was a social life, sports, and a fair degree of freedom available to those who wished to avail themselves of it.

Conclusion

The Failure of the Catholic University of Ireland

MICHAEL BUCKLEY, A JESUIT THEOLOGIAN WHO HAS WRITTEN on Catholic education, has provided a useful summary of the commonly assumed reasons that the Catholic University failed to 'perdure': 'Too much counted against it even from its birth: the intractable narrowness of its episcopal supporters, the inability to grant civil degrees, the incapacity to communicate its nature and its purpose, the lack of sufficient secondary schools from which to draw an adequate student body.'[1] As we have seen, Buckley's remarks about episcopal narrowness are unfounded. It is likewise difficult to understand his view that the CUI was unable to communicate its purpose; surely Newman's Dublin lectures amply fulfilled that goal. Buckley's other reasons are nevertheless valid, and they are also closely linked.

The primary reason for the university's failure was simple: it failed to attract enough students. Between its opening in 1854 and Newman's departure at the beginning of the 1858–59 academic year, only 106 students put their names to the university register.[2] Although this total excludes medical students and those attending the intermittent evening classes, the inability of the university to attract students is clear. What was worse, enrolments dropped, with one small upswing, in each year of Newman's tenure: in 1854–55 thirty-eight students registered, in 1855–56 there were twenty-five, 1856–57 saw three more students than the year before to make twenty-eight, and in 1857–58, Newman's last year, only fifteen students enrolled in the Catholic University.[3]

Despite its substantial endowment, the university was unable to sustain its outgoings without a substantial income from tuition. Cullen was thus perfectly justified in his concern over Newman's spending. He was never a spendthrift, but there was at least some truth to Cullen's charge that Newman spent 'as if he had the purse of Oxford behind him.'[4] Certainly, the number of professors Newman hired, though perhaps necessary to his vision of a first-class university, could not be justified given the university's rather precarious financial state and its inability to raise further funds from the country at large after 1855. Newman proved himself unwilling to pay any heed to Cullen's repeated cautions about expenditure, and the archbishop's frustration on this point must be considered reasonable.

The university was put in the position, however, of having to rely on tuition income by the actions of Cullen himself. As we have seen, Cullen, by centralising control over the university in the hands of the four archbishops (but with a casting vote for himself), forfeited the support of the remainder of the Irish hierarchy. Just as Patrick Leahy had suggested, the bishops were unwilling to support or engage in fundraising for an institution, supposedly national, over which they themselves had no control. Cullen was forced into this course of action, however, by the total inability of the bishops, acting as a body, to manage the university. Cullen knew that leaving the university to the tender mercies of an annual bishops' meeting, at which MacHale would have full scope for his wrecking tactics, could only spell disaster for the institution.

Essentially, Cullen took a calculated risk: only by centralising control in his own person could he assure that the university opened and was able to function. Such control would, he knew, drastically limit its ability to raise funds in the country; but, with a substantial endowment of £40,000, a reasonable number of students could have provided enough income for the university to survive and grow. What Cullen did not anticipate was the university's almost total inability to attract students; like everybody else, he knew numbers would initially be low, but nobody expected them to *decrease* with each passing year. Because of this, Cullen's gamble failed and the university's inability to raise substantial funds after 1855 effectively crippled it. Even the advent of the episcopal board in 1859 did little to increase incomes from the collection (despite the brief surge in Woodlock's first two years as rector). Despite this failure, it is difficult to see what Cullen might have done differently. If he had not caused Rome to remove the bench of bishops from their oversight of the university, it is questionable whether the CUI would have opened its doors at all; it is almost impossible to believe that it could have survived to provide at least the foundation for UCD.

The Catholic University failed to attract students for a number of reasons. Although Newman managed to attract by his name a number of foreign-born students (some thirteen from England and Scotland and fifteen from continental Europe)[5] during his time in Ireland, he was unable to make the Catholic University a truly transnational institution. In Ireland itself, as the Jesuit provincial Fr Curtis had warned Newman in 1854, there were not enough students of the sort whose parents might wish to send them to an institution such as the Catholic University.[6] Many of the Irish Catholic elite, and even the aspiring Catholic middle classes, either chose to educate their children at Trinity College, at Oxford or Cambridge (now slowly opening to Catholics), or on the continent, or they saw little need for a university education at all. Some parents sent their children, for reasons either practical or social, to the Queen's Colleges. Unlike Louvain, the Catholic University also suffered from the presence of a perfectly good seminary—Maynooth—that absorbed almost all the available ecclesiastical students, an important source of potential income. Catholic Ireland simply did not have the network of schools necessary to provide students for a university with a rigorously classical curriculum; such elite schools as Clongowes could not stock the university entirely on their own.

The Catholic University of Ireland suffered, too, from its attempt to create, *ex nihilo*, a proper university. Louvain had succeeded with such a strategy, but it had had the Belgian hierarchy fully behind it and a different situation on the ground than did the CUI. Its students also had the ability to gain degrees. A better model for the Catholic University, perhaps, was that offered by such American institutions as Notre Dame, where its founders combined a small university programme with a larger school. For many years, the school provided the student numbers to sustain the university, and the tuition income brought in by the school allowed the poorly endowed university, with its low student numbers, to survive.[7] Slowly, the school became less important to Notre Dame than the university and it was eventually phased out. Notre Dame had always thought of itself as a university, but by being in its early years primarily a school, it enabled itself to become one. Today, the University of Notre Dame is a conspicuous success, well-endowed and internationally respected. It is also, unlike the CUI's putative successor UCD, recognisably the same, very Catholic, institution. Other prominent American

Catholic universities, such as Georgetown and Boston College, followed similar approaches and, if they are not now as noticeably Catholic as Notre Dame, then they are certainly more so than is UCD.[8] It is of course impossible to know whether, if the CUI had followed the Notre Dame model, it would have succeeded. Notre Dame's example, however, at least shows that there were ways of overcoming poor student numbers and low tuition income.[9]

The primary difference between the Catholic University and Notre Dame, or Louvain, or any other Catholic university of the time, was its lack of a charter. The vexed issue of a charter looms large over any consideration of why the Catholic University of Ireland failed so signally. Despite all its other problems, it is possible that the Catholic University of Ireland, had it been granted a charter, might have been able to attract enough students to be successful.

Once Newman had left and taken his reputation with him, the Catholic University of Ireland had nothing to offer the prospective student. If few enough had come while Newman was there, even fewer would come once he was not. A charter could have given the university something to sell in an Ireland suddenly overflowing with choices for higher education. Without it, there was little hope of survival. Only the medical school thrived, and it did not need a charter. John Augustus O'Shea summed matters up when he wrote that the medical school 'was from the start prosperous. Reason: its lectures were recognized. The other houses were not flourishing. Reason: their lectures were not recognized.'[10]

Placed against the lack of a charter, all the other difficulties faced by the university pale into insignificance. It remains true that such problems as MacHale's obstructionism, the lack of episcopal enthusiasm for fundraising, and the difficulties that developed in the Newman-Cullen relationship after 1855 all played a part in the university's difficulties. However, even if MacHale and been a constructive supporter, even if the bishops had continued to raise money, even if Newman remained as a resident rector, and even if rector and archbishop had not fallen out, the university would most likely still have met the same fate. It might have taken a bit longer, but a university without students could never survive for long. And without a charter, the students simply wouldn't come.

CULLEN'S UNIVERSITY

The Catholic University of Ireland was in a real way Paul Cullen's own university. Although he did not suggest it, he quickly embraced the idea when it was first mooted and pushed it tirelessly while rector of the Irish College and bishops' agent. He bombarded Ireland with letters urging that it be established and did everything in his power to prevent the Queen's Colleges, the proposed university's rivals, from being approved by Rome. When he came to Ireland as archbishop of Armagh, he immediately set about making the university into a reality. By an impressive feat of diplomacy, he gained unanimous support for it at the Synod of Thurles. Following that victory he mounted a highly successful nationwide (and international) fundraising drive. And, by a careful manipulation of the university committee, he ensured that his chosen appointee would be selected as rector. He deserves the full and entire credit for selecting and appointing Newman to the post. And, in that sense, Cullen is entitled to his share of the credit for *The Idea of a University*.

When the university became caught up in the politics of Irish nationalism—becoming yet another stick with which MacHale could beat him—Cullen protected it and ensured that it would open with the rector and statutes he desired, and with £40,000 in the bank. Cullen's fulsome letter to Newman on the occasion of the University's opening was no doubt sincere in its expressions of pleasure. In 1854 Cullen had every reason to be hopeful; the university's problems all lay in the future. Although Cullen must, without question, assume his share of the blame for its failure with Newman and others (including the British government), it is clear that the university could never have existed if it were not for his tireless dedication to its cause. Both Newman and Cullen were devoted to the Catholic University. Both gave it many years of time and effort; Cullen gave the university life; Newman gave it, through the genius of his writings, a kind of immortality; but neither man could make it a practical success.

Nevertheless, Cullen was working to establish a Catholic University in Ireland long before he asked Newman to head it. And, long after Newman had given up the rectorship, Cullen was still devoting himself to somehow putting the university back on its feet. If Newman dedicated some seven years of his life to the university, Cullen can be said to have given nearly thirty-five years of his. Fergal McGrath, writing the history of the Catholic University of Ireland in 1951, called his book *Newman's University*. A more accurate title would have been "Cullen's University."

Notes

INTRODUCTION

1. Owen Chadwick, *The Spirit of the Oxford Movement: Tractarian Essays* (Cambridge: Cambridge University Press, 1990), 99.

2. G. M. Young, *Victorian Essays*, ed. W. D. Hancock (Oxford: Oxford University Press, 1962), 142.

3. John Henry Newman, *The Idea of a University*, ed. Frank M. Turner (New Haven: Yale University Press, 1996). The essays I mention here were written by Frank M. Turner, George Marsden, and George P. Landrow, respectively.

4. *Times Literary Supplement*, 2 April 1999, 16.

5. For a discussion of MacSuibhne, see 'Note on Sources'.

6. Fergal McGrath, *Newman's University: Idea and Reality* (London: Longmans, Green, 1951), 95.

7. Emmet Larkin, *The Making of the Roman Catholic Church in Ireland, 1850–1860* (Chapel Hill: University of North Carolina Press, 1980); Donal Kerr, *Peel, Priests and Politics* (Oxford: Oxford University Press, 1982), and *A Nation of Beggars? Priests, People and Politics in Famine Ireland, 1846–1852* (Oxford: Oxford University Press, 1994); Patrick J. Corish, 'Cardinal Cullen and Archbishop MacHale', *Irish Ecclesiastical Record* 91 (January–June 1959): 1–94; Ciaran O'Carroll, 'The Pastoral Politics of Paul Cullen', in *History of the Catholic Diocese of Dublin*, ed. James Kelley and Dáire Keogh (Dublin: Four Courts Press, 2000); E. D. Steele, 'Cardinal Cullen and Irish Nationality', *Irish Historical Studies* 19 (1974–75): 234–60; J. H. Whyte, 'Newman in Dublin: Fresh Light from the Archives of Propaganda', *Dublin Review* 483 (Spring 1960); Desmond Bowen, *Paul Cullen and the Shaping of Modern Irish Catholicism* (Dublin: Gill and Macmillan, 1983).

8. I am in the process of researching such a book.

9. Louis McRedmond, *Thrown Among Strangers: John Henry Newman in Ireland* (Dublin: Veritas, 1990).

10. Wilfrid Ward, *Life of John Henry Cardinal Newman*, 2 vols. (London: Longmans, Green, 1912).

11. See *AW*, 280–333.

12. The main biographies of Newman are: Ward, *Life of Newman*; Meriol Trevor, *Newman: The Light in Winter* and *The Pillar of the Cloud* (London: Macmillan, 1962); C. S. Dessain, *John Henry Newman* (London: Thomas Nelson, 1966); Ian Ker, *John Henry Newman: A Biography* (Oxford: Oxford University Press, 1989); and Sheridan Gilley, *Newman and His Age* (London: Darton, Longmans, Todd, 1990). None of these works deviates from the standard portrait of the Newman-Cullen relationship first put forward by Ward and based on Newman's own writings.

13. For example, see A. N. Wilson's comment in *God's Funeral* (London: John Murray, 1999) that Newman, 'when he joined the Church of Pio Nono and the Irish bishops ... discovered what bigotry and superstition really were', 111. Or Senia Pašeta's offhand remark that the Catholic University 'enjoyed little success as Cullen and Newman disagreed about the nature of university education.' *Before the Revolution: Nationalism, Social Change and Ireland's Catholic Elite, 1879–1922* (Cork: Cork University Press, 1999), 12.

14. McQuaid to Sir Shane Leslie, 27 May 1960, Cullen Papers, DDA, 64/16/3.

15. Alfred O'Rahilly, 'The Irish University Question, V—The Catholic University of Ireland', *Studies* 50, no. 200 (Winter 1961): 359.

1. First Conflicts: The National Schools and Charitable Bequests

1. Kerr, *Peel, Priests and Politics*, 1–67.

2. D. H. Akenson, *The Irish Education Experiment: The National System of Education in Nineteenth-Century Ireland* (Toronto: University of Toronto Press, 1970). The three previous paragraphs have been based on his account.

3. Bernard O'Reilly, *John MacHale, Archbishop of Tuam: His Life, Times, and Correspondence*, 2 vols. (New York: Fr. Pustet, 1890), 1:415.

4. MacHale's style can be seen in John MacHale, *Letters of the Most Rev. John MacHale, DD, Archbishop of Tuam* (Dublin: M. H. Gill and Son, 1893).

5. See, for example, Hilary Andrews' recent *Lion of the West: A Biography of John MacHale* (Dublin: Veritas, 2001).

6. MacHale to Russell, 12 February 1838, O'Reilly, *John MacHale*, 1:417.

7. William Meagher, *Notices of the Life and Character of His Grace Most Rev. Daniel Murray, Late Archbishop of Dublin* (Dublin: Gerald Bellew, 1853), 54.

8. See Ambrose Macaulay, *William Crolly: Archbishop of Armagh, 1835–49* (Dublin: Four Courts Press, 1994), 1–6.

9. John MacHale's surname was commonly spelled 'McHale' by a number of contemporaries, although even those who favoured 'McHale' would sometimes spell it 'MacHale'. The correct spelling is 'MacHale'. I have, however, left intact the spelling favoured by each individual correspondent.

10. Murray to Cullen, 28 April 1838, Cullen Papers, ICRA, #423.

11. MacHale to O'Connell, 27 February 1838, O'Reilly, *John MacHale*, 1:419.

12. After Cullen's arrival on the scene real power shifted back towards Ireland as the Propaganda, which still retained all its powers, tended to back, and was known to back, Cullen's decisions on the Irish Church. In the 1840s, however, no prelate retained anything like the degree of trust later reposed in Cullen.

13. For the history of the Irish Colleges in Europe, see James O'Boyle, *The Irish Colleges on the Continent* (Dublin: Browne and Nolan, 1935).

14. The evidence for this is circumstantial but convincing. MacHale was usually a fairly casual correspondent; only in formal letters or those intended for publication did he take great care with his structure and grammar. Also of note in this particular letter is the clarity of the writing. Although still obviously in MacHale's hand, it can be read easily by those unfamiliar with his normally execrable handwriting. The practice of a bishop writing to Cullen with the intent of the letter being shown in the Propaganda was not uncommon, and Cullen himself frequently used this procedure in writing to Kirby when the latter was rector.

15. MacHale to Cullen, 24 February 1838, Cullen Papers, ICRA, #406.

16. Higgins to Cullen, 10 March 1838, Cullen Papers, ICRA, #410.

17. Murray to Cullen, 13 June 1838, Cullen Papers, ICRA, #435.

18. Cullen to Slattery, 20 July 1838, Slattery Papers, CDA, P. 6001, 1839/6.

19. MacHale to Cullen, 15 September 1838, Cullen Papers, ICRA, #456.

20. Higgins to Cullen, 23 January 1839, Cullen Papers, ICRA, #483.

21. Murray to Cullen, 28 January 1839, Cullen Papers, ICRA, #485.

22. Crolly to Cullen, 4 February 1839, Cullen Papers, ICRA, #491.

23. Murray to Cullen, 13 March 1839, Cullen Papers, ICRA, #496.

24. See MacHale to Cullen, 26 March 1839, Cullen Papers, ICRA, #502.

25. Kerr discusses Cullen's role in the 1839 condemnation and seems to take it for granted that Cullen was opposed to the national system and in league with MacHale: 'Two factors favoured MacHale's party: the presence in Rome of Cantwell and Higgins and, even more important, the support furnished by Cullen.' *Peel, Priests and Politics*, 61. I do not think the evidence justifies so confident an assertion.

26. Macaulay, *William Crolly*, 189.

27. Ibid.

28. See Kerr, *Peel, Priests and Politics*, 62.

29. Quoted in Oliver P. Rafferty, *Catholicism in Ulster, 1603–1983, An Interpretative History* (London: Hurst, 1994), 121–22. See also Kerr, *Peel, Priests and Politics*, 62.

30. Macaulay, *William Crolly*, 189–91.

31. Murray to Cullen, 28 February 1840, Cullen Papers, ICRA, #585.

32. Cullen to MacHale, 12 January 1840, O'Reilly, *John MacHale*, 1: 422–23.

33. Ibid.

34. Draft of a report on the merits of the national system of education, 1840, Cullen Papers (New Collection), ICRA, box 3, folder 2, #1. Original in Italian.

35. Both Slattery and Kinsella were professors at Carlow College when Cullen was a student there.

36. Higgins to Cullen, 2 October 1844, Cullen Papers, ICRA, #956.

37. Ibid.

38. Murray to Cullen, 5 October 1844, Cullen Papers, ICRA, #958.

39. Murray to Slattery, 3 October 1844, Slattery Papers, CDA, P.6001, 1844/9.

40. Cullen to Murray (draft), 15 October 1844, Cullen Papers (New Collection), ICRA, carton 4, folder 3, #49.

41. Walsh to Cullen, 18 January 1845, Cullen Papers, ICRA, #1010.

42. See O'Reilly, *John MacHale*, 1:576.

43. Cullen to Walsh, 10 February 1845, DDA, 66/16.

2. 'GODLESS' EDUCATION FOR IRELAND

1. See Dermot Keogh, 'Catholics and the Godless Colleges, 1845–1995', in *Theology in the University: The Irish Context*, ed. Padraig Corkery and Fiachra Long (Dublin: Dominican Publications, 1997), 56.

2. Elizabeth I to Lord Deputy Fitzwilliam, 29 December 1592. Quoted in Fergal McGrath, *Newman's University: Idea and Reality* (London: Longmans, Green, 1951), 3.

3. Kerr, *Peel, Priests and Politics*, 290. Only some thirty Catholics entered Trinity each year as against some three hundred Protestants.

4. It would not be until 1967 that St Patrick's College Maynooth would once again welcome lay students. For the history of Maynooth, see Patrick J. Corish, *Maynooth College, 1795–1995* (Dublin: Gill and Macmillan, 1995).

5. See Finlay Holmes, 'Irish Presbyterians and the "Godless" Colleges', in Corkery and Long, *Theology in the University*, 15–26.

6. See McGrath, *Newman's University*, 131–32.

7. Kerr, *Peel, Priests and Politics*, 292–95.

8. Holmes, 'Irish Presbyterians', 20.

9. A third, western college (Galway) was to be added later.

10. Kerr, *Peel, Priests and Politics*, 302.

11. Quoted in McGrath, *Newman's University*, 59.

12. Kerr, *Peel, Priests and Politics*, 299–300.

13. MacHale to Peel, 24 January 1845, in O'Reilly, *John MacHale*, 1:570–71.

14. Crolly to Slattery, 14 May 1845, Slattery Papers, CDA, P.6001, 1845/3.

15. Resolution adopted by the Irish hierarchy on 23 May 1845, published in O'Reilly, *John MacHale*, 1:591.

16. 'Memorial of the Bishops to the Lord Lieutenant', 23 May 1845, quoted in Kerr, *Peel, Priests and Politics*, 304.

17. See Kerr, *Peel, Priests and Politics*, 308.

18. Despite Cullen's later reputation as an anti-nationalist, it is important to remember that he was a supporter and admirer of O'Connell's, and arranged, upon his death in Italy in 1847, for his heart to be buried in the Irish College. Indeed, a tablet marking the burial is still to be found in the present Irish College, where it was transferred when the college moved from St Agatha's to the Via Santi Quattro in the early part of this century. Oddly, O'Connell's heart (or what remains of it) seems to have been left behind.

19. Cullen to Kirby, 14 May 1845, Kirby Papers, ICRA, #360.

20. Cullen to Kirby, 3 June 1845, Kirby Papers, ICRA, #371.

21. Cullen to Kirby, 20 July 1845, Kirby Papers, ICRA, #390.

22. Cullen to Kirby, 3 August 1845, Kirby Papers, ICRA, #395.

23. See Macaulay, *William Crolly*, 360. Macaulay does not give a citation for this quotation, and it appears to be in the form of a report of Crolly's statements to the meeting. Kerr quotes the *Pilot* of 20 August 1845 with the same form of words (*Peel, Priests and Politics*, 319).

24. Kerr, *Peel, Priests and Politics*, 321.

25. Patrick Kennedy to Slattery, 23 August 1845, quoted in Kerr, *Peel, Priests and Politics*, 321.

26. Higgins to MacHale, 16 September 1845, O'Reilly, *John MacHale*, 1:567.

27. MacHale to Slattery, 18 October 1845, Slattery Papers, CDA, P.6001, 1845/17.

28. Cullen was telling Slattery the same thing; see Cullen to Slattery, 28 November 1845, Slattery Papers, CDA, P.6001, 1845/37: 'We have not had as yet any thing [official] about the new Colleges. Card. Fransoni is decidedly hostile to them'.

29. Cullen to MacHale, 27 November 1845, O'Reilly, *John MacHale*, 1:560.

30. Cantwell wrote a gloating letter to MacHale on the subject, see Cantwell to MacHale, 1 October 1845, O'Reilly, *John MacHale*, 1:577.

31. Kerr, *Peel, Priests and Politics*, 324.

32. MacHale to Slattery, 26 October 1845, Slattery Papers, CDA, P.6001, 1845/19.

33. Kinsella to Slattery, 2 November 1845, Slattery Papers, CDA, P.6001, 1845/23.

34. Cullen to Slattery, 13 December 1845, Slattery Papers, CDA, P.6001, 1845/41.

35. See Cantwell to Slattery, 8 January 1846, Slattery Papers, CDA, P.6002, 1846/3.

36. Cullen to Slattery, 13 December 1845, Slattery Papers, CDA, P.6001, 1845/41.

37. It is unclear if this letter was sent. It exists as a fair copy in the Slattery papers but does not seem to be preserved in Rome. Most likely it is the draft of the letter Cullen had requested from Slattery, and that the final copy was shown around by Cullen in Rome. This could account for its absence in the Irish College. The tone of the letter, its length, and its formal nature (Slattery was normally more informal in letters to Cullen) also lends support to this idea. However, regardless of whether Cullen read it, it still throws important light on Slattery's thinking.

38. Slattery to Cullen, 6 February 1846, Slattery Papers, CDA, P.6002, 1846/9.

39. Slattery to Cullen, 24 February 1846, Cullen Papers, ICRA, #1169.

40. Cooper to Slattery, 4 April 1846, Slattery Papers, CDA, P.6002, 1846/23.

41. Murray was offered but declined membership in the Irish privy council in 1846. Lord John Russell confirmed the offer in a statement to the House of Commons in 1852. Meagher, *Daniel Murray*, 63–64.

42. Macaulay, *William Crolly*, 387.

43. Cullen to Slattery, 2 June 1846, Slattery Papers, CDA, P.6002, 1846/30.

44. Cullen to Slattery, 18 June 1846, Slattery Papers, CDA, P.6002, 1846/37.

45. Cullen to Slattery, 16 July 1846, Slattery Papers, CDA, P.6002, 1846/42. See also Cooper to Slattery, 3 August 1846, Slattery Papers, CDA, P.6002, 1846/52.

46. Cullen to Slattery, 15 September 1846, Slattery Papers, CDA, P.6002, 1846/54.

47. Slattery to Cullen, 4 April 1846, Cullen Papers, ICRA, #1185.

48. Cooper to Cullen, 16 June 1846, Cullen Papers, ICRA, #1206.

49. MacHale to Cullen, 15 March 1846, Cullen Papers, ICRA, #1175.

50. The bishop of Derry, John McLaughlin, suffered from mental illness, experiencing a near total breakdown in 1845. Maginn was appointed to administer the diocese. McLaughlin, who was from time to time committed to an asylum, never fully recovered. Although Kerr described him as 'an ardent Repealer and Young Irelander' (*Peel, Priests and Politics*, 9), it must be noted that Maginn described the Young Irelanders as 'not less mad' than Young Italy. See Maginn to Cullen, 28 September 1848, Cullen Papers, ICRA, #1607.

51. Maginn to Cullen, 3 December 1846, Cullen Papers, ICRA, #1282.

52. See Donal Kerr, *A Nation of Beggars? Priests, People and Politics in Famine Ireland, 1846–1852* (Oxford: Oxford University Press, 1994), 283 n. 3.

53. See Macaulay, *William Crolly*, 402.

54. See McGrath, *Newman's University*, 63.

55. See Cullen to Slattery, 28 April 1847, Slattery Papers, CDA, P.6002, 1847/35.

56. Maginn to Cullen, 4 November 1847, Cullen Papers, ICRA, #1493.

57. Cullen to Slattery, 23 October 1847, Slattery Papers, CDA, P.6002, 1847/77.

58. Precisely where Cantwell intended to find this vast sum is unknown. Although Meath was the third most generous diocese behind Armagh and Dublin in the initial fundraising for the CUI (providing some £3,400), nothing like £10,000 was ever likely to appear. Cantwell's promise seems to have been quickly forgotten.

59. Cullen to Kirby, 29 October 1847, Kirby Papers, ICRA, M1 (52).

60. Macaulay, *William Crolly*, 404.

61. Cullen to Kirby, November 1847, Kirby Papers, ICRA, M1 (55). The date in November is illegible and the postmark has been worn away.

62. Cantwell to Cullen, 17 January 1848, Cullen Papers, ICRA, #1514.

63. McGrath, *Newman's University*, 43, 68.

64. Ibid.

65. Slattery to John O'Connell (copy), 9 November 1847, Slattery Papers, CDA, P.6002, 1847/87.

66. MacHale to Slattery, 29 October 1847, Slattery Papers, CDA, P.6002, 1847/83.

67. See chapter 5 for a discussion of Cullen's memorandum about the nature of the education provided at Louvain and the structure of that institution.

68. John O'Connell to Slattery, 6 November 1847, Slattery Papers, CDA, P.6002, 1847/87.

69. Kerr, *A Nation of Beggars?* 238–39.

70. Cooper to Slattery, 18 November 1847, Slattery Papers, CDA, P.6002, 1847/90.

71. Cullen to Slattery, 22 November 1847, Slattery Papers, CDA, P.6002, 1847/93.

72. McGrath, *Newman's University*, 66. See also MacHale to Cullen, 31 March 1848, Cullen Papers, ICRA, #1577.

73. O'Hanlon to Cullen, 18 May 1848, Cullen Papers, ICRA, #1594.

74. See Minute Book of the Catholic University Committee, UCDA, CU1, 1–2.

75. O'Hanlon to Cullen, 18 May 1848, Cullen Papers, ICRA, #1594.

76. Maher to Cullen, 20 May 1848, Cullen Papers, ICRA, #1597.

77. Miley to Cullen, 26 May 1848, Cullen Papers, ICRA, #1600.

78. Cullen to Slattery, 18 June 1848, Slattery Papers, CDA, P.6003, 1848/93.

79. Cullen to Slattery, 4 July 1848, Slattery Papers, CDA, P.6003, 1848/97.

80. Cooper to Slattery, 30 October 1848, Slattery Papers, CDA, P.6003, 1848/154.

81. Cooper to Slattery, 10 November 1848, Slattery Papers, CDA, P.6003, 1848/156.

82. Maher to Cullen, 13 October 1848, Cullen Papers, ICRA, #1658.

83. Cantwell to Slattery, 11 November 1848, Slattery Papers, CDA, P.6003, 1848/157.

84. Keating to Slattery, 23 November 1848, Slattery Papers, CDA, P.6003, 1848/161.

85. MacNally to Slattery, 28 November 1848, Slattery Papers, CDA, P.6003, 1848/167.

86. See Cullen to Slattery, 13 January and 21 January 1849, Slattery Papers, CDA, P.6003, 1849/1, 1849/2.

87. Cantwell to Slattery, 27 November 1848, Slattery Papers, CDA, P.6003, 1848/164.

88. Cooper to Cullen, 19 December 1848, Cullen Papers, ICRA, #1688.

89. Only Patrick MacNicolas, the elderly bishop of Achonry, failed to sign. It is probable that he failed even to attend.

90. See Cooper to Cullen, 1 February 1849, Cullen Papers, ICRA, #1707.

91. Copy of the Decrees of the Provincial Synod of Tuam, 26 January 1849, Slattery Papers, CDA, P.6003. This item carries no file number.

92. Cooper to Slattery, 31 January 1849, Slattery Papers, CDA, P.6003, 1849/10.

93. Cooper to Slattery, 14 [?] 1849, Slattery Papers, CDA, P.6003, 1849/24. To judge by its position in the Cashel filing system, the letter should date from April 1849. However, there is no other evidence for this dating, and it would seem unlikely, given the constant contact between Cullen, Cooper, and Slattery, that Cullen's views on the Tuam synod would be news on 14 April. However, the situation in Rome could have delayed such a letter to Cooper and thus his passing on the information to Slattery.

94. Cullen to Slattery, 24 January 1849, Slattery Papers, CDA, P.6003, 1849/4.

95. Slattery to Cullen, 4 February 1849, Cullen Papers, ICRA, #1708.

96. See Kerr, *A Nation of Beggars?* 219.

3. Enter the Ultramontane

1. January 1849, Cullen Papers, ICRA, #1696. His correspondent told Cullen that he would be killed unless he sacked the Jesuit lay brothers employed at the Propaganda College (where Cullen was acting rector) and the Irish College.

2. For Cullen as a model ultramontane, see Emmet Larkin, 'Paul Cardinal Cullen', in *Varieties of Ultramontanism*, ed. Jeffrey von Arx (Washington, D.C.: Catholic University of America Press, 1998).

3. Cooper to Slattery, 31 January 1849, Slattery Papers, CDA, P.6003, 1849/10.

4. It was not the Jansenists' rather stern moral code that Cullen had in mind. His remarks are more likely an historical allusion to the practice of the early Jansenists of meeting Roman condemnations of their doctrines by claiming that the doctrine Rome condemned could not, in fact, be found in their writings and that therefore nothing they said had been condemned.

5. Cullen to Slattery, 3 February 1849, Slattery Papers, CDA, P.6003, 1849/12.

6. Cooper to Cullen, 7 February 1849, Cullen Papers, ICRA, #1712.

7. See Corish, *Maynooth College,* 124.

8. Cantwell to Cullen, 10 June 1849, Cullen Papers, ICRA, #1749.

9. Higgins to Cullen, 7 July 1849, Cullen Papers, ICRA, #1757.

10. Slattery to Fransoni (copy), 30 July 1849, Slattery Papers, CDA, P.6003, 1849/53. See Kerr, *A Nation of Beggars?* 220.

11. For a detailed account of the events surrounding Cullen's appointment see Ambrose Macaulay, 'Dr. Cullen's Appointment to Armagh, 1849', *Seanchas Ard Mhancha* (1980–81): 3–36.

12. Kerr, *A Nation of Beggars?* 220.

13. Fransoni to Kirby, 12 February 1850, Kirby Papers, ICRA, #664.

14. Cullen to Walsh, 24 December 1849, DDA, 66/16.

15. In 1830 he was proposed as coadjutor bishop of Philadelphia. He was also twice considered for bishoprics in New York and once for a new diocese in Pittsburgh. In 1834 he turned down a nomination to be coadjutor bishop of Charleston, South Carolina. See Ciaran O'Carroll, 'The Pastoral Politics of Paul Cullen', in *History of the Catholic Diocese of Dublin,* ed. James Kelly and Dáire Keogh (Dublin: Four Courts Press, 2000), 295.

16. MacHale to Cullen, 10 January 1850, Cullen Papers, ICRA, #1843.

17. Murray to Cullen, 28 February 1850, Cullen Papers, ICRA, #1578.

18. Clarendon to Russell, 5 January 1850, quoted in Kerr, *A Nation of Beggars?* 221.

19. Clarendon to Russell, 20 October 1852, quoted in Kerr, *A Nation of Beggars?* 221.

20. Ibid.

21. Clarendon to Odo Russell, 25 January 1869, in Noel Blakiston, ed., *The Roman Question: Extracts from the Despatches of Odo Russell from Rome, 1858–1870* (Wilmington, Del.: Michael Glazier, 1980), 358.

22. MacHale to Cullen, 13 January 1850, Cullen Papers, ICRA, #1856.

23. Leahy to Kirby, 30 January 1850, Kirby Papers, ICRA, #660.

24. Leahy to Kirby, 15 February 1850, Kirby Papers, ICRA, #668.

25. Leahy to Kirby, 25 March 1850, Kirby Papers, ICRA, #693.

26. Cullen to Kirby, 7 May 1850, Kirby Papers (New Collection), ICRA, box 1, folder 2, #15.

27. Crolly had made a will making over his possessions (a bishop personally owned his palace and its contents under Irish law) to his successor, but had, under the provisions of the Charitable Bequests Act, died before that will could take effect. All his effects thus passed to his heir, a minor. It is somewhat ironic that Crolly's support in 1844 for an act that Cullen violently opposed led to his leaving his successor a house barren of all furnishings.

28. Cullen to Kirby, 16 May 1850, Kirby Papers, ICRA, #M2-18.

29. Cullen to Kirby, 4 June 1850, Kirby Papers (New Collection), ICRA, box 1, folder 2, #22.

30. After the death of Crolly, the hierarchy largely lost interest in the Belfast college. The demographics of Ulster ensured that the Queen's College, Belfast would be overwhelmingly Presbyterian.

31. Cullen to Slattery, 6 June 1850, Slattery Papers, CDA, P.6003, 1850/8.
32. Cullen to Kirby, 4 June 1850, Kirby Papers (New Collection), ICRA, box 1, folder 2, #22.
33. Timothy Murphy to Cullen, 6 June 1850, Cullen Papers (Armagh), DDA, 39/1/48. Cullen transferred his Armagh papers to Dublin when he was translated to that see in 1852. The Armagh diocesan archives hold, as a consequence, nothing from Cullen's time there.
34. Cullen to Kirby, 4 June 1850, Kirby Papers (New Collection), ICRA, box 1, folder 2, #22.
35. Slattery to Cullen, 10 July 1850, DDA, Cullen Papers (Armagh), 39/1/14.
36. For the above, see Emmet Larkin, *The Making of the Roman Catholic Church in Ireland, 1850–1860* (Chapel Hill: University of North Carolina Press, 1980), 30–31.
37. Cullen to Barnabò, 31 August 1850, quoted in Larkin, *Making of the Roman Catholic Church*, 31.
38. Cullen to Kirby, 31 August 1850, Kirby Papers (New Collection), ICRA, box 1, folder 2, #40.
39. Lyons to Kirby, 5 September 1850, Kirby Papers, ICRA, #763.
40. Slattery to Cullen, 29 October 1850, Cullen Papers, DDA, 39/1/24.
41. Slattery to Cullen, 21 November 1850, Cullen Papers, DDA, 39/1/26.
42. See Cullen to Slattery, 21 October 1850, Slattery Papers, CDA, P.6003, 1850/30.
43. Kirby to Cullen, 22 September 1850, Cullen Papers, DDA, 39/1/13.
44. Minute Book of the Catholic University Committee, UCDA, CU1.
45. Ibid.
46. List of Subscriptions and Donations, Catholic University of Ireland, D&CDA, D. 51/12. For Cullen's family tree, see M. J. Curran, 'Cardinal Cullen: Biographical Materials', *Reportorium Novum* 1 (1955): 213–27.
47. List of Subscriptions and Donations, Catholic University of Ireland, D&CDA, D. 51/12.
48. Cantwell to Cullen, 23 October 1850, Cullen Papers (Armagh), DDA, 39/1/70.
49. For example, see Cullen to Denvir, 10 May 1851, D&CDA, D. 51/12.
50. See Cullen to Peter Paul Lefevere (bishop of Detroit), John Baptist Purcell (archbishop of Cincinnati), and Anthony Blanc (bishop of New Orleans). All three letters are dated 8 July 1851, UNDA, III-2-h, II-4-1, and V-1-b.
51. Cullen to Kirby, 19 October 1850, Kirby Papers (New Collection), ICRA, box 1, folder 2, #50.
52. Leahy to Cullen, 10 November 1850, Cullen Papers, DDA, 45/3/12.
53. Slattery to Peter Cooper, 27 September 1850, Cullen Papers (Armagh), DDA, 39/1/19. This letter is in Slattery's hand and is marked 'Private and Confidential'. It is likely that it was passed to Cullen by Cooper.
54. Derry to Cullen, 4 January 1851, Cullen Papers (Armagh), DDA, 39/2/3.
55. Cullen to Slattery, 15 April 1851, Slattery Papers, CDA, P.6003, 1851/2.

56. Cullen to Kirby, 16 April 1851, Kirby Papers (New Collection), ICRA, box 1, folder 2, #89.

57. MacHale to Cullen, 12 January 1851, Cullen Papers (Armagh), DDA, 39/2/10. Although MacHale was no doubt more sympathetic than normal to English Catholics because of the controversy over ecclesiastical titles then brewing in England, he was more likely simply upset with the response of Irish Catholics. In his letter to Cullen he had complained about the unwillingness of the middle class and the wealthy to donate to the CUI. He followed his recommendation of the English connection up to Cullen in a letter, sent from Manchester, of 29 January. In it he said that the 'feeling there in favor of Catholic education and the university is most encouraging.' MacHale to Cullen, 29 January 1851, Cullen Papers (Armagh), DDA, 39/2/26.

58. Draft receipts, Cullen Papers, DDA, 45/3/9.

59. Meeting of 15 October 1851, Minute Book of the Catholic University Committee, UCDA, CU1.

60. There is an excellent discussion of the subject in Kerr, *A Nation of Beggars?* 242–48.

61. A useful summary of the affair can be found in E. R. Norman, *Anti-Catholicism in Victorian England* (London: George Allen and Unwin, 1968), 52–79.

62. Meeting of 26 June 1851, Minute Book of the Catholic University Committee, UCDA, CU1.

4. SEDUCTION: THE APPOINTMENT OF JOHN HENRY NEWMAN

1. Whitty had applied to become a member of the Birmingham Oratory, and had lived with the community for a time, but by 1849 was found to be unsatisfactory and was asked to leave by Newman in his role of superior of the Oratory. Despite this, Newman and Whitty remained friends.

2. Whitty to Cullen, 12 April 1851, Cullen Papers, DDA.

3. Cullen to Newman, 15 April 1851, BOA, Cullen File. Cullen to Kirby, 16 April 1851, Kirby Papers (New Collection), ICRA, box 1, folder 2, #87.

4. This was the only time that Cullen would contemplate a lay vice-rector. By 1857 he was adamantly opposed to such a thing. Cullen would also come to regret involving converts as such. In early 1861 he told Barnabò that he had long opposed giving positions of authority to converts based on his own experiences with Newman. Cullen's remarks came in the course of discussing the activities of Orestes Brownson, activities which were then worrying Rome. He even (falsely) took credit for blocking Brownson's appointment to the CUI. In fact, Newman actively pursued Brownson but was unable to tempt him to the university. See Cullen to Barnabò, 18 February 1861, UNDA, I-4-g. This is a copy of a letter held in the Propaganda archives.

5. Cullen to Kirby (?), 18 March 1851. Quoted in Larkin, *Making of the Roman Catholic Church*, 121. Larkin indicates that the letter was to Kirby but is

to be found in the Bernard Smith papers. It is unclear if Smith simply took the letter and kept it in his own papers or whether it was in fact addressed to Smith.

6. See Peter Cooper to Cullen, 3 November 1841, Cullen Papers, ICRA, #690. Cooper had written to tell Cullen of the controversy provoked by Tract 90 and Newman's response to his critics. It was not an entirely favourable report, with Cooper writing: 'poor Newman in a hurried & ill written Appendix fairly goes on his knees & asks pardon. not content with that, he writes an expiatory letter to the B. of Oxford . . . what hope from such a man? & yet he is perhaps the most favourable specimen of his class.' Faint praise indeed.

7. See Owen Chadwick, *From Bousset to Newman: The Idea of Doctrinal Development* (Cambridge: Cambridge University Press, 1957).

8. See diary entry for 5 February 1847, *LD* 12.

9. Newman to Cullen, 20 December 1848, *LD* 12.

10. Cullen to Newman, 8 January 1849, BOA, Cullen File.

11. Newman to Faber, 25 November 1849, *LD* 13. Newman had become caught up in Roman politics, and it seems that some at least among the English hierarchy objected to his approaching Cullen for help. See, for example, Newman to Faber, 25 December 1849, *LD* 13.

12. Cullen to Newman, 5 July 1850, BOA, Cullen File.

13. Newman to Cullen, 7 July 1850, *LD* 14.

14. Cullen to Kirby, 25 November 1850, Kirby Papers (New Collection), ICRA, box 1, folder 2, #57. Original in Italian.

15. Cullen to Newman, 15 April 1851, BOA, Cullen File.

16. Newman to Cullen, 16 April 1851, *LD* 14.

17. Newman to Cullen, 28 April 1851, *LD* 14.

18. Wiseman to Cullen, 21 May 1851, Cullen Papers (Armagh), DDA, 39/2/12.

19. Cullen to Fransoni, 7 July 1851, quoted in Larkin, *Making of the Roman Catholic Church*, 122.

20. Cullen to Kirby, 16 April 1851, Kirby Papers (New Collection), ICRA, box 1, folder 2, #87.

21. Smith to Cullen, 24 July 1851, Cullen Papers (Armagh), DDA, 42/3/21.

22. Fransoni to Cullen, 23 July 1851, Cullen Papers, DDA, 449/5/72.

23. Smith to Cullen, 11 July 1851, Cullen Papers (Armagh), DDA, 42/3/23.

24. J. O'Ferrall to Cullen, 7 June 1851, Cullen Papers (Armagh), DDA, 39/2/98.

25. See Cullen to Slattery, 8 July 1851, Slattery Papers, CDA, 1851/6.

26. Newman to Allies, 9 July 1851, *LD* 14.

27. The memorandum ('Memorandum of the subjects discussed at a meeting of several gentlemen with the Primate relating to the establishment of a Catholic University in Ireland', Cullen Papers, DDA, 45/3/6) is handwritten and gives the date of the meeting as '13 July. 185. .' A later hand has written in a '2' to make the date 1852. The document is also headed in a later hand '1852',

with the '2' being underscored. Trevor, Ker, and Gilley do not discuss the meeting at all; Ward refers to it in passing, but does not connect it with the decision to approach Newman. See Wilfrid Ward, *Life of John Henry Cardinal Newman*, 2 vols. (London: Longmans, Green, 1912), 1:310. McGrath is aware of the conference, and seems to understand its importance. But he clearly had not seen the memorandum of the meeting and thus seems to get the chronology wrong, implying that Cullen wrote to Newman at the same time as Hope wrote to Newman, in other words either on 12 July or on the 13th prior to the meeting. This can be seen by the fact that McGrath seems to think that Cullen wrote to Newman to propose a meeting with Manning, Hope, and the rest before actually meeting with them. In fact, it was decided by the group to invite Newman to a further meeting: something that had only been decided on 13 July. McGrath, *Newman's University*, 106–7. McRedmond mentions the conference, but does not connect it with the decision to approach Newman. Louis McRedmond, *Thrown Among Strangers: John Henry Newman in Ireland* (Dublin: Veritas, 1990), 49. Larkin, too, mentions the meeting, but follows McGrath in saying that the subject was '*apparently* Newman and the Rectorship' [emphasis added]; see Larkin, *Making of the Roman Catholic Church*, 123.

28. Cullen to Newman, 13 July 1851, BOA, Cullen File.

29. Newman to Cullen, 15 July 1851, *LD* 14.

30. Hope to Newman, 12 July 1851, quoted in McGrath, *Newman's University*, 106.

31. Memorandum of the subjects discussed at a meeting of several gentlemen with the Primate relating to the establishment of a Catholic University in Ireland, Cullen Papers, DDA, 45/3/6.

32. Ibid.

33. Ibid.

34. Cullen to Newman, 13 July 1851, BOA, Cullen File.

35. *AW*, 280. It is possible that Hope himself thought he was responsible for suggesting Newman. His biographer (and CUI professor), Robert Ornsby certainly reports events in this way. See Robert Ornsby, *Memoirs of James Robert Hope-Scott of Abbotsford, D. C. L., Q. C., late Fellow of Merton College, Oxford: With Selections from his Correspondence*, 2 vols. (London: John Murray, 1884), 2:98.

36. McGrath, *Newman's University*, 107.

37. Cullen to Smith, 12 July 1851. Quoted in Larkin, *Making of the Roman Catholic Church*, 122–23.

38. *AW*, 280.

39. Ibid., 281. McGrath, *Newman's University*, 109. Newman to Cullen, 23 July 1851, *LD* 14.

40. Newman to Allies, 25 July 1851, *LD* 14.

41. Cullen to Newman, 22 July 1851, BOA, Cullen File.

42. Newman to Ornsby, 11 September 1851, *LD* 14.

43. Newman to Cullen, 23 July 1851, *LD* 14.

44. Cullen to Newman, 12 August 1851, BOA, Cullen File. See also Meeting of 12 August 1851, Minute Book of the Catholic University Committee, UCDA, CU1.

45. For Newman's concern to gain for Allies a university salary, see Newman to Allies, 21 October 1851, *LD* 14.

46. Newman to Cullen, 28 August 1851, *LD* 14.

47. *AW*, 282.

48. Cullen to Newman, 15 September 1851, BOA, Cullen File.

49. Cullen to Newman, 20 September 1851, BOA, Cullen File.

50. Newman to Cullen 3 October 1851, *LD* 14.

51. Cullen to Newman, 28 October 1851, BOA, Cullen File.

52. Meeting of 12 November 1851, Minute Book of the Catholic University Committee, UCDA, CU1.

53. See *AW*, 283.

54. Cullen to Newman, 14 November 1851, BOA, Cullen File.

55. *AW*, 283.

56. See Newman to Cullen, 11 October, 14 October, and 5 November 1851, *LD* 14.

57. Smith to Cullen, 6 October 1851, Cullen Papers, DDA, 42/3/33.

58. Smith to Cullen, 20 November 1851, Cullen Papers, DDA, 42/3/34.

59. Cantwell to Cullen, 4 October 1851, Cullen Papers (Armagh), DDA, 39/2/124.

60. MacNally to Cullen, 5 October 1851, Cullen Papers (Armagh), DDA, 39/2/125.

61. Murray to Cullen, 29 October 1851, Cullen Papers (Armagh), DDA, 39/2/129.

62. Smith to Kirby, 10 March 24 November 1851, Kirby Papers, ICRA, #953. It is unfortunate that O'Reilly, the best and often the only source of information about MacHale in the 1850s, does not address the question of MacHale's attitude towards Newman's appointment at all.

63. Cullen to Walsh, 28 December 1851, Cullen Papers, DDA, 66/16.

64. Cullen to Walsh, 8 November 1851, Cullen Papers, DDA, 66/16.

5. The Idea of a University, in Ireland

1. David Newsome, *The Convert Cardinals: John Henry Newman and Henry Edward Manning* (London: John Murray, 1993), 217.

2. Richard Finnegan and Edward McCarron, *Ireland: Historical Echoes, Contemporary Politics* (Boulder, Colo.: Westview, 2000), 109.

3. O'Carroll, 'The Pastoral Politics of Paul Cullen', in *Catholic Diocese of Dublin*, ed. Kelly and Keogh, 295.

4. Cullen to Maher, 10 October 1829, Cullen Papers, DDA, 40/9(a).

5. Ibid.

6. See Peadar MacSuibhne, *Paul Cardinal Cullen and His Contemporaries*, 5 vols. (Naas, Co. Kildare: Leinster Leader, 1961–74), 1:3–11.

7. J. B. Taylor to Cullen, 30 October 1822, Cullen Papers, ICRA, #2.

8. F. S. L. Lyons, *Ireland since the Famine* (London: Fontana Press, 1971), 95.

9. See Murray to Cullen, 14 May 1834, Cullen Papers (New Collection), ICRA, 4/1/44. Quoted in Corish, *Maynooth College,* 89.

10. See J. McCann to Cullen, 8 April 1835, Cullen Papers, ICRA, #195, and Slattery to Cullen, 1 October 1835, Cullen Papers, ICRA, #221.

11. Meyler to Cullen, 2 January 1839, Cullen Papers, ICRA, #479.

12. Meyler to Cullen, 19 February 1838, Cullen Papers, ICRA, #405.

13. The former archivist of the college, the Rev. John Silke, tentatively dated the memorandum to 1850, but on what evidence is unclear. It certainly could not have been written any later, as it is held in Rome and predates Cullen's arrival in Ireland. However, it may have been composed at any time between 1847 and 1850.

14. Undated Memorandum, Cullen Papers (New Collection), ICRA, carton 3, folder 2, #12(c).

15. *AW,* 281.

16. BOA, Louvain University Working and Routine File, C.6.3.

17. Ibid. These notes clearly date between August and October 1851. Newman wrote to de Ram in August with his questions about Louvain and had his answers by September—in time for the early October meeting of the Thurles subcommittee, which explicitly cited Louvain's example.

18. Report of the subcommittee on the organization of the Catholic University of Ireland, printed in John Henry Newman, *My Campaign in Ireland: Catholic University Reports and Other Papers,* ed. William Neville (Aberdeen: A. King, 1896), 78.

19. Undated fragment, Cullen Papers, DDA, 43/7, File 2, #2.

20. 9 September 1850, Patrick Francis Moran, ed., *The Pastoral Letters and Other Writings of Cardinal Cullen, Archbishop of Dublin, etc. etc.,* 3 vols. (Dublin: Browne and Nolan, 1882), 1:56–59.

21. Ibid., 1:57.

22. Ibid.

23. Ibid., 1:58.

24. Undated fragment, Cullen Papers, DDA, 43/7, File 2, #14.

25. Moran, *Writings of Cardinal Cullen,* 1:59. It is far from clear that Cullen was wrong in his assessment of the products of Europe's universities. G. M. Trevelyan, in his hymn to the Roman Republic, has remarked that 'the [university] students were partisans of the movement of emancipation, and not only supplied the prophets, theorists, and statesman who redeemed Italy, but offered themselves by scores and hundreds as the common food for powder.' Having himself lived through the Roman Republic, Cullen would have been aware of this. G. M. Trevelyan, *Garibaldi's Defence of the Roman Republic* (London: Cassell, 1988), 94.

26. Moran, *Writings of Cardinal Cullen,* 1:58.

27. Pastoral letter to the Catholic Clergy of the Archdiocese of Armagh on Catholic Education, 1851, Moran, *Writings of Cardinal Cullen,* 1:70.

28. Cullen to Kirby, 21 December 1853, Kirby Papers (New Collection), ICRA, box 1, folder 3, #116. Original in Italian.

29. Cullen to unknown correspondent, undated, Cullen Papers, DDA, 43/7, file 2, #8. This letter was most likely written in 1850 or 1851.

30. Ibid.

31. Cullen to Monsell, 13 April 1853, Aberdeen Papers, BL, Add. Mss. 43.247, f. 190.

32. Cullen to Monsell, 22 April 1864, Monsell Papers, NLI, Ms. 8317 (3).

33. Cullen to Monsell, 26 December 1872, Monsell Papers, NLI, Ms. 8317(3). Cullen himself discussed at length his views on mixed education in testimony to the Powis Commission. See Moran, *Writings of Cardinal Cullen*, 2:517–802.

34. Undated fragment, Cullen Papers, DDA, 43/7, File 2, #14.

35. See Newman to Cullen, 16 September 1851, *LD* 14.

36. Cullen to Newman, 20 September 1851, BOA, Cullen File.

37. Newman to Ornsby, 18 April 1852, *LD* 15.

38. Ian Ker, 'The Idea of a Catholic University', paper delivered to the Newman Conference 'The Idea of a Catholic University in Mayo' (Ballina: n.p., 1996), 8.

39. G. M. Young, *Victorian Essays*, ed. W. D. Hancock (Oxford: Oxford University Press, 1962), 142–43.

40. John Henry Newman, *Discussions and Arguments* (London: Longmans, 1918), 259. Newman is quoting Peel.

41. Ibid., 261–62.

42. Ibid., 272.

43. A. Dwight Culler, *The Imperial Intellect: A Study of Newman's Educational Ideal* (New Haven: Yale University Press, 1955), 103–4, 109–10.

44. Newman to St John, 11 May 1852, *LD* 15.

45. Ian Ker, introduction to John Henry Newman, *The Idea of a University*, ed. Ian Ker (Oxford: Oxford University Press, 1976).

46. John Henry Newman, *Discourses on the Scope and Nature of University Education Addressed to the Catholics of Dublin* (Dublin: James Duffy, 1852), v, 39, v–vi.

47. Ibid., viii, x, xv.

48. Ibid., 11–13.

49. Ibid., 23–24.

50. Ibid., 25–26.

51. For the evolution of Newman's view on this subject, see *AW*, 320.

52. Newman, *University Education*, 39–40.

53. Ibid., 43–44.

54. *Pace* the modern 'multiversity'.

55. Newman, *University Education*, 44.

56. Ibid., 66.

57. Ibid., 104.

58. Ibid., 104–5.

59. Ibid., 55.

60. Moriarty was appointed coadjutor bishop of Ardfert and Kerry in 1854.

61. See McGrath, *Newman's University*, 170.

62. Moriarty to Newman, 21 July 1852, quoted in McGrath, *Newman's University*, 171.

63. V. A. McClelland, *English Roman Catholics and Higher Education, 1830–1903* (Oxford: Oxford University Press, 1973), 109.

64. See Newsome, *Convert Cardinals*, 217.

65. Newman's close friend T. W. Allies, who had been secretary to the Thurles subcommittee, was just as stern an opponent of mixed education as Newman, calling it 'a surrender to heresy, schism, and self-will . . . an abnegation of the highest end of our being', whereas a Catholic education 'is the realisation before all, and above all, of that highest end. But this secured, it proceeds to group around it the various sciences, accomplishments, and arts of social life.' Newman continually consulted Allies on the university in this early period, and the two men were in close sympathy on educational matters. See T. W. Allies, 'The Catholic University', *Dublin Review* 31 (December 1851): 587. Myles O'Reilly, who had sat with Allies and Newman on the same subcommittee, also held a similar view of a Catholic university education.

66. Cullen to Smith, 24 May 1852, The original of this letter (in Italian) is catalogued as being in the Kirby Papers (New Collection) of the Irish College. It does not seem, however, to be currently in that collection. Patrick Corish quotes from the letter in his guide to the Cullen Papers in Rome, from which I have drawn this quotation. Patrick J. Corish, 'Guide to Material of Public and Political Interest, 1836–1861, Irish College Rome: Kirby Papers', *Archivium Hibernicum* 31 (1973): 1–94.

67. Cullen to Kirby, 30 May 1852, Kirby Papers (New Collection), ICRA, box 1, folder 3, #28. Original in Italian.

68. Cullen to Fransoni, 11 June 1852. See MacSuibhne, *Paul Cullen*, 2:123.

69. Desmond Bowen, *Paul Cardinal Cullen and the Shaping of Modern Irish Catholicism* (Dublin: Gill and Macmillan, 1983), 150–51.

6. Delay—the University on Hold

1. Newman to Bowden, 26 August 1851, *LD* 14.

2. *AW*, 304.

3. Meagher, *Daniel Murray*, 108. Murray rightly suspected Cullen of hostility to Maynooth. Cullen had a long history, both in Rome and in Dublin, of suspicion of and borderline hostility towards Maynooth on various grounds— primarily the supposed Gallicanism of some of the staff. See Corish, *Maynooth College*, 142–43.

4. Murray to Cullen, 29 October 1851, Cullen Papers (Armagh), DDA, 39/2/129.

5. Murray to Cullen, 22 November 1851, Cullen Papers (Armagh), DDA, 39/2/135.

6. See MacSuibhne, *Paul Cullen*, 3:107.

7. *AW*, 321.

8. The description of Murray's last hours in Meagher's book tallies almost exactly with the symptoms of a severe stroke. See Meagher, *Daniel Murray*, 135–37.

9. Cullen to Newman, 27 February 1852, see *LD* 15:45n.

10. Newman to Cullen, 2 March 1852, *LD* 15.

11. Smith to Kirby, 10 March 1852, Kirby Papers, ICRA, #984.

12. Cooper to Kirby, 28 March 1852, Kirby Papers, ICRA, #981.

13. Halifax was made an archdiocese in early 1852.

14. Cullen to Walsh, 7 April 1852, Cullen Papers, DDA, 66/16.

15. McGrath, *Newman's University*, 128.

16. Newman to Cullen, 21 November 1851, *LD* 14.

17. Cullen to Newman, 25 November 1851, see *LD* 14:431.

18. Newman to Cullen, 4 February 1852, *LD* 15.

19. See Sheridan Gilley, *Newman and His Age* (London: Darton, Longmans, Todd, 1990), 270.

20. Ward, *John Henry Cardinal Newman*, 1:283.

21. Newman to Capes, 27 November 1851, *LD* 14.

22. See MacSuibhne, *Paul Cullen*, 2:129–30.

23. *AW*, 284.

24. Myles O'Reilly was also for an immediate beginning and claimed that Cullen believed that the university should take the model of the founding of a religious order in beginning on a small scale. O'Reilly, not unreasonably, noted that religious orders did not usually begin with £50,000 raised by public subscription. See O'Reilly to Newman, 26 October 1851, BOA, C.6.4.

25. *AW*, 286.

26. Newman to Bowden, 26 August 1851, *LD* 14.

27. Newman to St John, 3 October 1851, *LD* 14.

28. *AW*, 286.

29. Cullen to Walsh, 7 April 1852, Cullen Papers, DDA, 66/16.

30. Newman to Ornsby, 18 April 1852, *LD* 15.

31. Cullen to Smith, 24 January 1852, quoted in Larkin, *Making of the Roman Catholic Church*, 130.

32. Ulrick J. Bourke, *Life of John MacHale, Archbishop of Tuam* (New York: P. J. Kennedy, 1882), 141.

33. Cullen to MacHale, 16 February 1852, O'Reilly, *John MacHale*, 1:492.

34. Cullen to MacHale, 17 February 1852, O'Reilly, *John MacHale*, 1:494.

35. MacHale to Cullen, 20 February 1852, O'Reilly, *John MacHale*, 1:494.

36. Ibid.

37. Cullen to Kirby, 24 February 1852, Kirby Papers (New Collection), ICRA, box 1, folder 3, #16.

38. Cantwell to MacHale, 20 February 1852, O'Reilly, *John MacHale*, 1:496.

39. Newman, *My Campaign in Ireland*, 78–79.

40. See Emmet Larkin, *The Consolidation of the Roman Catholic Church in Ireland, 1860–1870* (Chapel Hill: University of North Carolina Press, 1987), chap. 4.

41. See Larkin, *Making of the Roman Catholic Church*, table 2, 'Factions among the Twenty-eight Irish Bishops', 169.

42. See Larkin, *Making of the Roman Catholic Church*, 108–12.

43. Ibid., 109.

44. Cullen to Walsh, 28 December 1851, Cullen Papers, DDA, 66/16.

45. Cullen to Walsh, 5 February 1852, Cullen Papers, DDA, 66/16.

46. Newman to Allies, 19 April 1852, *LD* 15. He had been warned off staying with Wilberforce by Robert Ornsby, on the advice of Lucas. See *AW*, 289.

47. Cullen to Newman, 25 April 1852, BOA, Cullen File.

48. Newman to Cullen, 11 October 1851, *LD* 14.

49. Newman to Allies, 27 April 1852, *LD* 15.

50. Newman to Allies, 19 April 1852, *LD* 15.

51. Newman to Dalgairns, 15 August 1849, *LD* 13.

52. McClelland, *English Roman Catholics*, 133–34.

53. Acton to Richard Simpson, 25 July 1858, *The Correspondence of Lord Acton and Richard Simpson*, 3 vols., edited by Josef L. Altholz and Damian McElrath (Cambridge: Cambridge University Press, 1971–73), 1:65.

54. This was not strictly true, as he took a close interest in getting Allies appointed to some sort of job within the university, preferably a professorship. See Newman to Cullen, 14 April 1852, *LD* 15.

55. Newman to Cullen, 4 July 1852, *LD* 15.

56. See *AW*, 284. Newman's letter to Manning (if that is in fact how he made the offer) on the subject does not seem to have survived.

57. *AW*, 292–93.

58. It is likely that this was the same Taylor who was writing to Cullen in 1822 about Carlow College.

59. *AW*, 294.

60. Ibid., 294.

61. Ibid., 297–98.

62. See Matthias Buschkül, *Great Britain and the Holy See, 1746–1870* (Dublin: Irish Academic Press, 1982), 92–95.

63. Cullen's views on the clerical role in politics is perhaps best summed up in a letter he wrote to Kirby in early 1854. 'The priests must have some share in political movements—but the church ought to be a sacred and neutral spot, where all worldly things are to be forgotten.' A primary component of the clerical role in the tenants' rights agitation was in speeches from the pulpit during the mass or in specially called meetings held in parish churches. See Cullen to Kirby, 12 January 1854, Kirby Papers (New Collection), ICRA, box 2, folder 1, #3.

64. For a discussion of the 'priests and politics' issue, see Larkin, *Making of the Roman Catholic Church*, 170–202.

65. Ibid., 202.

66. Cullen to Kirby, 9 December 1853, Kirby Papers (New Collection), ICRA, box 1, folder 3, #114.

67. The letter is only signed '+ Murphy', but is most likely from Timothy Murphy of Cloyne, who was a Cullen ally.

68. Murphy to Cullen, 3 July 1852, Cullen Papers, DDA, 325/1/82.

69. See Meeting of 14 May 1851, Minute Book of the Catholic University Committee, UCDA, CU1.

70. McGinnity to Cullen, 5 November 1852, Cullen Papers, DDA, 325/2/119.

71. See Minute Book of the Catholic University Committee, UCDA, CU1.

72. Cullen to Kirby, 17 October 1853, Kirby Papers (New Collection), ICRA, box 1, folder 3, #102.

73. For example, see Cullen to Slattery, 16 February and 6 May 1852, Slattery Papers, CDA, P. 6004, 1852/4 and 1852/14.

74. Dixon had been the candidate for Armagh whom MacHale and his allies had most opposed on the death of Crolly, and he had been passed over in favour of Cullen in 1849. He was himself, with Cullen's support, appointed to Armagh upon the latter's translation to Dublin in 1852. He never did anything to upset his patron. A good example of his subordination to Cullen came in 1857, when he actually wrote to Cullen to request the archbishop of Dublin write to Cornelius Denvir, the long-serving bishop of Down and Connor (Belfast), about the deployment of priests within his diocese. Down and Connor lay within Dixon's own province of Armagh and had nothing whatsoever to do with Cullen. Dixon's involvement of Cullen in the matter was indicative of his entire attitude towards the archbishop of Dublin. See Dixon to Cullen, 27 April 1857, Cullen Papers, DDA, 339/5/56. There has been only one biography of Dixon, a contemporary hagiography: M. F. Cusack (the 'nun of Kenmare'), *The Life of Most Rev. Joseph Dixon, D. D., Primate of All Ireland* (London: Burns, 1878).

75. Cullen to Kirby, 24 October 1853, Kirby Papers (New Collection), ICRA, box 1, folder 3, #104. This letter is misdated as 20 October 1853 by Corish in his guide to the Cullen/Kirby papers in Rome. Patrick J. Corish, 'Guide to Materials of Public and Political Interest, 1836–1861. Irish College Rome: Kirby Papers', *Archivium Hibernicum* 31 (1973): 49.

76. Meeting of 21 October 1853, Minute Book of the Catholic University Committee, UCDA, CU1.

77. *AW*, 303.

78. Meeting of 15 February 1853, Minute Book of the Catholic University Committee, UCDA, CU1.

79. Cullen to Newman, 4 February 1853, BOA, Cullen File.

80. Cullen to Kirby, 9 March 1853, Kirby Papers (New Collection), ICRA, box 1, folder 3, #64. Original in Italian.

81. Taylor's exact status remains somewhat unclear. What is clear is that he was never formally appointed as vice-rector of the university. In Bernard O'Reilly's biography of MacHale he reproduces a letter from John O'Hanlon (whom MacHale and Slattery had backed for the see of Armagh in 1849 before transferring their support to Cullen), in which he appears to throw some light on the question. O'Hanlon, who sat on the university committee, reported to MacHale that Francis Haly, bishop of Kildare and Leighlin, had proposed that Taylor be appointed as vice-rector of the CUI. According to O'Hanlon, the proposal was 'seconded by the Archbishop of Armagh [Dixon] and warmly supported by Dr. Cullen, Father Maher, Father Brennan, P.P., of Kildare, James O'Ferrell, Mr Errington, etc. . . .' In other words, Taylor's appointment was proposed and supported by Cullen and his allies on the committee. Again according to O'Hanlon, the proposed appointment of Taylor was opposed by some members of the committee on the grounds that it did not have the authority to make such an appointment as the right was to be reserved to the archbishops and rector conjointly. Cullen, according to this letter, then claimed that he had Newman's support for the appointment and James O'Farrell pointed out that, even if the committee as such had given up its authority over the matter to the archbishops, there could be no issue as three of the four were present and presumably in agreement as to the appointment. The upshot is that the meeting agreed to postpone discussion of Taylor's appointment and made him secretary to the university committee—the role in which he dealt with Newman—instead. The Minutes of the Catholic University Committee, preserved in the archives of University College Dublin (CU1) make no mention of these matters but might not be expected to record a failed appointment. Nor do any surviving letters of Cullen, Slattery, Leahy, or any other participants record such an attempt to appoint Taylor. In assessing O'Hanlon's letter it must be remembered that he was an ally of MacHale's and was writing in a strongly critical vein of the actions of the university committee. It is also highly unlikely that Cullen would baldly lie, for such it could only be, about Newman's support for Taylor's appointment as vice-rector. He would probably be caught out. Although it seems true that Cullen intended Taylor to be vice-rector, the evidence does not allow us to know exactly what steps, if any, he took to achieve that end. See O'Hanlon to MacHale, 29 January 1853, O'Reilly, *John MacHale*, 2:499–502.

82. Cullen to Kirby, 12 January 1854, Kirby Papers (New Collection), ICRA, box 2, folder 1, #3.

83. Cullen to Smith, 16 June 1854, MacSuibhne, *Paul Cullen*, 3:195.

7. Opening the University

1. Newman to Cullen, 2 March 1853, *LD* 15.
2. Quoted in McGrath, *Newman's University*, 203.
3. Vincent F. Blehl, 'Newman and the Missing Mitre', *Thought: Fordham University Quarterly* 35, no. 136 (Spring 1960): 111–23.

4. J. H. Whyte, 'Newman in Dublin: Fresh Light from the Archives of Propaganda', *Dublin Review* 483 (Spring 1960): 32–39.

5. See McGrath, *Newman's University*, 249.

6. *AW*, 304.

7. Ibid., 305.

8. Taylor to Newman, 17 January 1854, BOA, CUI General Correspondence.

9. Taylor to Newman, 26 January 1854, BOA, CUI General Correspondence.

10. Quoted in *AW*, 308.

11. See Newman to Cullen, 30 December 1853, *LD* 15.

12. Cullen to Kirby, 16 January 1854, Kirby Papers (New Collection), ICRA, box 2, folder 1, #4.

13. Cullen to Kirby, 25 August 1842, Kirby Papers, ICRA, #113.

14. Cullen to Kirby, 16 January 1854, Kirby Papers (New Collection), ICRA, box 2, folder 1, #4.

15. Cullen to Kirby, 28 January 1854, Kirby Papers (New Collection), ICRA, box 2, folder 1, #5.

16. See Whyte, 'Newman in Dublin', 32–33.

17. Wiseman, in a letter to Newman, addressed the question of English interference in Irish affairs. With almost spectacular naïveté, Wiseman informed Newman that while 'I am *in curiâ*, no one can consider me merely as an English Bishop, in whom it might be an impertinence to meddle in the affairs of another country or Church. As Cardinal, however unworthy, I am bound to assist the Holy See by my advice on any matters proposed to me by it, without reference to country' (Wiseman to Newman, 20 January 1854, *AW*, 315). Although no doubt technically correct, it is difficult to imagine that such an explanation would have satisfied MacHale or indeed any other Irish nationalist.

18. Scritture riferite nei congressi, Irlanda, 1854–56, ff. 116–17, vol. 234, no. 483. The original is in Italian and the translation is by J. H. Whyte, who quotes the document on 33–34 of his 'Newman in Dublin'.

19. In the his university memorandum Newman reports that many years after the event Hope-Scott had reported that it was Cullen who had blocked the appointment. Yet Newman had also heard it said that Barnabò was claiming that the whole matter had been a 'hoax'. Newman himself never expressed an opinion on what happened and does not seem to have himself blamed Cullen. See *AW*, 319.

20. For Newman's account of his proposed bishopric, see *AW*, 316–20.

21. Ibid., 319.

22. Cullen to Kirby, 4 March 1854, Kirby Papers (New Collection), ICRA, box 2, folder 1, #10.

23. Cullen to Kirby, 21 December 1853, Kirby Papers (New Collection), ICRA, box 1, folder 3, #116. Original in Italian.

24. Ibid.

25. Cullen to Kirby, 21 January 1854, Kirby Papers (New Collection), ICRA, box 2, folder 1, #5.

26. Cullen to Kirby, 28 January 1854, Kirby Papers (New Collection), ICRA, box 2, folder 1, #7.

27. Cullen to Kirby, 18 February 1854, Kirby Papers (New Collection), ICRA, box 2, folder 1, #8.

28. Cullen to Kirby, 12 March 1854, Kirby Papers (New Collection), ICRA, box 2, folder 1, #11.

29. Ibid.

30. Newman, *My Campaign in Ireland*, lxxxii–lxxxiii.

31. See Larkin, *Making of the Roman Catholic Church*, 241.

32. Entry of 13 February 1854, University Journal, 1854, BOA, A34.2.

33. See diary entries for 15, 16 February and 8, 14 March 1854, *LD* 16.

34. Newman to St John, 17 February 1854, *LD* 16.

35. Newman to James Laird Patterson, 9 March 1854, *LD* 16.

36. Newman to the Oratorians at Birmingham, 23 February 1854, *LD* 16.

37. Ibid.

38. Larkin, *Making of the Roman Catholic Church*, 243.

39. Cullen to Fransoni, 26 May 1854, Scritture riferite nei congressi, Irlanda, 1854–56, ff. 338–39, vol. 218. Quoted in Larkin, *Making of the Roman Catholic Church*, 247.

40. Ibid.

41. Ibid., 247–48.

42. Ibid., 248–49.

43. Cullen to Kirby, 5 July 1854, Kirby Papers (New Collection), ICRA, box 2, folder 1, #26.

44. Larkin, *Making of the Roman Catholic Church*, 252.

45. Ibid., 252–53.

46. The above figures are drawn from MacSuibhne, *Paul Cullen*, 2: 407–8. Emmet Larkin provides a useful diocese by diocese summary of donations, drawn from the same source. See his *Making of the Roman Catholic Church*, 432. It does seem, however, that a collection was made in Cashel in 1856, as Slattery forwarded some £560 (still a substantial decline) in early March of that year. See Slattery to Cullen, 1 March 1856, Cullen Papers, DDA, 339/1/24.

47. See Christopher O'Dwyer, 'Life of Dr. Leahy, 1806–1875' (M.A. thesis, St Patrick's College, Maynooth, 1970), 1–12.

48. E. R. Norman, *The Catholic Church and Ireland in the Age of Rebellion, 1859–1873* (Ithaca, N.Y.: Cornell University Press, 1965), 13. In his unpublished study of Leahy, Christopher O'Dwyer rightly takes Norman to task for this assertion.

49. The letter concludes with Leahy telling Slattery, 'I have said too much'. The letter (and envelope) had been addressed but not stamped. As the original appears in Leahy's papers, and as no sign of such a letter appears in Slattery's, it is probable that Leahy thought better of sending what was by any measure an extraordinarily intemperate attack on the most powerful man in the Irish church. Although Slattery might have been sympathetic, given the evolution of his views on the university since 1851, the risk must have seemed too

great that the contents might get out. Given the nature of the criticism of Cullen, it seems likely that this letter was written after Rome's revisions of the May synod had reached Ireland, in other words sometime after September. Christopher O'Dwyer dates this letter to early 1854 but gives no reason for this dating beyond its place in the Cashel filing system (O'Dwyer, 'Life of Dr. Leahy', 94). Leahy to Slattery, undated (filed under 1854), Leahy Papers, CDA, P.6005, 1854/2.

50. Ibid.

51. Ibid.

52. Entries of 5 November and 23 November 1853, 1854 University Journal, BOA, A34.2.

53. Renouf to his brother, 16 March 1854, Renouf Papers, PCA, 63/9/1/207.

54. Renouf to his parents, 'some day or other in April' (postmarked 13 April) 1854, Renouf Papers, PCA, 63/9/1/208.

55. Cullen to Newman, 14 April 1854, BOA, Cullen File.

56. Taylor had resigned to return to diocesan duties in the spring of 1854.

57. *AW*, 295.

58. Leahy to Newman, 22 May 1854, BOA, Catholic University General Correspondence.

59. O'Dwyer, 'Life of Dr. Leahy', 107.

60. Under Rome's amendments to the decrees of the synod, this was to become the permanent arrangement.

61. Cullen to Newman, 30 May 1854, BOA, Catholic University General Correspondence.

62. Cullen to Newman, 28 September 1854, BOA, Catholic University General Correspondence.

63. Arnold to Julia Arnold, 12 January 1859, *The Letters of Thomas Arnold the Younger*, ed. James Bertram (Auckland: Auckland University Press, 1980), 96.

64. Cullen to Newman, 30 September 1854, BOA, Catholic University General Correspondence.

65. The English appointees were Ornsby, Allies, Terrence Flanagan, J. B. Robertson, Renouf (from Guernsey), James Stewart, and Edward Healy Thompson. See McGrath, *Newman's University*, 324–25.

66. Here Newman's Anglican background shone through. 'Exegetics' was a term more in use in the Protestant theological world than the Catholic. One of Leahy's clerical friends asked him if he was to be professor of domestic economy. Newman later changed the name on Leahy's advice. See O'Dwyer, 'Life of Dr. Leahy', 101.

67. Newman to MacHale, 3 October 1854, O'Reilly, *John MacHale*, 2:505. Newman sent essentially the same letter naming the proposed appointees and asking for archiepiscopal approval to each of the four archbishops.

68. Cullen to Newman, 7 October 1854, BOA, Catholic University General Correspondence.

69. Dixon to Newman, 4 October 1854, BOA, Catholic University General Correspondence.

70. Renouf to his parents, 13 (?) April 1854, Renouf Papers, PCA, 63/9/1/208.

71. For MacHale's willingness to be placed on the university's books, see MacHale to Newman, 16 June 1854, O'Reilly, *John MacHale*, 2:503. MacHale also claimed, in this letter, that 'I shall not be wanting in taking an interest in the Catholic University, and I trust that its management will earn the confidence and support of the Catholics of Ireland.' Whether this sentiment reflects a genuine change of heart in MacHale as regards the CUI after at least partially getting his way in May (before Rome intervened) or whether this was simply a not terribly veiled warning to Newman is not clear. Given MacHale's temperament and later actions, the latter is by far the more likely.

72. See Cullen to Kirby, 8 October 1854, Kirby Papers (New Collection), ICRA, box 2, folder 1, #34.

73. O'Dwyer, 'Life of Dr. Leahy', 107.

74. Leahy to Newman, 10 September 1854, Catholic University General Correspondence, BOA.

75. Cullen to Kirby, 8 October 1854, Kirby Papers (New Collection), ICRA, file 2, folder 1, #34.

76. Cullen to Newman, 14 November 1854, BOA, Cullen File.

77. Catholic University Student Register, 1854–79, UCDA, CU5.

78. Ibid.

8. RUPTURE, FAILURE, AND DEPARTURE

1. Cullen to Newman, 20 December 1854, BOA, Cullen File.
2. Ibid.
3. Ibid.
4. Cullen to Newman, 12 January 1855, BOA, Cullen File.
5. MacSuibhne, *Paul Cullen*, 1:385–87.
6. McGrath, *Newman's University*, 355(n).
7. Moriarty to Newman, 1 May 1855, quoted in McGrath, *Newman's University*, 355.
8. Moriarty was badly mistaken about Pigot's supposed withdrawal from politics. Letters of Pigot's preserved in both the William Smith O'Brien Papers (NLI, Ms. 442,447) and the Gavan Duffy Papers (NLI, Ms. 5756) indicate that he had retained his active association with advanced nationalist politics, including after O'Brien had returned from his exile after the failed 1848 rising.
9. *AW*, 328–29. The extent of Pigot's involvement with Young Ireland is set out in Denis Gwynn, 'John E. Pigot and Thomas Davis', *Studies* (June 1949): 145–57.
10. *AW*, 328–29.
11. Pigot had written, apparently at Newman's request, a letter setting out how he thought the Catholic University should be organised and what it should

teach (his recommendation was that it pursue a classical curriculum). See Pigot to Newman, 11 May 1854, BOA, Suggestions for Organisation of the CUI, C.6.4.

12. Newman to Pigot, 5 March 1855, *LD* 16.

13. *AW*, 329.

14. After 'Young Ireland' had split from the mainstream O'Connellite nationalists with whom they had previously been allied.

15. Slattery to Cullen, 2 August 1846, Cullen Papers, ICRA, #1221.

16. Maginn to Cullen, 28 September 1848, Cullen Papers, ICRA, #1655.

17. Cullen to Thomas Cullen, 24 December 1848, Cullen Papers, DDA, 40/9(a).

18. Cullen to Slattery, 28 February 1848, Slattery Papers, CDA, P.6002, 1848/34.

19. Cullen to Walsh, 14 September 1849, Cullen Papers, DDA, 66/16.

20. Memorandum of Republican Atrocities, Cullen Papers (New Collection), ICRA, box 3, folder 2.

21. See M. J. Curran, 'Cardinal Cullen: Biographical Materials', *Reportorium Novum* 1 (1955), and MacSuibhne, *Paul Cullen*, 1:344–47.

22. Undated poem in Cullen's hand. Cullen Papers (New Collection), ICRA, carton 2 (loose, uncatalogued papers, mainly from the 1830s).

23. Cullen to Kirby, 25 June 1842, Kirby Papers, ICRA, #98.

24. Cullen to Hugh Cullen, 28 January 1848, quoted in MacSuibhne, *Paul Cullen*, 1:301.

25. Cullen to Barnabò, 12 July 1852, quoted in MacSuibhne, *Paul Cullen*, 3:131.

26. Cullen to Walsh, 28 December 1851, Cullen Papers, DDA, 66/16.

27. Cullen to Monsell, 10 May 1855, Monsell Papers, NLI, Ms. 8317(3).

28. See Lucas to Cullen, 15 May 1848, Cullen Papers, ICRA, #1592.

29. Cullen to Kirby, 9 December 1853, Kirby Papers (New Collection), ICRA, box 1, folder 3, #114.

30. Cullen to Kirby, 21 January 1854, Kirby Papers (New Collection), ICRA, box 2, folder 1, #5.

31. Cullen to Kirby, 30 May 1854, Kirby Papers (New Collections), ICRA, box 2, folder 1, #20.

32. Cullen to Haly, 21 December 1854, Kirby Papers (New Collection), ICRA, box 2, folder 1, #37. This letter is either a copy (albeit in Cullen's hand) or the original was never sent as it is preserved in Rome and is in Kirby's papers.

33. Journal of Frederick Lucas' 'Mission to Rome', Lucas Papers, NLI, Ms. 3738, undated, but probably January 1855.

34. Newman never did see any reason why he should sever relations with those of whom Cullen disapproved. As late as December 1856 (a year after Lucas had died), Newman would tell Wilberforce, 'I feel myself in no way indebted to Dr. Cullen or his support. On the contrary, I have served him faithfully, and have gone out of my way to do so. But I came to Ireland determined to belong to no party, whatever came of it. I felt I had a right to my own *opinions*, and to my own friends; nor will I ever give up an acquaintance be-

cause I differ from him.' See Newman to Wilberforce, 3 December 1856, *LD* 17.

35. *AW*, 328. Judging by Cullen's surviving letters to Newman, the latter had the order of events somewhat wrong: Cullen seems to have warned Newman against Lucas and then, when Newman ignored his warnings, grown cold towards him.

36. Newman to Cullen, 24 January 1855, *LD* 16

37. *AW*, 311.

38. Ibid.

39. Renouf to his parents, 22 January 1856, Renouf Papers, PCA, 63/9/1/220.

40. Lucas's friendship with Newman would not long be an issue, as he died on 22 October 1855, at the age of forty-four.

41. See Newman to Cullen, 23 February 1855, *LD* 16.

42. Ibid.

43. See Newman to Cullen, 5 July 1855, *LD* 16.

44. DeVere to Monsell, 8 February 1855, Monsell Papers, NLI, Ms. 8319(1).

45. Newman to Cullen, 26 July 1855, *LD* 16.

46. Newman to Cullen, 29 July 1855, *LD* 16.

47. Newman was able to meet with Cullen on 13 July (diary entry for 13 July 1855, *LD* 16), and he also enquired of Newman in writing as to whether one of the proposed professors of anatomy was a Catholic—Newman assured him that he was (Newman to Cullen, 1 August 1855, *LD* 16).

48. Scritture riferite nei congressi, Irlanda, 1854–56, f.510. The original is in Italian and the translation is by J. H. Whyte. Whyte, 'Newman in Dublin,' 34–35.

49. Ibid.

50. Cullen to Kirby, 9 August 1856, Kirby Letters (New Collection), ICRA, box 2, folder 1, #62. Original in Italian.

51. Cullen to Kirby, 3 September 1855, Kirby Papers (New Collection), ICRA, box 2, folder 1, #68.

52. Ibid.

53. The pope's brief establishing the university certainly implied the ability to grant degrees, and Cullen had reported previously to Newman that such a facility had been granted. What seems to have been at issue was exactly how the facility was to be exercised and the formalities of so doing.

54. Newman to Monsell, 4 September 1855, *LD* 16.

55. Monsell to Newman, 7 September 1855, BOA, Differences with Cullen File, C.6.27.

56. Cullen to Newman, 8 September 1855, BOA, Differences with Cullen File, C.6.27.

57. Unknown correspondent to Cullen, 28 August 1837, Cullen Papers, ICRA, #370. The Cullen papers catalogue in the Irish College has the writer of this letter as a 'Jas. Corr'. No such name appears in the letter and the attribution is most likely the result of a misreading of the final two words: 'jealous care'.

58. James Browne (bishop of Kilmore) to Cullen, 5 November 1838, Cullen Papers, ICRA, #466.

59. See Higgins to Cullen, 30 January 1839, Cullen Papers, ICRA, #487, and Murray to Cullen, 17 December 1838, Cullen Papers, ICRA, #475.

60. Newman seems to have had, in this matter, the support of precedent at Louvain (always important to Cullen). Myles O'Reilly, long a member of the university committee, told Newman in mid-1855 that the 'main point on which it [Louvain] seems to be an example to be studied is the discipline. It being perhaps the only example of one combining freedom in the students with the safeguard of Catholic Morality.' O'Reilly to Newman, 2 April 1855, BOA, Louvain Routine and Working File, C.6.3. Cullen, however, could have appealed to the disciplinary practice of the American Catholic Universities; for example, Notre Dame was 'seminary like in its rigour' during this period. See Heidemarie Weidner, 'Co-education and Jesuit "Ratio Studiorum" in Indiana: Rhetoric and Composition Instruction in Nineteenth Century Butler and Notre Dame' (Ph.D. diss., University of Louisville, 1991), 166–69.

61. Cullen's choice of billiards as an example of Newman's liberal approach to education and discipline is perhaps unfair. In 1880s Princeton, President James McCosh (no liberal) actually introduced billiards into the university as a means of maintaining discipline (by keeping the students on campus and away from nearby fleshpots). See George Marsden, *The Soul of the American University: From Protestant Establishment to Established Nonbelief* (New York: Oxford University Press, 1995), 201.

62. Cullen to Kirby, 15 January 1856, Kirby Papers (New Collection), ICRA, box 2, folder 1, #99.

63. Ibid.

64. Cullen to Kirby, 13 December 1856, Kirby Papers (New Collection), ICRA, box 2, folder 1, #154.

65. Culler, *Imperial Intellect*, 71–72.

66. Mark Pattison only left the house in the nick of time, managing to obtain a fellowship at the anti-Tractarian Lincoln College. See Mark Pattison, *Memoirs* (London: Centaur Press, 1969), 180–83.

67. For the above, see Larkin, *Making of the Roman Catholic Church*, 430–31.

68. *AW*, 327–28.

69. Ibid., 327.

70. See Newman to Monsell, 5 September 1855, *LD* 16, and also note, 539.

71. Christopher O'Dwyer, 'Life of Dr. Leahy, 1806–1875' (M.A. thesis, St Patrick's College, Maynooth, 1970), 97–98.

72. Cullen thought there would be no problem attracting students but, according to letters quoted by C. S. Dessain in the notes (page 545) to *LD* 16, such regular lectures (as opposed to the popular evening ones) only attracted a few Carmelites and were thus something of an embarrassment to Edmund O'Reilly, the professor of theology.

73. Cullen to Newman, 16 September 1855, reproduced in *LD* 16:545.

74. Cullen to Newman, 24 September 1855, BOA, Differences with Cullen File, C.6.27.

75. Particularly unfair was Newman's response to Cullen's remarks about discipline: '5 "Discipline!" then why did he not give me a Vice Rector?' Leahy, although not often resident, was still vice-rector and as such in charge of discipline. Newman seems to have been thinking of the period after Leahy's resignation, during which the vice-rectorship remained vacant. See *LD* 16:543.

76. Ibid.

77. O'Reilly to Newman, 12 October 1855, BOA, O'Reilly Correspondence.

78. Cullen to Kirby, 22 December 1855, Kirby Papers (New Collection), ICRA, box 2, folder 1, #94.

79. Cullen to Kirby, 15 January 1856, Kirby Papers (New Collection), ICRA, box 2, folder 1, #99.

80. Renouf to his parents, 22 January 1856, Renouf Papers, PCA, 63/9/1/220.

81. Renouf to his parents, 26 February 1856, Renouf Papers, PCA, 63/9/1/221.

82. Cullen to Kirby, 2 November 1856, Kirby Papers (New Collection), ICRA, box 2, folder 1, #147.

83. When, exactly, Leahy was appointed to these positions is unclear. Cullen reported the change to Kirby on 3 September (Cullen to Kirby, 3 September 1855, Kirby Papers [New Collection], ICRA, box 2, folder 1, #68) and told Newman on 24 September (Cullen to Newman, 24 September 1855, BOA, Differences with Cullen File, C.6.27). Leahy himself only made Newman aware of his new responsibilities on 5 October (Leahy to Newman, 5 October 1855, BOA, University Correspondence, C.6.26) in response to a letter from Newman (Newman to Leahy, 28 September 1855, *LD* 16). The reason for such a long delay is uncertain.

84. O'Dwyer, 'Life of Dr. Leahy', 23.

85. Leahy to Newman, 5 October 1855, BOA, University Correspondence, C.6.26.

86. O'Dwyer, 'Life of Dr. Leahy', 23.

87. Leahy to Newman, dated Feast of the Annunciation (thus 25 March) 1856, BOA, University Correspondence, C.6.26.

88. Cullen to Kirby, 2 November 1856, Kirby Papers (New Collection), ICRA, box 2, folder 1, #147.

89. Cullen to Kirby, 13 December 1856, Kirby Papers (New Collection), ICRA, box 2, folder 1, #154.

90. O'Dwyer, 'Life of Dr. Leahy', 25.

91. Ibid., 108.

92. Arnold to Captain Collinson, 19 September 1857, *Letters of Thomas Arnold the Younger*, 88.

93. Newman to Cullen, 23 July 1851, *LD* 14.

94. *AW,* 327.

95. Ibid.

96. Cullen to Kirby, 5 May 1856, Kirby Papers (New Collection), ICRA, box 2, folder 1, #120.

97. See Gilley, *Newman and His Age,* 284–89, for a full account of the question. Newman himself set out the Birmingham view of the controversy in a long letter to the Oratory fathers. See Newman to the Fathers of the Birmingham Oratory, 14 June 1856, *LD* 17.

98. *AW,* 327.

99. Cullen to Kirby, 22 December 1855, Kirby Papers (New Collection), ICRA, box 2, folder 1, #94.

100. MacHale to Newman, 3 August 1855, O'Reilly, *John MacHale,* 2:510.

101. Newman to MacHale, 8 August 1855, *LD* 16.

102. The amendments to the decrees of the May synod granted the power of appointment to the four archbishops, with the right to break any tie being given to the apostolic delegate (Cullen). Newman should certainly have been aware of this fact.

103. Cullen to Kirby, 13 December 1856, Kirby Papers (New Collection), ICRA, box 2, folder 1, #154.

104. See MacHale to Newman, 22 January 1856, O'Reilly, *John MacHale,* 2:511, and MacEvilly to Newman, 1 May 1856, O'Reilly, *John MacHale,* 2:511.

105. Derry to MacHale, 10 May 1856, O'Reilly, *John MacHale,* 2:513.

106. Cantwell to MacHale, 31 January 1857, O'Reilly, *John MacHale,* 2:515.

107. Cullen to Kirby, 15 May 1856, Kirby Papers (New Collection), ICRA, box 2, folder 1, #121.

108. Cullen to Newman, 26 June, (no year, but 1856), BOA, Differences with Cullen File, C.6.27. Cullen also met with Newman at least twice (on 18 June and 25 June) before Newman appeared before the assembled bishops, presumably to discuss tactics. See Newman to John Stanislas Flanagan, 18 June 1856, and Newman to Leahy, 25 June 1856, *LD* 17.

109. Lyons to Kirby, 27 June 1856, Kirby Papers (New Collection), ICRA, box 2, folder 1, #126.

110. Newman to St John, 26 June (2nd letter) 1856, *LD* 17.

111. Cullen to Kirby, 28 June 1856, Kirby Papers (New Collection), ICRA, box 2, folder 1, #129.

112. Cantwell to MacHale, 31 January 1857, O'Reilly, *John MacHale,* 2:514.

113. Cullen to Kirby, 11 January 1856, Kirby Papers (New Collection), ICRA, box 2, folder 1, #98.

114. Cullen to Kirby, 21 January 1856, Kirby Papers (New Collection), ICRA, box 2, folder 1, #100.

115. Lyons to Kirby, 27 June 1856, Kirby Papers (New Collection), ICRA, box 2, folder 1, #126.

116. Newman to St John, 26 June (1st letter) 1856, *LD* 17. He told Aubrey DeVere that 'much more work of the kind would go far to kill him [Cullen].' Newman to DeVere, 27 June 1856, *LD* 17.

117. Cullen to Kirby, 2 November 1856, Kirby Papers (New Collection), ICRA, box 2, folder 1, #147.

118. Catholic University Student Register, 1854–79, UCDA, CU5.

119. Cullen to Kirby, 2 November 1856, Kirby Papers (New Collection), ICRA, box 2, folder 1, #147.

120. Newman, *My Campaign in Ireland*, 65.

121. Fergal McGrath discusses the medical school at various points in his *Newman's University*. There are also two other treatments of the subject by William Doolin: 'The Medical School', *Struggle with Fortune, A Centenary Miscellany: Catholic University of Ireland, 1854/University College Dublin, 1954*, ed. Michael Tierney (Dublin: Browne and Nolan, 1954), and 'Newman and his Medical School', in *Studies* 42 (1953).

122. Newman, *My Campaign in Ireland*, 65.

123. Ibid.

124. *The Tablet*, October 1856.

125. See Cullen to Kirby, 13 April 1856, Kirby Papers (New Collection), ICRA, box 2, folder 1, #116.

126. Newman informed Ambrose St John in a letter dated 14 April 1856, that he had seen Cullen and 'mentioned my *leaving* in July year—and tho' at first he was startled or rather surprised, he quite acquiesced'. It is unclear how seriously Cullen took Newman's 'mention' of his intentions. There is no record of his considering a possible rectorial vacancy before December 1856, and he might not have, and indeed probably did not, take Newman's intentions seriously. See Newman to St John, 14 April 1856, *LD* 17.

127. Cullen to Kirby, 13 December 1856, Kirby Papers (New Collection), ICRA, box 2, folder 1, #154.

128. Ibid.

129. Cullen to Kirby, 1 February 1857, Kirby Papers (New Collection), ICRA, box 2, folder 2, #5.

130. McGrath, *Newman's University*, 423.

131. Newman to Wilberforce, 21 October 1856, *LD* 17.

132. Ibid.

133. Ibid.

134. Newman to St John, 30 October 1856, *LD* 17.

135. C. S. Dessain, in his notes to this letter, quotes a later note of Newman's to the effect that the secret enemies he had in mind were Wiseman and Faber. See *LD* 17:419n.

136. Newman to Wilberforce, 25 October 1856, *LD* 17.

137. Newman to St John, 26 October 1856, *LD* 17.

138. Newman to Forde, 28 October 1856, *LD* 17. Newman was urging Forde to postpone his own resignation until the end of the academic year and, by way of incentive, offered his own example of perseverance in the face of heavy trials.

139. Newman to St John, 30 October 1856, *LD* 17.

140. Newman continued to push Moriarty for the post, recommending him in fulsome terms to Dixon as late as July 1857. See Newman to Dixon, 2 July 1857, *LD* 18.

141. Newman to Flanagan, 19 November 1856, *LD* 17.

142. Newman to Moriarty, 25 November 1856, *LD* 17.

143. V. A. McClelland's comment that 'even David Moriarty . . . was totally opposed to his [Newman's] anglicizing policy' should be seen in the light of this quote. McClelland, *English Roman Catholics*, 126.

144. Moriarty to Newman, 28 November 1856, reproduced in *LD* 17:461–62.

145. Cullen to Kirby, 22 July 1857, Kirby Papers (New Collection), ICRA, box 2, folder 2, #35. Cullen's comments appear ironic in hindsight, given that Moriarty was possibly the only bishop more opposed to the Fenians than was Cullen himself.

146. Newman to Cullen, 2 April 1857, *LD* 18.

147. Browne to Newman, 10 April 1857, BOA, Correspondence with Irish Bishops File, C.6.29–30.

148. J. P. Leahy to Newman, 8 April 1857, BOA, Correspondence with Irish Bishops File, C.6.29–30.

149. It is worth noting that, of all the surviving letters from Irish bishops urging Newman to stay, all but that from George Browne (who had been bishop of Elphin since 1844) came from bishops appointed since Cullen had come to Ireland.

150. O'Brien to Newman, 4 April 1857, BOA, Correspondence with Irish Bishops File, C.6.29–30.

151. Leahy to Newman, 4 April 1857, BOA, Correspondence with Irish Bishops File, C.6.29–30.

152. Moriarty to Newman, 15 April 1857, BOA, Correspondence with Irish Bishops File, C.6.29–30.

153. St John to Newman, 6 May 1857, reproduced in *LD* 18:28. St John was writing in his capacity as dean of the Oratory.

154. Newman to St John, 6 May 1857, *LD* 18.

155. Newman to Wilberforce, 18 April 1857, *LD* 18.

156. Newman to St John, 12 May (2nd letter) 1857, *LD* 18.

157. See Leahy to Cullen, 7 May 1857, Cullen Papers, DDA, 339/5/62 and Leahy to Cullen, 5 November 1858, Cullen Papers, DDA, 319/1/143.

158. Newman to St John, 12 May (1st letter) 1857, *LD* 18.

159. Cullen to Kirby, 21 May 1857, Kirby Papers (New Collection), ICRA, box 2, folder 2, #25.

160. This option had evidently been canvassed in Rome in 1851, as Kirby, quoting Barnabò, told Cullen that there was a body of Roman opinion that favoured Cullen being the first president or rector. That role would be largely ceremonial, and Newman could 'have the direction of the studies under the most Rev. President.' Ironically, this proposal for Newman to be, effectively, prefect of studies was identical to the role Newman originally suggested for himself. Kirby to Cullen, 13 November 1851, Cullen Papers (Armagh), DDA, 39/2 box 1, file 6, #54.

161. Cullen to Kirby, 21 May 1857, Kirby Papers (New Collection), ICRA, box 2, folder 2, #25.

162. Ibid.

163. Leahy to Cullen, 25 May 1857, Cullen Papers, DDA, 339/5/70.

164. Cullen to Kirby, 26 May 1857, Kirby Papers (New Collection), ICRA, box 2, folder 2, #27.

165. Cullen speculated that this might be the result of Monsignor George Talbot, the agent of the English bishops in Rome, having passed on rumours of Cullen's views on Newman's performance.

166. Cullen to Kirby, 8 July 1857, Kirby Papers (New Collection), ICRA, box 2, folder 2, #32.

167. Cullen to Kirby, 22 July 1857, Kirby Papers (New Collection), ICRA, box 2, folder 2, #35. This promise was later temporarily withdrawn in October 1858, as it was thought unlikely that MacHale would approve the expenditure. Newman, then contemplating his final resignation, was furious.

168. Newman to Leahy, 21 May 1857, *LD* 18 (see note, 46).

169. Cullen to Newman, 27 March 1857, BOA, Cullen File. Newman had a hand in Arnold's conversion and seems to have been concerned to secure for him an income when Arnold returned from Tasmania after resigning as inspector of schools in the wake of his conversion. See Arnold to Newman, 23 October 1856, *Letters of Thomas Arnold the Younger*, 80–81.

170. Newman to Arnold, 23 July 1857, BOA. The correspondence between Newman and Arnold was not yet available at the time of the publication of the relevant volumes of the *LD* and has not been published elsewhere. It will appear in due course in volume 32 of the *LD*.

171. For the full text of the archbishops' letter to the Fathers of the Birmingham Oratory, see *LD* 18:112–13.

172. Newman to Hope-Scott, 5 August 1857, *LD* 18.

173. There is a draft in Newman's hand, and the letter itself is unmistakably Newman's work. See Dessain's note on the subject in *LD* 18:113.

174. The Fathers of the Birmingham Oratory to the Archbishops of Dublin, Armagh, and Cashel, 6 August 1857, *LD* 18.

175. Newman had by now given up dealing with Cullen except over necessary financial matters and addressed his letters on university business to the more sympathetic Leahy. Leahy himself was frustrated by the refusal of many officials of the CUI to deal with Cullen: 'I fear there is rather a disposition in a certain quarter to apply to your Grace only when it cannot be avoided.' Leahy to Cullen, December 1857, Cullen Papers, DDA, 339/5/141.

176. Newman to Leahy, 8 August 1857, *LD* 18.

177. Leahy to Cullen, 17 August 1857, Cullen Papers, DDA, 339/5/105.

178. Leahy to Newman, 13 August 1857, quoted in *LD* 18:116.

179. Newman to Leahy, 17 August 1857, *LD* 18.

180. Leahy to Newman, 25 August 1857, quoted in *LD* 18:120–21.

181. See Leahy to Newman, 28 August 1857, quoted in *LD* 18:121–22.

182. Newman to Leahy, 17 August 1857, *LD* 18.

183. Newman to Leahy, 26 August 1857, *LD* 18.

184. O'Dwyer, 'Life of Dr. Leahy', 121.

185. Leahy to Newman, undated (but early September 1857), quoted in *LD* 18:128.

186. Newman had told Leahy as early as May 1857 that Forde, although 'a man of talent, of decision, and of purpose' would be even more unpopular in the university community than would be a 'stranger'. See Newman to Leahy, 23 May 1857, *LD* 18. It is unclear why exactly Forde was so unpopular in the university. The most likely explanation is that he was an ally of Cullen's (and had been his student in Rome) and enjoyed the archbishop's support, not something that would engender much popularity in a faculty appointed by, and loyal to, Newman. Indeed, in early July 1857, Cullen told Kirby with some satisfaction that 'I believe we will make Dr Forde V[ice] Rector.' See Cullen to Kirby, 8 July 1857, Kirby Papers (New Collection), ICRA, box 2, folder 2, #32.

187. Memorandum for the answer to be made in October to Dr Leahy's letter of last month dated Templemore, quoted in *LD* 18:145.

188. McGrath, *Newman's University*, 448.

189. See Meeting of 18 December 1856, Minutes of the Council of the Faculty of Philosophy and Letters, UCDA, CU4.

190. Cullen to Kirby, 8 July 1857, Kirby Papers (New Collection), ICRA, box 2, folder 2, #32.

191. Newman to Butler, 19 November 1857, *LD* 18.

192. Butler to Newman, 7 December 1857, BOA, University Correspondence, C.6.26.

193. See Butler to Newman, 9 January 1858, BOA, University Correspondence, C.6.26. Butler's disappointed hopes for the vice-rectorship might go some way towards accounting for his comment that 'Dr. Cullen and the Irish Bishops, not having had themselves a University education, did not properly understand what it was, and with one or two exceptions, did not really want such a University as Newman had in mind, their idea was a glorified Seminary for the laity.' Butler's recollection was reproduced by his son, the Benedictine historian Cuthbert Butler, in his biography of Bishop Ullathorne. Cuthbert Butler, *The Life and Times of Bishop Ullathorne, 1806–1889*, 2 vols. (London: Burns Oates and Washbourne, 1926), 2:312–13. The question of whether Cullen wanted a 'lay seminary' has been addressed in chapter 5, but it is worth noting that Butler would have been aware that at no time during Newman's tenure did Cullen either interfere or attempt to interfere in either what was taught by the university or how it was taught.

194. Newman to Leahy, 3 February 1858, *LD* 18.

195. See, for example, Newman to Hope-Scott, 24 December 1857, *LD* 18.

196. Corish, *Maynooth College*, 155.

197. Leahy to Newman, 25 May 1858, quoted in McGrath, *Newman's University*, 461.

198. See Newman to DeVere, 5 March 1858. Although a copy is held in the BOA, this letter does not appear in the *LD*. The original is held at Trinity College Dublin, DeVere Papers, Ms.5053/40.

199. *AW*, 333.

200. Cullen to Kirby, 28 June 1858 (Copy), Kirby Papers (New Collection), ICRA, box 2, folder 2, #81.

201. Lyons to Kirby, 1 July 1858, Kirby Papers (New Collection), ICRA, box 2, folder 2, #82.

202. Murray to Kirby, 25 July 1858, Kirby Papers (New Collection), ICRA, box 2, folder 2, #88.

203. Cullen to Leahy, 19 July 1858, Leahy Papers, CDA, P.6005, 1858/34.

204. Cullen to Kirby, 24 July 1858, Kirby Papers (New Collection), ICRA, box 2, folder 2, #58. The Irish College in Paris was the responsibility of the four archbishops. MacHale had taken an active part in questions regarding it, and controversy had arisen over the behaviour of the rector, John Miley. Thomas MacHale, the archbishop's nephew, and other members of the faculty were opposed to Miley, a Cullen ally, and the affairs of the college became terribly unsettled. The nature of the conflict is not important for our purposes, but it is necessary to remember that Cullen was also under pressure on this issue. For a complete discussion of the controversy see Larkin, *Making of the Roman Catholic Church*, 410–28.

205. Cullen to Kirby, 24 July 1858, Kirby Papers (New Collection), ICRA, box 2, folder 2, #58.

206. Cullen did indeed write to Barnabò on the matter on 31 August. After again complaining of Newman's method of discipline and spending, which Cullen ascribed to his inability to see that the CUI, being poor, could not afford to behave as if it were Oxford, he told Barnabò that it was his belief that MacHale would use 'the mistakes of Father Newman' to justify attacks on himself. Cullen to Barnabò, 31 August 1858. The original is in Italian and the translation is by J. H. Whyte. Whyte, 'Newman in Dublin', 36.

207. Cullen to Kirby, 5 August 1858, Kirby Papers (New Collection), ICRA, box 2, folder 2, #90.

208. Monsell to Newman, 3 November 1858, BOA, Monsell Correspondence, box 2.

209. Leahy to Newman 20 October 1858, BOA, University Correspondence, C.6.26. Leahy had indeed been urging such a course on Cullen. See, for example, Leahy to Cullen, 1 February 1858, Cullen Papers, DDA, 319/1/18.

210. Cullen to Kirby, 9 August 1858, Kirby Papers (New Collection), ICRA, box 2, folder 2, #91.

211. Cullen to Newman, 27 September 1858, BOA, Correspondence with Irish Bishops File, C.6.29–30. The document is not in Cullen's hand.

212. Leahy to Newman, 3 October 1858, BOA, Correspondence with Irish Bishops File, C.6.29–30.

213. See Newman to Leahy, 2 October 1858, and 5 October 1858, *LD* 18.

214. Leahy to Newman, 8 October 1858, BOA, Correspondence with Irish Bishops File, C.6.29–30.

215. Newman to Ornsby, 7 October 1858, *LD* 18.

216. Leahy to Cullen, 5 October 1858, Cullen Papers, DDA, 319/1/133.

217. Leahy to Cullen, 5 November 1858, Cullen Papers, DDA, 319/1/143.
218. Newman to Ornsby, 11 October 1858, *LD* 18.
219. Newman to Ornsby, 17 October 1858, *LD* 18.
220. Newman to Monsell, 18 October 1858, *LD* 18.
221. Newman to the Archbishops of Ireland, 12 November 1858, *LD* 18.
222. Cullen to Leahy, 20 January 1859, Leahy Papers, CDA, P.6005, 1859/3. This letter shows that Archbishop Dixon was not, as William Rigney has claimed, the first to suggest Woodlock in 1861. William J. Rigney, 'Bartholomew Woodlock and the Catholic University of Ireland, 1861–1879', 2 vols. (Ph.D. diss., University College Dublin, 1995), 1:28 and note 1.

9. New Beginnings, Old Problems

1. 'Catholic University of Ireland 1854, University College Dublin 1954, Centenary Celebrations 18th–23rd July, 1954' (n.p., n.d.).
2. For the period of Jesuit control, see Thomas J. Morrissey, *Towards a National University: William Delaney SJ (1835–1924). An Era of Initiative in Irish Education* (Dublin: Wolfhound Press, 1983).
3. Quoted in Donal McCartney, *UCD: A National Idea. A History of University College, Dublin* (Dublin: Gill and Macmillan, 1999), 15.
4. McGrath, *Newman's University*, 467–68.
5. See John Augustus O'Shea, *Roundabout Recollections*, 2 vols. (London: Ward and Downey, 1892), 2:111–13.
6. Arnold to Newman, 6 November 1858, *Letters of Thomas Arnold the Younger*, 93–94.
7. McGrath, *Newman's University*, 468.
8. Arnold to Newman, 7 November 1859, *Letters of Thomas Arnold the Younger*, 103.
9. An extended treatment of the meeting can be found in Larkin, *Making of the Roman Catholic Church*, 466–71.
10. Ibid., 471.
11. Cullen to Kirby, 28 October 1859, quoted in Larkin, *Making of the Roman Catholic Church*, 471–72.
12. Ibid., 475.
13. Ibid. Derry's diocese of Clonfert gave nothing to the university between October 1859 and March 1861. Donations to the Catholic University of Ireland between October 1859 and March 1861. Cullen Papers, DDA, 45/4/3.
14. William J. Rigney, 'Bartholomew Woodlock and the Catholic University of Ireland, 1861–1879', 2 vols. (Ph.D. diss., University College Dublin, 1995), 1:60.
15. Arnold to Acton, 9 December 1859, *Letters of Thomas Arnold the Younger*, 105–6.
16. Gartlan to Cullen, 23 January 1861, Cullen Papers, DDA, AB4/45/4/2.

17. Kavanagh to Flannery, 25 June 1860, Woodlock Papers, DDA.
18. Donations to the Catholic University of Ireland between October 1859 and March 1861. Cullen Papers, DDA, 45/4/3.
19. Cullen to Kirby, 29 March 1861, quoted in Larkin, *Consolidation of the Roman Catholic Church*, 135–36.
20. Newman to Renouf, 3 May 1861, *LD* 19.
21. Cullen to Barnabò, 12 June 1861, quoted in Larkin, *Consolidation of the Roman Catholic Church,* 137–40.
22. See Rigney, 'Bartholomew Woodlock', 1:266–67.
23. Newman to Renouf, 3 May 1861, *LD* 19.
24. Rigney, 'Bartholomew Woodlock', 1:1–7.
25. Ibid., 1:29.
26. Woodlock to Cullen, 10 May 1861, Cullen Papers, DDA, AB4/45/4/5.
27. Calendar of the Catholic University for the Year 1861.
28. Ibid., 20.
29. Report of sub-committee on the affiliation of schools (1856), Woodlock Papers, DDA, 106/10.
30. The Calendar of the Catholic University of Ireland for the Session 1858–59.
31. Rigney, 'Bartholomew Woodlock', 1:202.
32. Ibid., 1:203–4.
33. Ibid., 1:7.
34. Woodlock to Moriarty, 12 December 1861, Monsell Papers, NLI, Ms. 8319(2).
35. Dorrian to Woodlock, 21 January 1862, Woodlock Papers, DDA.
36. Newman to Woodlock, 28 March 1862, *LD* 20.
37. See Donal Kerr, 'Dr. Quinn's School and the Catholic University, 1850–67', *Irish Ecclesiastical Record*, 5th ser., 108 (1967): 89–101.
38. The information for the above paragraphs comes from chapter 3 of Rigney, 'Bartholomew Woodlock', especially 1:142–99.
39. MacHale to Woodlock, 14 November 1861, Woodlock Papers, DDA.
40. See R. V. Comerford, *The Fenians in Context: Irish Politics and Society, 1848–82* (Dublin: Wolfhound Press, 1986), 79.
41. Cullen to Kirby, 23 July 1862, quoted in Rigney, 'Bartholomew Woodlock', 1:79.
42. Ibid., 1:252.
43. 'Catholic University of Ireland: Proposed Scheme of National Tribute For Its Support', Cullen Papers, DDA, 45/4/3.
44. Catholic University of Ireland: Diocesan Collections for 1862. Cullen Papers, DDA.
45. Report of the Rector on Annual Expenses, 11 November 1858, Woodlock Papers, DDA, 106/19.
46. I have been unable to locate any information on the circumstances of their appointment.
47. Errington to Scratton, 30 January 1860, Woodlock Papers, DDA.

48. Report of the Finance Committee of the Catholic University to the University Board, 18 September 1863, Cullen Papers, DDA, 45/4 file 3, #7A.

49. Ibid.

50. As early as 1862 Newman thought such consolidations were necessary and expressed to Woodlock the view that he would not have created so many chairs had he realised that student numbers would be so low. Newman to Woodlock, 7 March 1862, *LD* 20.

51. Report of the Finance Committee of the Catholic University to the University Board, 18 September 1863, Cullen Papers, DDA, 45/4 file 3, #7A.

52. Report to the Episcopal Board of the Catholic University of Ireland, 4 August 1865. Cullen Papers, DDA, 45/4 file 5.

53. Rector's Report, 1854–55, 26–27.

54. Badeley to Newman (?), 24 March 1856, Woodlock Papers, DDA, 106/8. Although Newman is not named in this memorandum as the recipient, it seems almost certain that he was and that he left the document in the university files as an official document.

55. William Woodlock to Woodlock, 24 March 1864, quoted in Rigney, 'Bartholomew Woodlock', 1:73.

56. Cullen to Monsell, 7 May (1st letter) 1858, Monsell Papers, NLI, Ms. 8317(3).

57. Cullen to Monsell, 7 May (2nd letter) 1858, Monsell Papers, NLI, Ms. 8317(3).

58. J. M. Capes, 'Ireland's Opportunity', *The Rambler* 20 (September 1857): 161–72.

59. Meeting of 2 April 1857, Minutes of the Meetings of the Council of the Faculty of Philosophy and Letters, UCDA, CU4.

60. Statement Submitted to the Board of Prelates by Henry Hennessy, F. R. S.. No date, but almost certainly early 1860s. Woodlock Papers, DDA.

61. Arnold to Newman, 12 January 1859, *Letters of Thomas Arnold the Younger*, 95.

62. William Flavelle Monypenny and George Earle Buckle, *Life of Benjamin Disraeli: Earl of Beaconsfield*, 6 vols. (London: John Murray, 1910–20), 5:5.

63. Robert Blake, *Disraeli* (New York: St Martin's Press, 1967), 435.

64. Quoted in McGrath, *Newman's University*, 41–42.

65. Blake, *Disraeli*, 342.

66. 'We caught Churchill young, and educated him in the Propaganda; but he has disappointed us [the speaker is an English monsignor]. At first all seemed well; he was reserved and austere; and we heard with satisfaction that he was unpopular. But now that critical times are arriving, his peasant blood cannot resist the contagion. He proclaims the absolute equality of all religions, and of the power of the state to confiscate ecclesiastical property, and alienate it for ever. For the chance of subverting the Anglican Establishment [in Ireland], he is favouring a policy which will subvert religion itself. In his eagerness he cannot see that the Anglicans have only a lease on our property, a lease which is rapidly expiring.' Benjamin Disraeli, *Lothair*, new ed. (London: Longmans, Green, 1870), 40.

67. The relationship between the Conservatives and English Catholics during this period is treated in Dermot Quinn, *Patronage and Piety: The Politics of English Roman Catholicism, 1850–1900* (Stanford: Stanford University Press, 1993), esp. chaps. 2 and 3. In my view Quinn misunderstands Disraeli's attitude towards Catholicism and sees too much cynicism (if that is possible with Disraeli) in his actions.

68. Matthias Buschkühl has argued that the 'prospect of a distinctly catholic Irish intelligentsia pumped fear into the hearts of the inner circle of the British ruling class and their political representatives in the liberal party under Gladstone.' Although Buschkühl is correct in noting the distaste of many Liberals for a specifically Catholic university, he puts his case far too strongly. Buschkühl, *Great Britain*, 123.

69. Woodlock to Cullen, 21 Febraury 1866, Cullen Papers, DDA, AB4/ 45/4–5, file 8, 45/4/12. Woodlock presented these remarks to Cullen as being verbatim.

70. James Whiteside was a Conservative MP for the University of Dublin and had been solicitor general for Ireland in 1852. He reentered Cullen's bad books when he was the trial judge in the libel action mounted by a Fr. Robert O'Keeffe against Cullen in 1871–72; Whiteside more than lived up to Cullen's early assessment of him. Richard Southwell Bourke held the courtesy title of Lord Naas before succeeding as the sixth earl of Mayo. He was chief secretary for Ireland under Conservative governments in 1852, 1858, and 1866. He became viceroy and governor-general of India and was assassinated there in 1872.

71. Cullen to O'Donoghue, 17 September 1859 (copy), Cullen Papers, DDA, Letterbook 3, 121/3.

72. Larkin, *Consolidation of the Roman Catholic Church*, 142.

73. Entry for 17 November 1861, *Disraeli, Derby, and the Conservative Party: Journals and Memoirs of Edward Henry, Lord Stanley, 1849–69*, ed. John Vincent (New York: Barnes and Noble Books, 1978), 177.

74. Woodlock to Monsell, 9 July 1861, Cullen Papers, DDA, AB4 45/4/4–5, file 1, 45/4/7.

75. Woodlock to Cullen, 7 June 1862, Cullen Papers, DDA, AB4/45/4–5, file 2, 45/4/4.

76. Woodlock to Cullen, 7 June 1863, Cullen Papers, DDA, AB4/ 45/4–5, file 3, 45/4/5.

77. O'Ferrall to Woodlock, 8 February 1862, Woodlock Papers, DDA.

78. Cullen had supported Matthew Kelly, who was later nominated as vice-rector of the CUI. The lay trustees chose to support instead Charles Russell for the post. (Russell, incidentally, was a friend of Newman and the latter, in his *Apologia Pro Vita Sua*, gave Russell much of the credit for his conversion.) Patrick Corish has written that 'Russell's election was possibly the last occasion on which the lay Trustees exercised an important influence.' Corish, *Maynooth College*, 155.

79. Proposals for Adding Laymen to the CUI Board, 25 November 1862, Cullen Papers, DDA, AB4/45/4–5 file 2, 45/4/9.

80. Ibid.

81. Cullen to Kirby, 11 August 1863, quoted in Larkin, *Consolidation of the Roman Catholic Church*, 169.

82. Ibid., 170.

83. Woodlock to Cullen, 13 June 1865, Cullen Papers, DDA, AB4/45/4–5, file 6, 45/4/4.

84. Woodlock to Cullen, 14 June 1865, Cullen Papers, DDA, AB4/45/4–5, file 6, 45/4/5.

85. Woodlock to Cullen, 19 June 1865, Cullen Papers, DDA, AB4/45/4–5, file 6, 45/4/7.

86. Woodlock to Cullen, 20 June 1865, Cullen Papers, DDA, AB4/45/4–5. file 6, 45/4/8.

87. Monsell to Woodlock, 22 June 1865, Cullen Papers, DDA, AB4/45/4–5, file 6, 45/4/10.

88. Cullen to Kirby, 30 November 1865, quoted by Rigney, 'Bartholomew Woodlock', 1:110.

89. Cullen to Kirby, 22 December 1865, quoted in ibid., 116.

90. Grey to Cullen, 30 January 1866, Cullen Papers, DDA, AB4/45/4–5, folder 7, 45/4/2.

91. Cullen to Kirby, 2 February 1866, quoted in Rigney, 'Batholomew Woodlock', 1:110.

92. Woodlock to Cullen, 13 February 1866, Cullen Papers, DDA, AB4/45/4–5, file 8, 45/4/1.

93. Woodlock to Cullen, 28 February 1866, Cullen Papers, DDA, AB4/45/4–5, file 8, 45/4/19.

94. Ibid.

95. Woodlock to Cullen, 1 March 1866 (2nd letter), Cullen Papers, DDA, AB4/45/4–5, file 8, 45/4/21.

96. Sullivan to Monsell, 27 March 1867, Monsell Papers, NLI, Ms. 8318(5).

97. Cullen to Leahy, 29 February 1868, Leahy Papers, CDA, P.6008, 1868/19.

98. That bill revived the idea, first mooted in 1845, of expanding the University of Dublin to include not only Trinity College but also the Queen's Colleges in Cork and Belfast (Galway would be disbanded) as well as the CUI. See H. C. G. Matthew, *Gladstone, 1809–1874* (Oxford: Oxford University Press, 1986), 198–201.

99. Cullen to Monsell, 26 February 1873, Monsell Papers, NLI, Ms. 8317(3).

100. Report to the Episcopal Board of the Catholic University of Ireland, 4 August 1865. Written by Woodlock. Cullen Papers, DDA, AB4/45/4–5, file 5, 45/4.

10. AN ACTUAL EXISTING UNIVERSITY

1. Report of the subcommittee on the Organization of the Catholic University of Ireland, printed in Newman, *My Campaign in Ireland*, 77–78.

2. Ibid., 80.

3. 'Letter of the Rector to the Dean of the Faculty of Philosophy and Letters on the Introduction of Religious Teaching into the Schools of that Faculty'. Printed in Newman, *My Campaign in Ireland*, 159.

4. Ibid., 163.

5. 'Substance of the Memorandum of the Rector, read in the Synodal Meeting, May 20, 1854', published in Newman, *My Campaign in Ireland*, 93–94. Hereafter Memorandum of the Rector.

6. Ibid., 95.

7. Ibid., 96.

8. Newman to Hope-Scott, 28 March 1857. Quoted in McGrath, *Newman's University*, 437.

9. This list is drawn from a lecture table for the faculty of philosophy and letters for the winter session, 1859. It can be found in the Woodlock Papers, DDA.

10. Rylands, W. H. G. Maspero, and E. Neville, eds., *The Life and Work of Sir Peter le Page Renouf*, 1st ser. (Paris: Leroux, 1907).

11. Henry Hennessy, *A Discourse on the Study of Science in its relations to individuals and society* (Dublin: W. B. Kelly, 1859), and *On a Uniform System of weights, measures, and coins for all nations* (London: Association for Obtaining a Uniform Decimal System of Measures, Weights and Coins, 1858).

12. Arnold's substantial publication record can be found in *Letters of Thomas Arnold the Younger*, 254–56.

13. Robert Ornsby, *The Greek New Testament: From Cardinal Mai's Edition of the Vatican Bible; with notes, chiefly philosophical and exegetical; a harmony of the Gospels, and chronological tables* (Dublin: James Duffy, 1860).

14. J. B. Robertson, *Lectures on Some Subjects of Modern History & Biography: Delivered at the Catholic University of Ireland, 1860–4* (Dublin: W. B. Kelly, 1864), and *Lectures on the Life, Writings and Times of Edmund Burke* (Dublin: McGlashen & Gill, 1875).

15. See Cullen to O'Curry, 14 August 1856, Woodlock Papers, DDA.

16. For episcopal support for the project, see Cullen to Woodlock, Leahy to Woodlock and Dixon to Woodlock, all 14 August 1862. Woodlock Papers, DDA.

17. Woodlock to the Catholics of the United States, 6 August 1864, Woodlock Papers, DDA, 106/48.

18. Memorandum of the Rector, 98.

19. Report to their Lordships the Archbishops and Bishops of Ireland, for 1854–55, 39. Printed in Newman, *My Campaign in Ireland*. Hereafter 'Rector's Report, 1854–55'.

20. Rector's Report, 1854–55, 16.

21. Ibid., 22.

22. Ibid., 22–24.

23. Rector's Report, 1855–56, 59.

24. Ibid., 59–60.

25. Ibid., 62–63.

26. Ibid., 67.
27. Rector's Report, 1856–57.
28. Ibid., 183.
29. Ibid., 99–100.
30. *Catholic University Gazette*, 1 February 1855.
31. Ibid.
32. Ibid.
33. *Catholic University Gazette*, 21 December 1854.
34. For the above, see the Transactions of the Catholic University of Ireland, UCDA, CU8, 15–16 (arts) and 32–33 (engineering).
35. Minutes of the Meetings of the Council of the Faculty of Philosophy and Letters, meeting of 28 June 1856, UCDA, CU4.
36. *Catholic University Gazette*, 20 July 1854.
37. *Catholic University Gazette*, 3 August 1854.
38. *Catholic University Gazette*, 17 August 1854.
39. 'Scheme of Rules and Regulations, submitted by the Rector to the Council in April, 1856, afterwards to be adapted to University use'. Published in Newman, *My Campaign in Ireland*.
40. Ibid., 135–37.
41. Ibid., 139.
42. Ibid., 140–45.
43. O'Shea, *Roundabout Recollections*, 2:121–22.
44. Minutes of the Meetings of the Council of the Faculty of Philosophy and Letters, meeting of 6 November 1856, UCDA, CU4.
45. The Calendar of the Irish Catholic University for the Session 1858–59.
46. For the above, see the Dublin University Calendar for 1856 (covering the year 1855).
47. For the above two paragraphs, see the Calendar, Queen's University in Ireland, Queen's College, Cork, Session 1854–55. Newman preserved this calendar in his files on education at the Birmingham Oratory.
48. Kerr, *A Nation of Beggars?* 216.
49. Catholic University Student Register, 1854–79, UCDA, CU5.
50. See Arnold to Julia Arnold, 21 November 1856, *Letters of Thomas Arnold the Younger*, 84.
51. Rector's Report, 1856–57, 181.
52. Robertson to Woodlock, 7 February 1862, Woodlock Papers, DDA.
53. Kerr, *Peel, Priests and Politics*, 238.
54. Kerr, 'Dr. Quinn's School', 90.
55. Walsh matriculated in 1856 at the age of sixteen and stayed for two years, leaving after his scholars' exam. He won the junior exhibition in mathematics. See Thomas J. Morrissey, *William J. Walsh: Archbishop of Dublin, 1841–1921* (Dublin: Four Courts Press, 2000), 6.
56. See O'Shea, *Roundabout Recollections*, 2:101, 2:119.
57. Senia Pašeta, in her *Before the Revolution: Nationalism, Social Change and Ireland's Catholic Elite, 1879–1922* (Cork: Cork University Press, 1999), has

discussed the role that University College and later University College Dublin played in the creation of a middle-class Catholic elite.

58. *Catholic University Gazette*, 1 February 1855.

59. O'Shea, *Roundabout Recollections*, 2:93–124.

60. Fellow-commoner is an Oxbridge term that refers to the sons of the aristocracy who, although technically junior members of the college, enjoyed special privileges—both social and academic.

61. O'Shea, *Roundabout Recollections*, 2:95.

62. Quoted in McClelland, *English Roman Catholics*, 131.

63. Ibid.

64. Ibid., 130–34. McClelland seems almost obsessed with this issue.

65. Thomas Arnold delivered himself of the most extraordinary attack on the Irish practice of ordaining 'the lowest of the people'. See Arnold to A. H. Clough, October 1858, *Letters of Thomas Arnold the Younger*, 92.

66. Culler, *Imperial Intellect*, 88.

CONCLUSION: THE FAILURE OF THE CATHOLIC UNIVERSITY
OF IRELAND

1. Michael J. Buckley, *The Catholic University as Promise and Project: Reflections in the Jesuit Idiom* (Washington, D.C.: Georgetown University Press, 1998), xvi.

2. Catholic University Student Register, 1854–79, UCDA, CU5.

3. Ibid.

4. Cullen to Kirby, 14 September 1858, Kirby Papers (New Collection), ICRA, box 2, folder 2, #99.

5. Catholic University Student Register, 1854–79, UCDA, CU5.

6. See *AW*, 323.

7. In 1854–55 Notre Dame had 111 students. By 1859–60 some 217 were enrolled from seventeen states and Canada. Yet by 1855 only four degrees had been awarded (and only twelve by 1860). Of the 463 students enrolled in 1864–65 only some 226 were of an age to be in the senior school (the university component for those over the age of sixteen); eighty-two were under the age of twelve and were thus in the 'minims' program. For degrees, see 'Chronological List of Degrees Awarded by the University of Notre Dame', *Bulletin of the University of Notre Dame*, 1907–8, Series 3, no. 4, 9. For student numbers, ages, and geographic distribution, see Enrolment Figures, Ages, Professions, Home states, etc. of Notre Dame Students, 1840s–1930, UNDA, 90-AC-3L.

8. For an excellent discussion of the growth of Boston College, see James Tunstead Burtchaell, *The Dying of the Light: The Disengagement of Colleges and Universities from Their Christian Churches* (Grand Rapids, Mich.: Eerdmans, 1998), chap. 6. By the time the Catholic University of Ireland opened in 1854 there were already some twenty-six Catholic colleges and

universities in the United States. Most originally had a substantial 'school' element.

9. For the early history of the University of Notre Dame, see Robert E. Burns, *Being Catholic, Being American: The Notre Dame Story, 1842–1934* (Notre Dame, Ind.: Notre Dame University Press, 1999), 3–40.

10. O'Shea, *Roundabout Recollections*, 2:95.

Bibliography

PRIMARY SOURCES

Private Papers

The British Library: Aberdeen Papers.
Dublin Diocesan Archives: Paul Cullen Papers; Daniel Murray Papers; Bartholomew Woodlock Papers.
University College, Dublin, Archives: Catholic University Papers.
Irish College Rome: Archives Paul Cullen Papers; Tobias Kirby Papers.
Archives of the Oratory of St Philip Neri, Birmingham: John Henry Newman Papers.
National Library of Ireland: Frederick National Library of Ireland: Frederick Lucas Papers; William Monsell Papers.
Cashel Diocesan Archives (microfilm copy held at the National Library of Ireland): Michael Slattery Papers; Patrick Leahy Papers.
Down and Connor Diocesan Archives: Cornelius Denvir Papers.
The Cardinal Tomas O Fiaich Memorial Library and Archive, Armagh: Joseph Dixon Papers.
Library of Trinity College, University of Dublin, Department of Manuscripts and Early Printed Books: Pamphlet Collections.
University of Notre Dame Archives: University Archives.
Archives of Pembroke College, Oxford: Peter le Page Renouf Papers.

Published

Allies, T. W. 'The Catholic University'. *Dublin Review* 31 (December 1851): 529–88.

Altholz, Josef L., and McElrath, Damian, eds. *The Correspondence of Lord Acton and Richard Simpson.* 3 vols. Cambridge: Cambridge University Press, 1971–73.

Bertram, James, ed. *The Letters of Thomas Arnold the Younger.* Auckland: Auckland University Press, 1980.

Blakiston, Noel. *The Roman Question: Extracts from the Despatches of Odo Russell from Rome, 1858–1870.* Wilmington, Del.: Michael Glazier, 1980.

Bourke, Ulrick J. *Life of John MacHale, Archbishop of Tuam.* New York: P. J. Kennedy, 1882.

Capes, J. M. 'The Catholic University: Its Difficulties and Prospects'. *The Rambler* 7 (n.s.) (February 1857): 83–98.

———. 'Ireland's Opportunity'. *The Rambler* 20 (September 1857): 161–72.

'Chronological List of Degrees Awarded by the University of Notre Dame'. *Bulletin of the University of Notre Dame*, 1907–8, ser. 3, no. 4.

Clarke, Richard F. *University Education in Ireland, A Retrospect and a Prospect.* London: Longmans, Green, 1890.

Crolly, George. *The Life of the Most Rev. Dr. Crolly, Archbishop of Armagh and Primate of Ireland; To which are appended some letters in Defence of his Character.* Dublin: James Duffy, 1851.

Corrigan, Dominic. *University Education in Ireland.* Dublin: Browne and Nolan, 1865.

Cusack, M. F. *The Life of the Most Rev. Joseph Dixon, D. D., Primate of All Ireland.* London: Burns, 1878.

Decreta Synodi Plenariæ Thurlesianæ, Episcoporum Hiberniæ, Habitæ Anno 1850. Dublin: J. M. O'Toole, 1873.

Dessain, Charles Stephen (primary editor). *The Letters and Diaries of John Henry Newman.* Oxford: Oxford University Press, 1961–.

Disraeli, Benjamin. *Lothair.* New edition. London: Longmans, Green, 1870.

Dublin University Calendars, 1850–1856. Dublin: Hodges Figgis.

Duffy, Charles Gavan. *My Life in Two Hemispheres.* London: Unwin, 1903.

———. *Young Ireland: A Fragment of Irish History, 1840–1850.* London: Cassell, Peter, and Galpin, 1880.

England, John. *The Catholic University and the Queen's Colleges.* Cork, 1865: TCD Library, Department of Early Printed Books, E.1.17 #7.

Fitz-Patrick, W. J. *The Life Times and Correspondence of the Right Rev. Dr. Doyle, Bishop of Kildare and Leighlin.* Dublin: James Duffy, 1880.

Formby, Henry. 'The University of Louvain'. *Dublin Review* 25 (September 1848).

Godkin, James. *Education in Ireland; Its History, Institutions, Systems, Statistics, and Progress, from the earliest times to the present.* London: Saunders, Oatley, 1862.

Lucas, Edward. *The Life of Frederick Lucas, MP.* London: Catholic Truth Society, 1887.

Meagher, William. *Notices of the Life and Character of His Grace Most Rev. Daniel Murray, Late Archbishop of Dublin.* Dublin: Gerald Bellew, 1853.

MacHale, John. *The Letters of the Most Rev. John MacHale, DD, Archbishop of Tuam.* Dublin: M. H. Gill & Son, 1893.

MacSuibhne, Peadar. *Paul Cardinal Cullen and his Contemporaries: With their letters from 1820–1902.* 5 vols. Naas, Co. Kildare: Leinster Leader, 1961–74.

Moran, Patrick Francis, ed. *The Pastoral Letters and Other Writings of Cardinal Cullen, Archbishop of Dublin, etc. etc.* 3 vols. Dublin: Browne and Nolan, 1882.

———. *Priests and People of Ireland in the Nineteenth Century.* Melbourne: Catholic Truth Society of Australia, n.d.

Neville, William P. *Addresses to Cardinal Newman and his replies, etc.* London: Longmans, 1905.

Newman, John Henry. *Autobiographical Writings.* Edited by Henry Tristram. New York: Sheed and Ward, 1957.

———. *Discourses on the Scope and Nature of University Education Addressed to the Catholics of Dublin.* Dublin: James Duffy, 1852.

———. *Discussions and Arguments.* London: Longmans, 1918.

———. *An Essay on the Development of Christian Doctrine.* London: James Toovey, 1845.

———. *Fifteen Sermons Preached before the University of Oxford between A.D. 1826 and 1843.* Notre Dame, Ind.: University of Notre Dame Press, 1997.

———. *The Idea of the University.* Edited by Ian Ker. Oxford: Oxford University Press, 1976.

———. *My Campaign in Ireland, Catholic University Reports and Other Papers.* Edited by William Neville. Aberdeen: A. King, 1896.

O'Reilly, Bernard. *John MacHale, Archbishop of Tuam. His Life, Times, and Correspondence.* 2 vols. New York: Fr. Pustet, 1890.

O'Reilly, Myles. 'Prospects of the Irish University'. *The Rambler* 12 (August 1853): 112–27.

Ornsby, Robert. *Memoirs of James Robert Hope-Scott of Abbotsford, D. C. L., Q.C., late Fellow of Merton College, Oxford: with selections from his correspondence.* 2 vols. London: John Murray, 1884.

O'Shea, John Augustus. *Roundabout Recollections.* 2 vols. London: Ward and Downey, 1892.

Pattison, Mark. *Memoirs.* Introduction by Jo Manton. London: Centaur, 1969.

Pollen, J. H. 'Newman in Dublin'. *The Month: A Catholic Magazine* 507 (n.s. 117) (September 1906): 317–20.

Pope Hennessy, John. *The Failure of the Queen's Colleges, and of Mixed Education in Ireland.* London: David Bryce, 1859.

Queen's University in Ireland, Queen's College Cork, Calendar, Session 1854–55.

Ullathorne, William Bernard. *From Cabin-Boy to Archbishop: The Autobiography of Archbishop Ullathorne: Printed from the Original Draft.* London: Burns and Oates, 1941.

———. *The Letters of Archbishop Ullathorne.* London: Burns and Oates, 1892.

Wiseman, Nicholas. *Cardinal Wiseman's Tour in Ireland.* Dublin: James Duffy, 1859.

————. *Lectures on Science and Revealed Religion*. London: Charles Dolman, 1851.

Vincent, J. R., ed. *Disraeli, Derby and the Conservative Party, The Political Journals of Lord Stanley 1849–69*. New York: Barnes and Noble, 1978.

Periodicals

The Catholic University Gazette, 1854–55.
The Freeman's Journal, 1845–63.
The Rambler, 1851–58.
The Tablet, 1852–58.

Reference Works

Boylan, Henry, ed. *A Dictionary of Irish Biography*. 3d ed. Dublin: Gill and Macmillan, 1998.

Cannon, John, ed. *The Oxford Companion to British History*. Oxford: Oxford University Press, 1997.

The Concise Dictionary of National Biography. Oxford: Oxford University Press, 1969.

Connolly, S. J., ed. *The Oxford Companion to Irish History*. Oxford: Oxford University Press, 1998.

SECONDARY SOURCES

Akenson, D. H. *The Irish Education Experiment: The National System of Education in the Nineteenth Century*. Toronto: University of Toronto Press, 1970.

Anderson, R. D. *Universities and Elites in Britain since 1800*. Cambridge: Cambridge University Press, 1995.

Andrews, Hilary. *Lion of the West: A Biography of John McHale*. Dublin: Veritas, 2001.

Arx, Jeffrey von, S. J., ed. *Varieties of Ultramontanism*. Washington, D.C.: Catholic University of America Press, 1998.

Blake, Robert. *Disraeli*. New York: St Martin's Press, 1967.

Blehl, Vincent F. 'Newman and the Missing Mitre'. *Thought: Fordham University Quarterly* 35, no. 136 (Spring 1960).

Bouyer, Louis. *Newman: His Life and Spirituality*. London: Burns and Oates, 1958.

Bowen, Desmond, *Paul Cardinal Cullen and the Shaping of Modern Irish Catholicism*. Dublin: Gill and Macmillan, 1983.

Bremond, Henri. *The Mystery of Newman*. Translated by H. C. Corrance. London: Williams and Northgate, 1907.

Brown, Stewart J., and David W. Miller, eds. *Piety and Power in Ireland, 1760–1960: Essays in Honor of Emmet Larkin*. Notre Dame, Ind.: University of Notre Dame Press, 2000.

Buckley, Michael J., S. J. *The Catholic University as Promise and Project: Reflections in the Jesuit Idiom.* Washington, D.C.: Georgetown University Press, 1998.

Burns, Robert E. *Being Catholic, Being American: The Notre Dame Story, 1842–1934.* Notre Dame, Ind.: University of Notre Dame Press, 1999.

Burtchaell, James Tunstead, C.S.C. *The Dying of the Light: The Disengagement of Colleges & Universities from Their Christian Churches.* Grand Rapids, Mich.: Eerdmans, 1998.

Buschkühl, Matthias. *Great Britain and the Holy See, 1746–1870.* Dublin: Irish Academic Press, 1982.

Butler, Cuthbert. *The Life and Times of Bishop Ullathorne, 1806–1889.* 2 vols. London: Burns, Oates, and Washbourne, 1926.

Chadwick, Owen. *From Bossuet to Newman: The Idea of Doctrinal Development.* Cambridge: Cambridge University Press, 1957.

———. *Newman.* Oxford: Oxford University Press, 1983.

———. *The Secularization of the European Mind in the Nineteenth Century.* Cambridge: Cambridge University Press, 1990.

———. *The Spirit of the Oxford Movement.* Cambridge: Cambridge University Press, 1990.

Cleary, Arthur P. *The Queen's Colleges in Ireland.* Dublin: Hodges, Smith, 1862.

Comerford, R. V. *The Fenians in Context: Irish Politics and Society, 1848–82.* Dublin: Wolfhound Press, 1998.

Condon, Kevin. *The Missionary College of All Hallows.* Dublin: All Hallows College, 1986.

Coolahan, John. *Irish Education: Its History and Structure.* Dublin: Institute of Public Administration, 1981.

Corish, Patrick J. 'Cardinal Cullen and Archbishop MacHale'. *Irish Ecclesiastical Record* 91 (January–June 1959): 393–408.

———. 'Guide to Material of Public and Political Interest, 1836–1861. Irish College Rome: Kirby Papers'. *Archivium Hibernicum* 31 (1973): 1–94.

———. *The Irish Catholic Experience: A Historical Survey.* Dublin: Gill and Macmillan, 1985.

———. *Maynooth College, 1795–1995.* Dublin: Gill and Macmillan, 1995.

Corkery, Padraig, and Fiancha Long, eds. *Theology in the University: The Irish Context.* Dublin: Dominican Publications, 1997.

Costello, Nuala. *John MacHale, Archbishop of Tuam.* Dublin: Talbot Press, 1939.

Costello, Peter. *Clongowes Wood: The History of Clongowes Wood College.* Dublin: Gill and Macmillan, 1989.

Culler, A. Dwight. *The Imperial Intellect: A Study of Newman's Educational Ideal.* New Haven: Yale University Press, 1955.

Curran, M. J. 'Cardinal Cullen: Biographical Materials'. *Reportorium Novum* 1 (1955): 213–27.

Davis, Richard. *The Young Ireland Movement.* Dublin: Gill and Macmillan, 1987.

Dessain, Charles Stephen. *John Henry Newman*. London: Thomas Nelson, 1966.
Doolin, William. 'Newman and His Medical School'. *Studies* 42 (1953): 151–68.
Earnest, James David, and Gerard Tracey. *John Henry Newman: An Annotated Bibliography of His Tract and Pamphlet Collection*. New York: Garland Publishing, 1984.
Finnegan, Richard, and Edward McCarron. *Ireland: Historical Echoes, Contemporary Politics*. Boulder, Colo.: Westview, 2000.
Foster, R. F. *Modern Ireland, 1600–1972*. London: Allen Lane, 1988.
———. *Paddy and Mr. Punch: Connections in Irish and English History*. London: Allen Lane, 1993.
Gilley, Sheridan. *Newman and His Age*. London: Darton, Longmans, Todd, 1990.
Gwynn, Denis. 'John E. Pigot and Thomas Davis'. *Studies* 38 (June 1949): 145–57.
———. *O'Connell Davis and the Colleges Bill*. Cork: Cork University Press, 1948.
Holland, C. H. *Trinity College Dublin and the Idea of a University*. Dublin: TCD Press, 1991.
Hoppen, K. Theodore. *Ireland since 1800: Conflict and Conformity*. 2d ed. London: Longmans, 1999.
Keenan, Desmond J. *The Catholic Church in Nineteenth-Century Ireland: A Sociological Study*. Dublin: Gill and Macmillan, 1993.
Kelley, James, and Dáire Keogh, eds. *History of the Catholic Diocese of Dublin*. Dublin: Four Courts Press, 2000.
Ker, Ian. 'The Idea of a Catholic University'. Paper delivered to the Newman Conference, 'The Idea of a Catholic University in Mayo' (Ballina: 1996).
———. *John Henry Newman: A Biography*. Oxford: Oxford University Press, 1989.
Ker, Ian, and Alan G. Hill, eds. *Newman after 100 Years*. Oxford: Oxford University Press, 1990.
Kerr, Donal. *The Catholic Church and the Famine*. Dublin: Columbia Press, 1996.
———. 'Dr. Quinn's School and the Catholic University, 1850–67', *Irish Ecclesiastical History*, 5th ser., 108 (1967): 89–101.
———. *A Nation of Beggars? Priests, People and Politics in Famine Ireland, 1846–1852*. Oxford: Oxford University Press, 1994.
———. *Peel, Priests and Politics*. Oxford: Oxford University Press, 1982.
Larkin, Emmet. *The Consolidation of the Roman Catholic Church in Ireland, 1860–1870*. Chapel Hill: University of North Carolina Press, 1987.
———. 'The Devotional Revolution in Ireland, 1850–75'. *American Historical Review* 72 (1967).
———. *The Making of the Roman Catholic Church in Ireland, 1850–1860*. Chapel Hill: University of North Carolina Press, 1980.
———. 'Paul Cardinal Cullen'. In *Varieties of Ultramontanism*, edited by Jeffrey von Arx, 61–84.

Lash, Nicholas. "'A Seat of Wisdom, A Light of the World'": Considering the University'. *Louvain Studies* 15 (1990): 188–202.

Lyons, F. S. L. *Ireland Since the Famine*. London: Fontana Press, 1971.

McCartney, Donal. *UCD: A National Idea. The History of University College, Dublin*. Dublin: Gill & Macmillan, 1999.

Macaulay, Ambrose. 'Dr Cullen's Appointment to Armagh, 1849'. *Seanchas Ard Mhancha* (1980–81): 3–36.

———. *William Crolly: Archbishop of Armagh, 1835–49*. Dublin: Four Courts Press, 1994.

MacSuibhne, Peadar. *The Good Cardinal Cullen*. Dublin: Irish Messenger Publications, 1979.

Marsden, George. *The Soul of the American University: From Protestant Establishment to Established Nonbelief*. New York: Oxford University Press, 1995.

Matthew, H. C. G. *Gladstone, 1809–1874*. Oxford: Oxford University Press, 1986.

McClelland, V. A. *English Roman Catholics and Higher Education, 1830–1903*. Oxford: Clarendon Press, 1973.

McDowell, R. B., and D. B. Webb. *Trinity College Dublin, 1592–1952: An Academic History*. Cambridge: Cambridge University Press, 1982.

McGrath, Fergal. *The Consecration of Learning: Lectures on Newman's Idea of a University*. New York: Fordham University Press, 1962.

———. *Newman's University: Idea and Reality*. London: Longmans, Green, 1951.

McRedmond, Louis. *Thrown Among Strangers: John Henry Newman in Ireland*. Dublin: Veritas, 1990.

Monneypenny, William Flavelle, and George Earle Buckle. *The Life of Benjamin Disraeli, Earl of Beaconsfield*. 6 vols. London: John Murray, 1910–20.

Moody, John. *John Henry Newman*. London: Sheed and Ward, 1946.

Moran, Gerard. *A Radical Priest in Mayo; Fr Patrick Lavelle, the Rise and Fall of an Irish Nationalist, 1825–86*. Dublin: Four Courts Press, 1994.

Morrissey, Thomas. *As One Sent: Peter Kenney SJ, 1779–1841, His Mission to Ireland and North America*. Dublin: Four Courts Press, 1996.

———. *Towards a National University: William Delaney SJ (1835–1924)*. Dublin: Wolfhound Press, 1983.

———. *William J. Walsh: Archbishop of Dublin, 1841–1921*. Dublin: Four Courts Press, 2000.

Murphy, John A. *The College: A History of Queen's/University College Cork*. Cork: Cork University Press, 1996.

Newsome, David. *The Convert Cardinals: John Henry Newman and Henry Edward Manning*. London: John Murray, 1993.

Nockles, Peter B. *The Oxford Movement in Context: Anglican High Churchmanship 1760–1857*. Cambridge: Cambridge University Press, 1994.

Norman, E. R. *Anti-Catholicism in Victorian England*. London: George Allen and Unwin, 1968.

———. *The Catholic Church and Ireland in the Age of Rebellion, 1859–1873*. Ithaca: Cornell University Press, 1965.

———. *The English Catholic Church in the Nineteenth Century*. Oxford: Oxford University Press, 1984.

O'Boyle, James. *The Irish Colleges on the Continent*. Dublin: Browne and Nolan, 1935.

O'Carroll, Ciaran. 'The Pastoral Politics of Paul Cullen'. In *History of the Catholic Diocese of Dublin*, edited by James Kelley and Dáire Keogh.

O'Dwyer, Christopher. 'The Life of Dr. Leahy, 1806–1875'. M.A. thesis, St Patrick's College Maynooth, 1970.

O'Rahilly, Alfred. 'The Irish University Question, V—The Catholic University of Ireland'. *Studies* 50, no. 200 (Winter 1961): 353–70.

Pašeta, Senia. *Before the Revolution: Nationalism, Social Change and Ireland's Catholic Elite, 1879–1922*. Cork: Cork University Press, 1999.

Pelikan, Jaroslav. *The Idea of a University: A Reexamination*. New Haven: Yale University Press, 1992.

Quinn, Dermot. *Patronage and Piety: The Politics of English Roman Catholicism, 1850–1900*. Stanford: Stanford University Press, 1993.

Rafferty, Oliver P. *Catholicism in Ulster, 1603–1983, An Interpretive History*. London: Hurst, 1994.

Rigney, William J. 'Bartholomew Woodlock and the Catholic University of Ireland, 1861–1879'. Ph.D. diss., University College Dublin, 1995.

Rothblatt, Sheldon. *The Modern University and Its Discontents: The Fate of Newman's Legacies in Britain and America*. Cambridge: Cambridge University Press, 1997.

Rylands, W. H., G. Maspero, and E. Neville, eds. *The Life and Work of Sir Peter le Page Renouf*, 1st ser. Paris: Leroux, 1907.

Steele, E. D. 'Cardinal Cullen and Irish Nationality'. *Irish Historical Studies* 19 (1974–75): 234–60.

Stockley, William F. P. *Newman, Education and Ireland*. London: Sands, 1933.

Thomas, Stephen. *Newman and Heresy: The Anglican Years*. Cambridge: Cambridge University Press, 1991.

Tierney, Michael, ed. *Struggle with Fortune, A Centenary Miscellany: Catholic University of Ireland, 1854/University College Dublin, 1954*. Dublin: Browne and Nolan, 1954.

———, ed. *A Tribute to Newman*. Dublin: Browne and Nolan, 1945.

Trevelyan, G. M. *Garibaldi's Defence of the Roman Republic*. London: Cassell, 1988.

Trevor, Meriol. *Newman: Light in Winter* and *The Pillar of the Cloud*. London: Macmillan, 1962.

Tristram, Henry. *Newman's Idea of a Liberal Education: A Selection from the Works of Newman*. London: George G. Harrap, 1952.

Ward, Wilfrid. *Life of John Henry Cardinal Newman*. London: Longmans, Green, 1912.

Whyte, J. H. 'Newman in Dublin: Fresh Light from the Archives of Propaganda'. *Dublin Review* 483 (Spring 1960): 31–39.

Wilson, A. N. *God's Funeral*. London: John Murray, 1999.

Wilson, Robert F. *Newman's Church in Dublin*. Dublin: Irish Industrial Printing and Publishing, 1916.

Young, G. M. *Victorian Essays*. Edited by W. D. Hancock. Oxford: Oxford University Press, 1962.

Index

Aberdeen, George Hamilton-Gordon, 4th Earl of, 80
Achilli, Giacinto, 94–96
Acton, John Emerich Edward Dalberg, 1st Baron, 103
All Hallows College, 184, 186
Allies, T. W., 69–70, 102, 124, 129, 208, 243n65, 245n54
Anderdon, W. H., 179
Anglican Church of Ireland, 10
Arnold, Thomas, 128, 152, 166–67, 179, 181, 195, 209, 218, 269n65
Atlantis, The, 191–92, 208

Badeley, Edward, 194
Baines, Peter Augustine, 28
Barnabò, Alessandro, 59, 66, 115, 165, 184
Belfast Academical Institute, 28
Belgium, Catholic education in. *See* University of Louvain
Bentham, Jeremy, 29
Bianconi, Charles, 190
Birmingham Oratory, 64, 94, 152–53, 165–66
Blake, Anthony, 30
Blake, Robert, 196
Blehl, Vincent, 111–12
Boston College, 224

Bourke, Ulrick J., 98
Bowen, Desmond, 4, 90
Browne, George, 161–62
Brownson, Orestes, 237n4
Bruce, Henry, 196–97
Buckley, Michael, 221
Buschkühl, Matthias, 265n68
Butler, Edward, 169–70, 185, 209

Cambridge University, 27–29, 38, 83, 198, 223
Campbell, Robert, 187
Cantwell, John: Armagh archbishopric selection and, 53; faculty/administrative appointments for CUI and, 71–72; formation committees for CUI and, 44–45, 47, 58, 71; funding/financial administration of CUI and, 41–42, 59, 154; governance of CUI and, 47–48, 100; location of CUI and, 45; national schools and, 20, 35; Queen's Colleges and, 35
Capes, J. M., 194–95
Cardwell, Edward, 201
Carlow College, 74–75
Catholic Church in Ireland: British concessions to, 14;

COLIN BARR lectures in modern European history at the National
University of Ireland, Maynooth.